THE AHMADIYYA IN THE GOLD COAST

THE AHMADIYYA IN THE GOLD COAST

Muslim Cosmopolitans in the British Empire

John H. Hanson

Indiana University Press

This book is a publication of

Indiana University Press
Office of Scholarly Publishing
Herman B Wells Library 350
1320 East 10th Street
Bloomington, Indiana 47405 USA

iupress.indiana.edu

© 2017 by John H. Hanson

All rights reserved

No part of this book may be reproduced or utilized in any form or by any means, electronic or mechanical, including photocopying and recording, or by any information storage and retrieval system, without permission in writing from the publisher. The Association of American University Presses' Resolution on Permissions constitutes the only exception to this prohibition.

The paper used in this publication meets the minimum requirements of the American National Standard for Information Sciences—Permanence of Paper for Printed Library Materials, ANSI Z39.48-1992.

Manufactured in the United States of America

Cataloging information is available from the Library of Congress.

ISBN 978-0-253-02619-4 (cloth)
ISBN 978-0-253-02933-1 (paperback)
ISBN 978-0-253-02951-5 (ebook)

1 2 3 4 5   22 21 20 19 18 17

Contents

Preface and Acknowledgments   *vii*
Note on Maps   *xi*
Note on Terminology and Spelling   *xiii*
List of Abbreviations   *xv*

Introduction   1

Part I. Preparing the Way in the Gold Coast

1. The Hausa Force and the Religious Marketplace in the Fante States   31
2. Binyameen Sam's Fante Muslim Community   60

Part II. Ahmadiyya Genesis and Expansion to London and Lagos

3. The Genesis of the Ahmadiyya in British India   95
4. Ahmadiyya Expansion to London and Lagos   123

Part III. Ahmadiyya Arrival and Consolidation in the Gold Coast

5. Ahmadiyya Arrival in the Gold Coast   163
6. Ahmadiyya Consolidation in the Gold Coast   181
7. Ahmadiyya Expansion to Asante   199
8. Ahmadiyya Expansion to Wa   218

Conclusion   240

Glossary   249
Bibliography   253
Index   277

Illustrations begin on page 142

Preface and Acknowledgments

VISIONARY EXPERIENCES and religious conversations brought West Africans and South Asians together into the Ahmadiyya, a Muslim movement with origins in British India. Dreams led to discussions that pointed to new religious horizons: nearly a century ago West Africans invited an Ahmadi missionary to visit, accepted the Ahmadiyya, and supported the founding of an Ahmadi mission and school in Ghana, then known as the Gold Coast. My interest in this past was sparked by my own experiences and conversations in Wa, a town in northwestern Ghana where I was conducting research. Shortly after arriving, I was on the back of Latif Khalid's motorbike when we hit a goat that darted in front of us. We survived, as did the goat, but Latif had a bloody gash on his leg. As I dressed his wound, Latif, my research assistant, asked about my first-aid kit, something I had not packed on previous outings. I replied that the night before I had dreamed about having an accident; I added, as an explanation, that my malaria prophylaxis caused me, someone who rarely dreamed, to do so vividly. But Latif, an Ahmadi Muslim, engaged me at length about the significance of dreams in the history of the Ahmadiyya. This exchange was the first of many discussions, in the months and years that followed, about visionary experiences and religious conversations involving pioneering Ahmadi Muslims in the Gold Coast. Ghanaians repeat these accounts to others, including Khalifatul Masih Masroor Ahmad, the current leader of the Ahmadiyya, who visited Ghana and heard about dreams in the company of Maulvi Abdul Wahab Adam, then head of the Ghanaian branch of the movement, in the Ahmadi cemetery at Ekrawfo, Ghana. I interpret these oral accounts and others as a historian, placing them in a context and listening in light of what I learn in written materials.

I build on the work of other historians, but the perspectives in Ahmadi accounts leads my analysis in a different direction than the approach taken in Humphrey J. Fisher's *Ahmadiyyah: A Study in Contemporary Islam on the West African Coast*. My analysis also differs from Ivor Wilks's chapter on the Ahmadiyya in *Wa and the Wala*. The Ahmadi narratives inspired me to probe more deeply than others had in archives and libraries, where I discovered texts that illuminated and amplified Ahmadi memories. I argue from this evidence for a long history of African initiative that preceded the arrival of the Ahmadiyya and paved the way for its success. The result is this book. As a historical account, much of the analysis is based on written materials, but the insights came from Ahmadi narratives. I am grateful to those who shared information with me, some listed in my bibliography and others not because their stories concerned the postcolonial past, beyond the chronological frame of this book.

Grants and fellowships allowed me to pursue this research. I was in Wa on a Fulbright fellowship, and the National Endowment for the Humanities funded "Friday Prayers at Wa," an audiovisual work on the CD-ROM *Five Windows into Africa*. Additional research was launched in subsequent summer trips to Ghana funded by Indiana University. Reflection on this project occurred at the Library of Congress's Kluge Center, where I was funded by a Rockefeller fellowship. Then I conducted an extended period of research in Ghana and the United Kingdom, supported by a Fulbright-Hays fellowship. Additional research and the drafting of several chapters occurred at the National Humanities Center through support from a National Endowment for the Humanities fellowship. I completed research in British archives and libraries and wrote the complete draft of the current manuscript with support from the Gerda Henkel Foundation. Indiana University's Institute for Advanced Study provided financial support as I made revisions and prepared the manuscript for publication.

The book is the result of numerous visits abroad, and it would not have been possible without the hospitality and support of many people. First and foremost, I must acknowledge the assistance of Ahmadi Muslims, who accepted me not as a fellow believer but as a researcher in their midst. I met the current leader, Khalifatul Masih Masroor Ahmad, near the completion of this book, and he and others assisted in providing access to issues of *Review of Religions* I could not find in libraries. Specific thanks is due to Umar Ahmad, Omair Aleem, Asif M. Basit, Amer Safir, and Hassan Wahab, who helped provide these materials and also assisted in the process of obtaining permissions to use images from *Review of Religions*. Crucial to my work at its outset was Maulvi Mohammed bin Salih, the current ameer and missionary-in-charge in Ghana, who assisted my initial research in Wa by opening many doors and discussing the Wala past at length. As my project expanded beyond Wa, I relied on the assistance, encouragement, and insights of the late Maulvi Abdul Wahab Adam, the previous ameer and missionary-in-charge in Ghana, a towering public intellectual whom I feel fortunate to have known: I lament not completing this book before he died.

Interviews in Ghana depended on the assistance of a great many people, who dropped other activities to assist me. In Asante I am grateful to the following: in Kumasi and neighboring villages, Nana Abubakar, Ismael Addo, Y. K. Agyare, Al-Hajjiya Ayesha Bonsu, Abdullah Nasir Boateng, Al-Hajj Adams Dawoode, Nana Muhammad K. Duah, Al-Hajj Yusuf Ahmad Edusei, A. Y. Fareed, I. K. Gyasi, Al-Hajj Nuhu Kofi, Opanin Tahir, Al-Hajjiya Ayesha Tiwaa, and Dr. Muhammad Zafrullah; in Asakore, Dr. Mahmud Ahmad Butt and Usman Mensah; in Asokwa, Ibrahim Addo and Tahir Hammond; in Fomena, Ahmad Boakye, Nazir A. Keelson, and Sadique Nuamah; in Kokofu, Dr. Hameed Nasullah; in

Mampon, Ibrahim Agyeman, Abdullah Nasir Boateng, and Al-Hajj Mahmud K. Bobbrey; in Peminase and Pramso, Alhassan Atta, Dr. Al-Hajj Mohammad bin Ibrahim, Fazlu Ilah, and Hakeem Kontor. In the Central Region, I am indebted to Usman Abekah, Jibreel Adam, Al-Hajj Hakeem Amissah, Al-Hajj Abubakar Anderson, Sarah Anderson, Tahir Andze, Adam Appiah, Zahoor Arthur, Hussain Assopiah, Al-Hajj Ismail Biney, Lateef Esuam, Nuruddeen Inkoom, Dr. Nasrullah Khan, Nana Muhammad Ogyefo-Yena, and Yusuf Quandze. In Wa I benefited from the assistance of Wa Na Momori Bondiri II, Limam Al-Hajj Yakubu Issaka, Latif Khalid, Mahmud Khalid, Malam Taslim Mahama, E. M. Salifu, Alhassan bin Salih, Abdul Rahman Yahaya, and Dawud R. Yahaya. If I inadvertently omitted someone, please accept my apologies.

Assistance provided by colleagues also was considerable. Those offering helpful advice and insightful commentaries include Francis Acquah, Robert Addo-Fening, Emmanuel Akyeampong, Jean Allman, Mikelle Antoine, Kofi Baku, Owusu Brempong, Louis Brenner, the late N. J. K. Brukum, Barbara Cooper, Peter Dery, Michel Doortmont, the late John K. Fynn, Sandra Greene, Rasheed A. K. Guar-Gorman, Sean Hanretta, Jan Jansen, Ray Kea, David Killingray, Jon Kirby, Martin Klein, Roman Loimeier, Gislaine Lydon, Takyiwaa Manuh, Irene Odotei, David Owusu-Ansah, Deborah Pellow, Akosua Perbi, Derek Peterson, Ammah Rabiatu, Richard Roberts, Patrick Ryan, Lamin Sanneh, Rüdiger Seesemann, Shobana Shankar, Ray Silverman, Simon Valentine, Rijk van Dijk, Dmitri van den Bersselaar, and Leonardo Villalòn. My Indiana University colleagues engaged my work and enhanced its development; they are too numerous to list, and I hope that I am forgiven for naming only those whose research is closest to mine, Akin Adesokan, A. B. Assensoh, George Brooks, Beth Buggenhagen, Gracia Clark, Maria Grosz-Ngaté, Lauren Maclean, Patrick McNaughton, Phyllis Martin, Marissa Moorman, Michelle Moyd, Patrick O'Meara, Diane Pelrine, Dan Reed, and Beverly Stoeltje. Encouragement and insights came from graduate students who also provided inspiration as they launched their careers; they are too numerous to name individually, and I mention here only those working on Ghana: Ebenezer Ayesu, Jennifer Hart, Fred Pratt, Kelly Tucker, and especially Muhammad al-Munir Gibrill and Nate Plageman, who offered extensive commentaries and assistance at crucial junctures. Historians produce historians: I owe a great debt to Franklin A. Presler, who set me on my scholarly path long ago, and to David Robinson, who has remained a trusted guide, insightful reader, and good friend over the years.

Facilitating my work were numerous archivists and librarians. In Ghana I owe gratitude to those at the Public Records and Archives Administration in Accra, Cape Coast, and Tamale, and at the University of Ghana at Legon's Balme Library and the Institute of African Studies library. In the United Kingdom I am grateful to those at the British Library, the National Archives, the Bodleian

Libraries at the University of Oxford, and the School of Oriental and African Studies Library at the University of London. At the Rhodes House Library (now the Bodleian Library of Commonwealth and African Studies), the senior archivist Lucy McCann was especially helpful. While I worked with microfilm copies of materials at the Basel Mission Archive, its staff assisted me in obtaining digital copies of several maps from their collection. At the National Humanities Center, where I won an informal award for the most interlibrary loan requests in an academic year, I am indebted to the librarians who assisted in acquiring those materials: Josiah Drewry, Jean Houston, and Eliza Robertson. I also placed a heavy load on the Wells Library at Indiana University, especially the interlibrary loan staff and Marion Frank-Wilson, the Africana librarian.

I incurred debts in preparing the final manuscript for publication. Matt Johnson created the maps, working from documents and hand-rendered versions. I was assisted in acquiring the images in the book from the staffs at the Bodleian Libraries at the University of Oxford, the British Library, the British National Archives, Cambridge University library, and the School of African and Oriental Studies Library; I note the special attention provided by Erich Kesse of the Digital Library Project at School of Oriental and African Studies Library. Last and certainly not least is Dee Mortensen at Indiana University Press, who as editor was ever-encouraging, provided invaluable advice at all stages of the project, and remained committed to the work as it took unexpected turns.

This book was long in the making. Historians often invoke the problem of sources in Africa, and I certainly was challenged in this regard, especially for materials before the arrival of the Ahmadiyya. Another reason is that the project kept growing beyond the boundaries I wanted to impose, and I did not have time to devote to the evolving research that was needed, serving as director of Indiana University's vibrant African Studies Program. Once I decided to leave the director's position to devote myself to this project, I was diagnosed with a rare and very aggressive cancer, endured an extensive series of invasive treatments, and then a long recovery to get, thankfully, to an enduring remission. I could not have done so without the care of oncologists and nurses, encouragement from colleagues and students, and assistance from family and friends. My last acknowledgment is for the love of my life, the artist Amie J. Campbell. I cannot begin to express adequately my appreciation for her love, care, support, and patience over the course of our lives together. I dedicate this book to her.

Note on Maps

THE MAPS WERE DRAWN by Matt Johnson. The placement of the administrative boundaries, towns, and cocoa production zone in map 1 was informed by the map in *The Gold Coast Census, 1931, Appendices, Containing Comparative Returns and General Statistics of the 1931 Census* (Accra: Government Printer, 1932). The placement of the towns, rivers, and the palm oil production zone in map 2 was informed by the map in Robin Law, ed., *From Slave Trade to "Legitimate" Commerce: The Commercial Transition in Nineteenth-Century West Africa* (Cambridge: Cambridge University Press, 1995), 2. The placement of the expedition routes in map 3 was informed by the map in the Papers of John Hawley Glover, 1861–1875, held by the Cambridge University library (and accessed through microfilm). The placement of villages and rivers in maps 4 and 5 was informed by map in the Basel Mission Archive, map D-31.1 #21. The placement of the administrative boundaries, towns, cocoa production zone, and railroad in map 6 was informed by the map in G. B. Kay, ed., *The Political Economy of Colonialism in Ghana: A Collection of Documents and Statistics, 1900–1960* (Cambridge: Cambridge University Press, 1972), 19. The placement of towns, villages, and rivers in map 7 was informed by the map in Harjot Oberoi, *The Construction of Religious Boundaries: Culture, Identity, and Diversity in the Sikh Tradition* (Chicago: University of Chicago Press, 1994), 41.

Note on Terminology and Spelling

Many scholars adopt the phrase "colonial Ghana" to refer to the British colonial territory, but I use "Gold Coast." I do so because this study begins and ends before Ghana became independent in 1957, and also because I discuss events that occurred before British colonial rule, when it would have been inaccurate to refer to "colonial Ghana." I refer to inhabitants of the Gold Coast as Africans, sometimes referenced by ethnic designation, occupation, region of origin, religion, and other relevant social and historical distinctions, but never as "Gold Coasters."

This book uses non-English words rendered into Roman script. Complications in spelling arise, and they are multiplied by the number of languages in this work: Akan, Arabic, Hausa, Hindi, Urdu, and others. These languages have vowels and consonants that are not used in English; a few are tonal languages; several have their own scripts; and Arabic has differences based on local pronunciations and regional conventions. Some Arabic words, too, have entered the English lexicon, such as hajj, jihad, and madrasa. British colonial rule also introduced spellings; often their renderings of place names have endured in the postcolonial era. Finally, personal names vary in spelling even though they have a source in one language, such variants of Muhammad including Mohamed, Mahamma, and others.

Guiding my use of terms are the values of clarity, simplicity, and consistency. I adopted widely used forms for clarity, and I avoided using diacritical marks in the body of the text and only used them, following scholarly conventions, to transliterate words in the glossary (and in the notes, for example, when I refer to the title of a book). Geographical terms are widely adopted forms, such as Punjab and not Panjab, Kumasi and not Kumase. I selected West African usage for Arabic terms except in chapter 3 concerning South Asia. I also Anglicized the pluralization of frequently used terms, such as *mallam*, *pir*, and *zongo* (i.e., I added an *s*). For personal names, I followed the choices of individuals, both living and deceased.

Abbreviations

Terms that appear frequently have been abbreviated as follows:

AHR	*American Historical Review*
BM	Basel Mission Archive, Basel, Switzerland
CCCP	Chief Commissioner of the Central Province
CCNT	Chief Commissioner of the Northern Territories
CMS	Church Missionary Society Archive, Birmingham University, Birmingham, UK
DC	District Commissioner
GBT	*Ghana Bulletin of Theology*
HA	*History in Africa*
JAH	*Journal of African History*
JRA	*Journal of Religion in Africa*
PDJ	Papers of Lieutenant-Colonel A. C. Duncan-Johnstone, Bodleian Library of Commonwealth and African Studies, Oxford University, UK
PG	Papers of John Hawley Glover, Cambridge University Library, Cambridge, UK
PRAAD	Public Records Archives and Administration Department, Ghana
PRO	Public Records Office, Kew, UK
RR	*Review of Religions*
THSG	*Transactions of the Historical Society of Ghana*
WMMS	Wesleyan Methodist Missionary Society Archive, School of Oriental and African Studies Library, University of London, UK

THE AHMADIYYA IN THE GOLD COAST

Introduction

MAULVI ABDUL RAHIM NAYYAR arrived at Saltpond in the British Gold Coast (colonial Ghana) on the ocean steamer SS *Burutu* as the sun was setting on February 28, 1921. His green turban attracted the attention of the harbor police, who escorted him to meet the British district commissioner. Maulvi Nayyar, a thirty-seven-year-old South Asian man, served as a missionary for the Ahmadiyya, a Muslim community formed in British India, and he was stopping at Saltpond on his way to Lagos, Nigeria.[1] Nayyar affirmed his peaceful intentions, and the district commissioner released him to meet his host, Amadu Ramanu Pedro, who himself had arrived recently at Saltpond from Lagos to start a trading venture. Pedro was an Afro-Brazilian Muslim who accepted the Ahmadiyya after reading the movement's English-language publications and mailing a membership form to India, as did other Muslims in Lagos during the mid-1910s. The Lagosian Ahmadi Muslims requested assistance in establishing an English-language school at Lagos, and Nayyar was on his way to help, visiting the Gold Coast at the request of the Fante Muslim community. Learning of the Ahmadiyya from Pedro, Fante Muslims joined the movement during Nayyar's visit and offered to support an Ahmadi missionary in the Gold Coast. Maulvi Nayyar sent this news to his superiors and continued to Lagos. Instructions followed, and before he returned to London, Nayyar stopped again at Saltpond to prepare for the posting of Maulvi Fazlul Rahman Hakeem, the first in a series of residential Ahmadi missionaries heading the movement's new mission in the Gold Coast (see figure 1).[2]

The Ahmadiyya expanded rapidly, attracting both Muslims and Christians in the Gold Coast. Fante Muslims, the first to accept, were former Methodists who had adopted Islam decades earlier. They spread news of the movement along trade routes into the heart of the rainforest, where Asante cocoa farmers, both Muslims and Christians, became members. From there word reached the savanna of the Gold Coast's Northern Territories, as immigrant Wala Muslim scholars and labor migrants accepted the Ahmadiyya in Asante and evangelized the movement upon returning to Wa (see map 1). By the mid-1940s the Ahmadiyya had more than twenty thousand members in the Gold Coast.[3] They built more than 150 mosques in the region, a number accounting for almost two-thirds of Ahmadi mosques outside South Asia at the time.[4] British officials, whose suspicions had led them to observe Maulvi Nayyar covertly during his two Gold Coast visits in 1921, came to refer to the Ahmadiyya as a modern Muslim movement and to laud its educational efforts as exemplary.[5] The administration provided financial support to five mixed-gender Ahmadi schools, just as it subsidized Christian missionary schools.[6] The Ahmadiyya message not only affirmed the compatibility of the Muslim faith with an English-language education but also asserted that the founder of the Ahmadiyya, Ghulam Ahmad, was the Mahdi and Messiah of the End Times.

Ghulam Ahmad, a Muslim scholar in British India, made numerous claims, the most controversial of which was that he received divine revelation.[7] Ghulam Ahmad did not advocate military action as the Mahdi, or "Guided One," of the End Times but insisted that he was a nonviolent leader serving simultaneously as the Messiah and ushering in a new religious era.[8] Ghulam Ahmad argued that Jesus had survived the crucifixion and died of natural causes in India: Ghulam Ahmad claimed to be the spiritual reflection of Jesus in serving as the Messiah, just as he was the spiritual reflection of the Prophet Muhammad in reforming Islam. Ghulam Ahmad forbade exuberant Sufi Muslim expressions and esoteric practices, widely accepted in Punjab, the region of northwest India where he lived. Ghulam Ahmad also encouraged his followers to attend English-language schools, such as the one he founded one at Qadian, his natal village and headquarters of the movement. Ahmadiyya reformism appealed to both Muslim notables and the poor in rural areas close to Qadian, and it also attracted Muslim middle classes in Lahore, Punjab's largest town.[9] But the movement split shortly after Ghulam Ahmad's death in 1908: the rural Ahmadi majority selected his son as the divinely inspired *khalifatul masih*, but some followers rejected his succession in 1914 and established a competing movement in Lahore. The Ahmadiyya Muslim Community, as the majority branch came to be known, was headed for more than fifty years by Ghulam Ahmad's son, Khalifatul Masih Bashir ud-Din Mahmud Ahmad, who made the Ahmadiyya a mass movement in South Asia.[10] The Ahmadiyya Muslim Community also established a missionary presence abroad. The London mission, one of its first, spread the Ahmadiyya message in Britain and beyond to the Americas and West Africa through the dissemination of English-language publications and missionary tours, such as the one taken by Maulvi Nayyar to West Africa in 1921.

Historians represent the Ahmadiyya as a foreign movement in West Africa. J. Spencer Trimingham relegated his discussion of the Ahmadiyya to an appendix in his influential history of Islam in West Africa, asserting that the movement "differs from all previous Islamic action on Africa in that it was a maritime importation into the forest region, and that meant an entirely different non-African Islamic tradition."[11] Humphrey Fisher added that "overseas control and expatriate management" of the Ahmadiyya's West African missions expressed "inalterable doctrinal necessity," a reference to the divine inspiration claimed by Ghulam Ahmad and his successors.[12] Fisher was pessimistic about the movement's future in West Africa and emphasized internal divisions and fragmentation, well documented for the history of the Nigerian branch. Optimism was merited, at least for Ghana, which Fisher discussed in a brief, four-page chapter: Ahmadiyya membership today in Ghana stands at half a million, and descendants of pioneering African converts have assumed leadership roles in an organization that operates more than a hundred primary, secondary, and tertiary institutions.[13] Scholars nevertheless still emphasize external influences rather than internal dynamism.[14]

This book places Africans at the center of its analysis of the Ahmadiyya in the Gold Coast. It does not neglect the role of South Asian Ahmadi missionaries, but I contend that the arrival and consolidation of the movement was a culmination of African efforts to found and sustain a local Muslim community. My argument is based on memories and written materials overlooked by previous historians. It is a story with many twists and turns, as a community of African Christians became Muslims, later accepted the Ahmadiyya, and then convinced others to do the same. It begins at the time of a British imperial war establishing the Gold Coast in 1874: some Fante Christians followed Binyameen Sam, a former Methodist, who accepted Islam after meeting a *mallam* associated with a militia of African recruits from Lagos.[15] The militia, known as the Hausa Force, fought with British armies against the Asante Empire and then returned to Lagos, and thereafter Binyameen Sam preached Islam from the Bible on his own in the Gold Coast. But *mallams* from the savanna, who migrated to the coast at the turn of the nineteenth century, asserted their superior religious credentials and criticized Sam's practices. Fante Muslims learned of the Ahmadiyya shortly after Sam's death and joined during Maulvi Nayyar's visit, thereafter collaborating with a succession of Ahmadi missionaries to open schools and to convey the End Times message to others, including Muslim and Christian cocoa farmers in Asante and Wala *mallams* and laborers who had migrated to Asante and returned to Wa.

These transformations express the initiatives of Muslim cosmopolitans. I define *cosmopolitans* as those parties conversing about universal religious values across cultural boundaries, drawing inspiration from the pragmatic ethics associated with cross-cultural exchanges discussed in Kwame Anthony Appiah's *Cosmopolitanism: Ethics in a World of Strangers*.[16] Muslims long have had exchanges with other Muslims in the wider Islamic world, but I distinguish those interactions from the conversations between Muslims and Christians in the British Empire that are the focus of this study.[17] The latter interactions decisively shaped the Fante Muslim community and the Ahmadiyya, two Muslim movements that engaged the expanding Christian missionary presence in British colonies. In contrast, most *mallams* in the West African savanna did not participate in religious exchanges with Christians; even contact with Ahmadi Muslims was discouraged, as evident in the strong opposition of *mallams* in Wa to the return of Wala Ahmadi Muslims, whom they condemned as having become Christians. Defining *cosmopolitan* in this sense allows me to place Fante Muslims, residential Ahmadi missionaries, and African converts to the Ahmadiyya in the same analytical frame: Fante Muslims interpreted the Bible in light of their knowledge of Islam, Ahmadi missionaries drew on the Bible and the Quran as they discussed Ahmadiyya beliefs and practices, and African converts to the Ahmadiyya were Christians and Muslims who compared religious traditions as they accepted the movement's message.

Cosmopolitanism often implies an urban sensibility, but much of the activity in this story occurred in rural contexts. Ghulam Ahmad resided in a Punjabi village far from the provincial capital of Lahore and drew most of his supporters from the region: they were aspirational Muslims interested in pursuing a pious path to material success in the colonial era.[18] Africans in the Gold Coast's cash-cropping regions also played lead roles in this history. The abolition of the transatlantic slave trade in the nineteenth century occurred simultaneously with expanding exports of West African agricultural products to new industries in Europe and North America.[19] Palm oil was a primary export of the early decades, but other tropical crops became important over time, such as cocoa in the twentieth-century Gold Coast.[20] British colonialism also created positions for those with English-language skills, such as clerks in colonial bureaucracies and in British firms. Scholars debate the long-term impact of British colonialism in West Africa; whatever its enduring influence, its arrival created opportunities for cash cropping and encouraged the acquisition of English, processes that facilitated the circulation of religious ideas between urban and rural contexts.

Muslim cosmopolitans from the British colony of Lagos played crucial roles in this history. Lagos was a Yoruba fishing village that became a major port during the era of the transatlantic slave trade and grew under British colonial rule, established in 1861, into a center of commercial and political significance (see map 2). Muslim communities in Lagos included repatriated Africans from Brazil and Freetown, a British colony receiving Africans liberated by the Royal Navy from slave ships bound for the Americas in the nineteenth century. Most immigrants from Brazil and Freetown were Christians, but some were Muslims. In Lagos these immigrants interacted with local residents, both indigenous practitioners and converts to Christianity and Islam. Historians of Lagosian Muslims concentrate on their activities in Nigeria and not their broader influences.[21] This book reveals the activities of two groups: Hausa Force Muslims who proselytized Islam among Fante Methodists during the 1870s and Afro-Brazilian Muslims who were at the vanguard of West African evangelism of the Ahmadiyya a half century later.[22]

West African cosmopolitans operated in wider networks extending to the imperial metropole of London and beyond. This context is discussed in Paul

Gilroy's *Black Atlantic*, which drew attention to the cultural initiatives of diasporic Africans in North America and Britain.[23] Others added West Africans into the Black Atlantic, but few have included West African Muslims in these exchanges.[24] This book situates them, as well as Ahmadi missionaries, into Black Atlantic cultural flows. Historians interested in early Ahmadiyya proselytism heretofore have focused on the dissident Lahori branch; one leading member was the lawyer Khwaja Kamal ud-Din, who helped establish an ecumenical mosque at Woking, south of London.[25] But the Ahmadiyya Muslim Community also was active in London at the time. Influencing these missionaries was Dusé Mohamed Ali, the pan-Africanist editor of *African Times and Orient Review*. Ali provided contacts to West Africans and those in the North American diaspora.[26] Afro-Brazilian Muslims in Lagos learned of the Ahmadiyya from literature disseminated through Dusé Mohamed Ali's networks connecting London to Lagos, and this exchange led to Maulvi Nayyar's 1921 tour of West Africa. The Ahmadiyya mission to African Americans in several northern cities of the United States similarly had marks of Ali's influence through the assistance he provided Mufti Muhammad Sadiq, an Ahmadi missionary who left London in 1920.[27]

This history challenges conventional representations of Muslims in the era of European imperialism. Historians often cast Muslims in reactionary roles, either fighting against imperial expansion or accommodating colonialism and turning inward to reform Islam.[28] West African Muslims certainly provided numerous examples of these two responses.[29] Muslim introversion was encouraged by colonial policies prohibiting Christian missions from operating in Muslim-majority areas in British territories in West Africa: Northern Nigeria is a well-known example, but Wa in the Gold Coast's Northern Territories is another. These British efforts did not prevent West African Muslims from reflecting on new ideas circulating in the Muslim world, and Islamic reformism became a major current in postcolonial West Africa.[30] But decades before, Muslims and Christians were interacting and discussing common aspects of their scriptural heritages in coastal West Africa. In the literature on Muslims in the Gold Coast, these exchanges are overshadowed by the "northern factor" or the historical influence of savanna Muslims in Asante and by extension in the Fante states.[31] The Ahmadiyya reversed this trajectory, not as a "non-African Islamic tradition," as Trimingham asserted, but as an initiative of African cosmopolitans who invited Ahmadi missionaries to the Gold Coast.

Cosmopolitans

Kwame Anthony Appiah's *Cosmopolitanism* addresses the relationship between absolute values and cultural relativity by proposing a pragmatic ethics that affirms universal human principles in a world of enduring cultural differences.

Appiah's cosmopolitanism is an ethical practice that responds eloquently to absolutists by advocating respectful conversations about shared principles across cultural boundaries. I draw inspiration from Appiah's ethics in my analysis of religious interactions in British imperial contexts by focusing on those seeking profound religious understandings through exchanges between Christians and Muslims.[32] The arrival of Christian evangelists in coastal West Africa during the nineteenth century opened the possibility for these religious exchanges, but most European and North American missionaries did not seize the opportunity. They were absolutists who imagined themselves as bringing a civilizing Christianity to the continent and were as dismissive of African Muslims as they were of followers of indigenous religious expressions. Nineteenth-century Christian proselytism, in West Africa as elsewhere, combined with British imperialism to create competitive religious arenas in which Christian missionaries aggressively sought converts. But the era nonetheless produced cosmopolitans.

One prominent cosmopolitan was Samuel Ajayi Crowther. He rose to become the first African Anglican bishop in a career that emerged during the era of the transatlantic slave trade and ended with British colonialism. Crowther was enslaved by African Muslims as a child in southwestern Nigeria, sold and put on a Portuguese slave ship at the coast, and then liberated at sea by a British naval vessel that took him to Freetown.[33] Crowther attended a Christian mission school at Freetown, returned to Nigeria as a Church Missionary Society missionary in the mid-nineteenth century, and rose through the society's ranks to become head of the Niger River mission. Crowther's evangelism among Muslims expressed an "African Christian approach to Islam in an African setting," according to Andrew Walls.[34] Crowther pursued a comparative textualism in which he showed a Bible translated into Arabic to Muslims, discussed Old Testament prophets that Christians shared with Muslims, and contrasted the New Testament teachings of Jesus with Muslim beliefs rooted in the Quran. Crowther's strategy is notable, not only because African Muslims had enslaved him as a youth but also, and more significantly, because he had been trained in an era when Freetown's European Christian missionaries were stridently hostile to African Muslims.[35]

Samuel Crowther's approach emerged, I contend, from his conversations with Muslim cosmopolitans. Crowther's initial missionary posting was at Badagry, just west of Lagos.[36] Within months of his arrival Crowther described a formative encounter with Mahamma, an Afro-Brazilian Muslim who was visiting Badagry from Lagos. His chance encounter with Crowther led Mahamma to pose questions about the spiritual status of Jesus in relation to Muhammad. Crowther spoke with Mahamma for three-quarters of an hour, until Crowther's compatriot, the British missionary Reverend Townsend, intervened with dismissive comments that abruptly ended the conversation. Before Mahamma left, however, Crowther gave him a copy of an Arabic Bible and invited Mahamma to return and continue the conversation. Mahamma did during his next visit to Badagry several months later.³⁷ These conversations with Mahamma contrasted with the heated confrontations that characterized most exchanges between Christian missionaries and Muslims in southwestern Nigeria at the time.³⁸ Buoyed by his early encounter with Mahamma, Crowther pursued an alternate path to interactions with Muslims from the one Reverend Townsend advocated, and he continued to interact with Muslims when he moved to Abeokuta, just north of Lagos.³⁹ By the late 1850s Crowther observed, after more encounters with Muslims during service on a British expedition up the Niger River, that mentioning shared prophets in the Quran and the Old Testament was "sufficient to rivet [Muslims] in the belief of their book being the same as ours."⁴⁰ Decades later Crowther implemented the formal evangelical strategy noted by Walls. It emerged from a series of interactions launched by conversations about shared religious values with Mahamma and other Muslim cosmopolitans.

Mahamma articulated an ecumenical religious ethos associated with the Afro-Brazilian community. Afro-Brazilians had been enslaved in West Africa, sent on slave ships to Brazil, and then returned to West Africa after securing emancipation.⁴¹ Most Afro-Brazilians were Catholic, but a few were Muslim. Afro-Brazilians resettled by the thousands in communities from Accra to Lagos, where the largest number resided during the nineteenth century.⁴² These immigrants came in several waves: a few arrived in the early nineteenth century as agents of Brazilian slave-trading firms, others left Brazil after an 1835 slave rebellion, and the majority migrated during the second half of the nineteenth century. Their ethnic identities included Yoruba, Nupe, Kanuri, and Hausa heritages: some returned to their regions of origin, but most remained on the coast, where they constituted a corporate group and provided one another communal security. These immigrants drew on skills they had gained in the diaspora and returned to assume key roles in bustling coastal towns. Afro-Brazilian architecture in West Africa, including Catholic churches and Muslim mosques, had a style that evoked both the Brazilian past and local expressions.⁴³ Scholars are coming to recognize the ecumenical ethos of the Afro-Brazilian communities in nineteenth-century West Africa.⁴⁴ Mahamma's discussions with Samuel Crowther were an expression of a widespread Afro-Brazilian openness to religious encounters between Muslims and Christians in West Africa.

Other West Africans were cosmopolitans. Many former slaves returned to the coastal regions of southern Nigeria from Freetown, as did Samuel Crowther, although they were traders more often than missionaries. Most Saro, as immigrants from Freetown were known in Nigeria, were Protestants, but some were Muslims. One was Muhammad Shitta, the son of an African liberated at Freetown. Shitta moved to Lagos and worked initially as an agent for English businessmen who called him "William," a name bestowed on him at a Freetown

Christian missionary school. He became a wealthy merchant and philanthropist who supported the construction of large mosques in Lagos and Freetown.[45] Shitta's experiences in the Freetown mission school gave him pause when British officials proposed opening a Muslim school with an English-language curriculum in Lagos during the late 1890s, but he agreed to try it on an experimental basis;[46] it gained Muslim support and existed for two decades before closing as Muslims increasingly attended Arabic schools.[47] Muhammad Shitta's collaboration with the British administration was matched by similar interactions with Saro Christians in Lagos. The ties between Freetown's Christian and Muslim immigrants were not as close as those between Afro-Brazilians, but they engaged in respectful exchanges across religious boundaries.[48]

Hausa Force Muslims were cosmopolitans, too. Some had been liberated at Freetown, but most had been slaves who fled their masters in southwestern Nigeria for Lagos, where British colonial officials organized this ethnically diverse group into a colonial militia in the 1860s.[49] British officials drew on widespread colonial ideas about martial races and stressed the military prowess of "Hausa" slaves whose Muslim identity made them, in their imaginings, a loyal force against non-Muslim African slave masters in the interior.[50] Historians have not gone beyond British imaginings to investigate how Hausa Force soldiers constructed their Muslim identity in the 1860s and 1870s. Members of the Hausa Force, I contend, expressed a variant of "barracks Islam" that included a demonstrative religious practice and engagement of *mallams* to receive esoteric protection and healing.[51] The force was influential beyond Lagos: its military accomplishments and demonstrative Muslim performances in the 1870s Gold Coast increased receptivity to Islam and opened a path for *mallams* associated with the force to convert locals.

Fante Muslims had a different social profile from that of the cosmopolitans discussed already. They did not have personal histories of enslavement: Afro-Brazilian Muslims, Muslims from Freetown, and members of the Hausa Force were Atlantic Muslims whose engagements with Christians arose out of the crucible of the transatlantic slave trade. Fante Methodists who became Muslims did not have experiences of liberation and return: their dislocation was elective, in that they chose to renounce their Christian heritage in a reaction against specific Methodist teachings. The genesis of the Fante Muslim community occurred in an era of religious change after the successful British invasion of Asante; thereafter, many coastal residents became Methodists, but some became Muslims. The leader of the Muslim movement, Binyameen Sam, was a Biblicist who interpreted Christian scripture to support Muslim beliefs and practices and to criticize some Methodist teachings. Later Fante Muslims became aware of the Ahmadiyya and joined the movement. The Ahmadiyya arrival did not produce a rupture in the Gold Coast, I contend, but it fit into the contours of a religious movement associated with Fante Muslim cosmopolitans. Ahmadiyya proselytism nonetheless elicited strong opposition from *mallams* in West Africa.

Muslim Scholars in the Savanna Tradition

West African Muslim scholars in the late nineteenth-century savanna saw themselves as custodians of a Muslim tradition that their ancestors had maintained for centuries.[52] One of the most prominent *mallams* was Al-Hajj Umar ibn Abi Bakr (d. 1934). He was born in northern Nigeria into a Hausa Muslim scholarly family and resided as an adult at Salaga and then Kete-Krachi in the middle Volta River region, the savanna north of Asante.[53] Al-Hajj Umar's life stretches over the span discussed in this book, giving him an opportunity to provide commentary on both the Hausa Force and the Ahmadiyya. Al-Hajj Umar's reference to the Hausa Force was only fleeting, a line in a poem about the British colonial conquest of the Asante Empire: he referred merely to "Hausa" who "accompanied the Christians," pointedly not mentioning the soldiers' religious status as Muslims even as he insisted on identifying British invaders as Christians.[54] Al-Hajj Umar judged the Hausa Force, whether because of its boisterous practices or its service to the British, to be distinct from the Muslim tradition that his Hausa Muslim scholarly family had transmitted over the centuries. Al-Hajj Umar was even more dismissive of the Ahmadiyya. At a meeting with Maulvi Hakeem, the first residential Ahmadi missionary in the Gold Coast who was visiting Kumasi in 1925, Al-Hajj Umar stood up, spat on the floor, and abruptly left in the middle of Hakeem's presentation at a British official's residence.[55] The Ahmadiyya and members of the Hausa Force, in Al-Hajj Umar's view, were outside the savanna Muslim tradition.

The savanna tradition invoked by Al-Hajj Umar arose after Muslims from north of the Sahara desert first convinced Africans in the savanna to adopt Islam more than a thousand years ago. The conversions produced religious advocates, organized into Muslim scholarly families, who traveled along trade routes and crossed cultural frontiers in the pluralist religious contexts of West Africa. These custodians of Islam continued to speak West African languages, such as Fulfulde, Hausa, and Juula, but they were specialists in Arabic and used their knowledge of the Quran and other Islamic texts to provide a variety of religious, pedagogical, and social services. Muslim scholars in the savanna followed legal recommendations in the Maliki tradition and were not divided by sectarianism. They shared an interest in esoteric practices, such as the provision of protective amulets and curative herbal medicinal washes.[56] This Muslim heritage included hierarchical relations between teachers and their students in the transmission of learning, esoteric practices, and other aspects of the tradition. The hierarchy was infused with intimacy, emphasizing face-to-face encounters between scholars and students who would form the next generation.[57] Reinforcing the tradition was the West African Muslim practice of recognizing a closed set of Muslim scholars in the transmission of Islamic texts in chains of religious authority.[58] West African Muslim scholarly families also had interests in the economy, usually as merchants and sometimes as farmers relying on slaves for labor, which freed them to focus on teaching and scholarship. Some Muslim scholars assisted rulers, serving as councilors and scribes, but others kept their distance. No tradition is static, and historical analysis of the West African Muslim past has noted numerous transformations, but the savanna tradition had resilience from the Senegal River basin to the shores of Lake Chad.

A series of militant movements encouraged the growing perception that the West African savanna was a Muslim domain by the nineteenth century. This call to arms was led by Muslim scholars who had refrained from political involvement and criticized Muslims who had forged alliances with established ruling elites. The first militant Muslim political movements occurred in the west, as the transatlantic slave trade in Mauritania and Senegambia led to religious condemnation of African elites who benefited from the enslavement of Muslims for sale in these commercial exchanges.[59] By the early nineteenth century the call to arms occurred in the eastern savanna in today's northern Nigeria, a region less fully influenced by Atlantic currents. The result was the founding of the Sokoto Caliphate, a Muslim federation of states formed after Shaykh Uthman dan Fodio declared "jihad of the sword" against the Hausa ruling elite in Gobir: Shaykh Uthman and his allies won, established a new capital and successor state at Sokoto, and gave flags to those who overthrew other Hausa city-states to create a new Muslim domain.[60] Other Muslim movements arose and established a series of Muslim states stretching from Senegal to Nigeria.[61] Although this militancy transformed the context, many Muslim scholars still refrained from political activism, and a few criticized the militants on religious grounds.[62]

Europeans imposed their rule over Muslims throughout West Africa in the late nineteenth century. Muslim reactions varied over time and even within the same context; groups within Muslim communities sometimes came to different conclusions about appropriate responses. Many leaders of Muslim states negotiated treaties with European agents in the initial period and later fought when European territorial ambitions were revealed; some leaders retreated strategically in the face of superior weaponry in hopes of finding a refuge; the majority eventually came to accommodation with European imperial powers and created opportunities for themselves as intermediaries in the colonial apparatus, in the process preserving Muslim control over some religious institutions and maintaining a semblance of political control over local affairs. Nevertheless, the European colonial era presented challenges to Muslims in the savanna tradition. Some historians argue that European colonial rule ruptured the tradition's esoteric worldview and encouraged Muslim reformers to adopt new pedagogical practices.[63] But the tradition of face-to-face encounters remained a core aspect of Muslim education in the West African savanna well into the twentieth century.[64] The savanna tradition was maintained and amplified by Muslims in the middle Volta River region and the rainforest to its south, two regions discussed in this book.

Muslims in the Middle Volta River Region

The savanna lands of the middle Volta River region included Muslim mercantile and scholarly families who settled in the region over the centuries.[65] The first Muslim immigrants were Mande-speaking Muslims who arrived from the heartland of the former Mali Empire in the fifteenth century, set down roots, and adopted local languages. They provided services as scribes and councilors to political elites atop states, such as Gonja, Dagomba, and Mamprusi, and small polities, such as Wa. Joining these Mande Muslim communities were Hausa-speaking Muslim traders and scholars arriving from the east in increasing numbers as trade with the Sokoto Caliphate and Bornu expanded, especially in the nineteenth century. Hausa-speaking Muslim scholars drew on a repertoire of religious and esoteric services similar to Mande Muslims, establishing their own reputations once they settled in the region.[66] Some scholars argue that Hausa Muslims, after the rise of the Sokoto Caliphate, were more assertive in their Muslim expressions than Mande Muslims, but calls to "jihad of the sword" were infrequent, as commercial interests predominated in the middle Volta region.[67]

Savanna Muslims were present in the rainforest of today's Ghana but rarely settled permanently until the twentieth century. While Akan speakers interacted with Muslims on the northern forest fringe, leaving traces of those early encounters in Akan material culture, Akan state formation in the rainforest did not include residential Muslims in political roles, as in the middle Volta region.[68] The rise of the Asante Empire provided Muslims with new opportunities: the imperial ruler (*asantehene*) sometimes favored nonresident Muslim merchants as a means to constrain the rise of an indigenous commercial class, but imperial policy also controlled Muslim travel, forcing Muslim merchants to live outside the rainforest in savanna trading towns, such as Salaga.[69] Asante control over Muslims also extended to *mallams*. Asante rulers turned to Muslim scholars to serve as scribes and councilors, and imperial conquests led to increasing use of *mallams* as providers of protective amulets for the Asante ruler and his soldiers. *Asante nkramo*, Muslim scholars of Mande heritage, resided at the Asante capital of Kumasi, but they were few in number and were subordinate to the *nsumankwaahene*, who provided cures and produced talisman known as *asuman*. *Asante nkramo* knew that they were guests who could be, and sometimes were, expelled when they fell out of favor.[70] Asante control of Muslim travel, residence, and proselytism also meant that few savanna Muslim scholars were present in the Fante states along the coast during the nineteenth century.

The rainforest opened to large-scale settlement by savanna Muslims only as British colonial influences increased beginning in the late nineteenth century. The British victory over Asante in 1874 led to the removal of travel restrictions on Muslims entering the Gold Coast, but few permanent Muslim settlements were established immediately.[71] Muslim residence in the south increased beginning in the 1890s, propelled by the outbreak of a civil war in Salaga and the lure of new economic opportunities along the coast.[72] British officials permitted immigrant Muslims to establish *zongos*, or immigrant wards, in coastal towns.[73] Asante's annexation by the British at the turn of the nineteenth century later opened Kumasi and other Asante towns to the creation of *zongos*.[74] Initial immigrants were laborers and Muslim traders, but *mallams* followed.[75] Muslim leaders in the Northern Territories, as well as leaders of *zongos* in southern towns, came to constructive working relations with British colonial officials, but the arrangements were more limited than the relations European colonial officials forged with Muslim elites in Senegal and northern Nigeria.[76] This accommodation allowed Muslims to maintain certain institutions, such as Arabic schools that taught the Quran by rote.[77] By the late colonial era, some Muslims began to challenge this pedagogical tradition and other aspects of the savanna tradition, and Muslim reformism gained momentum in the postcolonial era.[78] But well before these changes, Binyameen Sam founded an English-language school at a time when British officials encouraged Muslim schools along the coast.[79] Sam's Muslim school closed within a decade, but that initiative, and the subsequent Fante Muslim acceptance of the Ahmadiyya, expressed the initiatives of Muslim cosmopolitans operating in the religious marketplace of the Gold Coast.

Muslims, Christians, and Religious Marketplaces in the British Empire

Scholars often invoke the metaphor of encounters to analyze Muslim-Christian relations in Africa.[80] This approach has much to offer: conversations across religious boundaries, the focus of this book, occurred through such encounters. But Muslim-Christian interactions also are shaped by power relations and enduring religious attitudes. These factors are evident, for example, in the history of African Christians in Muslim majority contexts in twentieth-century Niger and northern Nigeria, where state policies and religious antagonism influenced encounters that unfolded over time.[81] I adopt a religious economy framework to underscore and illuminate the power dynamics of the colonial era: British officials affirmed religious liberty and gave Christian missionary access to most contexts, and the missions used this opening to define conversion as a matter of individual choice and to introduce new strategies and techniques for proselytism. Most West African Muslims did not engage in exchanges with Christians, but Muslims in coastal regions sometimes did. The religious marketplace approach frames those interactions in the British imperial era.

Christian missionary evangelism and British imperialism were distinct but intertwined processes in the nineteenth and twentieth centuries.[82] One provocative line of analysis stresses the ways Christian evangelism fostered the adoption of mentalities and practices associated with the British colonial order. Jean Comaroff and John Comaroff went beyond conventional recognition that mission schools imparted skills to work in the colonial economy and argued for a profound influence whereby Christian missionaries inculcated local converts into the habits of bourgeois colonial culture.[83] This interpretive move encouraged others to investigate how Christian missionary proselytism encouraged cultural transformations, bundled into the phrase "conversion to modernities" and referencing the adoption of new notions of the self that were deeply enmeshed in the institutions and processes of a globalizing world.[84] But while Christian converts often claimed to be modern, their definitions referred to many expressions: we need not adopt the concept of modernity to acknowledge that Christian evangelism contributed to the creation of new cultural orientations by its adherents.[85] These encounters were formative, even transformative, but only to the degree that converts were receptive to outside influences and constructed their own definitions of modernity.

Christian evangelism also produced Biblicists who drew on scripture to construct religious understandings that were meaningful and relevant in local contexts. Translating the Bible into other languages enabled Africans and Asians to inscribe local interpretations into scripture itself.[86] Converts also amplified and elaborated on Christian values by invoking biblical passages to describe their goals and aspirations. Some scholars argue that these local initiatives were "converting colonialism," altering the balance in the religious encounter to focus on the converts' initiatives.[87] John Peel's work offers a sophisticated analysis of how Yoruba Christians in southwestern Nigeria drew on interpretations of the Bible to contextualize their lives and guide their evangelism: the stories they told themselves and others were aspirational and decisively informed their activities.[88] Emphasis on the Bible had its limits, especially in contexts where local religious leaders had their own scriptures. Strident Christian missionary comparison of scriptures dominated exchanges with Muslims in British India, for example, with public religious debates in the heart of the former Mughal Empire that did not produce a groundswell of new converts to Christianity.[89]

Christian missionaries perceived that local Muslims had competitive advantages in the cultural domain. Many noted that Muslims made fewer religious demands than Christians and that they also tolerated polygyny and other local cultural practices.[90] In southwestern Nigeria during the early twentieth century, Christian missionaries were acutely aware that Islam often expanded into regions where their missions operated: they suspected that their proselytism created a spiritual opening that Muslims seized because strict Christian discipline became an obstacle to local participation.[91] Historians acknowledge instances in which these missionary apprehensions were merited, for example, when the Catholic Church in colonial Senegal lost converts to Muslims who allowed continued practice of life-cycle rituals when the church did not.[92] These examples reveal the results of Muslim evangelism through winning over former Christians, or at least those to whom Christians had made an appeal, but Muslim proselytism remains in the shadows, implied but not examined.[93] Studies of converts to Christianity in Muslim-majority contexts reveal the importance of biblical engagement over a long period, but no one has studied the reverse, how Christians might elect to become Muslims over an extended period of religious engagement.[94] This book fills that void by examining the Muslim preaching of Binyameen Sam, a former Methodist; the teachings of Ghulam Ahmad, who drew on biblical passages to construct his arguments about his role as the Messiah; and the initiatives of Ahmadi missionaries who drew on the Bible in their Gold Coast evangelism.

Competition to win converts across the Muslim-Christian divide raises broader issues about the nature of conversion. Scholars often differentiate the quality of acceptance, situating the experiences on a continuum from acculturation to fundamental transformation, with adhesion and syncretism as intermediary stages.[95] The depth of conversion was invoked in the debate between Robin Horton and Humphrey Fisher about religious change in colonial sub-Saharan Africa. Horton argued that converts usually did not undergo a "radical change in cosmology" and merely substituted the God of Christianity or Islam for the preexisting creator in their indigenous worldviews, which had been focused on the locality but shifted attention to the macrocosm with the social changes of the European colonial era.[96] Fisher countered that initial conversions were adhesion and stressed the "juggernaut" of religious change over time that ultimately led to fundamental reorientation.[97] Debates over gradations of conversion, however, presume insights into the internal life of believers that historical sources rarely provide. Fisher's insistence on eventual reform also is teleological, failing to recognize unstable religious commitments that characterized periods of social tumult. Instead of conversion, this book focuses on the religious context in which Christian evangelists emphasized religious choice and created competitive religious arenas in which other religious movements responded with vigor and new capacities. This approach avoids questions concerning the depth of the conversion experience and examines instead religious borrowings, adaptations, and transformations. Serial changes in the religious lives of Fante Muslims cannot be placed on a continuum in one religious tradition, nor can the rise of the

Ahmadiyya be understood without reference to the competitive religious context of the British Punjab.

Religious Marketplaces

Religious economy is a conceptual tool that analyzes religious change at a higher level of magnification than the evangelical encounter.[98] It does not reduce religious expressions to the ontological status of goods, and instead lays emphasis on competition and the exchange of strategies and techniques between religious movements. In a robust formulation of this approach, scholars conceive of religious leaders and their followers as producers and consumers, respectively, and compare religious movements as firms that respond to demand for religious services. Understanding religious change as the result of competition and comparison is most appropriate for pluralist religious contexts, especially where new religious movements arose in periods of social transformation.[99] *Bombay Islam*, Nile Green's analysis of Muslim expressions in British India, identifies Christian missionary societies as the catalyst for the competitive religious economy in nineteenth-century Bombay and reveals social differences between Muslim consumers: working-class Muslims, migrating from rural areas to work in industrializing Bombay, were interested in the enchanted services offered in Sufi festivals and other esoteric practices, whereas middle-class Muslims preferred the educational services offered by austere reformist Muslim movements. Green's analysis illustrates the interpretive power of the religious economy model for understanding the ways local Muslims operated in a newly competitive religious market of the British colonial era.[100]

This book adopts the term *religious marketplace* to refer to competitive religious arenas in British Punjab and the Gold Coast. I do not sustain the robust religious economy analyses of sociologists or even Nile Green's historical work on Bombay; instead, I refer to religious marketplaces as a means to illuminate the historical forces that shaped religious change in pluralist British colonial contexts. This approach frames the emergence of the Ahmadiyya in the competitive religious marketplace created after Christian missions arrived in Punjab during its incorporation into British India. It also contextualizes the Gold Coast religious arena at several historical moments: during the 1870s, the Hausa Force's military accomplishments and demonstrative Muslim expressions opened the religious marketplace and paved the way for Binyameen Sam's Muslim community to become a new religious provider in the Gold Coast; in the aftermath of the 1918 influenza pandemic, the Gold Coast religious marketplace was unsettled and made receptive to End Times messages, such as articulated by prophetic Christian movements and the Ahmadiyya; in the 1930s, the religious marketplace in Kumasi, which had been closed to the Ahmadiyya, opened to various new providers, including the Ahmadiyya. Adoption of a religious marketplace approach does not preclude other analyses, but it provides a historical context for a deeper appreciation of the activities of Muslim cosmopolitans who explored questions of religious practice and meaning in competitive religious arenas emerging in British India and the Gold Coast.

Sources

This history of the Ahmadiyya arrival and consolidation in the Gold Coast is based on sources internal and external to the movement. Residential Ahmadi missionaries in the Gold Coast provided contemporaneous accounts that appeared in the *Review of Religions*, an English-language publication of the Ahmadiyya Muslim Community, and in a few documents held in the mission's offices in Ghana: these Ahmadi sources are in English, the medium of communication for residential Ahmadi missionaries in the Gold Coast. Newspapers from London, Lagos, and the Gold Coast add external perspectives on the Ahmadiyya, as do British documents, such as Colonial Office records held in the British National Archives and Lieutenant-Colonel A. C. Duncan-Johnstone's papers at Oxford University.[101] African perspectives are more difficult to access. Binyameen Sam, though literate, left no writings for posterity, nor did other members of the early Fante Muslim community; African Ahmadi Muslims also produced few written materials during the early decades of the movement. Memories are the primary sources for African actors. In addition, texts by British officials, Christian missionaries, and others sometimes include references to statements made by Africans. These texts, as well as current memories, are mediated sources, providing voices from the past through the words of others.[102] This book builds its arguments on a broad canvassing of written and oral materials, and I discuss the limits of the extant evidence throughout my analysis.

Numerous individuals heard and recorded oral accounts of the Ahmadiyya past in Ghana over the past half century. Humphrey Fisher conducted research during the late 1950s and referenced local memories in his writings, usually without providing the names of informants and other details such as the place and date of the interviews. Rasheed A. K. Guar-Gorman, a Ghanaian Ahmadi Muslim, summarized Fante Muslim memories in the text of his master's thesis.[103] Mohammed bin Salih, the current head of the Ahmadiyya in Ghana, discussed Wala memories in his book.[104] Others have summarized what they heard in unpublished theses and essays.[105] I also conducted interviews among Ahmadi Muslims and others connected to this past. I taped private sessions, but large public meetings at mosques created logistical problems, and most were not recorded. English frequently was the medium of exchange, and when interviews occurred in African languages, I relied on assistants to transcribe and translate what informants related to me. In a few cases I received texts summarizing public memories that Ahmadi elders recounted at gatherings in mosques.[106]

Memories come in many forms. Private reminiscences often concerned events within living memory, but they sometimes had information, passed through families, about prominent ancestors, such as the first members to accept the Ahmadiyya. Usually an elder, often a woman in matrilineal Akan-speaking families, maintained these reminiscences. Public memories focused on the activities of leaders and usually were narrated by men at formal events, such as the presentations at Ahmadi mosques mentioned earlier. Another example of a public recounting occurred during the visit of Khalifatul Masih Masroor Ahmad, Ghulam Ahmad's great-grandson and fifth successor: he presided over public prayers at the grave of Mahdi Appah and heard stories about him, remembered as the first Ahmadi Muslim in Ghana for his role in inviting Maulvi Nayyar to the Gold Coast (see figure 2). Nearby Mahdi Appah's grave in the Ahmadi cemetery at Ekrawfo is Binyameen Sam's marker, which has the inscription "First Muslim Convert, Gold Coast Colony."

Public memories focus on visionary experiences associated with Binyameen Sam and Mahdi Appah. I heard an elaborate narrative of interconnected visions and dreams at Ekrawfo, the historical center of the Fante Muslim community.[107] Binyameen Sam, as a young Methodist walking along the shore of the Atlantic Ocean, reportedly encountered an apparition dressed in robes appearing from the sea and then, years later, converted to Islam after meeting a robed *mallam*. Later Mahdi Appah, shortly after Binyameen Sam's death, learned that one of Sam's relatives dreamed that he performed Muslim prayers with foreigners, and Appah interpreted it as pointing Fante Muslims to the Ahmadiyya. Contemporary narrators stress the connection between the visionary experiences of Sam and his relative leading to the Ahmadiyya arrival. The invocation of visionary experiences is not surprising, as the interpretation of visions and dreams have influenced public decisions at moments of social and political change throughout Africa.[108] Visionary experiences also are significant to Ahmadi Muslims.[109] Nonetheless, the Ekrawfo narrative is a complex account that requires careful analysis to understand its insights into the past.

This book is the result of my analysis of Ghanaian narratives regarding the history of the Ahmadiyya in the Gold Coast. In the case of the narrative about Binyameen Sam and Mahdi Appah recounted at Ekrawfo, the assertion of contemporary narrators that Sam, who died before Maulvi Nayyar's visit, influenced Appah's decision to invite the Ahmadiyya to the Gold Coast leads to the central question of this book: how did the Fante Muslim community shape the Ahmadiyya arrival and consolidation in the Gold Coast? The search for answers led me to analyze a broad range of materials, including contemporary memories, Methodist records, colonial documents, and other written accounts. These materials yielded information, but not without careful reflection on the nature of the source and its limitations. An example of my approach to these materials relates to the evidence regarding Binyameen Sam's acceptance of Islam.

Binyameen Sam left no written materials, but his voice appears in various texts. One was written by Reverend Jacob B. Anaman, a Fante Methodist who interviewed Sam and included a summary of his testimony in *The Gold Coast Guide* of 1902.[110] Anaman's text describes Sam's conversion as having occurred in the mid-1870s as a result of contact with a *mallam* associated with the Hausa Force. Humphrey Fisher did not refer to Anaman's text and instead drew on a report by the German missionary A. J. Lochmann, a member of the Basel Mission who visited the Fante Muslim community at Ekrawfo in 1913 and recounted Fante Christian rumors about Sam's conversion to Islam; from these reports Lochmann guessed that the conversion occurred in the mid-1880s, and Fisher (and others) have accepted this date for Sam's conversion.[111] How did I resolve the contradiction between the information in the texts of Anaman and Lochmann? I examined evidence from the 1870s. My efforts led me to Methodist missionary records, where I found contemporaneous descriptions of the genesis of the Fante Muslim community in the mid-1870s. I also investigated war records associated with Britain's 1873–1874 invasion of Asante, including the papers of John H. Glover, one of the British officers who helped form the Hausa Force and led a contingent in the 1870s; these materials provided crucial details about the Hausa Force's Muslim ethos and the activities of *mallams*.[112] This example illustrates the type of historical investigation that undergirds the arguments in this book: I examined contemporaneous records and written materials of diverse provenance to interpret the voices of Binyameen Sam and others whose statements are mediated through the words of others.

Organization of the Book

Maulvi Nayyar arrived in the middle of things in 1921. The Fante Muslim community was adrift after Binyameen Sam's death and facing criticism from savanna *mallams*, and the Ahmadiyya had split, leaving the largest branch to consolidate under the inspired but youthful leadership of Ghulam Ahmad's son. Both movements embraced English-language education and engaged Christian evangelists with Muslim interpretations of the Bible. The Ahmadiyya mission in the Gold Coast fused the two communities into one movement: residential Ahmadi missionaries and African members elaborated on Ahmadiyya theology and practices as the movement expanded and consolidated in the Gold Coast. I tell this story in eight chapters arranged in three parts.

The first part, "Preparing the Way in the Gold Coast," brings the Fante Muslim community to the eve of Maulvi Nayyar's visit. Chapter 1 discusses the arrival of the Hausa Force from Lagos, adopting the framework of the religious marketplace to highlight the activities of various religious providers and the opening of the Fante states to Muslim proselytism. Chapter 2 follows with the story of the Fante Muslim community. I contend that Sam was a Biblicist who criticized Methodism from within and preached Islam from Christian scripture after an encounter with a *mallam*. I also interpret current oral accounts of Sam's acceptance of Islam as fragments from conversion narratives that reveal the visual and religious culture of the early Fante Muslim community. The second part, "Ahmadiyya Genesis and Expansion to London and Lagos," discusses Ahmadiyya origins in British India and its expansion to London and Lagos. Chapter 3 represents the Ahmadiyya as filling a niche in the competitive and contentious religious marketplace of British Punjab by offering a combination of Muslim reformism and spiritualism. Chapter 4 places the missionary efforts of the Ahmadiyya Muslim Community mission into the wider Black Atlantic: the roles of Africans such as Dusé Mohamed Ali in London and the Afro-Brazilian M. L. B. Agusto in Lagos figure prominently in the history of Ahmadi expansion from London to West Africa. The third part, "Ahmadiyya Arrival and Consolidation in the Gold Coast," returns to the Gold Coast and takes the story from the arrival of Maulvi Nayyar to the 1940s, a quarter century of Ahmadi proselytism directed by a series of lone South Asian Ahmadi missionaries who worked closely with Africans to build schools, recruit new members, and introduce Ahmadiyya discipline in the Gold Coast. Chapter 5 begins with a discussion of changes in the Gold Coast religious marketplace, including the impact of the 1918 influenza pandemic that opened possibilities for religious providers with an End Times message. Fante Muslims accepted the Ahmadiyya, and Mahdi Appah, Binyameen Sam's successor, negotiated with Maulvi Nayyar to set the rules and regulations ensuring that financial donations remained in the Gold Coast. Chapter 6 concerns the movement's consolidation as Ahmadiyya ideas and practices were elaborated and new members joined in the Gold Coast colony. Chapter 7 discusses the expansion of the Ahmadiyya to Asante, initially among rural cocoa farmers and later in Kumasi, where Muslim opposition slowed progress until the religious marketplace opened in the mid-1930s. Chapter 8 examines Ahmadiyya expansion to Wa, where local opposition was even greater than in Kumasi and turned violent, but Wala Ahmadi Muslims persevered and established an enduring presence.

The book ends in the mid-1940s. It was the eve of the postcolonial era: independence broke British India into Pakistan and India in 1947, and a decade later the Gold Coast became the independent state of Ghana. The former event led the Ahmadiyya to move its headquarters from Qadian, India, to Rabwah, Pakistan, and the transition led to changes in the movement. Thereafter, larger numbers of South Asian Ahmadi missionaries served in the Gold Coast, expanding educational activities and transforming Ahmadi proselytism: the postcolonial era was different for the Ahmadiyya in both South Asia and Ghana. The conclusion reflects on the changes of the 1940s, reviews the religious transformations analyzed in the previous decades, and looks beyond to project the story of African initiative into the present with an overview of the Ahmadiyya in contemporary Ghana.

Notes

1. PRAAD, Cape Coast: ADM 1/23/353, 3 March 1921, Saltpond DC to CCCP.
2. Maulvi Nayyar's tour is discussed in a series of articles in *RR* 20–21 (1921–1922).
3. The 1948 Gold Coast census put the number of Ahmadi Muslims at 22,572. Gold Coast, *Census of the Population, 1948* (London: Crown Agents, 1950). Also see PRO CO 100/94: Blue Book, 1944.
4. Mubarak Ahmad, *Our Foreign Missions* (Rabwah: Ahmadiyya Foreign Muslim Missions, 1965), 58.
5. PDJ, box 5, "The Ahmadiyya Movement in the Gold Coast, 1921–31"; PRAAD, Cape Coast: ADM 23/1/353, 29 November 1926, Saltpond, "Report on the Ahmadiyya School."
6. PRO CO 96/814/3: Education Department report, 1948.
7. Some Muslims insist that the divine revelation received by the Prophet Muhammad ended these communications. Yohanan Friedmann, *Prophesy Continuous: Aspects of Ahmadi Religious Thought and Its Medieval Background* (Berkeley: University of California Press, 1989). For an overview of Ghulam Ahmad's religious claims, see Francis Robinson, "Ahmad and the Ahmadiyya," *History Today* 40, no. 6 (1990), 42–47.
8. Timothy Furnish, *Holiest Wars: Islamic Mahdis, Their Jihads, and Osama bin Laden* (Westport, CT: Praeger Publishers, 2005); Thomas Hodgkin, "Mahdism, Messianism, and Marxism in the African Setting," in *Sudan in Africa*, ed. Yusuf Fadl Hassan (Khartoum: Khartoum University Press, 1971), 109–127; Peter Clarke, "Islamic Millenarianism in West Africa: A 'Revolutionary' Ideology?," *Religious Studies* 16, no. 3 (1980), 317–339; Muhammad Sani Umar, "Muslims' Eschatological Discourses on Colonialism in Northern Nigeria," *Journal of the American Academy of Religion* 67, no. 1 (1999), 59–84.
9. Spencer Lavan, *The Ahmadiyyah Movement: A History and Perspective* (New Delhi: Manohar, 1974).
10. Adil Hussain Khan, *From Sufism to Ahmadiyya: A Muslim Minority Movement in South Asia* (Bloomington: Indiana University Press, 2015).
11. J. Spencer Trimingham, *A History of Islam in West Africa* (London: Oxford University Press, 1962), 231.
12. Humphrey J. Fisher, *Ahmadiyyah: A Study in Contemporary Islam on the West African Coast* (London: Oxford University Press, 1963), 187.
13. *Khilafat Centenary Jubilee Souvenir* (Accra: Ahmadiyya Muslim Mission, 2008).
14. Nathan Samwini, *The Muslim Resurgence in Ghana since 1950: Its Effects upon Muslims and Muslim-Christian Relations* (Berlin: Lit Verlag, 2006).
15. As is discussed later in this introduction and at length in chapter 2, contemporaneous sources, including Sam's own testimony to an African Methodist minister, conclusively date Sam's conversion to the mid-1870s. The current literature puts his conversion in the mid-1880s.

16. Kwame Anthony Appiah, *Cosmopolitanism: Ethics in a World of Strangers* (New York: Norton, 2007). I also have been influenced by C. A. Breckenridge, S. Pollock, H. K. Bhabba, and D. Chakrabarty, eds., *Cosmopolitanism* (Durham, NC: Duke University Press, 2002); and Stephen Vertovec and Robin Cohen, eds., *Conceiving Cosmopolitanism: Theory, Content, and Practice* (Oxford: Oxford University Press, 2002).

17. For Muslim cosmopolitans in the wider sense of interactions with other Muslims, see Edward Simpson and Kai Kresse, eds., *Struggling with History: Islam and Cosmopolitanism in the Western Indian Ocean* (London: Hurst and Company, 2007).

18. The most insightful analysis of the sociology of the Ahmadiyya movement at its origins is Avril Ann Powell, "Duties of Ahmadi Women: Educative Process in the Early Stages of the Ahmadiyya Movement," in *Gurus and Their Followers: New Religious Reform Movements in Colonial India*, ed. Antony Copley (New Delhi: Oxford University Press, 2000), 128–156.

19. Robin Law, ed., *From Slave Trade to "Legitimate" Commerce: The Commercial Transition in Nineteenth-Century West Africa* (Cambridge: Cambridge University Press, 1995); and Derek R. Peterson, ed., *Abolitionism and Imperialism in Britain, Africa, and the Atlantic* (Athens: Ohio University Press, 2010).

20. Polly Hill, *The Migrant Cocoa Farmers of Southern Ghana: A Study in Rural Capitalism* (Cambridge: Cambridge University Press, 1963). Also see Gareth Austen, *Labor, Land, and Capital in Ghana: From Slavery to Free Labor in Asante, 1807–1956* (Rochester, NY: University of Rochester Press, 2005).

21. H. O. Danmole, "The Crisis of the Lagos Muslim Community, 1915–1947," in *History of the Peoples of Lagos State*, ed. Ade Adefuye, Babatunde Agiri, and Jide Osuntokun (Lagos: Lantern Books, 1987), 290–305; Olokunde A. Lawal, "Islam and Colonial Rule in Lagos," *American Journal of Islamic Social Sciences* 12, no. 1 (1995), 66–80. Also see T. G. O. Gbadamosi, *The Growth of Islam among the Yoruba, 1841–1908* (London: Longman, 1978); and Patrick J. Ryan, *Imale: Yoruba Participation in the Muslim Tradition; A Study of Clerical Piety* (Missoula, MT: Scholars Press, 1978). Exceptions include works, cited here, focusing on Afro-Brazilian and Sierra Leonean Muslims.

22. Southwestern Nigeria produced a Mahdist movement in the mid-twentieth century, but it seems not to have been influenced by the Ahmadiyya's eschatology. See Peter B. Clarke, *Mahdism in West Africa: The Ijebu Mahdiyya Movement* (London: Luzac Oriental, 1995).

23. Paul Gilroy, *The Black Atlantic: Modernity and Double Consciousness* (Cambridge, MA: Harvard University Press, 1993).

24. Toyin Falola and Kevin D. Roberts, eds., *The Atlantic World, 1450–2000* (Bloomington: Indiana University Press, 2008); Robin Law and Kristin Mann, "West Africa in the Atlantic Community: The Case of the Slave Coast," *William and Mary Quarterly*, 3rd ser., 56, no. 2 (1999), 307–334; Charles Piot, "Atlantic Aporias: Africa and Gilroy's Black Atlantic," *South Atlantic Quarterly* 100, no. 1 (2001), 155–170; Philip S. Zachernuk, *Colonial Subjects: An African Intelligentsia and Atlantic Ideas* (Charlottesville: University Press of Virginia, 2000). For West African Muslims in the Americas, see Michael A. Gomez, *Exchanging Our Country Marks: The Transformation of African Identities in the Colonial and Antebellum South* (Chapel Hill: University of North Carolina Press, 1999).

25. K. Humayun Ansari, "The Woking Mosque: A Case Study of Muslim Engagement with British Society since 1889," *Immigrants and Minorities* 21, no. 3 (2002), 1–24; Purwez Salmat, *A Miracle at Woking: A History of the Shahjahan Mosque* (London: Phillimore, 2008). The activities of the Lahore branch are discussed in Eric Germain, "The First Muslim Missions on a European Scale: Ahmadi-Lahore Networks in the Inter-War Period," in *Islam in Inter-War Europe*, ed. Natalie Clayer and Eric Germain (London: Hurst and Company, 2008), 89–127;

and Gerdien Jonker, "A Laboratory of Modernity: the Ahmadiyya Mission in Inter-War Europe," *Journal of Muslims in Europe* 3 (2014), 1–25. The Ahmadiyya Muslim Community's early mission in London is mentioned in passing in Tarja Moles, "The Evolution of the Ahmadiyya Community in the UK," PhD diss., Royal Holloway, University of London, 2009.

26. Ian G. Duffield, "Dusé Mohamed Ali and the Development of Pan-Africanism, 1866–1945," PhD diss., Edinburgh University, 1971.

27. Moustafa Bayoumi, "East of the Sun (West of the Moon): Islam, Ahmadis, and African America," in *Black Routes to Islam*, ed. Manning Marable and Hishaam D. Aidi (London: Palgrave Macmillan, 2009), 69–78; and Richard B. Turner, "The Ahmadiyya Mission to Blacks in the United States in the 1920s," *Journal of Religious Thought* 44, no. 2 (2001), 50–66. Duffield mentions contact between Mufti Sadiq and Dusé Mohamed Ali in the United States in "Dusé Mohamed Ali and the Development of Pan-Africanism," 679.

28. David Motadel, introduction to *Islam and the European Empires*, ed. David Motadel (New York: Oxford University Press, 2014), 1–34.

29. Two illustrative examples in a vast literature are Yves Person, "Guinea-Samori," in *West African Resistance: The Military Response to Colonial Rule*, ed. Michael Crowther (New York: Africana Publishing Corporation, 1970), 111–143; and David Robinson, *Paths of Accommodation: Muslim Societies and French Colonial Officials in Senegal and Mauritania, 1880–1920* (Athens: Ohio University Press, 2000).

30. Two examples from a growing literature are Ousmane Kane, *Muslim Modernity in Postcolonial Nigeria: A Study of the Society for Removal of Innovation and Reinstatement of Tradition* (Leiden: Brill, 2003); and Ousman Murzik Kobo, *Unveiling Modernity in Twentieth Century West African Reforms* (Leiden: Brill, 2012). For an overview, see Roman Loimeier, "Patterns and Peculiarities of Islamic Reform in Africa," *JRA* 33, no. 3 (2003), 237–262. For Muslim engagements in French colonial Africa, see Rüdiger Seesemann and Benjamin Soares, "'Being as Good Muslims as Frenchmen': On Islam and Colonial Modernity in West Africa," *JRA* 39, no. 1 (2009), 91–120.

31. Ivor Wilks, *The Northern Factor in Ashanti History* (Legon, Ghana: Institute of African Studies, 1961); for a recent overview of this literature, see Raymond Silverman and David Owusu-Ansah, "The Presence of Islam among the Akan: A Bibliographic Essay," *HA* 16 (1989), 325–339.

32. Appiah, *Cosmopolitanism*.

33. Andrew F. Walls, "The Legacy of Samuel Ajayi Crowther," *International Bulletin of Missionary Research* 16, no. 1 (1992), 15–21.

34. Andrew F. Walls, "Africa as the Theatre of Christian Engagement with Islam in the Nineteenth Century," *JRA* 29, no. 2 (1999), 163–164. Also see P. R. McKenzie, *Inter-Religious Encounter in Nigeria: S. A. Crowther's Attitudes to African Traditional Religion and Islam* (Leicester: Leicester University Press, 1976). For a historical analysis of one mission under Crowther's administration, see F. J. Kolapo, "'Making Favorable Impressions': Bishop Crowther's Niger Mission in Jihadist Nupe Emirate, 1859–1879," in *Religion, History, and Politics in Nigeria: Essays in Honor of Ogbu U. Kalu*, ed. Chima J. Koriah and G. Ugo Nwokeji (Lanham, MD: University Press of America, 2005), 29–51.

35. Crowther described his initial approach to African Muslims, based on what he had learned in the missionary school at Freetown, as follows: "I had been well drilled, as I then thought, by reading and collecting arguments against Mohammedanism and heathenism, and went out with zeal, not yet tempered with experience." Crowther, *Experiences with Heathens and Mohammedans in West Africa* (London: Society for Promoting Christian Gospel, 1892), 6. For the Freetown missionary context and Christian attitudes toward Muslims, see Gibril R. Cole, *The Krio of West Africa: Islam, Culture, Creolization and Colonialism in the Nineteenth*

Century (Athens: Ohio University Press, 2013); and John Petersen, *Province of Freedom: A History of Sierra Leone, 1787–1870* (Evanston: Northwestern University Press, 1969).

36. Crowther and two other missionaries arrived at Badagry in January 1845, where they waited a year before going to found a mission at Abeokuta. J. F. A. Ajayi, *Christian Missions in Nigeria, 1841–1891: The Making of a New Elite* (London: Longmans, 1965), 34.

37. CMS CA2/031(b): Crowther journal entries for 25 June and 25 September 1845. Peel refers only in passing to this encounter. J. D. Y. Peel, *Religious Encounter and the Making of the Yoruba* (Bloomington: Indiana University Press, 2003), 209. Crowther did not mention it in *Experiences with Heathens and Mohammedans in West Africa*; he did refer in passing to exchanges with Muslims at Ilorin in 1872, but he otherwise avoided historical examples to concentrate on theological issues associated with his strategy.

38. Peel noted that "discussions between Christian evangelists and Muslims [in southwestern Nigeria] ranged in tone from abusive confrontations to serious attempts to explore their differences within a shared recognition of their common roots" and concluded that "not far beneath the surface of even friendly encounters . . . ran strong currents of rivalry and reserve." Peel, *Religious Encounter*, 207, 208.

39. CMS CA2/031(b): Crowther journal entry for 25 September 1850.

40. *The Gospel on the Banks of the Niger: Journals and Notices of the Native Missionaries Accompanying the Niger Expedition, 1857–1859*, ed. Samuel Crowther and John Christopher Taylor, 2nd ed. (London: Frank Cass, 1970), 236.

41. African slaves in Brazil secured emancipations more easily than elsewhere in the Americas, either through acts of liberation at the owner's death or through paying themselves from wages earned, often in urban contexts. For an overview of the extensive literature on Afro-Brazilians in West Africa, see Silke Strickrodt, "The Brazilian Diaspora to West Africa in the Nineteenth Century," in *AfrikaAmerika: Atlantische Konstruktionen*, ed. Ineke Phaf-Reinberger and Tiago de Oliveira Pinto (Frankfurt: Vervuert, 2008), 36–68. Also useful is Pierre Verger, *Flux et reflux de la traite des nègres entre le Golfe de Bénin et Bahia de Todos os Santos: Du XVIIe au XIXe siècle* (Paris: Mouton, 1968).

42. Lisa Lindsay, "'To Return to the Bosom of their Fatherland': Brazilian Immigrants to Lagos," *Slavery and Abolition*, 15, no. 1 (1994), 22–50; Ojo Olatunji, "Afro-Brazilians in Lagos: Atlantic Commerce, Kinship and Trans-Nationalism," in *Back to Africa I: Afro-Returnees and Their Communities*, ed. Kwesi Prah (Cape Town: Center for Advanced Studies of African Society, 2009), 232–260.

43. The pioneering work is Marianno Carneiro de Cunha, *Da senzala ao sobrado: Arquitectura brasileira na Nigéria e na Republica Popular do Benim* (São Paulo: Nobel Edusp, 1985). Recent work includes Brigitte Kowalski Oshineye, "Migrations, Identities, and Transculturation in the Coastal Cities of Yorubaland in the Second Half of the Second Millennium: An Approach to African History through Architecture," in *Movements, Borders, and Identities in Africa*, ed. Toyin Falola and Aribidesi Usman (Rochester: University of Rochester Press, 2009), 126–149.

44. Elisée Soumounni, "The Afro-Brazilian Communities of Ouidah and Lagos in the Nineteenth Century: A Comparative Analysis," in *Africa and the Americas: Interconnections during the Slave Trade*, ed. José Curto and Renée Soulodre-LaFrance (New York: Africa World Press, 2005), 231–242; also see Elisée Soumounni, "Afro-Brazilian Communities of the Bight of Benin in the Nineteenth Century," in *Trans-Atlantic Dimensions of Ethnicity in the African Diaspora*, ed. Paul E. Lovejoy and David V. Trotman (London: Continuum, 2003), 181–194.

45. For Shitta's biography, see Titilóla Euba, "Muhammad Shitta Bey and the Lagos Muslim Community, 1850–1895, Part 1," *Nigerian Journal of Islam* 2, no. 1 (1971–1972), 21–30; and id., "Muhammad Shitta Bey and the Lagos Muslim Community, 1850–1895, Part 2," *Nigerian*

Journal of Islam 2, no. 2 (1971–1972), 7–18. Shitta used William in his correspondence; see, for example, PG, 11 December 1873, William Shitta to John Glover.

46. Euba, "Muhammad Shitta Bey"; Gbadamosi, *Growth of Islam*, 164–177.

47. Many Yoruba Muslims attended Arabic schools in the twentieth century. See Razaq D. Abubakre and Stefan Reichmuth, "Arabic Writing between Global and Local Culture: Scholars and Poets in Yorubaland (Southwestern Nigeria)," *Research in African Literatures* 28, no. 3 (1997), 183–209.

48. Cole, *Krio of West Africa*, 138–40; Euba, "Muhammad Shitta Bey," part 2, 15; and Jean Herskovits Kopytoff, *A Preface to Modern Nigeria: the "Sierra Leoneans" in Yoruba, 1830–1890* (Madison: University of Wisconsin Press, 1965).

49. Kristin Mann, *Slavery and the Birth of an African City: Lagos, 1760–1900* (Bloomington: Indiana University Press, 2007), 110–113; Olatunji Ojo, "Islam, Ethnicity and Slave Resistance: Hausa 'Mamluks' in Nineteenth Century Yorubaland," in *Islam, Slavery and Diaspora*, ed. Behnaz A. Mirzai, Ismael Musah Montana, and Paul E. Lovejoy (Trenton, NJ: Africa World Press, 2009), 103–124; E. Adeniyi Oroge, "The Fugitive Slave Question in Anglo-Egba Relations, 1861–1886," *Journal of the Historical Society of Nigeria* 8 (1975), 61–80; and Tekena N. Tamuno, *The Police in Modern Nigeria, 1861–1965: Origins, Development and Role* (Ibadan: Ibadan University Press, 1970), 15–27.

50. David Killingray, "Imagined Martial Communities: Recruiting for the Military and Police in Colonial Ghana, 1860–1960," in *Ethnicity in Ghana: The Limits of Invention*, ed. Carola Lentz and Paul Nugent (London: Palgrave Macmillan, 2000), 119–136. For British imaginings in this era, see Heather Streets, *Martial Races: The Military, Race, and Masculinity in British Imperial Culture, 1857–1914* (Manchester: Manchester University Press, 2004).

51. I draw inspiration from Nile Green, who uses the phrase "barracks Islam" in his analysis of a similar Muslim expression in British India. See Green, *Islam and the Colonial Army in India: Sepoy Religion in the Service of Empire* (Cambridge: Cambridge University Press, 2009).

52. Sean Hanretta argued for a variant of an "Islamic tradition" in the western regions of the savanna in *Islam and Social Change in French West Africa: History of an Emancipatory Community* (New York: Cambridge University Press, 2009), 30–31. I draw on his work, as well as Mervyn Hiskett, *The History of Islam in West Africa* (London: Longmans, 1984); Nehemia Levtzion, "Islam in the *bilad al-sudan* to 1800," in *History of Islam in Africa*, ed. Nehemia Levtzion and Randall Pouwels (Athens: Ohio University Press, 2000), 63–92; Roman Loimeier, *Muslim Societies in Africa: A Historical Anthropology* (Bloomington: Indiana University Press, 2013); and David Robinson, *Muslim Societies in African History* (Cambridge: Cambridge University Press, 2004).

53. Al-Hajj Umar's autobiographical sketch is translated in Stanislaw Pilaszewicz, *Hausa Prose Writings in Ajami by Alhaj Umaru from A. Mischlich/H. Sölken's Collection* (Berlin: Dietrich Reimer, 2000), 64–74. The most complete biography is in Douglas E. Ferguson, "Nineteenth-Century Hausaland: Being a Description by Imam Imoru of the Land, Economy, and Society of His People," PhD diss., University of California, Los Angeles, 1973.

54. Arabic Collection, Balme Library, University of Ghana at Legon, Ghana, ms. 109 (v), line 63.

55. PDJ, box 5: "The Ahmadiyya Movement in the Gold Coast, 1921–31."

56. Louis Brenner discussed the esoteric practices of West African Muslim scholars in *Controlling Knowledge: Religion, Power, and Schooling in a West African Muslim Society* (Bloomington: Indiana University Press, 2001).

57. Rudolph T. Ware III, *The Walking Qur'an: Islamic Education, Embodied Knowledge, and History in West Africa* (Chapel Hill: University of North Carolina Press, 2014).

58. Ivor Wilks, "The Transmission of Islamic Learning in the Western Sudan," in *Literacy in Traditional Societies*, ed. Jack Goody (Cambridge: Cambridge University Press, 1968), 162–197.

59. Boubacar Barry, *Senegambia and the Atlantic Slave Trade*, trans. Ayi Kwei Armah (New York: Cambridge University Press, 1998).

60. Mervyn Hiskett, *The Sword of Truth: The Life and Times of Shehu Usuman dan Fodio*, new ed. (Evanston, IL: Northwestern University Press, 1994); and Murray Last, *The Sokoto Caliphate* (London: Longmans, 1967).

61. David Robinson, *The Holy War of Umar Tal: the Western Sudan in the Mid-Nineteenth Century* (Oxford: Clarendon Press, 1985).

62. Louis Brenner, "The Jihad Debate between Sokoto and Borno: An Historical Analysis of Islamic Political Discourse in Nigeria," in *People and Empires in African History: Essays in Memory of Michael Crowder*, ed. J. F. A. Ajayi and J. D. Y. Peel (London: Longman, 1992), 21–43.

63. Brenner, *Controlling Knowledge*.

64. Ware, *Walking Qur'an*.

65. Nehemia Levtzion, *Muslims and Chiefs in West Africa: A Study of Islam in the Middle Volta Basis in the Pre-Colonial Period* (London: Oxford University Press, 1968); and Holger Weiss, *Between Accommodation and Revivalism: Muslims, Society and the State in Ghana from the Colonial to the Postcolonial Era* (Helskini: Finnish Oriental Society, 2008).

66. Ismail Hussein Abdalla, "Islamic Medicine and Its Influence on Traditional Hausa Practitioners in Northern Nigeria," PhD diss., University of Wisconsin, 1981.

67. Hausa Muslim assertions are stressed by Pilaszewicz, *Hausa Prose Writings*, 2.

68. Raymond Silverman, "History, Art, and Assimilation: The Impact of Islam on Akan Material Culture," PhD diss., University of Washington, 1983.

69. Kwame Arhin, *West African Traders in Ghana in the Nineteenth and Twentieth Centuries* (London: Longman, 1979); and Paul Lovejoy, *Caravans of Kola: The Hausa Kola Trade, 1700–1900* (Zaria, Nigeria: Ahmadu Bello University Press, 1980).

70. David Owusu-Ansah, *Islamic Talismanic Tradition in Nineteenth-Century Asante* (Lewiston, NY: Edwin Mellen Press, 1991).

71. British officials noted that most Muslims arriving in the Gold Coast were itinerant traders and returned without settling. For the first Hausa settlements, see Mahdi Adamu, *The Hausa Factor in West African History* (Ibadan: Ibadan University Press and Oxford University Press Nigeria, 1978).

72. J. A. Braimah and Jack Goody, *Salaga: The Struggle for Power* (London: Longmans, 1967). For Muslim immigration to the coast after the Salaga civil war, see Misbahudeen Ahmed-Rufai, "The Muslim Association Party: A Test of Religious Politics in Ghana," *THSG*, n.s., no. 6 (2002), 105–106; Mervyn Hiskett, "Commissioner of Police v. Musa Kommenda and Aspects of the Working of the Gold Coast Marriage of Mohammedans Ordinance," *Journal of African Law* 20, no. 2 (1976), 128; and Samuel Aniegye Ntewusu, *Settling in and Holding On: A Socio-Economic History of Northern Traders and Transporters in Accra's Tudu, 1908–2008* (Leiden: African Studies Centre, 2012), 10–12, 19–20, 27–28.

73. John Parker, *Making the Town: Ga State and Society in Early Colonial Accra* (Portsmouth, NH: Heinemann, 2000); Deborah Pellow, *Landlords and Lodgers: Socio-Spatial Organization in an Accra Community* (Chicago: University of Chicago Press, 2008).

74. Enid Schildkroudt, *People of the Zongo: The Transformation of Ethnic Identities in Ghana* (Cambridge: Cambridge University Press, 1978).

75. A few Hausa Muslims scholars arrived earlier. K. O. Odoom, "A Document on Pioneers in the Muslim Community of Accra," *Institute of African Studies Research Review* 7, no. 3 (1971), 1–31.

76. Weiss, *Between Accommodation and Revivalism.*

77. B. A. R. Braimah, "Islamic Education in Ghana," *GBT* 4, no. 5 (1973), 1–16.

78. David Owusu-Ansah, Mark Sey, and Abdulai Iddrisu, *Islamic Learning, the State and the Challenges of Education in Ghana* (Trenton, NJ: Africa World Press, 2012); Abdulai Iddrisu, *Contesting Islam in Africa: Homegrown Wahhabism and Muslim Identity in Northern Ghana, 1920–2010* (Durham, NC: Carolina Academic Press, 2013); and Kobo, *Unveiling Modernity.*

79. David E. Skinner, "The Incorporation of Muslim Elites into the Colonial Administrative Systems of Sierra Leone, the Gambia and the Gold Coast," *Journal of Muslim Minority Affairs* 29, no. 1 (2009), 91–108.

80. Benjamin Soares, "Muslim-Christian Encounters in Africa," in *Muslim-Christian Encounters in Africa*, ed. Benjamin Soares (Leiden: Brill, 2006), 1–16.

81. Barbara M. Cooper, *Evangelical Christians in the Muslim Sahel* (Bloomington: Indiana University Press, 2006); and Shobana Shankar, *Who Shall Enter Paradise? Christian Origins in Muslim Northern Nigeria, ca. 1890–1974* (Athens: Ohio University Press, 2014). For similar developments in Egypt and the Sudan, see Heather J. Sharkey, "Empire and Muslim Conversion: Historical Reflections on Christian Missions in Egypt," *Islam and Christian-Muslim Relations* 16, no. 1 (2005), 43–63; and id., "Missionary Legacies: Muslim-Christian Encounters in Egypt and Sudan during the Colonial and Post-Colonial Periods," in *Muslim-Christian Encounters in Africa*, ed. Benjamin Soares (Leiden: Brill, 2006), 57–88. An overview historical work also stressing historical difficulties in relations between Muslims and Christians in African contexts is Charlotte Quinn and Frederick Quinn, *Pride, Faith, and Fear: Islam in Sub-Saharan Africa* (Oxford: Oxford University Press, 2003).

82. Andrew Porter, *Religion versus Empire? British Protestant Missionaries and Overseas Expansion, 1700–1914* (Manchester: Manchester University Press, 2004).

83. Jean Comaroff and John Comaroff, *Of Revelation and Revolution*, vol. 1, *Christianity, Colonialism, and Consciousness in South Africa* (Chicago: University of Chicago Press, 1991); id., *Of Revelation and Revolution*, vol. 2, *The Dialectics of Modernity on a South African Frontier* (Chicago: University of Chicago Press, 1997). For their influence, see Elizabeth Elbourne, "Word Made Flesh: Christianity, Modernity, and Cultural Colonialism in the Work of Jean and John Comaroff," *AHR* 108, no. 2 (2003), 435–459. Some argue for greater African agency, such as Paul Landau, *The Realm of the Word: Language, Gender, and Christianity in Southern African Kingdom* (Portsmouth, NH: Heinemann, 1995); and Meredith McKitterick, *To Dwell Secure: Generation, Christianity, Colonialism in Ovamboland* (Portsmouth, NH: Heinemann, 2002).

84. Peter van der Veer, ed., *Conversion to Modernities: The Globalization of Christianity* (New York: Routledge, 1996).

85. Lynn M. Thomas, "Modernity's Failings, Political Claims, and Intermediate Concepts," *AHR* 116, no. 3 (2011), 727–740.

86. Lamin Sanneh, *Translating the Message: The Missionary Impact on Culture*, 2nd ed. (Maryknoll, NY: Orbis, 2009). Also see Gerald O. West, "Mapping African Biblical Interpretation: A Tentative Sketch," in *The Bible in Africa: Transactions, Trajectories, and Trends*, ed. Gerald O. West and Musa W. Dube (Leiden: Brill, 2000), 29–53.

87. Dana L. Robert, ed., *Converting Colonialism: Visions and Realities in Mission History, 1706–1914* (Grand Rapids, MI: William B. Eerdmans, 2008).

88. J. D. Y. Peel, "For Who Hath Despised the Day of Small Things? Missionary Narratives and Historical Anthropology," *Comparative Studies in Society and History* 37, no. 4 (1995), 581–607.

89. Powell, *Muslims and Missionaries.*

90. J. Spencer Trimingham, *The Christian Church and Islam in West Africa* (London: Student Christian Movement, 1955); and Elwood M. Wherry, *Islam and Christianity in India and the Far East* (New York: Fleming H. Revell, 1907).

91. J. B. Webster, *The African Churches among the Yoruba* (Oxford, UK: Clarendon Press, 1964), 99–100.

92. James F. Searing, "The Time of Conversion: Christians and Muslims among the Sereer-Safèn of Senegal, 1914–1950s," in *Muslim-Christian Encounters in Africa*, ed. Benjamin Soares (Leiden: Brill, 2006), 115–141.

93. Pioneering work on postcolonial Muslim evangelism is examined in Chanfi Ahmad, "The Wahubiri wa Kislamu (Preachers of Islam) in East Africa," *Africa Today* 54, no. 4 (2008), 3–18; and John A. Chesworth, "Fundamentalism and Outreach Strategies in East Africa: Christian Evangelism and Muslim *Da'wa*," in *Muslim-Christian Encounters in Africa*, ed. Benjamin Soares (Leiden: Brill, 2006), 159–186.

94. Avril Ann Powell, "Processes of Conversion to Christianity in 19th Century North Western India," in *Religious Conversion Movements in South Asia: Continuities and Change 1800–1900*, ed. Geoffrey A. Oddie (London: Curzon Press, 1997), 15–55; and Shobana Shankar, "A Fifty-Year Muslim Conversion to Christianity: Religious Ambiguities and Colonial Boundaries in Northern Nigeria, c. 1906–1963," in *Muslim-Christian Encounters in Africa*, ed. Benjamin Soares (Leiden: Brill, 2006), 89–114.

95. Marc David Baer, "History and Religious Conversion," in *The Oxford Handbook of Religious Conversion*, ed. Lewis H. Rambo and Charles E. Farhadian (New York: Oxford University Press, 2014), 25–47.

96. Robin Horton, "African Conversion," *Africa* 41, no. 2 (1971), 85–108; and id., "On the Rationality of Conversion," *Africa* 45, nos. 3–4 (1975), 219–235 and 373–399.

97. Fisher expressed his indebtedness to A. D. Nock's views on adhesion in "Conversion Reconsidered: Some Historical Aspects of Religious Conversion in Black Africa," *Africa* 43, no. 1 (1973), 33; and id., "The Juggernaut's Apologia: Conversion to Islam in Black Africa," *Africa* 55, no. 2 (1985), 158.

98. L. A. Young, ed., *Rational Choice Theory and Religion: Summary and Assessment* (New York: Routledge, 1997).

99. R. Andrew Chestnut, *Competitive Spirits: Latin America's New Religious Economy* (Oxford: Oxford University Press, 2003); Nile Green, *Bombay Islam: The Religious Economy of the West Indian Ocean, 1840–1915* (Cambridge: Cambridge University Press, 2011); Tong Chee Kiong, *Rationalizing Religion: Religious Conversion, Revivalism, and Competition in Singapore* (Leiden: Brill, 2007); and Peter van der Veer, *Gods on Earth: The Management of a Religious Experience and Identity in a North Indian Pilgrimage Centre* (London: Athlone Press, 1988).

100. Green, *Bombay Islam*.

101. Duncan-Johnstone's papers include his report "The Ahmadiyya Movement in the Gold Coast, 1921–31," as well as contemporaneous materials about his encounters with Ahmadi missionaries, African converts, and Muslim opponents of the Ahmadiyya.

102. David William Cohen, Stephan Miescher, and Luise White, "Introduction: Voices, Words, and African History," in *African Words, African Voices*, ed. Luise White, Stephan Miescher, and David William Cohen (Bloomington: Indiana University Press, 2001), 1–27.

103. Rasheed A. K. Guar-Gorman, "Islam in Fantiland," MA thesis, University of Ghana, Legon, 1971.

104. Mohammad bin Salih, *A History of the Wala: The Ahmadiyya Factor* (Accra: Salihsons, 2000).

105. Richard Abu Abudu, "The Contribution of the Ahmadiyya Muslim Mission to the Development of Western Education in Ghana: A Case Study of the Asante Region," postgraduate degree in education thesis, University of Cape Coast, 1998; Francis Acquah, "The Impact of Traditional Religious Beliefs and Cultural Values on Christian-Muslim Relations in Ghana from the 1920s through the Present: A Case Study of Nkusukum-Ekumfi-Enyan Areas of the Central Region," PhD diss., University of Exeter, 2011; Mikelle Antoine, "Practice and Conversion of Asante Market Women to the Ahmadiyya Muslim Mission in the Late 20th Century," PhD diss., Michigan State University, 2010; Khadijah Boateng, "The Establishment of Ahmadiyya Muslim Mission at Asafo, Kumasi, and Its Influence on the People," long essay, Kwame Nkrumah University of Science and Technology, 1990; Johnson Apenad Mbillah, "The Causes of Present Day Muslim Unrest in Ghana," PhD diss., University of Birmingham, 1999; M. A. Morgan, "The History of the Ahmadiyya Movement in Ashanti," BA thesis, Kwame Nkrumah University of Science and Technology, 1990; and Ahmad Seidu, "Accountability in Religious Circles: A Case Study of the Kumasi Central Mosque," MA thesis, Kwame Nkrumah University of Science and Technology, 2012.

106. On these materials, see "Interviews" in the references list.

107. Hanson interviews in Ekrawfo: public meeting in the mosque and a private discussion with Hakeem Kofi Yamoah, 1 June 2005. Yamoah also gave me a text titled "The Advent of Ahmadiyyat in Ekumfi Ekrawfo," based on the memories of Ahmad Afful. I discuss this narrative more fully in chapter 2.

108. David Chidester, "Dreaming in the Contact Zone: Zulu Dreams, Visions, and Religion in Nineteenth-Century South Africa," *Journal of the American Academy of Religion* 76, no. 1 (2008), 27–53; Humphrey J. Fisher, "Dreams and Conversion in Black Africa," in *Conversion to Islam*, ed. Nehemia Levtzion (New York: Holmes and Meier, 1979), 217–235. Fisher's essay surprisingly does not include any Ahmadiyya examples.

109. Marzia Balzani, "Dreaming, Islam, and the Ahmadiyya Muslims in the UK," *History and Anthropology* 21, no. 3 (2010), 293–305.

110. Anaman, *The Gold Coast Guide* (London: Christian Herald, 1902), 85–86. For Anaman's career as a Methodist, see Dennis Kemp, *Nine Years on the Gold Coast* (London: Macmillan, 1898), 271–272. For Anaman's role in developing Fante lyrics for Methodist hymns, see Abamfo Atiemo, "'Singing with Understanding': The Story of Gospel Music in Ghana," *Studies in World Christianity* 12, no. 2 (2006), 142–163. Anaman later founded an independent church.

111. An English translation of Lochmann's report is in Hans Debrunner, H. H. A. Fisher, and Humphrey J. Fisher, "Early Fante Islam," *GBT* 1, no. 7 (1959), 23–35; and id., "Early Fante Islam [continued]," *GBT* 1, no. 8 (1960), 13–29. Lochmann's date for Sam's conversion is accepted in Fisher, *Ahmadiyyah*, 117; and Debrunner, *A History of Christianity in Ghana* (Accra: Waterville Publishing House, 1967), 241. Subsequent works adopt this date; for a recent example, see David E. Skinner, "Conversion to Islam and the Promotion of 'Modern' Islamic Schools in Ghana," *JRA* 43, no. 4 (2013), 431.

112. Glover's papers include details about the Hausa Force in Lagos as well as their Gold Coast deployment.

PART I

Preparing the Way in the Gold Coast

1 The Hausa Force and the Religious Marketplace in the Fante States

REVEREND T. B. PICOT, chairman of the Wesleyan Methodist Mission in the Gold Coast, went to Kumasi, the Asante capital, in 1876 to press the *asantehene* to relax constraints on Methodist evangelism. Picot traveled shortly after British imperial troops had returned from their invasion of Asante in 1873–1874, a war that left Kumasi looted and burned but Asante still outside the domain of the newly declared British Gold Coast colony. Buoyed by the British victory, Picot sought to build on the Methodist presence in the Fante states of the Gold Coast, where they had been active from the 1830s and had won adherents among traders and others in coastal towns. Immediately after the war, tens of thousands of Fante rural residents began to attend Methodist services for the first time, a religious surge that led the Methodists to establish new mission stations and schools in interior villages. The revival's timing suggests that Fante villagers were persuaded by the British victory to seek access to the Christian God, and Picot hoped that Asante residents similarly would be open to the Methodist message of personal salvation.

Asantehene Mensa Bonsu was undeterred by the war's outcome and did not agree to Reverend Picot's request. Reaffirming long-standing Asante restrictions on Christianity, Mensa Bonsu insisted that "God at the beginning gave the Bible to the white people, another book to the Muslims, and *abosom* to us."[1] *Abosom* are spiritual forces believed to make contact with humans through ritual specialists known as *akomfoo*. Asantehene Mensa Bonsu asserted that Methodist proselytism had "ruined" the Fante states because Fante Christians no longer accorded proper respect to Fante rulers and *akomfoo*. Left unstated was that Asante religious restrictions also applied to Muslims: *mallams* were forbidden from proselytizing and expected to serve the *asantehene* by providing protective amulets and herbal cures. Asante rulers also prevented savanna Muslims from traveling to the coast, largely to protect Asante commercial interests.[2] Muslim access to the Fante states opened, however, during the British invasion of the 1870s: arriving by sea were *mallams* who accompanied the Hausa Force, a colonial militia based in Lagos. These *mallams* provided esoteric healing, and conversations between Muslims and Christians led some Fante Methodists to find parallels in the Bible and the Quran.

Historians have not examined this era of religious change. Methodists remembered the postwar Gold Coast revival for decades, but recent historical works rarely mention the surge in Christian affiliation.[3] Scholars also have not analyzed the Muslim influences of the Hausa Force and its *mallams*, either in the Gold Coast or in Lagos.[4] Reluctance to do so is related in part to awareness of British "martial races" thinking associated with their constitution based on imaged ethnic identities.[5] David Killingray convincingly argued that the Gold Coast Constabulary, modeled on the Hausa Force, was diverse ethnically and was Muslim only in the imagination of its British officers.[6] But the Hausa Force, I contend, was distinct from the Gold Coast Constabulary and practiced a demonstrative "barracks Islam."[7] The force also drew on the services of *mallams*, who introduced Muslim ideas and practices to Fante communities in the Gold Coast.

This chapter analyzes transformations in the late nineteenth-century religious marketplace of the Fante states of the Gold Coast. It begins by reviewing the history of the Fante states and describing the features of the religious marketplace. The following section examines the Hausa Force's formation in Lagos and its role in the British invasion of Asante in the 1870s. Then the chapter turns to the force's exuberant Muslim performances in the Gold Coast. The final section concerns the era of religious change after the British victory over Asante.

The Fante States

Akan speakers, including the Fante people (*mfantsefoo*), came to dominate the rainforest in today's southern Ghana over the past half millennium. The processes associated with this expansion are multiple, and scholars still are investigating patterns of migration, settlement, and assimilation of others.[8] Encouraging social absorption was the Akan cultural practice of matrilineal reckoning that allowed outsiders to marry and have their offspring incorporated into the mother's kinship group. Akan polities also integrated diverse peoples into an expanding political culture: new communities emerged around Akan-speaking adventurers known as *abirempon*, often remembered as hunters who founded new settlements in virgin forest. As these communities attracted others, the settlements eventually became enduring polities led by *ahene* (singular, *ohene*), rulers associated with matrilineal royal lines. Akan political culture included elaborate court rituals that conferred legitimacy and supported numerous courtesans. Asante had become the dominant Akan state by the eighteenth century, but its rise did not eliminate all other Akan polities; the Fante states endured and contested Asante assertions of authority along the coast.

Fante oral historians narrate the founding of the Fante states as an epic tale of migration from Tekyiman (see map 1), a savanna settlement just north of the rainforest. These migrants, known as Borbor Fante, reportedly arrived at

Mankessim (maps 3 and 4) near the coast. The remains of spiritual guides leading these immigrants were buried near Mankessim, at a sacred grove known as Nananom Mpow. Some Borbor Fante families left Mankessim to found Fante polities nearby, but they retained a connection to Nananom Mpow and political elites at Mankessim. Fante states proliferated, including city-states along the coast, but they never formed a centralized or unitary state.[9] Acknowledging Nananom Mpow as a sacred site cemented a loose political charter in the southern rainforest and coast, enabling Mankessim to serve as a meeting place to affirm shared political interests, to discuss crises facing the region, and to develop military and other strategies to cope with external threats.

Historians situate the rise of the Fante states into global developments. Gold mined in the rainforest connected the region to commercial networks. The initial contacts were to the savanna and trans-Saharan routes to North Africa, Europe, and the Middle East. Later gold entered the Atlantic world on European ships after Portuguese merchants arrived at the coast in the late fifteenth century. Following them were British, Danish, and Dutch merchants, who leased land and built forts along what became known as the Gold Coast.[10] The forts became sites for the exportation of war captives to the Americas as demand for slaves increased in the eighteenth century. These historical processes were complex, including both internal and external factors: the result was that small rainforest polities gave way to larger states as warfare increased to provide captives to European merchants along the coast.[11] The Asante Empire became the dominant power in the rainforest and extended its military campaigns into the savanna, initially capturing its own prisoners of war and later receiving annual tribute in the form of captives from tributary states in the savanna. Political leaders in the Fante states assumed roles as brokers in the exchange of Asante war captives to European merchants at the coast: Cape Coast and Anomabu were major markets for enslaved Africans heading to British possessions in the Americas. As Asante became an empire, its relations with the Fante states grew uneasy: Asante armies invaded the coast on numerous occasions to undermine the Fante states, to challenge Europeans in the forts, and to secure favorable terms of trade.[12]

Social rank was an important element in the Fante states. Akan speakers established polities in which *ahene* and other royals (*adehyee*; singular, *odehyee*) had higher standing than commoners and outsiders. *Ahene*, *adehyee*, and commoners had slaves, Akan social dependents including pawns working off indebtedness, convicted criminals serving victims' families, and hostages taken in war; each had a distinct term designating their type of subordinate status.[13] Demand for dependent labor in expanding Akan settlements was the reason the first Portuguese merchants exchanged slaves obtained elsewhere in Africa for gold in the Gold Coast.[14] The flow reversed during the era of the transatlantic slave trade, and warfare led Akan speakers to develop new categories of subordinates, such as *nnonkofoo*, prisoners of war taken from the savanna.[15] Most *nnonkofoo* were sold into the transatlantic slave trade during the eighteenth century, but during the nineteenth century *nnonkofoo* remained and worked in the Gold Coast as the transatlantic slave trade ended and new opportunities opened for commerce in cash crops and other commodities.[16]

Fante entrepreneurs were involved in the economic changes of the nineteenth century Gold Coast. Their influence increased as Fante *ahene* lost the ability to accumulate wealth from tolls on the passage of slaves to coastal markets with the end of the transatlantic slave trade. Fante innovators established new businesses associated with the export of cash crops, such as palm oil, and forest products, such as timber and rubber, to meet demand for these items in an industrializing Europe. Facilitating the rise of Fante merchants were two other economic changes: British firms developed a system in which credit flowed more easily to African merchants, and British steamers, brought into West African service in the 1850s, began to take orders directly from African firms.[17] Fante entrepreneurs seized these opportunities and made considerable profits, for example, in accumulating and selling palm oil or in making canoes for use as surfboats servicing European steamers. Wealth concentrated in the hands of several hundred Gold Coast merchants, who relied on slaves and other dependents as workers in their firms and homes. These affluent merchants usually were not sitting *ahene* but often were *adehyee* whose connections facilitated access to land and labor. Expanding trade also benefited commoners who earned small sums working for affluent merchants, starting small businesses peddling European goods in the interior, and serving as brokers between palm oil merchants and Africans collecting wild palm kernels in the interior.[18]

Increasing wealth led to new forms of Fante self-presentation. Sartorial practices reflected rank and status. *Ahene* and *adehyee* wore elegant, locally produced cloths, woven in African looms and expressing Fante styles; *ahene* added golden regalia to mark their political office during ceremonial events. Commoners and slaves wore plain local cloths. But in the mid-nineteenth century, European clothing became fashionable. Fante merchants and traders adopted dresses for women and pants, shirts, and jackets for men, and others aspired to this new style and other aspects of European material culture. Affluent merchants also formed new social organizations, such as Freemason and Temperance societies, modeled along European lines but expressing local perspectives and interests. British law, too, interested the elite, who studied abroad and returned to engage the British on local rights. Coastal residents published newspapers and produced written histories to counter British representations in an era of growing European disregard of Africa's past.[19] These changes reflected wider Fante social transformations that also were evident in religious expressions.

The Religious Marketplace in the Mid-Nineteenth-Century Fante States

British imperialism and Methodist proselytism combined to create a new religious marketplace in the Fante states during the mid-nineteenth century. British dominance in the region expanded gradually over the course of the nineteenth century, even as Asante remained a major regional power for most the era. The 1807 Asante invasion of the Fante states destroyed Abora, the most powerful Fante state at the time, and the Asante army temporarily occupied Mankessim and other Fante towns. Although the Fante states reclaimed autonomy by the 1820s, they did so with British assistance. As cash cropping gained momentum in the Gold Coast, British imperial interests were whetted, and by 1844 Fante *ahene* agreed to allow British judicial assessors the right to prosecute serious offenses, such as murder and robbery, anywhere in the Gold Coast.[20] This legal concession led to the opening of prisons and the establishment of an armed force in British forts. The latter proved difficult to maintain, as the pay was too low to attract many local applicants: British officials turned to various external solutions, such as deploying forces of the West Indian Regiment and ultimately members of the Hausa Force in the early 1870s. British domination in the Gold Coast continued to expand as they consolidated control over coastal forts that Denmark and Netherlands had occupied for centuries. The formal declaration of the Gold Coast colony in 1874 was the culmination of decades of formal and informal British influence in the affairs of the coast.

English-language schools expanded with rising British imperialism in the Gold Coast. These schools initially operated in the British forts, where sons of local elites received an English-language education. Fante *ahene* also needed literate members of the court to communicate with the British in writing, instead of relying on courtiers, known as *akyeame*, who spoke on behalf of political elites. Over time the need for literate clerks increased: they did not displace *akyeame*, who remained influential in local contexts, but added a new role to the retinue serving Fante royalty in the mid-nineteenth century.[21] Expanding Fante businesses also wanted workers who could speak English. Increasing demand for English-language skills was met by the schools established by the Wesleyan Methodist Missionary Society. The mission was the second factor in the formation of a religious marketplace through its emphasis on salvation, individual conscience, and religious choice. The Methodist role in the formation of the Gold Coast religious marketplace is discussed after an overview of indigenous religious expressions along the coast.

Indigenous Religious Practices

The religious lives of *mfantsefoo* and other Akan speakers in the rainforest were shaped by an "arena of belief" that identified spiritual forces and defined religious practices.²² Fante traditions of emigration from Tekyiman to Mankessim stressed the role of *akomfoo* in guiding this journey, and the religious shrine at Nananom Mpow reinforced the connections between political and religious elites in the Fante states. Nineteenth-century Fante *ahene* maintained a close association with *akomfoo*, but they never exercised the strict control over religious expressions that the *asantehene* did in the interior: Fante *akomfoo* had relative autonomy to establish their own networks and provided ritual services to local residents as well as political elites. The activities of *akomfoo* enter the historical record in vague and unsympathetic European references to "the fetish," and these glimpses into religious activities suggest an influential presence of *akomfoo* as healers of the ill, ritual experts at family life-cycle events, and public servants at harvest festivals and political transitions.²³ Methodist missionaries lamented that all Fante settlements had sacred groves attended by *akomfoo*, attesting to the pervasive influence of indigenous religious practices in the Fante states.

John Mensah Sarbah provides insight into Fante indigenous religious practices and ideas. Mensah Sarbah, an early twentieth-century Gold Coast lawyer raised in a prominent African Christian family, acknowledged the significance of harvest festivals and sacred groves in the lives of coastal residents. He stressed the superordinate spiritual force, *onyankupon*, or "Great Friend," in the heavens, and repeated the Fante proverb "Speak to the winds, and God will hear thee."²⁴ The indigenous arena of belief drew on Akan concepts regarding a creator, *onyankupon* (or *onyame*, the more widely invoked term).²⁵ In Akan imaginings *onyame* formed the world and stepped back from involvement in human affairs. Men and women were not alone, and Sarbah's proverb indicates that humans could express their concerns to God by speaking to the wind, but no formal shrines or religious specialists were devoted to serving *onyame*. The Methodist missionary John Martin grasped this aspect of the arena of belief, conceding in his journal that "they believe in the existence of the Supreme, but regard him with the feelings of a deist."²⁶ The historian Thomas McCaskie added from his research on nineteenth-century Asante that "*onyame* was the final arbiter of justice, but in this, as in other matters, he was remote and allocative rather than approachable and flexible."²⁷

Abosom, the general Akan term for accessible spiritual forces, were the focus of most religious practices along the coast. These forces, understood to be the children of *onyame*, were in nature and intervened in human affairs arbitrarily; *abosom* usually were associated with water, vegetation, and the sky. Each Fante state claimed to have nearly a hundred manifestations of *abosom* in rivers, sacred groves, and other sites. Shrines were constructed after reported appearances of *abosom*, and another manifestation was a possession experience. Men and woman who had been possessed could be initiated into the ranks of the *akomfoo*, religious specialists who knew how to communicate with *abosom*. Initiation took years and included mastery of a dance that was preparatory for possession. Once called and initiated into the group, *akomfoo* marked themselves apart by dressing distinctively, living on the outskirts of settlements, and conducting rituals in the forest. These specialists formed a diffuse network of practitioners who provided a range of services. Women who could not have children often went to *akomfoo* for cures of their bareness. *Akomfoo* also performed a prophetic role at oracles by revealing communications from *abosom*. Some Fante religious specialists were experts in healing through herbs, but they were distinct from *akomfoo*, who had the ability to communicate with *abosom*.[28] *Akomfoo* cut a powerful figure with their distinctive dress and expressive actions, appearing publicly during harvest festivals and at ceremonies associated with the *oman*.

Asuman, or power objects, had spiritual force and were ubiquitous along the coast, but these objects were inferior to *onyame* and *abosom*. *Asuman* took the form of amulets used for personal purposes, for example to protect, harm others, or obtain a beneficial outcome. The nineteenth-century Methodist missionary Reverend Martin described one as "a stone with some cordage entwined around it."[29] *Asuman* took various forms: they were worn on clothing, hung on fences, buried in the ground, and placed wherever humans hoped to direct spiritual power. Soldiers often wore *asuman* on smocks to protect them in battle. Their power was only temporary, specific to the intended purpose for which it was made. The manufacture and use of these objects indicated a secondary status; the source was ambiguous and often understood to be derivative, coming from *abosom*. That *asuman* were sold underscores their subordinate religious status, as *abosom* could not be controlled in that way.

Human spirits also were a focus in the cosmologies of the Akan-speaking world. John Mensah Sarbah acknowledged that "ancestor worship even now permeates the actions of all, although some persons will deny it," and he referred to the widespread practice of pouring libations and making "prayers to the spirits of the departed ones."[30] In Fante imaginings the interior spiritual core of humans included several elements, some of which became a *saman* (spirit) at death and joined other ancestral spirits in *samanadze*, the "land of the spirits," believed to be under the earth.[31] In the mid-nineteenth century, heads of households were buried under the floors of their former residences, and surviving family heads were responsible for pouring libations to the deceased ancestors. Concern for ancestors was pervasive, but it did not divert attention from *abosom* and *akomfoo*.

This arena of belief offered a general conceptualization of the supernatural realm and human access to it. While religious ideas and practices were shared widely in the Akan-speaking world, important differences were evident. Asante was a centralized state, and its leaders sought to control *akomfoo*: challenges could arise nonetheless, and *akomfoo* daring to defy the Asantehene were dealt with harshly.[32] The political order of the Fante states was not centralized, and *akomfoo* associated with Nananom Mpow could exercise influence over political matters. Rebecca Shumway argued that Nananom Mpow rose above its initial association with Borbor Fante and became a regional "protector god" for all coastal peoples during the intensive warfare of the Atlantic slave-trading era.[33] In the nineteenth century, Nananom Mpow was attended by more than fifty *akomfoo* differentiated by rank and function. Access to its *abosom* occurred during annual ceremonies and in individual consultations on major issues, after appropriate sacrifices had been offered and accepted. Ceremonies occurred at night, with a sacred fire burning. *Abosom* became manifest through a wind that shook the trees and pulled up sacrifices into the air: *akomfoo* revealed what was communicated to them in a hoarse and stuttering voice.[34] Nananom Mpow was a potent oracle, and its *akomfoo* were respected leaders who provided guidance to residents of the Fante states in the nineteenth century.[35] Fante *ahene* and *akomfoo*, however, could not prevent the arrival of new religious providers, the Wesleyan Methodist Missionary Society.

Methodist Proselytism

The Wesleyan Methodist Missionary Society founded a mission in the Gold Coast in the mid-1830s, and the Methodist Church became an integral part of the religious arena of the Fante states over the years. Methodism has roots in the preaching of the British evangelist John Wesley, who inspired a movement of lay preachers to spread his message of personal salvation through rebirth and sanctification. The Methodist movement in the eighteenth and nineteenth centuries grew quickly in Britain and North America, attracting members through its emphasis on good works, education, and communal discipline.[36] Thomas Coke, Wesley's successor, pushed for Methodist proselytism in new frontiers, and the Wesleyan Methodist Missionary Society formed in the early nineteenth century.[37] The Methodists, as other missionary societies of the era, used abolition of the slave trade as a rallying cry for contributions to their African missions. The Methodist arrival in the Gold Coast, however, was rooted in African initiative. Members of the Meeting for Promoting Christian Knowledge, a group of young African men who received an English-language education at a school in Britain's Cape Coast fort, requested a Methodist missionary in 1831.[38] Thereafter, Africans joined and became prominent Methodists, serving as catechists, teachers, and ministers in a network of mission stations, chapels, and English-language schools along the coast. Methodism in the mid-nineteenth-century Gold Coast was an African appropriation of a European missionary organization.[39]

Methodism in the Gold Coast benefited from the inspired leadership of Thomas Birch Freeman.[40] He was the son of a former African slave and a British mother, and he directed the Gold Coast mission for two decades. Freeman arrived in 1837 in the wake of the deaths of the initial Methodist missionaries, all Europeans who perished from tropical diseases. He built on their early efforts, retaining a base at Cape Coast and continuing their focus on the Fante states. The Methodists also had a small presence at Accra, and Freeman hoped to expand into other regions, but the Fante states remained the heart of the mission in the early decades. Freeman was assisted by several young Africans who had attended the English-language school at the Cape Coast fort. One was William De Graft, who was assistant missionary at Winneba in the late 1830s before rising to become a minister. De Graft described his preaching in the inland village of Kwakwatia:

> I went and took my stand under a Fetish Grove in the market place and after singing a few verses of a Hymn and prayed [sic], I proclaimed to the assembled people who came to hear me that "God is love." I endeavored all I could to bring the subject home to their minds and I bless the Lord of the vineyard who manifested his presence and proved my sufficiency.[41]

De Graft was devoted to the Methodist cause, and several other Africans followed his path, producing a sizable African clergy by the 1870s.[42]

The Methodist commitment to education was a signature aspect of their presence in the Gold Coast. Methodist schools offered English-language instruction; local teachers sometimes used Fante informally.[43] Methodists were slow to develop Fante language translations of the Bible and hymns, which drew criticism from some Fante Methodists. English-language education nevertheless remained an attraction for many children interested in careers in which English was essential. By the 1860s eleven thousand children attended Methodist schools, which were mixed-sex but attended overwhelmingly by boys. This number of students so exceeded instructional capacity that Methodist schools relied on advanced students as teaching mentors in the lower grades. Instructional quality may have plunged, but the schools provided sufficient instruction for students to land positions with commercial firms wanting clerks to complete paperwork in English. They also served Fante political elites, who engaged in English-language correspondence with British officials in the region. Methodists exposed so many to Christianity at an early age that membership increased over the years as former students became active again after they founded households.

Individual salvation and communal discipline were defining features of Methodist theology and practice in the Gold Coast. The Wesleyan Methodist Missionary Society guide instructed missionaries to promote personal piety through example and imposing discipline on others. These recommendations, consistent with the movement's evangelical goals, forced Africans to renounce social practices, such as polygyny and the consultation of Fante *akomfoo*. Thomas Birch Freeman was a pragmatist, according to Brodie Cruickshank, a British merchant and longtime coastal resident: Cruickshank noted that the first British missionaries "burned with an intemperate enthusiasm approaching fanaticism," whereas Freeman combined "the wisdom of the politician with the active zeal of the missionary, and possessed an elastic buoyancy of temperament."[44] The first decades of Methodist proselytism drew in converts through Freeman's willingness to relax aspects of communal discipline in hopes of gaining the individual salvation of as many Africans as he could persuade to become Methodists.

Freeman's successors tended to hone more closely to the general recommendations for Methodist missionaries. In addition to polygyny and indigenous religious practices, Methodists insisted on payment of fees to attend Sunday services and schools, "ticket money" and "class money," respectively, in the Methodist parlance of the era. Payment led to a printed receipt or "ticket," often with a biblical quote. Ministers designated members to enforce discipline in the purchase and display of "tickets."[45] This collection led to severed memberships and dissident movements over the course of the late nineteenth century. J. E. Casely Hayford, an early twentieth-century Gold Coast lawyer raised in a prominent Methodist family, commented on the challenges facing Methodists. He wrote in 1903:

> Now, when the missionary comes along, simple soul that he is, and gives the would-be converted Native the comprehensive command to give up all fetish as a thing abominable in the sight of God, his reason reels, and the foundations of his faith are, for the first time, shaken. But he soon finds himself on *terra firma*: and when he remembers the lessons of his youth and considers that, after all, the missionary may be wrong in a matter that affects the vital interests of the life beyond, he remains forever afterwards only a Christian worshipper in form, if he does not openly revolt. Where he remains a formal worshipper, it does not necessarily follow that he is a hypocrite. The fact is that he likes the music and the ceremonials of the Christian Church, and would fain continue to enjoy them, while at heart he remains true to the faith of his fathers.[46]

Casely Hayford's perspective expressed a widespread view that Methodism sometimes pressed uncomfortably against social customs. Missionaries countered this trend by casting a broad net to bring in as many members as possible in hopes that personal salvation would occur before converts were lost because of their failure to abide the demands of communal discipline.

Members of all social ranks became Methodists in the Gold Coast, but the organization was controlled by Fante elites in alliance with British Methodists. Thomas Birch Freeman and William West, his successor, encouraged religious outreach to all members of coastal society. Slaves were among the initial Methodist converts, but their numbers decreased over time. The historian Anne Hugon argued that slaves still attended services for decades and came to be represented as "domestic" servants by the missionaries. Another explanation is that slaves left as more affluent residents became Methodists and made them feel unwelcome: at least one missionary report acknowledged that slaves were intimidated by their masters and stopped attending services.[47] Commoners were the largest group of Methodists. In contrast to its "low church" status in Britain, the Methodist Church became an establishment institution run by members of elite Fante families and a few British missionaries.

Fante *akomfoo* challenged Methodist missionaries when they first arrived on the coast, but British officials acted to support religious freedom and Methodist activities. John Beecham, reporting from Methodist missionary accounts, noted the opposition at Nananom Mpow where an *okomfo* "had been caught up by the fetish into the air, and had received a message for the people, to the effect that, if they did not immediately reject the new religion, the fetish would not send any more rain."[48] Methodist missionaries were undeterred. At a village near Mankessim, a lay Methodist secretly entered Nananom Mpow and cut down one of its trees in the early 1850s. *Akomfoo* responded by burning the mission station and scattering the Fante Methodists with the help of the leader of Mankessim. The British judicial assessor, Brodie Cruickshank, intervened and assessed a fine on the Mankessim leader, and when he refused Cruickshank oversaw a trial in which Fante Christians presented extensive evidence of fraudulent practices at Nananom Mpow.[49] Methodists won the case and opened a new missionary station. The Mankessim mission endured challenges in its early years, but with the support of British officials, Methodists persevered and made it a thriving station with a chapel and school by the 1860s.[50]

The Nananom Mpow conflict with Methodists underscored the trajectory of religious change in the mid-nineteenth-century Gold Coast. Thomas McCaskie contended that the episode was a "leading indicator of the crisis of cultural identity that afflicted mid-nineteenth century Fante society," a crisis he attributed to the expansion of Christianity, British intervention, rising merchant wealth, and the diminishing authority of political elites.[51] McCaskie perhaps overstated the decline of Nananom Mpow, but he captured the sense that British imperialism and Methodist proselytism had created a new religious marketplace along the coast.

Muslims in the Fante States

African Muslims were not numerous in the mid-nineteenth-century Gold Coast. They resided in small groups or as individuals in a coastal context dominated by sacred groves and Christian missions. Some Muslims were *nnonkofoo*, uprooted from the savanna and limited in their Muslim practices by their non-Muslim masters: they lived without community support and did not constitute a distinct group. Other Muslims were former slaves who settled near the Dutch forts at Elmina and Accra. The group at Elmina included *nnonkofoo* who had been sold to Dutch officials recruiting men for military service in Indonesia: they returned after this service to collect pensions in Elmina's "Java Hill" neighborhood.[52] The Muslims at Accra included Afro-Brazilians who arrived from the Americas in several migrations beginning in the first half of the nineteenth century.[53] By the 1870s aspirational Afro-Brazilians at Accra sought English-language education as the British formally declared colonial rule over the Gold Coast;[54] Muslims in this group often became Christians. Another group of Muslims arrived at Accra during the latter half of the nineteenth century: they were led by Mallam Naino, a Muslim scholar who relocated from Katsina in today's northern Nigeria with several members of his family.[55] These small Muslim communities did not have much influence along the coast in the mid-nineteenth century, and they had little contact with residents of the Fante states.

Muslims visited the Fante states briefly in the late 1860s. Missionaries from the Basel Mission noted Muslim visitors when they arrived in 1870 at Akyem, an inland Akan polity, and again when then departed Akyem in 1872.[56] These missionaries added that the Muslims had passed through the Fante states, but no Methodist mentioned the visit at the time. The Muslims presumably arrived from Lagos by British steamers at Cape Coast or Saltpond and made their way to Akyem.[57] These visitors may have been in the region to explore the expansion of the kola nut trade: wild kola nuts went uncollected from the southern regions of the rainforest at the time, and the first exports were sent on steamers from Accra to Lagos in 1872.[58] The infrequency of Muslim visitors to the Fante states during the middle decades of the nineteenth century made this visit seem significant to the Basel Mission. Just a few years after this visit, the Hausa Force and their *mallams* arrived and transformed the religious marketplace.

The Hausa Force

The Hausa Force, also known as the Armed Hausa Police, was a colonial militia at Lagos.[59] Warfare in its hinterland made Lagos a major market for the transatlantic slave trade in the mid-nineteenth century, and the creation of the Hausa Force was an outgrowth of British abolitionism. Once a British colony was established at Lagos in 1861, the first British administrators, H. S. Freeman and his successor John H. Glover, sought to end the slave trade and to promote British commerce. They pursed several initiatives, such as establishing a customs service and courts as well as expanding access to trade routes into the hinterland. Glover had a long tenure in Lagos, beginning in the early 1860s and then serving as administrator from 1866 to 1872. Kristin Mann argued that Glover adopted the airs of an African "big man," governing through patron-client relationships: he provided a small group of Africans (and a few Europeans serving in Lagos) with positions and economic rewards and protected them through informal adjudication of disputes backed up by force of arms. Glover's enforcers included the Hausa Force.[60]

Genesis

The men of the Hausa Force often are called "Glover's Hausa," but the force was not solely Glover's creation.[61] The African influences are evident if one takes the long view. This more complex story begins in the late 1850s during W. B. Baikie's exploratory expedition up the Niger River: several Africans associated with this expedition later became integral to the Hausa Force at Lagos. After Baikie's ship grounded up the Niger, his expedition returned to Lagos, whereupon Baikie sent John Glover, then his assistant, to obtain supplies at Freetown. There Glover recruited Africans who identified themselves as "Hausa" liberated from slave ships. Once in Lagos these men joined others recruited from the servile population of the region: the former masters reportedly attacked Baikie's entourage as it was leaving Lagos, and Glover led the former slaves in repulsing the attack.[62] This experience influenced Glover, who thereafter argued for the value of a Hausa militia aiding British imperial projects.[63] Several Africans associated with the Baikie expedition later became Hausa Force officers: Yakubu, son of a Hausa leader Baikie encountered; Yakubu's brother Abdul Karim, who served as one of Baikie's escorts; and Harri Zenoah, who claimed Bornu origins, met Glover at Freetown in 1858, and returned with him to Lagos.[64] These men, all Muslims, shaped the Hausa Force as much as Glover.

The Hausa Force was constituted in 1862 after the administrator H. S. Freeman received authorization to found a small militia. Major Leveson initially led this force, but John Glover assumed its command in 1863 and developed it into a cohesive unit: the Hausa Force grew under Glover from a small force of forty to several hundred regular members in the mid-1860s.[65] Rank-and-file members were former slaves who had fled bondage to Lagos or had been liberated by the Hausa Force during its expeditions on the frontier of the colony. Soldiers were not necessarily Hausa in ethnicity, but they were former captives who usually had savanna origins and were "outsiders" in Lagos. Former soldiers remained connected to the unit even after completing their service: many were reservists, members of a group of several hundred whom Glover maintained and compensated for two months annual duty. Glover imagined the reservists as "guardians of the peace," creating a defensive buffer on an expanding colonial frontier: he acquired land as "Crown grants" from local chiefs and gave reservists access to farm.[66] Glover also had a fund to provide financial assistance to these reservists: violations of discipline by active forces were fined, and Glover distributed the accumulated funds to reservists needing capital to start a farm or launch enterprises.⁶⁷ Through these efforts Glover ensured that service in the force led to an autonomous life through continued ties to him. Marriages in the force are undocumented, but Glover seems to have condoned the "liberation" of female captives from local slave owners and their marriage to members of the force: this practice occurred frequently during the force's Gold Coast deployment. Glover also paid stipends to wives who accompanied the men to the Gold Coast in advance of the campaign, and one imagines that he was similarly generous with his support over the years in Lagos.

The Hausa Force reflected the historical experience of Lagos, a town defined by the slave trade and its abolition. British colonial rule eliminated international slave dealing in Lagos, and the arrival of Sierra Leoneans, former captives liberated by the British Navy from slavers off the coast, reversed the flow as Africans educated in Christian missionary schools in Freetown arrived as traders and missionaries during the mid-nineteenth century.⁶⁸ Ending slavery was another matter. Various forms of servitude thrived in the region, some based on long-standing practices, such as pawning, and others reflecting innovations in local slave holding as new firms arose to produce palm oil and other cash crops for international markets. Wars produced captives in the interior, and regional trading networks funneled some to the coast. Fugitive slaves who made it to Lagos could appeal for assistance, but overall the regime led by Freeman and Glover was not actively seeking to abolish slavery. Many of Glover's clients were prominent commercial leaders with vested interests in the status quo. At the same time, Glover espoused anti-slavery rhetoric and applied it to the Hausa Force: he understood his role as their liberator and hoped that they would be loyal to the British thereafter. Glover's abolitionist paternalism is evident in remarks he made to the men in the Gold Coast, after their service in the British invasion of Asante: he asked them to swear allegiance to "the Great White Queen" and fight "against her enemies for all time" because they had been "a downtrodden and oppressed people" before their liberation by the British.⁶⁹

The Hausa Force was Muslim by self-expression as much as by British design. John Glover and other British officers were influenced by "martial races" ideas and imagined the "Hausa" as Muslims who would fiercely fight their former masters. The British outfitted the force in a modified Zouave uniform, including a fez, short vest, and loose pants, associated with Muslim colonial armies;⁷⁰ Major Leveson, who fought in the Crimean War when the Zouave uniform first gained British awareness, may have selected this style for the men.⁷¹ But Africans asserted a Muslim identity, too. Glover drilled them in a schedule associated with the lunar Muslim calendar; he would not have known the dates, and African officers probably were the ones to propose it to him.⁷² These officers also were the likely source of putting *mallams* on the Hausa Force payroll.⁷³ The force's buglers played to instill discipline when fighting and at ceremonial functions, but they also used their instruments to announce the times to perform Muslim *salat*, as was reported during their deployment in the Gold Coast. The force's own expression of its Muslim identity was not clearly apparent in the historical record from Lagos, but evidence of their Muslim practices exists for the period of their deployment in the Gold Coast, as will be discussed later.

The military exploits of the Hausa Force attracted the attention of British administrators in the Gold Coast. They were most interested in the lower cost compared to regular military troops. Eventually members of the Hausa Force were deployed in the Gold Coast to fight in the British invasion of Asante, and later some remained to form the core of the new Gold Coast Constabulary. The majority of men, however, returned to Lagos and found that circumstances had changed. Glover no longer was administrator in Lagos, and the Hausa Force had been integrated into the Civil Police; the men lost their elevated roles, and they no longer wore distinctive uniforms. Reservists' settlements of former Hausa Force members, however, remained a source of accumulation for several decades.[74] The Hausa Force practice of having *mallams* serving African soldiers also continued into the late nineteenth century (figure 3).

Gold Coast Deployment

Proposals to recruit locally to form a Gold Coast version of the Hausa Force were made in 1871, but pressing military concerns curtailed those plans and forced the deployment of members of the Hausa Force to the Gold Coast in 1872.[75] The pressing issue was that the Dutch had ceded their fort at Elmina to Britain, and British colonial officials feared an attack from Asante, as its rulers considered Elmina to be within its realm. The Gold Coast was defended at the time by units of the West Indian Regiment; the British bolstered their defenses by transferring more than 150 members of the Hausa Force to their Gold Coast forts at Elmina and Cape Coast in 1872.[76] The Hausa Force remained distinct from the West Indian Regiment, and its first mission involved Akyeampon Yaw, the Asante royal and former envoy at Elmina whom the Dutch transferred to Assini, a nearby town. In October 1872 fifty Hausa Force soldiers, led by Colonel G. F. Foster, put Akyeampon Yaw and his entourage onto a British military steamer; once at Cape Coast and under the cover of evening darkness, they escorted Yaw to Asante territory.[77] Their success in this sensitive mission increased the force's stature in British eyes, and an additional hundred members were sent from Lagos in early 1873, increasing the Gold Coast contingent to more than 220 soldiers.[78]

The history of the 1873–1874 British invasion of the Asante Empire has been told in detail by others and is only summarized here.[79] The Asante army, after the transfer of the Dutch fort at Elmina to the British, crossed into the Gold Coast in early 1873 but did not attack the British forts, which were defended by the Hausa Force and local African allies. Two British-led forces arrived to invade Asante, both armed with artillery. The main force was headed by Garnet Wolseley, who commanded a force of 2,500 British soldiers, 2,000 additional West Indian Regiment forces, and several hundred Hausa Force members. The other force was led by John Glover, who recruited nearly a thousand Hausa Force soldiers and others in the Gold Coast and Lagos to launch a flanking operation from the Volta River (see figure 4). Wolseley's force engaged the Asante army as it marched from Cape Coast to Kumasi; the Asante army fought admirably, but it ultimately remained too long on the march to keep itself well and adequately fed. Glover's flanking operation arrived in Kumasi, too, after Wolseley's forces had started back to Cape Coast, and the Hausa Force looted and torched the town. The Anglo-Asante peace treaty of 1874 ended hostilities and defined a boundary between Asante and the Gold Coast, which just months later became a formal British colony.

The Hausa Force's military performance received praise from British officials. Both Garnet Wolseley and John Glover gave members of the Hausa Force medals for their service. Historians speculate that Wolseley might have eliminated the expense of a long campaign with British forces if he had deployed the Hausa Force against Asante when its army was weakened from its long residence in the Gold Coast.[80] Perhaps aware of similar criticisms expressed at the time, Wolseley claimed that Glover, by removing most of the Hausa Force men from Elmina and Cape Coast to the Volta before Wolseley's arrival, forced him to call more British troops to fight.[81] Glover himself argued that the Hausa Force members under his command were instrumental to the campaign's success and lamented his inability to recruit as many as anticipated.[82] This debate underscores the significance of the Hausa Force to the British invasion of Asante.

British colonial officials formed a Gold Coast militia along the lines of the Hausa Force. This militia eventually became known as the Gold Coast Constabulary, a fighting force that assisted in British military operations during the late nineteenth century and was integrated into the West African Frontier Force in the early twentieth century. The first move toward the formation of the Gold Coast Constabulary was the 1873 British ordinance forming the Gold Coast Armed Police Force. This unit formalized the merging of members of the Hausa Force into the Gold Coast Police in the buildup to the invasion. But Glover's assumption of command over some Hausa Force members, and Wolseley's subsequent recruitment of additional Hausa Force men from Lagos, transformed the force during the invasion. At the end of the war, Lord Kimberly in the Colonial Office wanted men from the Hausa Force to remain and ordered that concrete plans be made for their deployment in the Gold Coast.[83] These postwar efforts set in motion the formation of the Gold Coast Constabulary, modeled on the Hausa Force and including some of its members.

The Gold Coast Constabulary was distinct from the Hausa Force. Most Hausa Force soldiers from Lagos returned after the war and did not join the Gold Coast Constabulary: John Glover argued successfully that the men he recruited from Lagos earned the right to return, and almost two-thirds of the Lagosian members departed in mid-1874.[84] Original Hausa Force members who remained in the Gold Coast were outnumbered by members recruited in the Gold Coast, some added during the war and more recruited in the late 1870s. The change in personnel meant that the ethos of the original Hausa Force was lacking in the new force. The loss of solidarity is revealed by the desertions from the force during the late nineteenth century and the constant need to recruit new members. British recruitment efforts targeted regions where few Hausa-speaking peoples lived, reducing further the force's solidarity. Not even Islam was a shared value among recruits.[85] Drunkenness was a problem, and by the late 1880s the British hoped that reinforcing the force's presumed Muslim identity would help: they employed *mallams* and built a mosque (figures 5 and 6), but the mosque was used by Muslims from the town and not constabulary members in the late nineteenth century.[86] This era has left an enduring impression of an imagined Muslim force in the historical literature, but most Hausa Force members in the early 1870s were Muslims, and their Gold Coast deployment included many examples of an exuberant performance of their distinctive Muslim identity.[87]

Muslim Expressions in the Gold Coast

The Hausa Force asserted a Muslim identity beyond the forts where they resided in the Gold Coast. Within weeks of the force's arrival, the administrator of the Gold Coast reported seeing men "mixing with the people" in the evenings.[88] These interactions sometimes produced graphic displays of Hausa Force disgust at seeing pigs freely roaming about town. These animals were regarded as unclean to Muslims, and at least once Hausa Force members shouted loudly to frighten pigs from coming close to the garrison's water source at the Cape Coast fort.[89] Demonstrative expressions were an element of the barracks Islam practiced by the force: their Muslim identity was a matter of social practice as much as theology. The Hausa Force performed Muslim rituals, but they also engaged in activities that other West African Muslims avoided, such as consuming alcohol and playing Christian hymns on their bugles to call Muslims to prayer. They were former slaves who became abolitionists, securing liberation of servile women they claimed as wives. The Hausa Force, whatever the servile experiences of any individual member, was a community of Atlantic Muslims who operated in the shadow of the transatlantic slave trade.

Glimpses into the daily routine of Hausa Force Muslim rituals are provided by British war correspondents. They offered descriptions of force members shouting praises to Allah before engaging opponents.[90] The Muslim identity of the Hausa Force was evident in other domains. Frederick Boyle noted that in the evenings the force performed "ballads and drum songs in honour of the moon, especially when she is new."[91] Boyle did not know that he was describing observance of Eid al-Adha, a Muslim holiday: its timing is defined by the moon's movement, and that year it fell in November, 1873, when Boyle noted the activities. Others were unknowing witnesses to the force's call to prayer. George A. Henty, a British correspondent for *The Standard*, and A. E. Ellis, a member of the British military expedition, both independently reported that members of the force's band played bugles before dawn.[92] Henty noted that the bugles were blown "before the sun was up," well before morning military drills. Ellis added that buglers marched back and forth repeatedly playing the first two stanzas of the hymn, "Old Father Paul Came from the Holy Land," for more than ten minutes. These references do not make a connection with the Muslim call to prayer or describe its performance after the bugle blowing. Nevertheless, the bugling occurred before sunrise, the time for the day's first performance of *salat*: it is likely that the buglers were calling men to pray before their military drills. The choice of a Christian hymn repeated excessively was the buglers' efforts to emulate a muezzin's calls to prayer in Arabic by using a Christian hymn and repeating its lyrics.

Mallams provided religious services to members of the Hausa Force. John Glover had employed *mallams* in Lagos, and some accompanied the men to the Gold Coast. William Winwood Reade, war correspondent for the *Times* of London, described their activities:

> Each company has attached to it a Mahomedan priest, who enjoys extraordinary influence with the Houssas. These priests are also, as a rule, usurers. The men are all generally in their debt, as they are inveterate gamblers. The priests' costume consists of a long flowing white robe and a white turban. They have numerous texts of the Koran fastened to their turbans and hung around their necks. They accompany the Houssas into battle and show the same disregard for danger as they do. They encourage the men, reading verses from the Koran.... It is always necessary for the officers commanding them to be on good terms with the Mahomedan priest attached to his command.[93]

Reade's description of the dress and usage of the Quran is consistent with the activities of Hausa *mallams* of the era: white robes were widely used, but the Gold Coast Constabulary adopted blue robes for its *mallams* in the late nineteenth century (compare figures 3 and 5). The reference to usury speaks perhaps to complementary economic roles as traders, a common activity among *mallams*. Leisure activities of gambling, smoking, and drinking, reported by Reade and others, were tolerated, if not condoned, by Hausa Force *mallams*.[94] No other detailed description of *mallams* in the force exists, and recent memories are vague and usually recount events after Britain's invasion of Asante in the 1870s.[95]

Members of the Hausa Force sometimes resisted the demands of their British officers in graphic displays. Dr. Samuel Rowe, John Glover's close associate in Lagos, was recruited to the Gold Coast to serve as an informal adviser because Rowe knew the "wishes and customs" of the force. Rowe wrote frequently about their complaints, noting that they resented serving as "town-police" with nonmilitary duties. He also reported at length about a dispute between Colonel Foster, the force's commander in Elmina, and Ensign Gerard, who had commanded them in Lagos and was transferred to Elmina. Gerard clashed with Foster over who could give orders, and Foster secured Gerard's removal. Hearing of Gerard's removal, members of the Hausa Force threatened to march back to Lagos. Rowe calmed the situation. He also advised the Gold Coast administrator to assume personal authority over the force and hold a public ceremony in which Gerard's departure was announced as the administrator's own decision. Rowe added that the administrator needed to replace Colonel Foster with Dr. McKellar, Rowe's colleague as surgeon. This decisive action dissipated the conflict, but the force's threatened return to Lagos no doubt circulated publicly as an act of insubordination, adding to its local reputation as a colonial militia with a distinctive ethos.[96]

The Hausa Force liberated *nnonkofoo* women as their partners. Administrator Pope Hennessy cited the force's taking of "wives" within weeks of their arrival.[97] Dr. Samuel Rowe reported numerous acts of liberation by its members.[98] In one instance Rowe was thrust into an intermediary role, as the force member came to him with his long-lost "wife," who happened to be claimed by an African clerk in Rowe's office: Rowe agreed to host the young woman at his Cape Coast residence until the dispute was settled, but then allowed the soldier and young woman to return to the Elmina barracks under the cover of darkness. The next day Rowe explained to the clerk that he had saved his life because the soldier would have killed the clerk.[99] These liberations multiplied over the months: the British war correspondent George Alfred Henty visited the camp of the Hausa Force at Ada, near the mouth of the Volta River, as they marched in campaign with Glover in late 1873: Henty reported that it was "an encampment of married people, for scarcely a Houssa but had some young woman following his fortune."[100] Some residents of Accra physically restrained their *nnonkofoo* in shackles as Glover marched from Accra to camp at Ada.[101] Mrs. Bannerman, the wife of a prominent African leader from Accra, went to Ada to reclaim two servants; Glover reluctantly returned them because he depended on her spouse's leadership in the war effort.[102] Others masters at Accra did not have this leverage, and *nnonkofoo* liberations were a source of resentment for its affluent residents.

The force's liberations were an expression of Muslim social justice. Dr. Samuel Rowe, in recounting the liberation associated with his clerk's servant, wrote that the Hausa Force soldier asserted that it was God's will that spouses be reunited with former husbands.[103] While the influence of British Christian abolitionism cannot be discounted, the soldier represented his action in Islamic terms: it was an effort to bring a Muslim family together as God's will. The role of *mallams* in giving an explicit Muslim justification for these actions is unclear. Reade noted that *mallams* exercised religious authority over the force, so much that British officers had to remain on their good terms with *mallams* if they wanted to have the soldiers' loyalty; one guesses that *mallams* condoned the acts of liberation, if not giving them explicit sanction. Other West African Muslims from servile background became abolitionists, situating their arguments in a Sufi understanding.[104] Hausa Force members were not Sufis but rather Muslim cosmopolitans who integrated Christian abolitionist ideology with their understanding of Islam's emphasis on equality before God to assert a universal value in liberating slaves from bondage.

The Hausa Force's Muslim assertions in the Gold Coast occurred in the context of their participation in the British invasion of Asante. The outcome was uncertain, as Asante was a regional hegemon that had suffered few defeats in the past. The temporary occupation of Kumasi by the forces of Garnet Wolseley and John Glover brought the war to a conclusion that led to a peace treaty and demarcation of a clear boundary between the Asante Empire and the Gold Coast colony, declared by the British in the invasion's aftermath. The war also was followed by a period of unsettled religious affiliations, as residents of the Gold Coast explored new options in the years that followed. The Methodists were the primary beneficiaries, but *mallams*, new suppliers in the religious marketplace, attracted consumers by offering esoteric healing that the Methodists did not provide.

Postwar Religious Change

Methodist missionaries reported a "revival" in several Gold Coast communities almost immediately after the conclusion of the war. The initial reports came from villages close to the Asante frontier, where Fante refugees returned after fleeing to coastal towns.[105] The Asante army had destroyed Methodist chapels at several villages, and missionaries at these outstations had dour assessments of Methodism's prospects. But instead, they found that open-air Methodist services received increased participation from the refugees. At Abora Ekrawfo in the months immediately after the British victory, its minister wrote that "emphatically we have a revival, and far and wide it is spreading."[106] Thomas Birch Freeman, returning to missionary service in the 1870s after his retirement in 1857, encouraged the revival in the Anomabu circuit that he supervised. At Mankessim, the market town and home to Nananom Mpow, Methodist attendance jumped in 1874, and Freeman visited repeatedly to deliver guest Sunday sermons in Mankessim's chapel and to lead open-air meetings at nearby villages. The increasing numbers pressing to attend services led Freeman to request more membership forms because he had given out more than two thousand in just a few months.[107]

Rising membership led the Methodists to establish new stations in the interior. In Thomas Birch Freeman's Anomabu circuit, for example, Mankessim and Abaasa had been the only permanent interior missions in the early 1870s; during the mid-1870s the Methodists added Enyamem, a few miles north of Mankessim, and opened new stations at Mando, Otobiadzi, and Ampia Ajumako, within the orbit of Abaasa. Expansion had its costs. Freeman observed in his 1878 report that Methodist membership must involve the "positive obligation of paying class and ticket money" as one of the "just and vital proofs of sound conversion to God."[108] Payments were not provided regularly, however, and by the late 1870s Methodist leaders began to terminate memberships of those unwilling to contribute ticket money. The Methodists could take this disciplined approach because, despite several swings at individual missions, an overall increase occurred from 1874 to 1889 in terms of attendance, membership, and baptisms; the last factor was the basis for future growth as children became married adults with their own offspring.

New members brought their own understandings of religious expressions with them. The exuberance of new members was evident at Mankessim, where a messianic movement developed within the Methodist congregation. Thomas Birch Freeman described the situation at Mankessim as follows: "the minds of several of the most earnest professed to have strange dreams and visions," and then some female members claimed that "they were some of the Apostles again in the flesh."[109] Freeman sent his son, also employed by the Methodists, to investigate. Even before his son returned, Freeman learned of a more dramatic occurrence at Mankessim: "one of the female members was fancying and declaring herself to be Jesus Christ come again in the flesh." Pilgrims from outside Mankessim started to visit her, and one Methodist agent was overtaken by his dreams and abetted the woman: he reportedly allowed vapors to fill the interior of the Mankessim chapel during a prayer meeting. The excitement spread to Saltpond's Methodist chapel, where a local worker rang the bells as her envoy was relating news of Jesus' return to a large congregation. The elder Freeman dispatched Methodist agents to counteract the claims and subdue the perpetrators. He also held a Methodist inquiry into events, during which the woman repented and was allowed to remain in the fold. The inquiry was much less generous to the Methodist agents involved in the incident: one was expelled and several others disciplined. Already before the Mankessim incident, the Methodists had moved to "exercise our church discipline on the insincere," as the 1877 General Report on the Gold Coast district described these efforts.[110] Six years later the General

Report commented on the expulsions that followed and acknowledged that the losses were "chiefly among those . . . whose religion never became fixed upon the true foundations."[111] Thereafter, especially with increasing numbers of British missionaries and fewer Africans in leadership roles, Methodists stressed rigorous education of new members and enforcement of rules on monogamy and the payment of ticket money.

Religious change was not confined to the Methodists. Almost as soon as the revival occurred, *akomfoo* organized themselves in opposition to the rising attendance at Methodist services. In 1877, Thomas Birch Freeman wrote about "the powers of darkness" associated with the increasing activities of *akomfoo*.[112] At the new missionary station at Essikuma, for example, the harassment of those attending Methodist services, as well as the local leader's refusal to support founding a school, prompted Freeman to seek the intervention of the British colonial government. Freeman was moved after receiving several letters outlining the escalating disruption of Methodist services and the use of *asuman* to intimidate Methodist agents. British invention was only a short-term remedy, however, and Methodist efforts in Essikuma were stymied: its Methodist membership remained under ten members for well over a decade thereafter.[113] Essikuma was merely the most dramatic and well-reported such incident involving *akomfoo*. While missionary reports celebrated the successes of the Methodist revival in introductory statements, their individual discussions of mission stations reveal that they never were successful in convincing more than a minority of rural residents to convert to Christianity in the late nineteenth-century Gold Coast.

Coastal residents were receptive to the esoteric services of *mallams* in this era of religious change. They had been aware of the reputed efficacy of these Muslim practices from rumors circulating about Muslim amulets and cures monopolized by the *asantehene*.[114] The arrival of *mallams* along the coast in the 1870s expanded access to these religious services. Hausa memories refer to Fante interest in a Muslim immigrant known only as Mallam Tibu, a title referring to *tibb*, the Arabic word for "medicine." Mallam Tibu reportedly was from Bornu and may not have arrived with the Hausa Force, but he operated along the coast in the early 1870s and, according to local memories, provided esoteric cures to Fante residents of Saltpond and nearby villages before his arrival at Cape Coast. Memories of Mallam Tibu are limited in part because he died not long after the war's conclusion and seems not to have had family in the region.[115] References to Mallam Tibu's activities, vague though they are, point to the willingness of enterprising *mallams* to extend their services beyond the Hausa Force and to meet with Fante residents who were interested in their cures. The legacy of Mallam Tibu and *mallams* associated with the Hausa Force was the emergence of the Fante Muslim community in the mid-1870s.

Conclusion

Methodist proselytism and British imperialism worked together to create a competitive religious marketplace in the mid-nineteenth-century Fante states. Merchants and other residents of coastal towns had become Christians in the middle decades of the century, and thousands more joined in the aftermath of Britain's invasion of Asante. Muslims were a very small minority and had virtually no presence in the Fante states, but this situation changed with the arrival of the Hausa Force in the early 1870s. The force's military accomplishments and demonstrative Muslim performances elevated its status and enhanced the reputations of *mallams* associated with the force: their esoteric cures had proven to be efficacious against the powerful Asante army. Binyameen Sam converted to Islam under the guidance of a *mallam* associated with the Hausa Force, and he brought other Fante Methodists into his Muslim community during the period of unsettled religious affiliations immediately after the war. Fante Muslims expressed a different ethos than those joining the Methodist revival. The woman claiming to be the returned Jesus, for example, continued to believe that religious power was expressed through spirits inhabiting the bodies of living persons. Fante Muslims may have been attracted by the esoteric healing of *mallams*, but they also were Biblicists moved by parallels they saw between the Bible and the Quran. The next chapter turns to the activities of Binyameen Sam and the emergence of the Fante Muslim community.

Notes

1. WMMS: 3 May 1876, T. B. Picot to W. B. Boyce. This exchange between Picot and Mensa Bonsu also is quoted in G. G. Findlay and W. W. Holdworth, *The History of the Wesleyan Methodist Missionary Society* (London: Epworth Press, 1921), 4:175; and T. C. McCaskie, *State and Society in Pre-Colonial Asante* (Cambridge: Cambridge University Press, 1995), 140. The passage uses two terms that I translate: the original passage used *Cramo* or *nkramo*, the Akan word for "Muslim," and *fetish*, a European word referencing *abosom*.

2. Wilks, *Asante in the Nineteenth Century*, 267–269, 276. Also see Adamu, *Hausa Factor*, 166; Ntewusu, *Settling in and Holding On*, 2, 20; and Mervyn Hiskett, "Commissioner of Police v. Musa Kommenda," 129 (relying on Jack Goody, *The Ethnography of the Northern Territories of the Gold Coast, West of the White Volta* [London: Colonial Office, 1954], appendix 4).

3. The 1870s revival is not mentioned in F. L. Bartels, *The Roots of Ghana Methodism* (Cambridge: Cambridge University Press; Accra: Methodist Book Depot, 1965); or Arthur E. Southon, *Gold Coast Methodism* (London: Cargate Press, 1934). It is mentioned only in passing in Allen Birtwhistle, *Thomas Birch Freeman: West African Pioneer* (London: Cargate Press, 1950), 102–107; and F. Deaville Walker, *Thomas Birch Freeman* (London: Student Christian Movement, 1929), 209–211. The 1870s revival falls outside the period analyzed by Anne Hugon, *Un protestantisme africain au XIXe siècle: L'implantation du méthodisme en Gold Coast (Ghana), 1835–1874* (Paris: Karthala, 2007).

4. David Killingray, "Guarding the Extending Frontier: Policing the Gold Coast, 1865–1913," in *Policing the Empire: Government, Authority, and Control, 1830–1940*, ed. D. M. Anderson and D. Killingray (Manchester: Manchester University Press, 1991), 106–125; Mann, *Slavery and the Birth*, 110–113; Ojo, "Islam, Ethnicity and Slave Resistance"; Oroge, "Fugitive Slave Question"; Tamuno, *Police in Modern Nigeria*, 15–27.

5. Streets, *Martial Races*.

6. Killingray, "Imagined Martial Communities."

7. "Barracks Islam" is a phrase used by Nile Green to define a similar Muslim expression in British India. Green, *Islam and the Colonial Army*.

8. James Anquandah, "Urbanization and State Formation in Ghana during the Iron Age," in *Archaeology of Africa: Foods, Metals and Towns*, ed. Thurston Shaw (New York: Routledge, 1993), 642–651; Gérard L. Chouin and Christopher R. Decorse, "Prelude to the Atlantic Trade: New Perspectives on Southern Ghana's Pre-Atlantic History, 800–1500," *JAH* 51, no. 2 (2012), 123–145; Florence Dolphyne, "Akan Language Patterns and Development," *Tarikh* 7, no. 2 (1982), 35–45; Ivor Wilks, "The State of the Akan and Akan States," *Cahiers d'études africaines* 22, nos. 3–4 (1982), 231–249.

9. John K. Fynn, *Asante and Its Neighbors* (Evanston, IL: Northwestern University Press, 1971); for the traditions, see id., *Oral Traditions of Fante States*, 7 vols. (Legon, Ghana: Institute of African Studies, 1974–1976).

10. Kwame Y. Daaku, *Trade and Politics on the Gold Coast, 1600–1720* (London: Oxford University Press, 1970).

11. Ray A. Kea, *Settlements, Trade and Polities in the Seventeenth-Century Gold Coast* (Baltimore: Johns Hopkins University Press, 1982).

12. Rebecca Shumway, *The Fante and the Transatlantic Slave Trade* (Rochester, NY: University of Rochester Press, 2011).

13. Akosua A. Perbi, *A History of Indigenous Slavery in Ghana: From the 15th to the 19th Centuries* (Accra: Sub-Saharan Publishers, 2004).

14. Walter Rodney, "Gold and Slaves on the Gold Coast," *THSG* 10 (1969), 13–28.

15. The etymology of *odonko* is unclear, according to McCaskie, who was not convinced that it meant "love to run away," as R. S. Rattray argued. McCaskie, *State and Society*, 95–96. Gilbert suggested that it may be based on *odo*, "he has joined us," and *nko*, "not to go back." Michelle Gilbert, "Names, Cloth and Identity: A Case from West Africa," in *Media and Identity in Africa*, ed. Kimani Njogu and John Middleton (Bloomington: Indiana University Press, 2009), 239.

16. Ray A. Kea, *A Cultural and Social History of Ghana From the Seventeenth to the Nineteenth Century: The Gold Coast in the Age of the Trans-Atlantic Slave Trade* (Lewiston, NY: Edwin Mellen Press, 2012).

17. Martin Lynn, "Technology, Trade, and 'A Race of Native Capitalists:' The Krio Diaspora of West Africa and the Steamships, 1852–95," *JAH* 33, no.3 (1992), 421–440.

18. Raymond Dumett, "African Merchants of the Gold Coast, 1800–1905: Dynamics of Indigenous Entrepreneurship," *Comparative Studies in Society and History* 25, no. 4 (1983), 261–264; Mary McCarthy, *Social Change and the Growth of British Power in the Gold Coast: The Fante States, 1807–1874* (New York: University Press of America, 1983); Edward Reynolds, *Trade and Economic Change on the Gold Coast, 1807–1874* (London: Longman, 1974).

19. Ray Jenkins, "Gold Coast Historians and Their Pursuit of the Gold Coast Pasts, 1882–1917," PhD diss., University of Birmingham, 1985.

20. J. B. Danquah, "The Historical Significance of the Bond of 1844," *THSG*, 3, no. 1 (1957), 3–29; Roger S. Gocking, *Facing Two Ways: Ghana's Coastal Communities Under Colonial Rule* (Lanham: University Press of America, 1999).

21. Brodie Cruickshank, *Eighteen Years on the Gold Coast, Including an Account of the Native Tribes, and Their Intercourses with Europeans* 2nd ed. (New York: Barnes and Noble, 1966), 2:263–264.

22. I draw on McCaskie's historical reconstruction of the nineteenth-century Asante "arena of belief" as I discuss similar Fante practices. See McCaskie, *State and Society*, 102–135.

23. For the history of the European use of *fetish* in West Africa, see William Pietz, "The Problem of the Fetish, I," *Res*, no. 9 (1985), 5–17; id., "The Problem of the Fetish, II: the Origin of the Fetish," *Res*, no. 13 (1987), 23–45; id., "The Problem of the Fetish, III: Bosman's Guinea and the Enlightenment Theory of Fetishism," *Res*, no. 16 (1988), 105–123.

24. John Mensah Sarbah, *Fanti National Constitution: A Short Treatise on the Constitution and Government of the Fanti, Asanti, and Other Akan Tribes of West Africa*, 2nd ed. (London: Frank Cass, 1968), 13, 51, 52.

25. J. B. Danquah, *The Akan Concept of God: A Fragment of Gold Coast Ethics and Religion* (London: Lutterworth, 1944).

26. A. J. N. Tremearne, "Extracts from the Diary of the Late Rev. John Martin, Wesleyan Missionary in West Africa, 1843," *Man* 12 (1912), 139.

27. McCaskie, *State and Society*, 107.

28. Herbalists are called *edurusinyi* in Fante Twi. See James Boyd Christensen, *Double Descent among the Fanti* (New Haven, CT: Human Relations Area File, 1954), 91.

29. Tremearne, "Extracts from a Diary," 139.

30. Mensah Sarbah, *Fanti National Constitution*, 5, 51.

31. Christensen, *Double Descent*; Anthony Ephirim-Donkor, *African Spirituality: On Becoming Ancestors* (Trenton, NJ: Africa World Press, 1997); George P. Hagan, "An Analytical Study of Fanti Kinship," *Research Review* (Institute of African Studies, University of Ghana at Legon) 5 (1968), 50–90.

32. McCaskie, *State and Society*, 125.

33. Rebecca Shumway, "The Fante Shrine of Nananom Mpow and the Atlantic Slave Trade in Southern Ghana," *International Journal of African Historical Studies* 44 (2011), 27–44.

34. T. C. McCaskie, "Nananom Mpow of Mankessim: An Essay in Fante History," in *West African Economic and Social History: Studies in Memory of Marion Johnson*, ed. David Henige and T. C. McCaskie (Madison, WI: African Studies Program, 1990), 139–143.

35. Shumway, "Nananom Mpow and the Atlantic Slave Trade in Southern Ghana."

36. David Hempton, *Methodism: Empire of the Spirit* (New Haven, CT: Yale University Press, 2005).

37. Andrew Porter, *Religion versus Empire?*, 32; Hempton, *Methodism*, 116–117. Porter describes initial British Methodist missionary efforts as a "fragile one-man band" led by Coke. Hempton added that the London Missionary Society's success in receiving donations from Methodist congregations prompted the Methodist leader Jabez Bunting to seek such support to put the Methodist missionary effort on a surer footing than Coke had instituted.

38. Methodist accounts stress the role of Captain Potter, a Methodist captain operating a ship between Britain and the Gold Coast, but Ray Kea refers to an 1831 document, before Potter's involvement in 1833, referencing an African request for a missionary. Kea, "Modernity and Identity: William de Graft and John Halm and the Social Imaginary in Nineteenth Century Fanteland (the Gold Coast)," in *Mondes Akan/Akan Worlds*, ed. Pierluigi Valsecchi and Fabio Viti (Paris: L'Harmattan, 1999), 228n28.

39. This point is the central argument of Hugon, *Un protestantisme africain*.

40. The secondary literature on the Methodist mission in nineteenth-century Gold Coast includes Bartels, *Roots of Ghana Methodism*; Birtwhistle, *Thomas Birch Freeman*; Hugon, *Un protestantisme africain*; Kea, "Modernity and Identity"; Bengt Sundkler and Christopher

Steed, *A History of the Church in Africa* (Cambridge: Cambridge University Press, 2000), 201–218; Southon, *Gold Coast Methodism*; and Walker, *Thomas Birch Freeman*.

41. William De Graft's account is quoted in Kea, "Modernity and Identity," 231.

42. Biographies are in Hugon, *Un protestantisme africain*, 373–389; and Southon, *Gold Coast Methodism*, 91–95.

43. Debrunner, *Christianity in Ghana*, 142.

44. Cruickshank, *Eighteen Years* 2, 116–117.

45. Hugon, *Un protestantisme africain*, 189–190.

46. J. E. Casely Hayford, *Gold Coast Native Institutions, with Thoughts upon a Healthy Imperial Policy for the Gold Coast and Ashanti* (London: Sweet and Maxwell, 1903), 104–105; the reference to a "national Church" is at 105–106.

47. WMMS: Annual Report, Anomabu and Domanasi Circuits, 1844; Hugon discusses the participation of slaves in *Un protestantisme africain*, 278–279.

48. John Beecham, *Ashantee and the Gold Coast, Being a Sketch of the History, Social State and Superstitions of the Inhabitants of those Countries with a Notice of the State and Prospect of Christianity Among Them* (London: Dawsons of Pall Mall, 1968), 279.

49. Cruickshank, *Eighteen Years* 2:262–298.

50. WMMS: Annual Report, Anomabu Circuit, undated (textual evidence points to 1853 or 1854) and 1859.

51. McCaskie, "Nananom Mpow of Mankessim," 147.

52. Larry W. Yarak, "New Sources for the Study of Akan Slavery and the Slave Trade: Dutch Military Recruitment in the Gold Coast and Asante, 1831–72," in *Source Materials for Studying the Slave Trade and the African Diaspora*, ed. Robin Law (Stirling, UK: University of Stirling Press, 1997), 35–60; W. Walter Claridge, *A History of the Gold Coast and Ashanti*, 2nd ed. (London: Frank Cass, 1964), 1:558–559.

53. Alcione Amos and Ebenezer Ayesu, "'I am Brazilian': A History of the Tabom, Afro-Brazilians in Accra, Ghana," *THSG*, n.s., no. 6 (2002), 35–58; Kwame Essien, "African Diaspora in Reverse: The *Tabom* People in Ghana, 1820s–2009," PhD diss., University of Texas–Austin, 2010; Ray Jenkins, "West Indian and Brazilian Influences in the Gold Coast-Ghana, c. 1807–1914: A Review and Reappraisal of Continuities in the Post-Abolitionist Links between West Africa and the Caribbean and Brazil," Society for Caribbean Studies, conference paper, 1988; Samuel Quarcoopome, "The Brazilian Community in Accra," BA honors essay, University of Ghana at Legon, 1970; Marco Aurelio Schaumloeffel, *Tabom: The Afro-Brazilian Community in Ghana* (Bridgetown, Barbados: Custom Books Publishing, 2009).

54. Parker, *Making the Town*, 82.

55. Odoom, "Pioneers"; Pellow, *Landlords and Lodgers*, 47–48.

56. BM: October 1870, Third Quarter Report, submitted by Kromer; and 13 April 1872, First Quarter Report, submitted by Lodholtz. Also see English summaries in "Abstracts from Correspondence in the Basel Mission Archive, 1852–1898, made by P. Jenkins," 560, 571–572.

57. Thomas Birch Freeman alludes to Muslims "from Lagos" visiting "seven or eight years ago" in his 1877 report on the Fante Muslim community: he likely drew on information from Basel missionaries who reported on the visiting Muslims at Akyem. WMMS: 27 December 1877, Thomas Birch Freeman to General Secretary.

58. William Winwood Reade noted in the late 1860s that kola nuts were abundant but uncollected in Gold Coast's rainforest. The first shipment of kola from Accra to Lagos was sent in 1872, the same year the Muslim delegation left Akyem; kola exports had a hiatus until 1877, and kola exports expanded significantly from the 1880s. Reade, "Extracts of Letters from W. Winwood Reade, Esq. to Andrew Swanzy, Esq., F. R. G. S., Relating to His Journeys in Western

Africa," *Proceedings of the Royal Geographical Society of London* 13, no. 5 (1868–1869), 359; Edmund Abaka, *Kola Is God's Gift: Agricultural Production, Export Initiatives, and the Kola Industry in Asante and the Gold Coast, c. 1820–1950* (Oxford, UK: James Currey, 2005), 45–48, 100. For early kola exports from Accra, see Ntewusu, *Settling in and Holding On*, 139–164.

59. Mann, *Slavery and the Birth*, 110–113; Ojo, "Islam, Ethnicity and Slave Resistance"; Tamuno, *Police in Modern Nigeria*, 15–27.

60. Mann, *Slavery and the Birth*, 106.

61. Killingray, "Guarding the Extending Frontier," 107; Pellow, *Landlords and Lodgers*, 50. The British war medals for the 1873–1874 Asante campaign were inscribed with "Glover's Force." Gillespie, *Gold Coast Police*, 12.

62. A. C. G. Hastings, ed., *The Voyage of the Dayspring: Being the Journal of the Late Sir John Hawley Glover, R.N., G.C.M.G., Together with Some Account of the Expedition up the Niger River in 1857* (London: John Lane, 1926), 205–211; W. D. McIntyre, "Commander Glover and the Colony of Lagos, 1861–1873,"*JAH* 4, no. 1 (1963), 60n18; Robert S. Smith, *The Lagos Consulate, 1851–1861* (Berkeley: University of California Press, 1979), 107, 170n78.

63. Elizabeth R. S. Glover, "Early Days in Nigeria, I: the Niger Expedition of Half-a-Century Ago," *West Africa* (12 May 1917), 256; id., *Life of Sir John Hawley Glover, R.N., G.C.M.G*, ed. Richard Temple (London: Smith, Elder & Co., 1897), 83–84.

64. W. B. Griffith, *The Far Horizon: Portrait of a Colonial Judge* (London: Stockwell, 1951), 82–84; David Killingray, "Bald Biographies of the Barely Reclaimable: Native Officers of the Gold Coast Constabulary, 1874–1907," *Bulletin, Ghana Studies* 3 (1985), 14–15. "Harri Zenoah," *Gold Coast Gazette*, no. 50 (14 August 1920), 1023; Alan Burns, *History of Nigeria*, 7th ed. (London: George Allen and Unwin, 1969), 230n2. See also Oroge, "Fugitive Slave Question," 65.

65. Glover received approval to increase the size of the Hausa Force by one hundred in April 1865 and asked for another increase months later: PRO CO 147/8: 9 April 1865, Lt. Gov. to Edward Cardwell; PRO CO 147/9: 14 August 1865, Lt. Gov. to Edward Cardwell (with two enclosures).

66. Oroge, "Fugitive Slave Question," 74.

67. Glover, *Life*, 84.

68. Kopytoff, *Preface to Modern Nigeria*.

69. Elizabeth R. S. Glover, "An Imperial Pioneer, VI: Close of the Ashanti Campaign and a Touching Farewell," *West Africa* (16 June 1917), 339. The men reportedly referred to Glover as their "father." PG: 24 June 1873, Isaac Willoughby to Glover; William Winwood Reade, *The Story of the Ashantee Campaign* (London: Smith, Elder & Co., 1874), 204, 374–375.

70. The Zouave uniform is described in Thomas S. Abler, *Hinterland Warriors and Military Dress: European Empires and Exotic Uniforms* (London: Bloomsbury Academic, 1999), 99–103.

71. Leveson was colonial secretary from 1862 to 1863 and led the Hausa Force on at least one expedition. His service record is discussed in PRO CO 147/10: 5 July 1865, Leveson to Cardwell (undated attachment with marginalia referring to Mr. Wedgewood as the author).

72. PRO CO 147/4: 10 October 1863, Glover to Newcastle.

73. PG: 12 July 1876, "State of the Houssa Force at Lagos." The document refers to Muslim "priests."

74. Mann, *Slavery and the Birth*, 113.

75. PRO CO 96/87/2478: 31 January 1871, Ussher to Kennedy, and 11 March 1871, Minute (attached to 17 February 1871, Kennedy to Kimberly).

76. PG: 12 July 1872, Isaac Willoughby to Glover. For the buildup to the war, see Claridge, *History* 2, 3–8; and Wilks, *Asante in the Nineteenth Century*, 230–235.

77. PRO CO 96/95/3118: 30 October 1872, Foster to Administrator.

78. Henry Brackenbury, *The Ashantee War: a Narrative Prepared from the Official Documents* (London: W. Blackwood and Sons, 1874), 1:58; Claridge, *History* 2:20; PG: 13 March 1873, Goldsworthy to Glover (Goldsworthy puts the figure at ninety-nine).

79. Claridge, *History* 2; Allen Lloyd, *The Drums of Kumasi: the Story of the Ashanti Wars* (London: Longman, 1964); W. D. McIntyre, "British Policy in West Africa: The Ashanti Expedition of 1873-4," *Historical Journal* 5, no. 1 (1962), 19–46; W. E. F. Ward, *A History of the Gold Coast* (London: George Allen & Unwin, 1946), 261–281; Wilks, *Asante in the Nineteenth Century*, 235–242.

80. Claridge, *History* 2:168–169.

81. Garnet Wolseley, *The Story of a Soldier's Life* 2 (London: Scribner's, 1904), 295–296.

82. John H. Glover, "The Volta Expedition during the late Ashantee Campaign," *Journal of the Royal United Service Institution* 18 (1875), 317–330.

83. Brackenbury, *Ashantee War* 2:276–280; Claridge, *History* 2:157; PG: 13 February 1874, Kimberly to Wolseley (copy).

84. PG: no date, "Names of Lagos Houssas who served with Glover's Expedition during the late Ashantee War"; Gillespie, *Gold Coast Police*, 13.

85. Killingray, "Imagined Martial Communities," 123.

86. Adamu, *Hausa Factor*, 167–168, 175n16 and 175n17; Gillespie, *Gold Coast Police*, 20.

87. Former Hausa Force members, retired as Gold Coast Constabulary officers land in early twentieth-century Accra, reportedly lobbied the British colonial government to receive land to build a mosque. Adamu, *Hausa Factor*, 168; James P. Dretke, "The Muslim Community in Accra (An Historical Survey)," MA thesis, University of Ghana at Legon, 1968, 39–40.

88. PRO CO 96/93/6426: 31 May 1872, Pope Hennessy to Kimberly.

89. "The Houssa Force," *The Times* (London), 3 September 1873, 4 (the correspondent was William Winwood Reade, who had traveled extensively in West Africa before the war).

90. Reade, *Ashantee Campaign*, 178; "Houssa Force," *The Times*, 4.

91. Boyle, *Through Fanteeland to Coomassie*, 244.

92. Henty, *March to Coomasie*, 272; Alfred Burdon Ellis, *Land of the Fetish* (London: Chapman & Hall, 1883), 269–270.

93. "Houssa Force," *The Times*, 4.

94. Boyle, *Through Fanteeland to Coomassie*, 72, 244.

95. Adamu, *Hausa Factor*, 170–171.

96. PRO CO 96/95/1467: 8 February 1872, Kennedy to Kimberly; CO 96/95/1433: 9 February 1872, Minute; CO 96/95/2342: 11 March 1872, Minute; PG: 3 and 21 July 1872, Rowe to Glover.

97. PRO CO 96/93/6426: 31 May 1872, Pope Hennessy to Kimberly.

98. PG: 9 July 1872, Rowe to Glover.

99. PG: 22 October 1872, Rowe to Glover. A much-abbreviated version of this story appears in Glover, *Life*, 140.

100. Henty, *March to Coomasie*, 273.

101. Glover, "Volta Expedition," 318–319; and Glover, *Life*, 378. An account of the incident also appears in an undated manuscript in the PG.

102. PG: Order book for Volta Expedition, entries for 1 and 4 December 1873 at Ada.

103. PG: 22 October 1872, Rowe to Glover.

104. Hanretta, *Islam and Social Change*.

105. The first Methodist reference to a "revival" appears in WMMS: Annual Report, Cape Coast Circuit, 1874. A useful retrospective overview appears in WMMS: Annual Report, Aburah Circuit, 1884. Note that Ekrofol, the village where the revival began, should not be confused with Ekrawfo, the village that became the base of the Fante Muslim community.

106. WMMS: 29 September 1975, Joseph Hayford to District Supervisor.
107. WMMS: 5 December 1875, Thomas Birch Freeman to General Secretary.
108. WMMS: Annual Report, Anomabu Circuit, 1878.
109. WMMS: 15 September 1878, Thomas Birch Freeman to General Secretary.
110. WMMS: General Report, the State of our Societies in Each Circuit, 1877.
111. WMMS: 17 January 1883, Minutes of the Annual Meeting.
112. WMMS: 27 December 1877, Thomas Birch Freeman to General Secretary (attachments include two letters from Joseph Ammoko in October 1877 regarding events).
113. WMMS: Annual reports reference the decline in membership at Essikuma.
114. Reade, *Ashantee Campaign*, 327.
115. Adamu, *Hausa Factor*, 171. It is possible that Mallam Tibu was associated with the Muslims, discussed earlier, who passed through the Fante states before arriving in Akyem. I discuss Mallam Tibu's possible encounters with Binyameen Sam in chapter 2.

2 Binyameen Sam's Fante Muslim Community

Binyameen sam came upon Kwabena Abeka in Narebehi, a rainforest village in the Gold Coast. Abeka was a decade younger than Sam, but they shared the experience of having attended the Methodist primary school at the coastal town of Anomabu in the mid-nineteenth century. The cash-crop boom in neighboring regions led them to leave: Binyameen Sam became a palm oil broker in Ekumfi, and Abeka was a trader further east in Gomoa. They met when Sam toured Gomoa in hopes of recruiting new members into the Fante Muslim community. Drawing on their shared Methodist upbringing, Binyameen Sam convinced Abeka that Fante Muslims worshiped "the same God as the Wesleyans." Abeka could not attend Sunday services because he did not live close to a Methodist church, and he learned from Sam that he could practice "purer" Muslim devotions, *salat*, on his own without having to attend church. Abeka adopted Musa as his new Muslim name and joined a small but growing community of former Christians accepting Islam through the preaching of Binyameen Sam.[1]

The Fante Muslim community formed immediately after the British invasion of Asante. Thomas Birch Freeman, a Methodist missionary who had resided in the Gold Coast for decades, was the first to describe what he called a "strange compound" in 1877: Fante Muslims used the Old Testament to practice a "spurious Mohammedanism" based on "the ceremonial laws of Moses."[2] They embraced polygyny as a biblical mandate and saw no basis in scripture for the collection of "ticket money," the Methodist requirement of regular financial contributions for the right to attend Sunday services. Freeman did not mention any Fante Muslim by name, but he noted that the movement was based at Gyinankoma, where Sam resided before moving the community to Ekrawfo. Decades later Sam met a Fante catechist of the Basel Mission and asked him if he used the same Bible as Methodists: the catechist told Sam that the Basel Mission did, and Sam reportedly exclaimed, "I see, you believe rightly!"[3] Sam was a Biblicist interpreting the Old Testament in light of his conversion to Islam.

Binyameen Sam did not leave written materials for posterity, but others wrote about what Sam told them. One was the Reverend Jacob B. Anaman, who summarized Sam's account in the 1902 edition of *The Gold Coast Guide*: Sam claimed to have been converted to Islam in the mid-1870s by Abu Bakr, a *mallam* who ministered to the Hausa Force brought from Lagos by Captain John Glover during the British invasion of Asante.[4] Elaborate stories about Sam's conversion circulate today, stressing encounters with mysterious robed figures followed by a meeting with Abu Bakr.[5] These stories begin with Sam as a young Methodist who was walking the Atlantic shore at night near Anomabu: an apparition circled above, Sam fell unconscious on the beach, and he was found the next morning by relatives, who convinced him to leave employment with the Methodists. Sam moved to Ekumfi to work for a relative in the palm oil trade, but he continued to have dreams of robed figures until he met Abu Bakr, a *mallam* who impressed Sam by being able to heal the ill. Sam accepted Islam and learned its beliefs and practices, and then Abu Bakr left and had no further contact with him. These memories contribute to the widespread contemporary view that Binyameen Sam was the "First Muslim Convert, Gold Coast Colony," the epitaph inscribed on his gravestone in the cemetery next to the Ahmadiyya mosque at Ekrawfo.

This chapter analyzes Binyameen Sam's acceptance of Islam and his efforts to create a Muslim community in the Gold Coast. Humphrey Fisher acknowledged Sam's role as founder of the Fante Muslim community, but he did not cite either Anaman's summary of Sam's testimony in *The Gold Coast Guide* or contemporaneous Methodist materials.[6] Fisher relied instead on a report written by A. J. Lochmann of the Basel Mission who visited Ekrawfo after Sam's death: it dated Sam's acceptance of Islam in the mid-1880s on the basis of rumors Lochmann heard from a Fante Christian.[7] But a conversion in the mid-1880s is contradicted by Sam's own testimony and Freeman's 1877 report. I draw on a broad canvassing of evidence to place Binyameen Sam's conversion in the 1870s and argue that he was a Biblicist who became a Muslim and preached Islam to Fante Methodists from Christian scripture. I also contend that current memories of Sam's conversion are elaborations of conversion narratives articulated at the founding of the Fante Muslim community. This chapter begins with Binyameen Sam's early life and the Biblicism of the Fante Methodist community of that era. The next section analyzes Sam's voice in Anaman's text, contemporaneous accounts, and current memories regarding Sam's acceptance of Islam. The genesis of the Fante Muslim community is the topic of the next section, and the following section examines the consolidation and expansion of the Fante Muslim community, including the founding of English-language schools. The chapter ends with an analysis of generational divisions in the Fante Muslim community and a discussion of Sam's death and its implications for the Fante Muslim community.

Binyameen Sam before His Acceptance of Islam

Binyameen Sam, or "Benjamin" as he was known before he accepted Islam, was born in the mid-1830s in the coastal fishing village of Egyaa (see map 4).[8] His parents were among the first converts to Methodism in the Gold Coast, and they sent their son to Anomabu's Methodist school, located just a mile from Egyaa. Sam received a basic education, became fluent in English, and may have worked for the Methodist mission at Anomabu after graduation (see figure 7). Then he moved in the 1850s to reside at Nakwa and other small villages along the coast in Ekumfi, a neighboring Fante state, where his cousins worked in the expanding trade in palm oil (see map 5). By the 1860s Sam eventually came to reside at Gyinankoma, an Ekumfi village fifteen miles from the coast. There palm oil was harvested, put into barrels, rolled to the Amissa and Nakwa rivers, and floated down to Saltpond on the coast. A British visitor described Saltpond as having "an air of business about it that was quite strange to see on the Gold Coast. On every side were people employed in melting the palm-oil, or in filling, heading, and moving puncheons for shipment."[9] Sam was a broker who connected palm oil producers at Gyinankoma with purchasers at Saltpond, advancing cash in exchange for promises of future deliveries and sharing in profits when the oil was delivered. Binyameen Sam thrived by creating personal networks based on mutual interest and trust in an era when new fortunes were being made in the Gold Coast.

Methodist missions had not yet been founded at Gyinankoma and other nearby Ekumfi villages in the 1860s, but Christianity nonetheless grew through the proselytism of former Methodist students working in the region. Most graduates took jobs in commerce, and their Methodist education remained an influence on their lives. The most devout sometimes returned to serve in the Methodist mission as teachers and ministers later in life. One was Isaac Hayford, a contemporary of Binyameen Sam who also was a pioneering graduate of Methodists schools: he changed course at midlife and became a Methodist minister. Hayford's application for the ministry explained that he had been "harassed continually with the thought that I had missed my providential way" until "God's great love for man was revealed to me in my inmost soul."[10] Sam did not follow Hayford in becoming a Methodist minister or teacher, but he was involved in lay evangelism in Ekumfi at "preaching places," informal gatherings at which regular Sunday services and midnight prayer vigils occurred. Sam also taught English informally in Ekumfi's rural villages.[11] Sam pursued a career as a palm oil broker in Ekumfi, but he also evangelized Christianity on the frontiers of the Methodist presence in the Gold Coast.

Methodist Biblicists in the Gold Coast

An emphasis on personal salvation through Bible study was at the heart of Methodist proselytism in the mid-nineteenth century.[12] The first Methodist missionaries found a receptive audience in the Gold Coast, where their efforts were preceded by the activities of Africans who formed the Meeting for Promoting Christian Knowledge. One of its members was William De Graft, who showed its charter to John Beecham, the general secretary of the Wesleyan Methodist Missionary Society; De Graft had become a Methodist and met Beecham in Britain during the early 1840s. Beecham was impressed by the Biblicism expressed in the charter, passages of which he quoted at length. One was as follows:

> As the word of God is the best rule a Christian ought to observe, it is herein avoided framing other rules to enforce good conduct, but that the Scriptures must be carefully studied, through which, by the help of the Holy Spirit and faith in Christ Jesus, our minds will be enlightened and find the way to eternal salvation.[13]

This commitment to careful study and prayerful reflection defined an approach to scripture that stirred controversy along the coast in the early nineteenth century. Members of the Meeting for Promoting Christian Knowledge challenged Joseph Smith, their teacher at the British school in the Cape Coast fort, who advocated a literalist reading as opposed to an analytical approach. The conflict was resolved by Governor George Maclean, who fined and imprisoned De Graft and another student in the Cape Coast fort. They remained unbowed and got other prisoners to join them in singing "hymns of praise to their Lord."[14] De Graft and other Meeting members expressed a Christian ethos of spiritual rebirth through Bible study well before the arrival of Methodist missionaries from Britain.

The arrival of Methodist missionaries reinforced this local impulse and led to the emergence of an "interpretive community of devotees," a phrase adopted by Ray Kea to define the religious changes in the mid-nineteenth-century Gold Coast.[15] Isaac Hayford's account of his decision to return to the Methodists, cited earlier, reveals the inner life of those moved by scripture. Outward expressions of African converts also conveyed these religious transformations: Thomas Birch Freeman came upon some Fante merchants on the road to Kumasi who sang Methodist hymns into the night.[16] Freeman encountered what another missionary called lay ministry by "preachers of righteousness" who, wherever they traveled, "sing our hymns, erect a family altar, read and expound according to their several abilities the sacred scripture."[17] Proselytization and attendance at Methodist services and schools, according to Kea, "had become normative conventions and internalized values—necessary practices—among growing sections of the rural and urban population" of the Fante states.[18] One must be cautious about imputing inner transformations for all African Methodists, but a significant number of the 2,500 adherents in the mid-1870s had experiences that they would claim were salvation through Bible study.[19]

Engaging the Bible in prayerful contemplation sometimes produced alternate readings that challenged Methodist teachings. One group, known as the

"Methodist Society," emerged in the late 1860s and caused an upheaval in several rural congregations in the Fante states.[20] Alan Taylor, a British missionary, noted that the dissidents left the congregation because they rejected the collection of "ticket money" for attending services, the sale and consumption of alcohol, and the performance of some Methodist rituals not referenced in the Bible, such as baptisms and the sacrament.[21] This group may have been influenced by Akonomnsu ("water-drinking people"), a local temperance movement launched at Anomabu by R. J. Ghartey, a merchant who returned from travels to Britain in 1861 to challenge the drunkenness of some Methodist ministers.[22] The Methodist Society, in contrast to Akonomnsu, did not leave much evidence about its theology and practices. Contemporaneous Methodist accounts place its genesis in the coastal fishing community of Kintu and its spread to the nearby village of Assafa; whether it expanded to other Fante villages is unknown. The Methodist Society did not become a major challenge, and it had disbanded by 1870, as most of its members rejoined the Methodists.[23]

The history of the Methodist Society reveals that some Biblicists were prepared to remove themselves from the church on religious grounds by the late 1860s. This movement drew on Akonomnsu's condemnation of Methodist drunkenness and aired other concerns, such as the collection of ticket money. The Methodist Society, according to the historian Anne Hugon, expressed a "double rupture": the first was when Africans broke from indigenous religious practices, and the second was when they left the Methodists to form an autonomous Christian community.[24] The shift from indigenous practices certainly was a rupture, a sense of personal salvation leading to Bible reading and interpretation, but the second break never manifested for members of the Methodist Society, as the movement quickly dissolved and most members rejoined the church after only two years of active dissent. Nevertheless the Methodist Society revealed that the Gold Coast had entered a new religious era when African Biblicists were willing to contemplate forming dissident communities around a commitment to their own scriptural interpretations. Just a few years later Binyameen Sam built on the arguments of the Methodist Society and broke from the Methodists by arguing against the collection of ticket money and in favor of Muslim practices that Sam associated with the teachings of the Bible. Whether Sam was directly influenced or not by the Methodist Society, he expressed the dissident views that were circulating in that movement.

Binyameen Sam's Acceptance of Islam

Binyameen Sam told Reverend Jacob B. Anaman that he accepted Islam after an encounter with Mallam Abu Bakr sometime in the mid-1870s.[25] Thomas Birch Freeman, a Methodist missionary at the time, described the Fante Muslim community that was forming at Sam's home village of Gyinankoma, noting its reliance on the Old Testament and criticism of the Methodist practice of collecting ticket money.[26] These materials, and others, help situate the conversions in an era when tens of thousands attended Methodist services for the first time, likely convinced by the British victory over Asante that *akomfoo* had not protected Asante against the Christian God of the British. But the esoteric healing of *mallams* also had allure, and their reputation was enhanced by the Hausa Force's role in the British defeat of Asante. This aspect of Sam's conversion is expressed in memories pointing to Mallam Abu Bakr's healing powers. These memories also focus on Abu Bakr's clothing and its association with Sam's visions of meeting robed strangers. This section situates what we can know about Sam's conversion from all these materials: Sam's voice in Anaman's words, contemporaneous accounts, and current memories of Sam's acceptance of Islam.

Memories

Memories of Binyameen Sam's conversion to Islam circulate with related stories about the conversion of his closest follower, Adoagyir Appah, who took Mahdi as his Muslim name. These accounts are articulated by Fante Muslims, both Ahmadi Muslims and the smaller number who are not. The Ahmadi versions emphasize Binyameen Sam's visionary experiences before his conversion and focus on Abu Bakr's esoteric healing powers, which impressed Sam and brought Appah to Islam when he and his wife surmounted infertility and had a child. The non-Ahmadi version, written by Al-Hajj Hamied, whose father broke from the Ekrawfo Muslim community after the arrival of the Ahmadi missionary in 1921, does not mention Sam's visions and concentrates only on esoteric healing.[27] Complicating a binary division into Ahmadi and non-Ahmadi versions are stories repeated by Ahmadi Muslims, often as asides and not elaborated, noting that Binyameen Sam and Mahdi Appah were able to provide esoteric Muslim healing. All accounts agree that esoteric healing was an aspect of Islam's appeal.

These reminiscences can be interpreted as fragments from "conversion narratives," stories told to elaborate on personal religious decisions and to convince listeners to follow the same path. As conversion narratives, the stories contain literary devises. One genre emphasizes the interior life of visionary experiences, and the other stresses pragmatic concerns such as infertility. References to visions, associated with Binyameen Sam's conversion, appealed to Methodists, whereas stories about Muslim cures, linked to the conversion of Mahdi Appah, were most relevant for those interested in esoteric healing. Of course, these two interests overlapped. Sam, Appah, and other pioneering Fante Muslims probably told variants of these conversion narratives as they sought to convince others to accept Islam. Current accounts have been embellished over the years by members of the Fante Muslim community and combined into a historical narrative about the genesis of the community.

One of the earliest Ahmadi accounts, heard in the late 1950s by Humphrey Fisher, elaborates on a meeting between Abu Bakr and Binyameen Sam. In Fisher's version, Abu Bakr went to Sam's uncle at Cape Coast and requested that he call Sam to his natal village of Egyaa. Abu Bakr went to Egyaa to wait for Sam and reportedly recognized him without prior introduction. Abu Bakr eventually asked Sam to convert to Islam, and Sam replied:

> He had been preparing to be ordained, but that he had visions concerning Abu Bakr, and would follow him. One vision had been on the road returning from Cape Coast when Ben Sam had gone to pay his ticket money to the Wesleyans. Three times he met a tall figure in Muslim dress, and finally collapsed in fear. The figure circled him thrice and vanished. Yabore [Sam's brother-in-law] found Ben Sam, and carried him to Anamabu [sic] for treatment. Later Ben Sam dreamt that he was with Muslims and was asked to lead the prayer. He protested that he did not know how, and was told to say, "Bismillāhi-rrahmāni-rrahīm [sic]." . . . Thus prepared, Ben Sam became a Muslim at the hands of Abu Bakr. Memories are uncertain now, but Ben Sam apparently stayed with Abu Bakr only about eight days, and then returned to [Ekumfi].[28]

More recent versions of the Ahmadi account do not mention the second dream about leading prayers and instead concentrate on the encounter with a robed figure along the coast. One recent version is included in Haneef Keelson's *Early History of the Ahmadiyyat in Ghana*, which is much abbreviated but captures the main action of a vision and subsequent conversion after meeting a visiting Muslim.[29] Another recent version, similar in structure but more elaborate in details, expresses the memories of Ahmad Afful, who was assisted by Hakeem Kofi Yamoah, a retired school teacher: I heard this account at Ekrawfo's mosque in 2005, and Yamoah subsequently gave me a written version of the narrative.[30] Both recent accounts focus on Binyameen Sam's visions of a robed figure emerging from the ocean as central to his acceptance of Islam.

The current pervasiveness of the story about Binyameen Sam's vision along the coast speaks to its evocative power, but it also relates to its common source. Haneef Keelson and Ahmad Afful drew on the memories of Haleema Adjoa Yansewa, who was Keelson's sister and Afful's mother. Haleema Yansewa was Binyameen Sam's granddaughter and Adoagyir Appah's daughter, the child of a marriage cementing relations between the two leading figures of the Fante Muslim community at Ekrawfo.[31] Unfortunately, Haleema Yansewa never wrote or taped an account before her death in 1985. Current narrators, drawing on the authority of hearing stories from her, stress Sam's visions in dramatic accounts, sometimes elaborating that it was not one but three robed figures emerging from the sea. Beyond its evocative quality, this story of a robed stranger conveys the religious life of Binyameen Sam as a Christian: he was a faithful Methodist preoccupied with mysterious visions. One can never prove that Sam had visionary experiences, but his granddaughter recounted stories that express threads of what she remembered having heard either directly from her grandfather or related to her by family members after Sam's death.

Ahmadi accounts move from Binyameen Sam's conversion to Adoagyir Appah's acceptance of Islam. Haneef Keelson's version mentions Appah's conversion in passing, and other Ahmadi accounts provide elaborate narratives. Informants in the 1950s referred to Ekuwa Endow, Appah's second wife, who was unable to have a child. This account notes:

> Ben Sam, now a Muslim, went back with the couple to Agyaa II [sic], where they stayed for a day or two enlisting the prayers of Abu Bakr. The woman conceived, and when Abu Bakr left shortly afterwards, he asked that the child be named for him. (He disappears from the story at this point). The baby proved to be a girl and was called Sadua. . . . Ado Agiri [Appah] of course became a Muslim.[32]

Another version stresses Binyameen Sam's role: Ahmad Afful's account states that Abu Bakr was aware of Ekuwa Endow's barrenness and instructed Sam to write a verse from the Quran in an herbal wash and have her drink it. Both these accounts stress the healing powers of the Quran and merely differ on the actor associated with the practice. Reminiscences of other early Fante converts to Islam mention similar experiences of children born through esoteric healing.

Acceptance of polygyny in Islam is an undercurrent in these stories about Adoagyir Appah and Ekuwa Endow. Note that it was Ekuwa Endow, Appah's *second* wife, who was barren and received the blessing of a child. This element of the story would not have been lost on listeners in the nineteenth-century Gold Coast, given that Methodists recognized only monogamous unions in their religious community. Some members had wives whom the church did not recognize, but Methodist preaching was insistent on the moral value of monogamy. The conversion narrative associated with Adoagyir Appah stressed two aspects of Islam that Methodism did not provide: esoteric healing for barren couples and tolerance of polygamy. As with the conversion narrative of Binyameen Sam, one cannot prove that Mahdi Appah and Ekuwa Endow were barren and cured by Muslim healing, but certainly this story was repeated numerous times: the trope of fecundity through esoteric intervention came to be associated with Binyameen Sam's Fante Muslim community.

Non-Ahmadi Fante Muslim accounts similarly invoke Islam's esoteric healing powers in the conversions of Binyameen Sam and Adoagyir Appah. The non-Ahmadi Fante Muslim community arose after the 1921 arrival of an Ahmadiyya missionary at Saltpond: those who did not accept the Ahmadiyya congregated at Obonster, a village northwest of Ekrawfo in the Fante state of Enyan. The Fante Muslim community at Obonster came to be led by Hamidu, who passed leadership at his death to Al-Hajj Hamied, Hamidu's son. Al-Hajj Hamied wrote a Fante text that includes a brief historical account of Binyameen Sam as founder of the Fante Muslim community. Al-Hajj Hamied's account does not mention visionary experiences and instead focuses on a *mallam*, named Sheibu in his account, who settled at Sam's natal village of Egyaa.[33] Al-Hajj Hamied's account continues that Sam, serving as a Methodist catechist in Ekumfi, heard about the *mallam* and brought Appah and another person to meet him at Egyaa: all received medicine against infertility and accepted Islam after the cure proved successful. Al-Hajj Hamied's account, important for the views of those who broke from the majority of the Fante Muslim community at the arrival of an Ahmadi missionary, reveals that the narrative emphasizing Islam's esoteric power is widely recounted among Ahmadi and non-Ahmadi Fante Muslims.

These accounts are based on memories of the Fante Muslim community, both the Ahmadi and the non-Ahmadi branches. Haleema Adjoa Yansewa, the granddaughter of Binyameen Sam and the daughter of Mahdi Appah, was one of those recounting this past. Her connection to key members of the Fante Muslim community lent authority to her accounts, especially for the two families. As a historian, I interpret them as conversion narratives: at their genesis they were efforts to persuade others to accept Islam and not historical accounts. What remains, too, are not the complete narratives but fragments, elements of the stories that had enduring meaning for the Fante Muslim community and those remembering the past. They help contextualize the emergence of the Fante Muslim community, as will be discussed below, but these accounts do not provide much evidence of Sam's conversion. Thankfully Binyameen Sam gave an interview that provides details about the circumstances of his conversion to Islam.

Abu Bakr and Binyameen Sam's Acceptance of Islam

Binyameen Sam told Reverend Jacob B. Anaman that a *mallam* named Abu Bakr converted him to Islam. Abu Bakr disappears from Fante Muslim accounts shortly after Sam converts to Islam, adding an aura of mystery to his identity.[34] Abu Bakr left few traces in the historical record, and one is left to analyze what Anaman recounted based on what Sam told him:

> The history of the rise and progress of the Mahometan religion in this country dates from a period when the Protectorate was greatly agitated by rumours of an Ashanti invasion. In consequence of this threatened blow native auxiliary forces were recruited by the British Government, among whom was a body of Hausas, the result of Captain Glover's successful recruiting mission in the

interior of Lagos. These men were followers of the great Prophet [Muhammad]. The elders of the faith at Tacadama in the Hausa country consequently sent in 1872 Abu Bukur [sic], a missionary, to minister to the spiritual wants of the faithful few. Among the early converts of this missionary was one Benjamin Sam, known amongst his fellow believers as Bonyaminu [sic] Sam, who together with Mahdi Appah, has been eminently instrumental in the spreading of the Moslem faith on this coast. The foregoing is extracted from a long account furnished by the Priest, Bonyaminu Sam.[35]

Anaman had historical interests and added details, such as a reference to the Gold Coast being "greatly agitated by rumours of an Ashanti invasion" and perhaps even the reference to 1872 as the date of Abu Bakr's arrival. But Anaman must have done so based on Sam's reference to a *mallam* associated with the Hausa Force: whether Sam or Anaman added that it was led by John Glover is not clear. What only Sam could have known was that Abu Bakr told him that he was sent by the "elders of the Faith at Tacadama in the Hausa country." The records of the Glover expedition do not provide the names of *mallams* who accompanied the soldiers from Lagos.[36] But Sam's reference to Tacadama is a clue. In Hausa *ta kadama* means "from Kadama," which suggests that Abu Bakr told Sam that he was from the town of Kadama in the Kanuri state of Bornu. Abu Bakr likely was a Kanuri Muslim, as were many members of the Hausa Force who were recruited by Harri Zenoah, a Kanuri Muslim himself. Glover first met Zenoah in Freetown in the late 1850s, and Zenoah helped form the Hausa Force in Lagos during the 1860s. Glover recruited Zenoah from Lagos to fight in the Gold Coast during the early 1870s, and Zenoah may have convinced Abu Bakr to join him on the expedition, but that is not certain.[37] What is certain is that Abu Bakr was a *mallam* associated with the Hausa Force and likely a former resident of Kadama in the Kanuri state of Bornu.

Descendants of the pioneering Hausa settlers of the Gold Coast's coastal towns have memories of the earliest *mallams*. One of the first *mallams* at Cape Coast was Musa, a Kanuri Muslim and veteran of the Hausa Force who was head of the Hausa community at Cape Coast.[38] Another was remembered by his title, Mallam Tibu, a reference to his provision of Muslim esoteric healing, as discussed in chapter 1. Mallam Tibu reportedly was a Kanuri Muslim who settled at Cape Coast "shortly after the soldiers returned from the 1874 war" and died not long thereafter. What Hausa elders remembered in the 1970s was that Mallam Tibu interacted with Fante residents as a "missionary . . . in the Saltpond area, where he used to travel from village to village talking to non-Muslims and converting a few to Islam."[39] It is tempting to suggest that Mallam Tibu was Abu Bakr, given their similar ethnic backgrounds and interactions with Fante residents of the Saltpond hinterland. Such an identification would explain how Sam came to know so much about Islam and why he lost contact with Abu Bakr: Sam interacted with him for several months, and then Abu Bakr died shortly after the war's conclusion. But Hausa elders stated that Mallam Tibu had "no connection with the army," and Sam's voice in Anaman's account insists on a connection by stating that Abu Bakr was sent to minister to the soldiers. Perhaps the memories of Hausa elders are inaccurate, or perhaps Mallam Tibu and Abu Bakr are not the same person.[40] At the very least, Hausa memories of Mallam Tibu's activities suggest that Sam's account of having visions of robed strangers may be an allusion to his awareness of Mallam Tibu before meeting Mallam Abu Bakr.

Accounts by both Ahmadi and non-Ahmadi Muslims place Binyameen Sam's encounter with a *mallam* at Egyaa, Sam's natal village on the coast. It reportedly was a dramatic meeting in front of Sam's family, when the *mallam* demonstrated his esoteric powers. Sam may have been at Egyaa during the British invasion, having fled Ekumfi for the security of residence with maternal relatives near the British garrison at Anomabu. This return put him in a prime location to meet the Hausa Force immediately after the war: Anomabu, only a mile from Egyaa, was where members commanded by John Glover and those led by Garnet Wolseley assembled before returning to Lagos (see map 3).[41] Perhaps Sam met Abu Bakr for the first time in the dramatic circumstances in the story, but one must remember that it is an embellished fragment from a conversion narrative. More plausible is that Sam had met Abu Bakr earlier, accepted Islam, and then introduced him to his relatives. An earlier conversion is likely if Mallam Tibu and Abu Bakr were the same person. What can be drawn from memories is that Abu Bakr's encounter with Sam in front of his relatives perhaps was the first *public* demonstration of Sam's conversion to Islam. Whatever the exact circumstances and timing of Sam's conversion, the immediate postwar era was when Sam's acceptance of Islam became public, initially to relatives at Egyaa and later to Fante Methodists in Ekumfi when Sam returned to Gyinankoma.

Binyameen Sam's public acceptance of Islam occurred on the eve of an era of religious change in the Gold Coast. As Sam began to convince others to join the Fante Muslim community, the Methodists were having a revival: many attended church services and prayer vigils, some were possessed, and a few were convinced that Jesus had returned from heaven. In this context, Binyameen Sam offered a different path. He was a Biblicist who interpreted Islam in ways that appealed to Fante Methodists: Sam criticized some Methodist practices, such as the collection of ticket money and insisting on monogamy, and he offered access to Muslim practices, such as esoteric healing, that Methodists did not provide. As Sam preached, Christians speculated as to the motivation for his break from the Methodists. A. J. Lochmann reported that some Fante Christians alleged that Sam was ambitious for religious leadership and renounced Christianity to assume that role as a Muslim.[42] The precise reason for Sam's conversion is unknown, and his voice as reported in Anaman's words does not address this issue.

Nor did Anaman's account mention Abu Bakr's clothing, which is a focus of current memories. But the discussion of Muslim sartorial style points to the emergence of a Fante Muslim visual culture associated with Sam's preaching.

Fante Muslim Visual Culture

Memories insist that Abu Bakr wore long, white robes. He probably did, as it was the common attire for *mallams* at the time (figure 3).[43] In these memories, Abu Bakr's robes serve as a literary device to remind listeners of Binyameen Sam's youthful apparition of mysterious robed figures. Sam himself discussed Muslim clothing in his preaching. Elderly informants in the 1970s told Rasheed Guar-Gorman that Sam taught that "illustrations in Bibles portrayed the type of dress worn by Muslim religious leaders."[44] This visual culture is evident in A. J. Lochmann's report of his 1913 meeting with Salomon Asamang, a Fante Muslim residing at Mando:

> In the high street stands a fine house. Over the entrance is written in English, "Priest Salomon Asamang." A lad led me into the house. I introduced myself briefly to the owner as a [Christian] missionary. Scarcely had I sat down when the examination began. He passed me a picture and asked, "Who is in the picture?" "Abraham and son," I gave the answer. Then he brought pictures of Noah's ark and Moses. As he took them back, he said emphatically: "All good Mohammedans!"

Asamang chose Christian pictures that he knew Lochmann would identify so that Asamang could confidently assert that they were Muslims. Lochmann does not describe the images, but religious pictures of the era depicted Abraham, Moses, and Noah in robes.[45] Asamang's insistence that the Old Testament prophets were Muslims illustrated the influence of Binyameen Sam's preaching about Muslim clothing.

Fante Muslim visual culture built on Methodist proselytism in the nineteenth-century Gold Coast. Methodist missionaries encouraged their members to interpret visions as expressions of the Holy Ghost. One such event occurred in the village of Abakrampa, on the main road from Cape Coast to Kumasi, where John Solomon was the African Methodist agent in the mid-1850s. Reverend Daniel West, a visiting British Methodist, recounted the experiences at an open-air prayer service, where some participants reported seeing an apparition, clothed in a robe inside the small Methodist chapel. Solomon had a non-Methodist witness profess publicly to having seen the apparition to doubters: he hoped to use this public admission to convert this witness to Christianity, but instead the man fled into the forest and died when a tree fell on him.[46] Reverend West related the account, not to comment on African superstitions, but rather to reveal a spiritual visitation at a Methodist revival in the Gold Coast. West does not discuss local interpretations of events, but his account underscores the ways Methodists encouraged Africans to interpret visual experiences in biblical terms.

West African Muslim clothing and its visual similarity to the religious pictures of Old Testament prophets allowed Binyameen Sam to reassure former Fante Methodists that joining his Muslim community was not a complete break from the past. Religious images, according to David Morgan in *Visual Piety*, had the power to convey a sense of the "real" to believers in nineteenth-century North America. This analysis has salience for nineteenth-century Gold Coast: religious images performed a "world-making" function at times of social change by creating a bridge to a new religious worldview through images associated with the past.[47] The robes worn by Muslims struck Sam as reflecting the sartorial style of prophets depicted in Christian pictures. He used this visual insight to connect the Old Testament to Islam. When preaching from his Bible, Sam likely reinforced his arguments by pointing to religious pictures, a practice that his followers adopted, as seen in Salomon Asamang's encounter with Lochmann. References to pictures of Old Testament prophets helped construct and maintain a new religious community among former Methodists who were practicing Islam under Sam's guidance in the Fante Muslim community.

Muslim Healing

Residents of the Gold Coast were aware of the esoteric powers of Muslim scholars from the West African savanna. Even before the arrival of the Hausa Force and its *mallams*, stories circulated in the Gold Coast about the mysterious but efficacious remedies provided by *mallams* in the court of the *asantehene*. William Winwood Reade, the European explorer and correspondent for *The Times* during the British invasion of Asante, reported a story concerning the activities of a Muslim "doctor" in Kumasi who

> wrote certain words on paper, sewed them up in leather cases, and sold them as charms against wounds in the war. He fumigated the nostrils of the sick with the smoke of mysterious herbs set on fire, he wrote the texts of the Koran on a wooden board, washed off the ink into water, and gave it to patients as a draught; he cupped for fever, inoculated for small-pox, applied the hot iron; he also divined future events from a book filled with diagrams, or from figures drawn in sand.[48]

Reade dramatized some of the description for European readers of his book, but he nonetheless described activities in the repertoire of savanna Muslim scholars. Hausa Force *mallams* provided these services, too, and their reputations were enhanced after the British invasion of Asante. Contemporaneous reports do not reference an interest in Muslim healing among Methodists, but memories do. Confirming specific details is impossible, but what is without doubt is that

Methodists had no esoteric credentials to compete with *mallams*. From the 1870s, *mallams* provided these services to those who had known about them through rumors.

Fante Muslims continued to seek Muslim cures even after Abu Bakr was no longer associated with their community. Abu Bakr may have taught Sam the rudiments of Muslim healing, just as he instructed him in basic Arabic so that he could perform *salat*. Another possibility is that Binyameen Sam adapted Abu Bakr's practices into his own version of Muslim healing: one reference along the coast refers to an amulet with a page from the Bible inside, and Sam may have adopted this practice after Abu Bakr left.[49] Alternately the early Fante Muslim community may have turned to itinerant *mallams* who may have visited the coast. Memories focus not on subsequent visiting Muslims, but instead on the leadership of Binyameen Sam. Whatever the exact circumstances, memories insist that esoteric healing, initially provided by Abu Bakr and later by Binyameen Sam, was an aspect of Islam's appeal among Methodists joining the Fante Muslim community.

The British victory over Asante produced an era of religious change along the coast. Fante villagers returning to interior villages after fleeing to coastal towns began to attend Methodist services. But Binyameen Sam accepted Islam and used the era of religious change to convince other Fante Methodists to become Muslims. At Anomabu, where the Hausa Force mustered, Binyameen Sam made his acceptance of Islam public, perhaps with a dramatic encounter witnessed by his maternal relatives at Egyaa. Thereafter, Binyameen Sam returned to Gyinankoma and founded a religious movement that offered new services and drew on local criticisms of Methodism. Sam already had established bonds of trust with residents of Ekumfi through his Methodist proselytism. Sam eased the transition to Islam by preaching from his Methodist Bible and pointing to pictures of Old Testament prophets to reassure his followers that they were worshiping the same God as they had as Methodists.

The Early Fante Muslim Community

The Fante Muslim community at Gyinankoma faced challenges as it emerged in the 1870s. Methodist missionaries responded to Binyameen Sam's preaching with various measures. Thomas Birch Freeman, an experienced Methodist missionary and long-time resident of the region, clearly was alarmed by Sam's success in convincing Fante Methodists to join his movement. He made a recommendation in 1877 to counter "this false form of religion" by putting into the hands of Methodists missionaries "some little book, in the form of, or answering the purpose of, a Manual of Mohammedanism." Freeman's request for a Manual of Mohammedanism is not discussed in subsequent correspondence, so it is unclear whether this measure was adopted. Methodists did increase their presence in Ekumfi. They established a school with a residential teacher at Gyinankoma in 1875.[50] In 1876 another Methodist mission station was opened at Otobiadzi, six miles north of Gyinankoma. In 1877 two more Methodist stations were established at Esakyir and Ekotsi, both four miles from Gyinankoma.[51] Binyameen Sam, who proselytized Christianity at informal Methodist "preaching places" in Ekumfi without the support of a mission station or school, now found himself, as he preached Islam from his Bible, surrounded by a growing Methodist presence established shortly after his acceptance of Islam (see map 5).

Relations between religious communities at Gyinankoma were tense. After the Methodist presence had been bolstered in Ekumfi, Reverend Richard Rossall, Thomas Birch Freeman's successor as superintendent of the circuit, traveled to Gyinankoma in 1879. In an open-air sermon, Reverend Rossall warned Fante Muslims that eternal salvation awaited only those who accepted Jesus. Reverend Rossall, an exuberant missionary on his first tour, claimed to have secured the return of one Methodist from the Muslim fold, who publicly renounced his marriages to several wives after Rossall's sermon.[52] But his words also inflamed the situation at Gyinankoma: for the following two years, annual circuit reports referred to "wild Mahommedanism" at Gyinankoma, as Christians struggled to "maintain [themselves] against the inroads of Mohammedans . . . in their midst."[53] But references to Fante Muslims at Gyinankoma stop in 1882. The only subsequent mention of Fante Muslims at Gyinankoma was passing acknowledgment of their opposition to the construction of a large Methodist church in the late 1880s.[54] Methodist activities in and around Gyinankoma led Fante Muslims to find safe harbor elsewhere.

Fante Muslims moved to Ekrawfo, another village in Ekumfi. Ekrawfo was one of four Ekumfi villages reportedly founded by Borbor Fante leaving Mankessim: the first migrants settled at Gyinankoma, and population growth led to the subsequent creation of villages at Attakwaa, Ekrawfo, and Otobiadzi. Ekrawfo did not have a Methodist church in the 1880s and was an ideal new location for Fante Muslims, who resided in their own neighborhood in the village. Their main street was named *kyiri akomfoo*, or "*akomfoo* are forbidden"; this street name suggests that the conflict with the Christians was matched by opposition to Fante Muslims from *akomfoo*.[55] The move to Ekrawfo from Gyinankoma ultimately put the Fante Muslim community in a secure position and allowed for its expansion, eventually including the building of a large mosque (see figure 8). Current memories do not mention conflict with Christians at Gyinankoma, and informants merely state that Ekrawfo was the first Fante Muslim settlement in the Gold Coast.

Binyameen Sam's most important early convert to Islam was Adoagyir Appah.[56] He was a young member of the royal family at Attakwaa. Sam provided brokerage services to senior members of his family and tutored Adoagyir in English. Sam also convinced Appah, who was at least fifteen years younger than him, to become a Methodist. Current memories add that Appah, recently married to his second wife and childless, converted to Islam after receiving a remedy for infertility from either Sam or Mallam Abu Bakr. Appah was a crucial early convert because his royal connections likely helped convince the *ohene* at Ekrawfo to accept the Fante Muslim immigrants from Gyinankoma. His elevated status in current memories is related to Appah's subsequent role in inviting the Ahmadiyya to the Gold Coast. Fisher complained of a "transparent Ahmadi gloss" in memories about Appah, including the claim that his Muslim name, Mahdi, had been chosen because "Abu Bakr preached of the Mahdi and Messiah."[57] Ideas about the Mahdi were circulating in West Africa and may have informed the choice of Appah's Muslim name, but no contemporaneous Methodist observer mentioned messianic aspects in Sam's preaching. Instead he preached about the roots of Muslim practices in the Old Testament and provided esoteric Muslim cures.

The early Fante Muslim community grew through informal preaching, especially at market towns near Ekrawfo. Binyameen Sam had engaged in Methodist evangelism at informal "preaching places," and he adapted the practice to make the case for Islam. Methodist sources reported on Fante Muslim preaching, without specifically mentioning Sam, in the market towns of Mankessim and Mando in the early 1880s.[58] Memories of pioneering Fante Muslims confirm that traders associated with these two towns were among the first to accept Islam. Kwesi Gyan, known before his conversion by his Methodist name James Ainoo, resided at Ekotsi and traded regularly at Mankessim, where family memories locate his conversion by Binyameen Sam.[59] The first Muslim in Breman Asikuma, Muhammad "Kofi Maama" Amini, accepted Islam at Mando, where he regularly traveled for business and met Mahdi Appah.[60] The ability to convert others through proselytism at market towns bolstered the Fante Muslim community as it strove to consolidate a permanent home at Ekrawfo.

Women as well as men converted in the early years. Memories of women's acceptance of Islam often are mediated through stories about the conversion of their husbands and children. One theme in these accounts is the women's desire for esoteric medicine to address infertility. Another theme is the agency of senior women, usually mothers of Fante Muslim converts, who destroyed *asuman* and other indigenous religious objects in the household after being convinced to convert by their sons.[61] The most elaborate stories concern the wives and offspring of Binyameen Sam and Mahdi Appah. Rukiyya Akua Mansah, Sam's daughter, is a key figure, in part because she married Mahdi Appah and later divorced him: she not only links the two early leaders but also provides the vehicle for commentary about a dispute between the two men, discussed later in this chapter. Another prominent woman is Haleema Adjoa Yansewa, Rukiyya Mansah's daughter. Haleema Yansewa played an important role as conciliator in the Fante Muslim community and later became the primary repository of memories of Binyameen Sam. Accounts of the conversion of Fante Muslim women point to significant transformations, such as the destruction of *asuman* and other religious objects. These activities rarely are mentioned in other accounts, written or oral, so the details of these transformations elude historians.

The social diversity of the early Fante Muslims is difficult to determine, as memories often focus on pioneers in wealthy commercial families or those with royal connections. Acknowledgment of past status as slaves, for example, is not forthcoming in contemporary Ghana, and no one suggests that early Fante Muslims included former slaves. The acceptance of Islam among communities of Fante fisherfolk in coastal villages is one measure of the diversity of membership in the early Fante Muslim community. Fishing communities had provided stiff opposition to Methodist proselytism in the nineteenth century, so their adoption of Islam often was not preceded by an earlier conversion to Christianity, as was the case with other pioneering Fante Muslims.[62] Memories sometimes stress conflicts over failure to participate in indigenous religious activities; the appeal of esoteric healing also was another theme in these memories.[63] Some of the fishing communities providing pioneering Fante Muslims were near the mouth of the Nakwa River. It is possible that Binyameen Sam came into contact with them through his commercial activities as a palm oil broker: small quantities of oil reached market by floating barrels down the Nakwa River to the coast, and memories from the 1950s place Sam's relative as a merchant there.[64] Whatever the reason for the conversion of members of Fante fishing communities, they contributed to the social diversity of membership in the early Fante Muslim community.

Binyameen Sam provided education to these pioneering Fante Muslims, who did not know the details of Muslim beliefs and practices. Sam's stewardship is captured evocatively in the memories of the Ekotsi Muslim community. Seven prominent men converted to Islam under Sam's influence and made the weekly trip to Ekrawfo to perform the congregational Friday prayers with other Muslims, walking by foot for nearly an hour from Ekotsi to Ekrawfo. Binyameen Sam reportedly assigned each of them the task of memorizing one verse from the *sura al-fatiha*, the Quran's first chapter: its seven verses are repeated by Muslims in the performance of *salat*. Memorizing the verses improved their ritual practice and reportedly made the walk seem to go by more quickly. It also built a sense of community among believers.[65] Memories of the conversion of the first Muslims in Fante families are punctuated with accounts of the adoption of Muslim names and clothing. For the latter, former Christians often wore British-style clothing, which they replaced with robes. Amid the adoption of new rituals and clothing, one aspect of the Methodist service carried over: the singing of hymns, which occurred after the conclusion of congressional prayers on Fridays.[66] Sam's pedagogy also anchored his preaching about Islam from the Bible, the scripture most converts knew from their time as Methodists.

Preaching Islam from the Bible

Binyameen Sam preached from the Bible to convince Fante Methodists to join his new movement. He left no written materials to give us insight into his use of scripture, and current memories do not provide details. Thomas Birch Freeman mentioned the invocation of the Old Testament by Fante Muslims in 1877, and a logbook from the English-language Fante Muslim school notes continued use of Methodist Bibles and hymnals at the turn of the nineteenth century.[67] Sam retained an attachment to the Bible, as mentioned in the introduction when Sam learned that Methodists and Presbyterians shared the same scripture and exclaimed, "I see, you believe rightly."[68] Binyameen Sam relied on the English-language Bible as a matter of necessity because he was not literate in Arabic and could not root his teachings in the Quran. But it was an effective strategy, as his primary target for proselytism were former Methodists who would have known the Bible and been persuaded by references to it.

While Binyameen Sam's exegesis of the Bible was distinctive, it was not unusual. Classical Muslim scholarship acknowledges previous scriptural revelation from God, in the Torah and Bible, even as it insists on the finality of God's revelation in the Quran. Scholars are only beginning to understand Muslim engagement with the Bible over the centuries. Certainly, Muslim exegesis of the Bible was in the repertoire of Ghulam Ahmad, who developed an extensive Ahmadi exegesis of the Bible, as will be discussed in chapter 3. Nineteenth-century West Africa was another context in which scriptural comparisons occurred: as discussed in the introduction, Samuel Crowther, adopted an evangelical strategy based on using an Arabic Bible to reveal similarities between Islam and Christianity before pointing to theological differences.[69] Crowther's approach arose through encounters with an Afro-Brazilian Muslim known as Mahamma, who asked Crowther to discuss the Protestant perspective on Jesus. Mahamma's cosmopolitan interest in engaging Crowther expressed the openness of Afro-Brazilian Muslims arising from their intimate relations with Afro-Brazilian Catholics along the West African coast.

Binyameen Sam may have been influenced by awareness of Arabic Bibles. These texts began to circulate along the West African coast with the arrival of European missionaries in the early nineteenth century.[70] One of these Bibles was in the Gold Coast by the mid-nineteenth century: Presbyterian missionaries in the Basel Mission reported that an Afro-Brazilian Muslim in Accra possessed one.[71] No reference to Sam's knowledge of the Arabic Bible exists, but as a palm oil trader he could have learned of its existence through discussions with Afro-Brazilian Muslims merchants along the coast. Alternately, Binyameen Sam might have learned of the Arabic Bible from Abu Bakr, the *mallam* who converted him; if Abu Bakr passed through Lagos, then the Hausa Force barracks was located next to the Afro-Brazilian neighborhood, thus facilitating encounters between the two groups of Muslims. Future research on the history of Arabic Bibles in nineteenth-century West Africa may uncover an extensive tradition of Muslim exegesis of the Bible, perhaps in the Afro-Brazilian community but also in other communities that received copies of the Arabic Bible in the era of expanding Christian proselytism and comparison of religious traditions.

Even if Binyameen Sam was stimulated to interpret his Bible through knowledge of the Arabic Bible, he brought his own understanding of Christian scripture to his evangelism of Islam. Thomas Birch Freeman's reference to Fante Muslim condemnation of Methodist teachings and practices strongly suggests that Sam was not merely repeating what he may have learned from Abu Bakr or an Afro-Brazilian Muslim. Sam's decades as a Biblicist meant that he would have been able to make contrasts between Christianity and Islam, once he became a Muslim and started to learn its beliefs and practices. Sam drew on a wave of African criticism of Methodist teachings, expressed in the Methodist Society. Sam's conversion to Islam, however, enhanced the criticism by articulating the dissent not within the tradition but from a Muslim perspective. Instead of using an Arabic Bible to convince Muslims to accept Christianity, as Samuel Crowther did, Sam drew on an English Bible to argue that Islam was rooted in the Old Testament. Both Samuel Crowther and Binyameen Sam were cosmopolitans, but Sam reversed Crowther's conceptual move to find new meanings in an era of religious comparisons.

Expansion of the Fante Muslim Community

The Fante-speaking Muslim community extended beyond Ekumfi in the last decades of the nineteenth century. One direction of expansion was to the east and the neighboring regions of Gomoa and Agona (see map 4). These regions shared Ekumfi's history of economic expansion through palm oil production. Binyameen Sam was not the only Muslim to proselytize Islam in these regions, as local memories credit Hausa Muslims at Winneba with the conversions of a few Fante speakers. But Binyameen Sam eventually became identified by local residents through his proselytism. The Presbyterian missionary A. J. Lochmann visited Ekrawfo from his Basel station at Nsaba in Agona, traveling eleven hours by bicycle in 1913 because he had learned that Ekrawfo was the center of "Mohamedan propaganda" in the region.[72] Lochmann compiled a list of Muslim communities in Fante areas, and it included more villages in Gomoa and Agona than in Ekumfi. The geographical weighting of Gomoa and Agona reflected Lochmann's knowledge of regions close to his mission base; local memories stress a wider network of Fante Muslim communities than Lochmann details.[73] Nonetheless, Lochmann's perspective highlights the extent to which Sam and Appah had made the Muslim movement at Ekrawfo into a regional development.

Binyameen Sam targeted Christian traders in Gomoa and Agona who operated along trade routes from Winneba, a major market in the nineteenth-century palm products trade. This strategy may have been an elaboration of the initial proselytism at Mankessim and Mando by extending informal proselytism to markets farther east. Binyameen Sam had no reason to enter that region as a trader, as presumably his own activities in Ekumfi supported him, so his travels were for Muslim evangelism. He could have heard of local conversions to Islam from Hausa-speaking Muslims in coastal ports, or Sam himself may have visited the region on his own initiative. Whatever the source of inspiration, Lochmann's list of Muslim communities and his discussion of Binyameen Sam's activities suggest that he operated along a north-south axis from Winneba.[74] Sam continued to preach Islam from the Bible in Gomoa and Agona. The conversion of Kwabena Abeka, discussed in the introduction, illustrates Binyameen Sam's style of appealing to a shared knowledge of Christianity before extolling the advantages of Islam. Lochmann personally interviewed Abeka, a resident of Narebehi, a village in Gomoa just a few miles south of the Basel Mission station at Nsaba. He told Lochmann that he took the Christian name John Tobia and then launched his career as a trader in Gomoa. But "one day Ben Sam came" and Abeka converted to Islam.[75] Lochmann mentions other villages near Nsaba with Muslim converts personally initiated into Islam by Binyameen Sam, strongly suggesting that he targeted that area in a preaching tour. Sam would have relied on contacts from his involvement in the palm oil trade, as most of the conversions occurred in the interior, twenty miles inland from the coast, where palm oil was collected. Binyameen Sam clearly had success in converting Christian traders, whose lives mirrored his own after he left Anomabu. The isolation Abeka communicated in his account points to the attraction of Islam for uprooted Methodists seeking a religious community.

Binyameen Sam recruited agents to continue his work when he was not on tour. In Winneba, for example, a Fante Muslim regularly attended street preaching sessions organized by the Methodists and made a competing case for Islam. Methodists report that this agent admitted, as Binyameen Sam did, that Christianity was an appropriate religious path given that it was a monotheism rooted in scripture, even as he recruited Methodists to Islam.[76] Fante Muslim proselytism, including an element of religious negotiation, expressed the activities of Muslim cosmopolitans that stood in contrast to the rigid formulations of most European

Christian missionaries at the time. This evangelical style brought increasing numbers of Fante Christians to Islam. Lochmann conceded in his 1913 report that Islam "has already made greater progress than the Basel Mission in the same length of time."[77] The number of Muslims in the Fante Muslim community, according to Sam, was approximately 1,600 in 1902.[78]

Another area of Muslim expansion was Breman, a Fante region to the north of Ekumfi (see map 4). Local memories stress the role of Mahdi Appah and his cousins in the process. Appah and his cousins used to hunt in the forests of that region as youths. When Breman Bedum later fell into a land dispute with a neighboring community, its leaders turned to Mahdi Appah for assistance. Appah organized an expedition to remove the offending parties from the land and also aided the aggrieved residents of Breman Bedum by encouraging them to plead their case in the British colonial courts. When the residents of Breman Bedum won the case, Appah and his cousins received land at several villages near Wasabiampa, outside of Breman Bedum. Mahdi Appah eventually moved to the region, built a mosque at Wasabiampa, and brought several Breman families of the region into the Muslim fold (see figure 9). Memories associated with the first Muslim converts, such as Kwaabo Yeboawa of Amoanda, attest to the use of esoteric healing to provide fertility to families unable to have children; some attribute the provision of those Muslim services to Mahdi Appah himself.[79]

Muslim English-language Schools

Binyameen Sam and Mahdi Appah opened English-language schools for Fante Muslims. One was at Ekrawfo, and it closed within a decade of its founding. A. J. Lochmann, who visited Ekrawfo shortly after Sam's death, blamed the closure on a disagreement between Sam and Appah over the value of English-language education.[80] Humphrey Fisher agreed with Lochmann's assessment, and he added that Appah also objected to Sam's lax attitudes toward the consumption of alcohol, on the basis of local memories he heard in the late 1950s.[81] Another factor, I contend in the following section, was generational change in the Fante Muslim community: the pioneering generation of Fante Muslims largely was not concerned with the views of other Muslims, but a younger generation, and even a few long-standing members such as Mahdi Appah, came to question Binyameen Sam's teachings. The founding of an English-language school was a concern, as Lochmann and Fisher argued, but the larger issue was the desire to reform religious practices in light of savanna Muslim norms associated with *mallams* migrating to Gold Coast towns in the late 1890s.

British officials encouraged West African Muslims to open English-language schools and offered government financial assistance if the schools met colonial standards.⁸² The first Muslim school opened at Ekrawfo in 1896, and it received government assistance for eight years and finally closed in 1908: enrollment averaged forty boys and two girls annually until it fell precipitously in the last two years. Another school was at Ekotsi, the second largest Fante Muslim community at the time and just a few miles from Ekrawfo: it was placed on the government registry from 1901 to 1905 and received financial assistance in 1904. The other two schools were outside Ekumfi: one was at Obonster in Enyan, and the other was at Kroboase in Bedum. They had low enrollments and never received any government assistance. Official records do not indicate the religious affiliation of the students, but one presumes that Fante Muslims were in the majority, given that others in the village had the option of sending their children to nearby Christian missionary schools. The Muslim schools closed within years of opening, despite the possibility of continued governmental financial assistance.⁸³

Current memories of these Muslims schools are lost; the opening of Ahmadi schools in the 1920s and 1930s is foremost on the minds of informants. Indirect memories are mentioned by Rasheed Guar-Gorman, who heard accounts in the 1970s of financial support for the early Fante Muslim community provided by Ogyadziyi Quansah of Kwansakwaa.⁸⁴ Guar-Gorman mentioned no specific activity, but it is possible that Quansah's generosity helped fund Fante Muslim schools. Sam's initiative had an advocate in Edward Blyden, who served as Government Agent for Native Affairs in Lagos between 1896 and 1897: Fisher reported that "it is said that Blyden tried to meet the Fante Muslims, but it was prevented through a fault in the mails."⁸⁵ Reference to a potential visit suggests that Sam was in correspondence with Blyden about the Muslim schools; unfortunately written materials that might shed light on this contact have not come to light.⁸⁶ What is clear is that Binyameen Sam opened Muslim schools, modeled on Methodist schools and supported by Fante Muslims before obtaining British financial support. It was an initiative by Muslim cosmopolitans who drew on Methodist models to establish Muslim schools.

The operations at Ekrawfo's school were reported in a logbook. No similar document exists for the other Fante Muslim schools: its details are the sole means to learn about activities at these institutions. Humphrey Fisher examined Ekrawfo's logbook in the late 1950s, when he described it as being in a "decrepit" state; additional deterioration did not preserve it for my consultation in 2005. Fisher's summary describes it as having numerous entries, dated and signed by Binyameen Sam or Mahdi Appah, providing descriptions of pedagogical activities, enrollment and attendance figures, and summaries of comments made by British examiners. These logbook entries identify Sam as the person to whom the Gold Coast director of education addressed his comments about the terms of colonial government assistance, confirming his role as the initiator of the school.

The entries also reference Mahdi Appah as involved, sometimes as the manager, in entries continuing until 1905. Colonial government financial assistance brought regular inspections in advance of approval and thereafter: the logbook refers to such inspections beginning in 1898, including the visit of the Saltpond district commissioner in early 1899. Government funds were released in January 1900, which allowed for an increase in teacher salaries and other outlays. The support and inspections continued until 1908, the year the logbook entries stop and the school closed; 1908 also is the year that Ekrawfo's school dropped from the official list of schools.[87]

The curriculum and schedule of Ekrawfo's English-language school met British colonial government requirements. The logbook mentions coverage of reading, writing, arithmetic, geography and music, and it notes the delivery of books and supplies from the Methodist Book Depot, a major provider of educational materials to the government-assisted Methodist schools. These materials included, in addition to school primers and copybooks, Methodist Bibles and catechisms. Binyameen Sam preached Islam from these materials, but the exact uses to which they were employed are unclear from the logbook entries. One of the entries notes the "interesting lectures" provided by Binyameen Sam: his cosmopolitan interpretation of Christianity and Islam, no doubt, occurred on those occasions. Ekrawfo's school followed the British schedule with a long vacation at Christmas, but it also included a "fasting holiday," sometimes mentioned explicitly as Ramadan, and a "feasting holiday," presumably Eid al-Adha. Government funding also led to other celebrations, such as the observance of Empire Day and the singing of songs such as "Hurrah for England's King" and "Holy Father, Mighty God" during the visit of the government inspector in 1902. Judging from the names of the teachers, they were young men educated in Methodist missionary schools and perhaps Christians: only one of the teachers had an explicitly Muslim name. The frequent recruitment of new teachers to address departures suggests that instructors sought higher compensation elsewhere. Attendance declined in the last few years, and especially as the decade neared its end, and Ekrawfo eventually joined the other Muslim schools in closing and ending the Fante Muslim pedagogical initiative.[88]

The Presbyterian missionary A. J. Lochmann visited Ekrawfo in 1913 from his Basel Mission station at Nsaba in neighboring Agona. It was after Binyameen Sam's death, and Lochmann argued that when Sam

> was at the height of his effectiveness, schools also were founded. He even managed that three of them came under government supervision. . . . The farsighted view of Ben Sam . . . was not shared by the majority of his comrades in the faith, who were illiterates. Above all not by Mahdi Apaa [sic] . . . [who] demanded that in a proper Mohamedan school only Arabic or Hausa should be taught.[89]

Despite Lochmann's negative view of Mahdi Appah, the logbook indicates that Appah had served as manager of Ekrawfo's school for several years. Additionally, the opening of a Muslim English-language school at Kroboase, near Appah's cocoa farm in Breman, likely was the result of Appah's effort. What changed, perhaps, was the increasing pressure on Appah and other Fante Muslims to conform to norms stressed by other Muslims in the Gold Coast. Lochmann's passage alludes to such pressure to conform in his reference to "a proper Mohamedan school."

Generational Divisions among Fante Muslims

The closing of the Fante Muslim schools offers a glimpse into broader conflicts emerging in the Fante Muslim community during the early twentieth century. Informants discussed the closings with Humphrey Fisher in the late 1950s. Fisher named his informants, all young adults at the time of closings. They included descendants of Binyameen Sam and Mahdi Appah, as well as M. A. Ishaque and Jibraeel Gyan, prominent Ahmadi Muslims of the era. Fisher summarized their oral testimony as follows:

> Clerics continued to come from the north. One in particular, Mallam Tijani, taught that English would certainly entail damnation. Apaa [sic] became convinced of this, and quarreled with Ben Sam. It is said that Apaa refused to pray behind Ben Sam, who was Imam of the community, if Ben Sam persisted in his attachment to English education; this is probably a later Ahmadi gloss, separate prayer being the distinguishing sign of the Ahmadi. The quarrel was involved with another one, about alcohol, concerning which Ben Sam was apparently not so strict as Apaa and the visiting Hausa would wish.[90]

Fisher summarized only the gist of what he heard and does not provide direct quotations from individuals. He concluded, on the basis of these memories as well as Lochmann's statements and the information in the logbook, that a dispute over English-language education led Appah to move from Ekrawfo, which contributed to the school's collapse in 1908.[91]

Mahdi Appah's grandson, Ahmad Afful, provided a different perspective on the dispute between Mahdi Appah and Binyameen Sam. In 2005 Afful narrated an account, which he had heard from his mother, Haleema Adjoa Yansewa. Afful did not mention English-language schools and stated that the conflict was a family matter: Rukiyya Akua Mansah, Sam's daughter and Haleema's mother, married Appah but later divorced him in an acrimonious separation sometime after Appah had left Ekrawfo to reside in Breman, a region north of Ekrawfo. After the divorce, when Appah returned from Breman to celebrate Muslim holidays at Ekrawfo, the two families no longer celebrated together. The family impasse ended, according to Afful, when a sheep Appah had brought to slaughter for Eid al-Adha got loose and was found eating grass next to the sheep Sam had obtained. The two agreed that, if the sheep could eat together, then they could put their dispute aside and celebrate together.[92] I heard a similar account of the dispute and its reconciliation from residents of Asikuma, close to where Appah resided in Breman.[93]

These memories add significant details about the reasons Mahdi Appah left Ekrawfo for Breman: he went to farm cocoa with his cousins. Appah and his kin were first-generation Fante cocoa farmers who joined others in settling in virgin forests and planting cocoa trees during the late 1890s.[94] Appah received his land from Breman royalty as recompense for his assistance in a previous dispute, and he chose virgin forestlands at Harage ("here is fine") near Wasabiampa (see maps 4 and 6). Current residents of Wasabiampa remember that Appah built the first mosque in the region, initially a temporary structure at Harage and then a larger, permanent one that still stands today in Wasabiampa.[95] Appah probably planted his first cocoa trees at Harage in the late 1890s but retained a primary residence at Ekrawfo until 1902, when Appah's entries in the Ekrawfo logbook became infrequent and he started to devote more time to his maturing cocoa trees at Harage. Appah's departure from Ekrawfo, according to Ahmad Afful and residents of Wasabiampa, had to do with cocoa farming and not a dispute over English-language education at Ekrawfo.

The information from Humphrey Fisher and these memories is best reconciled by analyzing the social groups involved in the narration. Descendants of Mahdi Appah and residents near his former cocoa farm in Harage locate the conflict in the contours of Appah's domestic life and do not reference a larger Muslim dispute. They put no emphasis on English-language education and offer a chronology of Appah's life that explains his departure from Ekrawfo in terms of his cocoa farming. Reminiscences heard by Fisher in the 1950s included members of both families, but also prominent members of the Ahmadiyya community. These memories stressed the religious dimensions of the conflict, including Sam's tolerance of alcohol consumption by Fante Muslims. The Ekrawfo logbook also references the use of Methodist Bibles and hymnals, other practices condoned by Binyameen Sam but not keeping with savanna Muslim norms. The dispute between Sam and Appah likely involved both family matters and religious issues. The visiting Muslim may have preached about the evils of English-language education, but Fisher placed too much emphasis on that issue as the basis for Appah's disagreement with Sam. One even wonders if English-language education even divided the two, as Appah later was such a strong supporter of Ahmadiyya English-language schools in the 1920s.

Mahdi Appah's conflict with Binyameen Sam was an element of a larger generational cleavage emerging in the Fante Muslim community. Appah had become a pioneering cocoa entrepreneur just as Sam was entering the last years of his life. Whether the marital dispute preceded or followed the religious dispute, Appah's conflict with Sam reflected his growing awareness of savanna Muslim norms. As elsewhere in colonial West Africa, contact between Muslims of diverse backgrounds produced aspirations for standardization.[96] Humphrey Fisher's informants, all young men during the early twentieth century, freely recounted Sam's faults before Fisher, an outsider, revealing the depth of their conviction that Sam did not practice Islam well. One of Fisher's informants, Al-Hajj M. A. Ishaque, attended the Arabic school at Ekrawfo in the 1910s and likely was one of those revealing Sam's shortcomings. These memories, associated with boys and young men in the early twentieth century, attest to the generational divide that had emerged within the Fante Muslim community. Younger elders such as Appah had left to cocoa farm, and youths in Ekrawfo interacted with other Muslims and came to question Sam's religious leadership. The conflict over Muslim norms may have contributed to the closing of the English-language schools at Ekrawfo, Ekotsi, and Kroboase, but it was a general debate about appropriate Muslim practice and not specifically English-language education that divided Fante Muslims.

Binyameen Sam spent the last days of his life at Ankorakwaa, a village a few miles from Ekrawfo, before he died around 1909.[97] Ankorakwaa was the home of his second wife, and his departure from Ekrawfo may well have reflected recognition of the generational divisions in the Fante Muslim community. He died at Ankorakwaa, and his body was buried at Ekrawfo. Ekua Obowa, Sam's eldest daughter from his deceased first wife, organized the event and read from the Quran at his gravesite. A wondrous event reportedly occurred, as Ekua Obowa completed her recitation: a thunderclap struck, Sam's body turned white, and he raised his arms and blessed everyone before slumping into a lifeless form as his normal color returned. After the service some funeral participants returned to collect the mud created from washing his body. These curative practices, no longer observed, reference an esoteric repertoire that the Fante Muslim community observed in the past.[98]

Savanna Muslim scholars established an Arabic-language school at Ekrawfo after Binyameen Sam died. When Lochmann visited in 1913 he noted that Mallam Musa, a Hausa Muslim scholar from Kano, taught a small number of students and served as the community's imam; memories from the 1950s suggest that Musa arrived shortly after Sam's death and was the first savanna Muslim scholar teaching Arabic at Ekrawfo.[99] The number of students at this school was a handful and never approached forty-nine, the highest annual enrollment of Ekrawfo's English-language school. Mallam Yakubu, a Hausa Muslim scholar who succeeded Musa, ran the school at Ekrawfo in the late 1910s.[100] One of the students at these Arabic schools, M. A. Ishaque, gained fluency and was able to converse in Arabic with Maulvi Nayyar when he visited in 1921. But Fante Muslim students who aspired for advanced Islamic training had to leave Ekrawfo to study at Saltpond and other coastal towns. Ekrawfo, a center for Fante Muslims during Sam's era, had become the lowest rung in a network of Muslim educational institutions run by savanna Muslim scholars in the early twentieth-century Gold Coast.

Fante Muslims were at a crossroads in the 1910s. Binyameen Sam had died, and Mahdi Appah no longer resided at Ekrawfo. Mallam Yakubu, a Hausa Muslim scholar, was Ekrawfo's religious leader. But just before he could consolidate his position, an influenza pandemic swept through West Africa, claiming as many as one hundred thousand lives in the Gold Coast in late 1918.[101] This pandemic caused Africans to question the efficacy of existing religious practices, and many new Christian movements emerged throughout West Africa where the pandemic had taken a great toll. It was in this context that an Ahmadi Muslim arrived to trade at Saltpond and that Yusuf Nyarko, a relative of Binyameen Sam, dreamed about praying with foreign Muslims.

Conclusion

One of the first African Methodist ministers in the Gold Coast was Reverend John Oboboam Hammond, whose pioneering role is commemorated in his stained-glass image at the Methodist church at Saltpond. Reverend Hammond's acts of faith included the deathbed conversion of a Fante Muslim, who wanted to return to his Christian roots and be placed back in the Methodist registry in the late 1890s. Hammond asked the reasons for his change of heart, given that "there is but one God, who is the God of Mohammedans and Christians alike." The Fante Muslim responded that he had gained nothing from his acceptance of Islam "but doubt of heaven and fear of hell." Hammond added his name so that he "died in hope," and thereafter Hammond convinced a few other Muslims to return to the Methodist fold.[102] These conversions were exceptions, but they illustrate the enduring imprint that Methodism had made on Fante Muslims.

The Fante Muslim community faced greater challenges than the loss of its members to the Methodists. The Basel missionary A. J. Lochmann noted in 1913 that Hausa Muslims did not recognize Fante Muslims as "Mohamedans of equal rank."[103] The Hausa leader in Winneba proudly asserted that savanna *mallams* were teaching Fante Muslims "how to be proper Muslims."[104] These attitudes led savanna Muslim scholars to criticize Binyameen Sam's preaching of Islam from the Bible, to condemn his tolerance of alcohol consumption, and to question other activities. Before the large-scale migration of savanna Muslims to the coast from the savanna in the 1890s, the Fante Muslim community had little or no contact with *mallams*: the first memories of interactions with *mallams* are from the late nineteenth century. But after Binyameen Sam's death, a Muslim from the savanna tradition resided at Ekrawfo and taught Arabic to a handful of Fante Muslim young men. Shortly thereafter, however, news of the Ahmadiyya arrived, and the Fante Muslim community invited a missionary to visit the Gold Coast. That invitation and the visit it engendered is discussed in chapter 5; the next two chapters turn to the genesis of the Ahmadiyya and its expansion to London and Lagos.

Notes

1. Abeka related his story to Lochmann. See Debrunner, Fisher, and Fisher, "Early Fante Islam [continued]," 1, no. 8 (1960), 17. Lochmann refers to Abeka by his birth name, Kwabena Abeka, his Christian name, John Tobia, and his Muslim name, Musa Kula Mulashi.

2. WMMS: 27 December 1877, Thomas Birch Freeman to General Secretary. Freeman noted that this development began two years earlier. He did not mention an encounter with a Hausa Force *mallam* and wondered whether it may have been associated with the report of Muslim visitors to the region from Lagos in the late 1860s and early 1870s (probably conveyed from the Basel Mission).

3. Debrunner, Fisher, and Fisher, "Early Fante Islam," 1, no. 7 (1959), 28.

4. Anaman, *Gold Coast Guide*, 85–86. For Anaman's biography, see introduction, note 110.

5. Contemporary memories are mentioned in *Ahmadiyya Movement in Ghana* (Saltpond: Ahmadiyya Movement, Ghana, 1961); 1; Guar-Gorman, "Islam in Fantiland," 58–63; and Haneef Keelson, *Early History of Ahmadiyyat in Ghana* (Accra: Ahmadiyya Muslim Mission, 2003), 1–8. Fisher heard stories of Sam's conversion in the 1950s, and his most comprehensive discussion of these memories is in Debrunner, Fisher, and Fisher, "Early Fante Islam [continued]," 1, no. 8 (1960), 23–26. Also see Fisher, *Ahmadiyyah*, 117; and id., "Early Muslim-Western Education," 288. I heard an account in Ekrawfo's mosque on 1 June 2005 based on the memories of Ahmad Afful. After the presentation I received a handwritten text, "The Advent of Ahmadiyyat in Ekumfi Ekrawfo," written for Afful by Hakeem Kofi Yamoah.

6. Fisher made a passing reference to Sam's conversion in one of his early articles that suggested the influence of Anaman's account, but he never cited Anaman in any publication and adopted Lochmann's date of the mid-1880s for Sam's conversion (see note 7). The influence of Anaman's text on Fisher might have been from an article by Addo-Aryee Brown that seems to draw on Anaman's account, but it does not refer explicitly to Sam, Anaman or *The Gold Coast Guide*. See Fisher, "Early Muslim-Western Education," 289; and A. Addo-Aryee Brown, "Historical Account of Mohammedanism in the Gold Coast," *Gold Coast Review* 3, no. 2 (1927), 196–197. Another early source that seems to draw on Anaman without mentioning *The Gold Coast Guide* as a source is Joseph William de Graft Johnson, *Historical Geography of the Gold Coast* (London: Headley Brothers, 1929), 118.

7. Lochmann's passage draws on information from a Fante informant and states: "Benjamin Sam went with the Mohamedan to the north, where he was initiated into the secrets of Islam. In the year 1885 or 1886 he returned as a fanatical disciple of Mohamed and unfolded an astonishing propaganda." Debrunner, Fisher, and Fisher, "Early Fante Islam," 1, no. 7 (1959), 25. A conversion date in the mid-1880s is repeated in Debrunner, *Christianity in Ghana*, 241; and Fisher, *Ahmadiyyah*, 117. Others follow their lead in dating Sam's conversion to the mid-1880s.

8. Binyameen Sam's gravestone notes a birth in 1822, but this date is not definitive: the practice of putting dates on graves was not widely followed at the time of Sam's death, and the current marker was erected after his burial and has been refurbished at least twice since

the 1950s. Dating his birth is best estimated by anchoring it in a known event, such as his attendance at Anomabu's Methodist school. This school opened only in the mid-1840s. If Sam was among its initial generation of graduates, such as Isaac Asuman Graham, Robert John Hayfron, and Isaac Hayford, then he likely was born in the 1830s, as their birth dates range from 1832 to 1839. Assigning Sam a birth in c1835 would make him seventy-four when he died around 1909. For the birth dates of Graham, Hayfron, and Hayford, see WMMS: "Character of Candidate" statements for Isaac Asuman Graham (c. 1884), Robert John Hayfron (c. 1873), and Isaac Hayford (1881) (dates of application for ministry in parentheses). Note that today Egyaa has grown and there are two villages, Egyaa I and Egyaa II.

9. A. B. Ellis, *West African Sketches* (London: Samuel Tinsley and Co., 1881), 220–221. For Saltpond's role in the palm oil trade, see Kwamina B. Dickson, *Historical Geography of Ghana* (Cambridge: Cambridge University Press, 1969), 144, 254.

10. WMMS: 17 January 1881, "Personal statement," in Isaac Hayford's application to the ministry.

11. Lochmann asserted that Sam was a teacher at the Methodist mission school at Gyinankoma, but the Methodists did not open a school there until after Sam became a Muslim. Debrunner, Fisher, and Fisher, "Early Fante Islam," 1, no. 7 (1959), 25.

12. Hempton, *Methodism*.

13. Beecham, *Ashantee and the Gold Coast*, 260.

14. Southon, *Gold Coast Methodism*, 29–30.

15. Kea, "Modernity and Identity," 221.

16. Thomas Birch Freeman, *Journal of Various Visits to the Kingdoms of Ashanti, Aku, Dahomi, in Western Africa*, 2nd ed. (London: J. Mason, 1844), 18–20.

17. John Watson to his superiors in 1842, quoted in Kea, "Modernity and Identity," 221.

18. Kea, "Modernity and Identity," 219.

19. Hugon, *Un protestantisme africain*, 195 and chart on 196.

20. K. A. Dickson, "The 'Methodist Society:' A Sect," *GBT* 2, no. 6 (1964); Hugon, *Un protestantisme africain*, 330–335.

21. Hugon provides a French translation of the key passage from Alan Taylor's letter in *Un protestantisme africain*, 330–331.

22. Bartels, *Roots of Ghana Methodism*, 82; the movement published the report of its first meeting at Anomabu in *First Report of the Anomaboe Temperance Society Total Abstainers* (Birmingham, UK: Hudson and Son, 1864).

23. WMMS: Annual Reports, Anomabu Circuit, 1868, 1869, 1870. The 1870 report noted regarding Assafa, one of the villages associated with the Methodist Society, that "all of the fanaticism here has at last disappeared" but provides no details.

24. Hugon argued against Dickson's view that the members of the Methodist society were not well-informed of Methodist teachings and practices. See Hugon, *Un protestantisme africain*, 334–335.

25. Anaman, *Gold Coast Guide*, 85–86.

26. WMMS: 27 December 1877, Thomas Birch Freeman to General Secretary.

27. Al-Hajj Hamied's text is discussed in Acquah, "Impact of African Traditional Religious Beliefs," 145–150. For the Fante Muslim community at Obonster, also see Guar-Gorman, "Islam in Fantiland," 88–91.

28. Debrunner, Fisher, and Fisher, "Early Fante Islam [continued]," 1, no. 8 (1960), 24–25.

29. Keelson, *Early History of Ahmadiyyat in Ghana*.

30. Yamoah, "The Advent of Ahmadiyyat in Ekumfi Ekrawfo," based on Ahmad Afful's memories.

31. Haleema Adjoa Yansewa, born in the early twentieth century, was the daughter of Rukiyya Akua Mansah, Binyameen Sam's daughter, and Mahdi Appah.

32. Debrunner, Fisher, and Fisher, "Early Fante Islam [continued]," 1, no. 8 (1960), 25.

33. Al-Hajj Hamied's account has Sheibu offering his esoteric services to Elmina during its war with the Fante states.

34. Fisher never reflected extensively on the question of Abu Bakr's background. Deborah Pellow and David Skinner suggested that he was related to Mallam Naino, a Hausa scholar from Katsina who is remembered as the first Hausa settler in Accra: Mallam Naino had a brother known as Abu Bakr. But if the Muslim who converted Sam had been Mallam Naino's brother, then Anaman surely would have made the connection in *The Gold Coast Guide*, as Abu Bakr was a prominent Muslim in the Gold Coast at the time. Deborah Pellow, "The Power of Space in the Evolution of an Accra *Zongo*," *Ethnohistory* 38, no. 4 (1991), 444n23; and David Skinner, "Muslim Elites," 100 (Skinner actually refers to Abu Bakr as Mallam Naino's nephew and not his brother). For Mallam Naino, see Odoom, "Pioneers"; and Pellow, *Landlords and Lodgers*, 47–48.

35. Anaman, *Gold Coast Guide*, 85–86.

36. GP: no date, "Names of Lagos Houssas who served with Glover's Expedition during the late Ashantee War."

37. Zenoah deployed to the Gold Coast with other members of the Hausa Force and remained to serve as a native officer in the Gold Coast Constabulary. Zenoah had left the force in 1870 to serve Glover as a government agent in Lagos, but he reenlisted after Glover's term as administrator ended. Zenoah wrote Glover to recount difficulties he encountered after Glover left Lagos. GP: August, 1872, Harry Maxwell to Captain Glover. Zenoah was known as Harry Maxwell, a name given him in Freetown. See "Harri Zenoah," *Gold Coast Gazette*, no. 50 (14 August 1920), 1023; Glover, *Life*, 78; and Killingray, "Bald Biographies," 14–15.

38. Adamu, *Hausa Factor*, 170.

39. Ibid., 171.

40. Mallam Tibu may be one of the Muslim visitors mentioned by members of the Basel Mission as having passed through the Fante states on their way to Akyem, where the Muslims arrived in late 1870. Either Mallam Tibu stayed behind in the Fante states as the others went to Akyem or he returned to the Fante states after a two-year residence in Akyem. Methodist reports and correspondence from this era, however, make no mention of Muslim visitors, so the connection between Mallam Tibu and this visit is uncertain. But the villages of Ekumfi where Sam resided were on the periphery of the Methodist presence at the time, so Mallam Tibu's visit might have escaped Methodist notice. If Mallam Tibu did have contact with Sam and played a role in his conversion to Islam, then the postinvasion aftermath was less relevant to Sam's conversion than it was to the vast majority of Fante Muslims who converted after the invasion. For them, the unsettled affiliations of the era were salient, as was the enhanced status of *mallams* after the Hausa Force participated in the successful occupation of Kumasi.

41. Gillespie, *Gold Coast Police*, 13; GP: no date, Glover to Wolseley; Glover, *Life*, 280.

42. Debrunner, Fisher, and Fisher, "Early Fante Islam," 1, no. 7 (1959), 25.

43. William Winwood Reade described the attire of Hausa Force *mallams* in the mid-1870s as consisting of "a long flowing white robe and a white turban." See "The Houssa Force," *The Times* (London), 3 September 1873, 4.

44. Guar-Gorman, "Islam in Fantiland," 63.

45. Frederica Beard, a Christian pedagogue of the turn-of-the-century United States, instructed Christian school educators in the use of religious pictures. See her *Pictures in Religious Education* (New York: George H. Doran, 1920).

46. Thomas West, *The Life and Journals of the Rev. Daniel West, Wesleyan Minister and the Deputation to the Wesleyan Mission Stations on the Gold Coast, Western Africa* (London: Hamilton, Adams and Co., 1857), 197–198; for nineteenth-century Methodist views of spiritualism and visions, see Ann Taves, *Fits, Trances, and Visions: Experiencing Religion from Wesley to James* (Princeton, NJ: Princeton University Press, 1999), 50–58, 71–75.

47. Morgan, *Visual Piety*.

48. Reade, *Ashantee Campaign*, 327.

49. Ellis, *West African Sketches*, 128.

50. WMMS: Annual Report, Anomabu Circuit, 1876 (circuit and district names changed as reorganization occurred with the expansion and then consolidation of new Methodist mission stations).

51. WMMS: Annual Reports, Anomabu Circuit, 1876, 1877.

52. WMMS: Annual Report, Adansi Circuit, 1879.

53. WMMS: Annual Reports, Adansi Circuit, 1880, 1881.

54. WMMS: Annual Reports, Anomabu District, 1886, 1889; the latter noted that the church was "almost completed" despite "fierce and determined opposition from the Mohammedans."

55. Guar-Gorman, "Islam in Fantiland," 61–62; Debrunner, Fisher, and Fisher, "Early Fante Islam [continued]," 1, no. 8 (1960), 26.

56. Hanson interviews at Ekrawfo and Breman Asikuma: respectively, Ahmad Afful and Nuhu bin Mahdi, 1 June 2005 and 6 June 2005; "Advent of Chief Mahdi Appah, also known as Kwadwo Aduagyir from Ekumfi Attakwaa, and Occupation of Breman Bedum Stool Land" (manuscript given to the author by Nuhu bin Mahdi on 6 June 2005).

57. Debrunner, Fisher, and Fisher, "Early Fante Islam [continued]," 1, no. 8 (1960), 27. Note that Anaman refers to Appah as "Mahadi," so he had this Muslim name before becoming an Ahmadi Muslim. Anaman, *Gold Coast Guide*, 86.

58. WMMS: Annual Reports, Mankessim Circuit, 1880, 1881.

59. Hanson interview at Ekotsi: Usman Kojo Otoo and Kwesi Abdullah Saeed, 2 June 2005; "How Islam Ahmadiyyat was Introduced to the Citizens of Ekumfi Ekotsi in the Central Region of Ghana, Compiled by Bro. Usman Koko Otoo and Bro. Kwesi Abdullah Saeed" (manuscript given to the author by the compilers on 2 June 2005).

60. Hanson interview at Breman Asikuma: Nuhu bin Mahdi, 6 June 2005; "Advent of Chief Mahdi Appah, also known as Kwadwo Aduagyir from Ekumfi Attakwaa, and Occupation of Breman Bedum Stool Land" (manuscript given to the author by Nuhu bin Mahdi on 6 June 2005).

61. My interpretation of the local meaning of women's conversion stories benefitted from my conversations with Maulvi A. Wahab Adam and Fatima Yusif. Hanson interview at Accra: Maulvi A. Wahab Adam, 28 May 2005; Hanson interview at Ebubonko: Fatima Yusif, 5 June 2005. Note that the destruction of indigenous objects also is a theme in memories related to me in Asante. See chapter 7 for elaboration on its meaning for Asante Ahmadi Muslim households.

62. Hugon, *Un protestantisme africain*, 279–281.

63. Hanson interview at Immuna: Ahmad Saeed Anderson, 1 June 2005.

64. Debrunner, Fisher, and Fisher, "Early Fante Islam [continued]," 1, no. 8 (1960), 24.

65. Hanson interview at Ekotsi: Usman Kojo Otoo and Kwesi Abdullah Saeed, 2 June 2005; "How Islam Ahmadiyyat was Introduced to the Citizens of Ekumfi Ekotsi in the Central Region of Ghana, Compiled by Bro. Usman Koko Otoo and Bro. Kwesi Abdullah Saeed" (manuscript given to the author by the compilers on 2 June 2005).

66. Debrunner, Fisher, and Fisher, "Early Fante Islam," 1, no. 7 (1959), 32.

67. WMMS: 27 December 1877, Thomas Birch Freeman to General Secretary; Fisher, "Early Muslim-Western Education," 289.
68. Debrunner, Fisher, and Fisher, "Early Fante Islam," 1, no. 7 (1959), 28.
69. Walls, "Africa as the Theatre of Christian Engagement with Islam," 163–164.
70. The Society for the Promotion of Christian Knowledge started circulating Arabic Bibles along the West African coast in the early nineteenth century. The first shipment arrived in Freetown during the second decade of the nineteenth century. See Daniel L. Brunner, *Halle Pietists in England: Anthony William Boehm and the Society for Promoting Christian Knowledge* (Gottingen: Vandenhoeck & Ruprecht, 1993), 161; and Charles Hole, *The Early History of the Church Missionary Society for Africa and the East to the End of A.D. 1814* (London: Church Missionary Society, 1896), 598–600. For Arabic publishing in Britain in this era, see Geoffrey Roper, "Arabic Printing and Publishing in England before 1820," *Bulletin (British Society for Middle Eastern Studies)* 12, no. 1 (1985), 12–32.
71. "Abstracts from Correspondence in the Basel Mission Archive, 1828–1851, Made by Hans Debrunner," 107, citing the 2 January 1851 report by Zimmermann.
72. Debrunner, Fisher, and Fisher, "Early Fante Islam," 1, no. 7 (1959), 24.
73. Yusuf K. Effah, "History of Ahmadiyya Movement in Ghana," *RR* 84, no.10 (1989), 29–30.
74. Hanson interviews in Gomoa Potsin: Sarah Anderson (niece of Isa Quantson), 31 May 2005, and N. Inkoom (descendant of Adam Kofi Quarm), 31 May 2005; also see "History of Islam at Potsin" (manuscript given to the author by N. Inkoom on 31 May 2005).
75. Debrunner, Fisher, and Fisher, "Early Fante Islam [continued]," 1, no. 8 (1960), 17.
76. WMMS: Report on the State of the Societies, Winneba Circuit, 1897: entry for Kyireku.
77. Debrunner, Fisher, and Fisher, "Early Fante Islam [continued]," 1, no. 8 (1960), 19.
78. Anaman, *Gold Coast Guide*, 85–86.
79. Hanson interviews at Breman Asikuma: Nuhu bin Mahdi; and Ahmad Afful, 6 June 2005. Also see "Advent of Chief Mahdi Appah, also known as Kwadwo Aduagyir from Ekumfi Attakwaa, and Occupation of Breman Bedum Stool Land" (manuscript given to the author by Nuhu bin Mahdi on 6 June 2005).
80. Debrunner, Fisher, and Fisher, "Early Fante Islam," 1, no. 7 (1959), 27.
81. Fisher, *Ahmadiyyah*, 118; Fisher, "Early Muslim-Western Education," 288–289, 295; Debrunner, Fisher, and Fisher, "Early Fante Islam [continued]," 1, no. 8 (1960), 26–27.
82. Skinner, "Muslim Elites."
83. Fante Muslim schools are listed Blue Books in: PRO CO 100/49–100/61.
84. Guar-Gorman, "Islam in Fantiland," 66.
85. Humphrey Fisher, "Planting Ahmadiyya in Ghana," *West Africa*, no. 2226 (30 January 1960), 121.
86. Edward W. Blyden mentions visiting the Gold Coast twice in *West Africa before Europe, and Other Addresses Delivered in England in 1901 and 1903* (London: C. M. Phillips, 1905), 11, 106. My search in Ghanaian archives produced no materials about Blyden visiting Ekrawfo.
87. Fisher, "Early Muslim-Western Education."
88. Ibid., 290.
89. Debrunner, Fisher, and Fisher, "Early Fante Islam [continued]," 1, no. 8 (1960), 27.
90. Ibid., 26–27.
91. Fisher conjectured that Appah resided in Mando with Suleiman Asamang, but Appah lived in Bedum.
92. Hanson interview at Ekrawfo: Ahmad Afful, 1 June 2005.
93. Hanson interview at Breman Asikuma: Nuhu bin Mahdi, 6 June 2005; "Advent of Chief Mahdi Appah, also known as Kwadwo Aduagyir from Ekumfi Attakwaa, and Occupation of

Breman Bedum Stool Land" (manuscript given to the author by Nuhu bin Mahdi on 6 June 2005).

94. For passing reference to pioneering Fante cocoa farmers, see Polly Hill, "The History of the Migration of Ghana Cocoa Farmers," *THSG* 4, no. 1 (1959), 25.

95. Hanson interview at Wasabiampa: Tahir Quainon (descendant of Mahdi Appah), 6 June 2005.

96. Robert Launay and Benjamin Soares, "The Formation of an 'Islamic Sphere' in French Colonial West Africa," *Economy and Society* 28 (1999), 497–519.

97. Sam's gravestone in the Ekrawfo puts his death at 1915, but it is not definitive, as I similarly argued for its dating of his birth. Lochmann reported after his 1913 visit to Ekrawfo that Sam had died four years earlier, which would be in 1909. See Debrunner, Fisher, and Fisher, "Early Fante Islam," 1, no. 7 (1959), 25. Corroborating this date is the British colonial official J. L. Atterbury, who referred in 1915 to Sam's death having occurred six years earlier. See Thora Williamson and Anthony Kirk-Greene, eds., *Gold Coast Diaries: Chronicles of Political Officers in West Africa, 1900–1919* (London: Radcliffe Press, 2000), 95, citing Atterbury's diary entry for 16 September 1915 at Saltpond.

98. Hanson interview at Ekrawfo: Hakeem Kofi Yamoah, 1 June 2005.

99. Debrunner, Fisher, and Fisher, "Early Fante Islam," 1, no. 7 (1959), 31–33; id., "Early Fante Islam [continued]," 1, no. 8 (1960), 27–28.

100. For Mallam Yakubu as the Muslim scholar at Ekrawfo in the late 1910s, see Debrunner, Fisher, and Fisher, "Early Fante Islam [continued]," 1, no. 8 (1960), 27–28; and Acquah, "Impact of African Traditional Religious Beliefs," 145–150. Guar-Gorman identified "Mallam Qasim," reportedly a Hausa speaker of Zugu ethnicity, as the Muslim teacher residing at Ekrawfo after Sam's death in "Islam in Fantiland," 87–88.

101. K. David Patterson, "The Influenza Epidemic of 1918–1919 in the Gold Coast," *JAH* 24 (1983), 485–502.

102. WMMS: Annual Report, Ayan Main Circuit, 1889; the story is retold in Kemp, *Nine Years*, 82–84.

103. Debrunner, Fisher, and Fisher, "Early Fante Islam," 1, no. 7 (1959), 29.

104. PRAAD, Cape Coast: ADM 1/23/353, no date, "Ahmadia Movement in the Gold Coast."

PART II

AHMADIYYA GENESIS AND EXPANSION TO LONDON AND LAGOS

3   The Genesis of the Ahmadiyya in British India

GHULAM AHMAD HAD a series of visionary experiences that inspired him to found the Ahmadiyya in 1889. One occurred in early adulthood when the Prophet Muhammad reportedly appeared as a light in Ghulam Ahmad's dream and nurtured him with words and fruit from his garden.[1] This dream, evocative of the pinnacle of Sufi mystical experiences, did not lead to an embrace of Sufism, the dominant Muslim expression in Punjab at the time. Instead, Ghulam Ahmad received additional visions and became convinced that he was God's choice to reform Islam and to win new converts through nonviolent means as the Mahdi and Messiah. Ghulam Ahmad established the Ahmadiyya as a Muslim movement that encouraged followers to eliminate local customs that Sufi leaders tolerated. The movement also opened primary schools with English-language instruction to provide skills to navigate the British colonial order. The Ahmadiyya, named after the Quran's reference to Ahmad being Muhammad's beautiful manifestation, attracted Punjabi urban middle classes, rural landowners, and the poor in a region where Muslims, Hindus, Sikhs, and Christians competed for followers. Ghulam Ahmad's death in 1908 ultimately led to a succession crisis. The Ahmadi majority accepted Ghulam Ahmad's son, Bashir-ud-Din Mahmud Ahmad, as *khalifatul masih*, or "successor of the Messiah," but some broke away and founded a competing Ahmadiyya movement in Lahore, Punjab's capital. After the split in 1914 Khalifatul Masih Bashir-ud-Din Mahmud Ahmad moved decisively to consolidate his position as the charismatic leader of the Ahmadiyya Muslim Community, as the majority branch came to be known.

The Ahmadiyya defies precise classification.[2] Many cast it as a variant of a Sufi order, whereas others define it as a Muslim reform movement.[3] Complicating either categorization was Ghulam Ahmad's teaching that diverged from Sufism and Muslim reformism in significant ways: he claimed to be the Mahdi and Messiah, combining diverse threads into one religious movement that followed its own path. In the context of the current analysis, Ghulam Ahmad and his followers were Muslim cosmopolitans who engaged Christians and others. The religious marketplace of British Punjab was competitive, and the various movements sharpened their rhetoric and produced "rival forms of cosmopolitanism," a term used by scholars of the Indian Ocean world in reference to religious interactions in contexts with sectarian divisions.[4] Ghulam Ahmad and his followers acknowledged universal human standards, even as their arguments pressed Ghulam Ahmad's claims in the intensely competitive religious marketplace of Punjab.

This chapter provides an overview of the Ahmadiyya from its genesis under Ghulam Ahmad to the 1914 succession of Khalifatul Masih Bashir ud-Din Mahmud Ahmad. It begins with background on Punjab, a region of northwestern India where the Ahmadiyya was based, and its diverse religious heritages. The next section adopts the metaphor of the religious marketplace to discuss the competitive Punjabi religious context of the late nineteenth century when British imperialism and Christian proselytism helped foster the emergence of Hindu and Sikh reform movements. Next it presents Ghulam Ahmad's life and his founding of the Ahmadiyya, referencing Muslim reform movements emerging elsewhere in India, developing Ghulam Ahmad's theological claims, and discussing the movement's organizational and sociological dimensions. It ends with Ghulam Ahmad's preparations for the succession after this death, the internal divisions that appeared, and the fragmentation produced by Khalifatul Masih Bashir ud-Din Mahmud Ahmad's succession in 1914.

Punjab in the Nineteenth Century

Punjab is located in the westernmost region of the northern Indian plains (see map 7). The Himalayas are to the north, and several rivers flow south and converge in Punjab at the midpoint of the Indus River. These rivers define the boundaries of several Punjabi regions, known as *doabs*, referring to the land between rivers.[5] Farming and herding have been the primary activities for more than five millennia in Punjab, a region where some of the first settled societies appeared in the greater Indus River region several millennia ago. Cultivation expanded over the centuries with the introduction of new technologies, such as ironworking and the waterwheel. Competing to control these productive lands were local elites, regional powers, and Central Asian immigrants, primarily Afghans and Turks. Punjab's largest town, Lahore, has been the capital of a local polity, a provincial center, and occasionally an imperial capital, as well as the residence for scholars and merchants situated along the 1,500-mile road connecting Central Asia to Bengal. The dominant language of the region is Punjabi, an Indo-Aryan language related to classical Sanskrit, Hindi, and other North Indian languages: its numerous dialects reflect the region's cultural interactions as diverse groups settled and came to speak variants of a shared language over the past two millennia.[6]

The rise and fall of the Mughal Empire made Punjab an imperial province and then an autonomous polity. The Mughals were Muslim groups arriving in northern India from Central Asia: they consolidated power during the early sixteenth century and extended it, over the following two centuries, into peninsular

India. The Mughal Empire maintained connections with the broader Muslim world, especially the Persian-speaking regions, but it also forged local arrangements in ways that engaged South Asian social groups. Dissolution began in the eighteenth century; in Punjab Persians and Central Asians invaded from the west and severed it from Mughal control. Later the Sikh military leader Ranjit Singh united the *doabs* of Punjab into a single state in the early nineteenth century. British imperialism lurked to the east in the form of the British East India Company, which expanded to claim Delhi, the Mughal capital, and lands up to the Sutlej River, the easternmost river in Punjab, by the early nineteenth century.[7]

Early nineteenth-century Punjab was a rural social order. It had few towns and large tracts of rural areas in which landowners and kin-based social groups dominated social life. Most landowners held small or medium plots and formed patron-client relations with other rural residents, including artisans and a landless population of laborers. Merchants also were influential property owners, often in towns, as were religious specialists controlling land at Hindu, Sikh, and Muslim religious sites. Descent was an important social marker, and claims of common heritage defined membership in kin-based communities: these groups often were associated with occupational status, such as farming, artisanal production, commerce, and other activities, and members of these communities tended to marry within the same group.[8] The collapse of the Mughal Empire and the subsequent consolidation of Ranjit Singh's state scrambled the rural social order, and each *doab* had a distinctive social composition and landholding pattern in the early nineteenth century.

Hinduism, Islam, and Sikhism in Punjab

Hinduism is a diverse set of beliefs and practices with a long history in Punjab as well as in India generally. It springs from the Vedas, oral expressions of knowledge that eventually were written in Sanskrit texts in the first century BCE, as well as subsequent Sanskrit works, including texts elaborating on the Veda's teachings and more popular works eulogizing various deities. Brahmans were religious specialists who organized rituals at temples, interpreted religious texts, and taught seekers of religious knowledge. The plethora of texts meant that Brahmans and other specialists pursued many paths: over the centuries several Hindu traditions emerged and laid emphasis on different texts and condoned diverse ritual practices. Reform movements within the various streams arose at several historical moments. The two most significant reforms were adopting South Asian languages in rituals and challenging notions of ritual purity that elevated Brahmans and excluded others from rituals. Sometimes reform movements produced new religious traditions, such as Buddhism in earlier centuries and Sikhism in more recent centuries. Hinduism nevertheless remained an important religious expression in nineteenth-century Punjab, as past eras of reformism added Punjabi as a widely accepted devotional language; Brahman interpreters of the Vedas also remained influential in supervising a vibrant ritual life centered on temples and shrines.[9]

Islam became a religious practice in Punjab after the arrival of Central Asian Muslims. From the tenth century groups of Muslim elites consolidated power in local contexts as social outsiders: religious differences were less salient than linguistic and cultural distinctions.[10] Punjab's Muslim rulers were patrons of Muslim scholars serving as judges, teachers, poets, and physicians. The largest concentration of scholars was in Delhi and the Mughal heartland, but small groups resided in Lahore and other Punjabi towns. Muslim scholars wrote in Arabic and Persian, and a few produced works in Punjabi. The most influential Muslim scholars were Sufi seekers who propagated a mystical form of Islam as members of the Chishtiyya, Naqshbandiyya, Qadiriyya, and other orders. Sufi mystics known as *pirs* or religious guides were cultural brokers in rural areas, drawing on their charisma as recipients of blessings from God and attracting a following to their exuberant ritual activities. Descendants of notable *pirs*, known as *sajjada nishin*, or "those who sit on prayer rugs," came to influence Muslim practice in rural areas by maintaining tombs that served as loci of religious activity and local festivals. As Mughal power collapsed in eighteenth-century Delhi, Muslim reformers such as the scholar Shah Waliullah and the Sufi leader Shah Fakhruddin sought to reform and revitalize Islamic practice. Shah Waliullah focused on knowledge conveyed in *ahadith* (singular, *hadith*) or "reports" from companions of the Prophet Muhammad, and Shah Fakhruddin reorganized the Chishtiyya order to concentrate on the active propagation of core Islamic rituals and practices. These Islamic currents from the Mughal heartland circulated among some Punjabi Muslims. Nevertheless, *sajjada nishin* and *pirs* of local Sufi orders retained considerable followings, especially in the western and central *doabs* of nineteenth-century Punjab.[11]

Sikhism is associated with the teachings of Guru Nanak. A fifteenth century Punjabi spiritual leader, Nanak broke from Hinduism by stressing a strict monotheism, equality before God, and praying at a *gurdwara*, or place of worship, without statues, incense, and other items associated with Hindu temples. Later Amritsar became a spiritual center, home to a *gurdwara* known as the Harmadir Sahib, or Golden Temple. In the late seventeenth century Guru Gobind Singh, Nanak's tenth successor, announced the end of living gurus and instructed followers to follow the text known as the Guru Granth. Gobind Singh also founded the *khalsa*, a disciplined community adopting distinctive practices and seeking to defend Sikhs at time of religious oppression under late Mughal rule. Khalsa Sikhs, those adopting the new practices of the *khalsa*, formed several polities in the *doabs* as the Mughal Empire declined. Ranjit Singh united these Khalsa Sikhs into a single polity in the early nineteenth century, but he did not impose religious homogeneity. Most Sikhs did not adopt *khalsa* discipline and were known as Sahajdhari Sikhs.[12] Several new Sikh movements also emerged, such as the one established in the early nineteenth century by Baba Dayal Das, who founded a reform movement to challenge what he interpreted as eclecticism in Sikh religious practice.[13] Ranjit Singh's Sikh state did not impose one Sikh practice but tolerated various streams, most outside the *khalsa* discipline.

Hindu, Sikh, and Muslim religious specialists maintained extensive religious networks in nineteenth-century Punjab. Muslims were more prevalent in the western and central *doabs*, and Sikhs and Hindus were more concentrated in the central and eastern *doabs*, but Hindus, Sikhs, and Muslims lived and traveled throughout the region. Seers and healers also operated in the region, drawing on popular beliefs in sorcery and the efficacy of unseen forces associated with sacred sites: these religious specialists claimed to foretell the future, cure illnesses, and provide other religious services, often as members of social groups with connections to patrons and others in the rural Punjabi context. These beliefs and practices operated in the margins of Hinduism, Islam, and Sikhism, contributing to a Punjabi religious sensibility that tolerated diversity.[14] Challenges to religious eclecticism began in the eighteenth century and expanded as British colonial rule and the arrival of Christian missionaries in the mid-nineteenth century accelerated calls for religious reform in Punjab.

The Emergence of the Religious Marketplace in British Punjab

British colonial policies and Christian missionary proselytism fostered the emergence of a competitive religious marketplace in nineteenth-century Punjab. After the annexation of the region into British India in 1849, colonial officials maintained religious neutrality, ultimately turning to census data on religious affiliation as a basis for filling government positions through quotas related to religious affiliation in the late-nineteenth century. British officials also encouraged Christian missionary societies, and what followed an "ecclesiastical conquest" of Punjab.[15] The missionaries conceptualized religious conversion as a matter of personal conscience and encouraged individuals to accept Christianity based on comparison and individual choice. They pressed their ideas through public preaching, used the printing press to propagate their religious message, and built institutions that provided social services such as education, health care, and charity. Local reformers responded and produced the largest number of South Asian religious reform movements of any region of British India.[16] Kenneth W. Jones described these Punjabi movements as "acculturative," meaning that each one "originated in the colonial milieu and was led by individuals who were products of cultural interaction" or at least had a following that was literate in English.[17] This section discusses the emergence of the religious marketplace in nineteenth-century Punjab by reviewing British colonial rule, Christian proselytism, and Hindu and Sikh reform movements; the next section examines Muslim involvement in the religious marketplace and the rise of the Ahmadiyya.

British Colonial Rule

The chartered East India Company was an agent of British imperialism in India. Its commercial activities initially were confined to outposts at coastal towns such as Mumbai, Madras, and Kolkata, but competition with other European firms and the outbreak of the Seven Years' War led to expansion, not only along the coast but also into the interior of Bengal, where the East India Company allied with local commercial groups and convinced the Mughal governor to cede to the company the right to collect revenue in the mid-eighteenth century. Thereafter, the East India Company steadily pushed into the interior, its expansion facilitated by the gradual collapse of the Mughal Empire due to provincial secession and Central Asian invasions: through political, diplomatic, and military means the East India Company extended its reach over north India and the southern peninsula. In the north, company rule began in 1803 as a protectorate over Delhi and the former heartland of the Mughal Empire, leaving Punjab on the northwestern frontier outside imperial control. Britain's annexation of Punjab in 1849 occurred as strategic concerns, including Russian advances in Central Asia, led to British wars in Afghanistan, the lower Indus River valley, and then Punjab itself as Ranjit Singh's successors were defeated in a series of British military campaigns during the late 1840s. The British government assumed control over India from the East India Company after a revolt in Delhi and its environs in 1857.

Colonial rule brought political and economic changes in Punjab. British officials established accommodations of convenience with selected landowners, leaders of kin-based groups, and even a few religious leaders, who served as intermediaries with tax-collecting and judicial authority at the bottom ranks of a tiered system of administration in the five *doabs*. British officials hoped that a stable social order in the rural areas would promote increased cash-crop production and the purchase of consumer goods in the new colonial economy. Encouraging cash-crop production was the colonial expansion of the canal system through the repair of existing canals and the construction of new canals to increase cultivable land in the arid western and southern regions. New "canal colonies" opened to migrants from within Punjab, increasing mobility and circulation in the region. Economic change also occurred in Punjab's towns, which expanded light manufacturing and developed new capacities. Rural areas were connected to towns, not only for the marketing of foodstuffs but also for access to credit, which sometimes fostered rural indebtedness through complex financial arrangements with urban merchants. British colonial policy in Punjab unleashed economic forces that transformed Punjabi lives, but its reliance on local intermediaries fixed in place a patriarchal political structure, especially in rural contexts.[18]

British rule created opportunities for South Asians literate in English. Colonial positions initially were greatest in Punjab's towns, where the administrative apparatus depended on South Asians to staff its lower ranks. Bengalis with English-language education filled these positions in the immediate colonial consolidation, but British educational policies eventually encouraged the opening of schools and colleges to provide skills to Punjabi residents interested in an "Anglo-vernacular education," that is, a British curriculum in South Asian languages at the lower levels and English-language instruction at the higher levels. Graduates literate in both English and South Asian languages constituted a "new elite," a group drawing on both British and South Asian cultures to construct transformed identities in the colonial context.[19] Members of the new elite were diverse, claiming various geographical, social, and religious backgrounds. Their exposure to new ideas and practices made them agents of change articulating a vision of a reformed Indian society of deracinated, rational individuals. Lahore was the focal point for reformism in Punjab, a colonial center where members of the new elite interacted with British officials and merchants in workplaces and new voluntary societies, such as the Anjuman-i-Punjab, an association open to both British and South Asian members in the mid-nineteenth century.[20] Drawing on these experiences and others, the new elite formed their own voluntary organizations to discuss new ideas, criticize established conventions, and push for social and religious reforms in colonial Punjab.

The lithographic press allowed for the circulation of new ideas from beyond Lahore into Punjab's smaller towns and rural areas. This new technology was introduced in Punjab by Christian missionaries, who developed typefaces to print South Asian languages in local scripts in their efforts to deliver their religious teachings to potential converts.[21] These hand-driven presses were affordable, and South Asian merchants, associations of the new elites, and others purchased them and made Lahore a publishing center for newspapers, pamphlets, and other printed materials: by the early 1880s nearly three dozen presses had been licensed to businesses and others in Lahore.[22] The new elites were not alone in supplying materials to the publishing industry; numerous Urdu-language poets, for example, resettled in Lahore from Delhi after the 1857 revolt and made it the center for popular Urdu poetry.[23] The printing industry was not confined to Lahore, as smaller Punjabi towns also had printing presses as did other regions of India. The railroad facilitated the wide circulation of published materials to and from every corner of colonial India. Print culture was influential in urban contexts, but it also reverberated into Punjab's rural areas, where religious leaders and others read newspapers and mass-produced books aloud in public fora.

Christian Missionary Proselytism

Christian missionaries first arrived in northwest India in 1834 at Ludhiana, a town in the British sphere just to the east of the Sutlej River, the boundary between Ranjit Singh's state to the west and the region under East India Company administration. The British agent at Ludhiana invited missionaries from the Presbyterian Church in the United States, known locally as American Presbyterians, to establish schools in Ludhiana: they provided education and more, building a chapel for worship and importing a printing press to propagate the Christian message in English and South Asian languages. The American Presbyterians expanded from Ludhiana into the eastern and central *doabs* immediately after the British annexation of Punjab. Others joined them, including missions associated with the Anglican Church, the Church of Scotland, the Catholic Church, and two American organizations, the Methodist Episcopal Church and the United Presbyterian Church.[24] In 1862 the Christian missionary societies held a conference in Lahore to address common concerns and coordinate their missionary activities, discussing issues such as proselytism, the provision of social services, and relations with the British colonial administration. Encouraged by British officials in Punjab, the missionaries saw the region as a frontier where proselytism and the provision of social services could transform society.[25]

Christian missionaries arrived with strategies and practices honed by earlier efforts in India. Prior engagements with Hinduism focused Christian criticism on polytheism and social practices such as ritual exclusiveness and sati (self-immolation of widows on the funeral pyre of deceased husbands).[26] Christians drew on understandings of Muslims rooted in the era of the Crusades and noted that the Muslim prophet had died but that Jesus resided in heaven and would return. Karl Gottlieb Pfander, a missionary with the Church Missionary Society at Agra south of Delhi, for example, distributed Bibles translated into Arabic and Persian, wrote apologetic works in Arabic, and engaged in public debates with Muslims, including the widely attended affair with the South Asian Muslim Rahamatullah Kairanawi in 1854.[27] These aggressive activities received critical commentary from Sayyid Ahmad Khan, the nineteenth-century Muslim scholar who blamed the 1857 revolt in part on the "new forms of preaching" and "controversial religious books" making comparisons "in a most offensive manner."[28] Missionaries in Punjab followed Pfander's lead: Elwood M. Wherry, an American Presbyterian posted at Ludhiana and serving for four decades, earned a reputation as a forceful opponent of Islam, and the Church Missionary Society at Amritsar organized a fifteen-day debate in 1893 involving Ghulam Ahmad and Abdullah Athim, a Muslim convert to Christianity.[29]

The provision of education, assistance to orphans, and other social services was an important aspect of Christian missionary activity in colonial Punjab.

The British colonial administration in Punjab relied on Christian missionary schools to a greater extent than in other regions of British India, and most missions accepted financial support and agreed to meet colonial standards in the provision of an Anglo-vernacular education.[30] The medium of instruction long had sparked debate among missionaries, with the pioneering Baptist missionary William Carey favoring South Asian languages and the Church of Scotland missionary Alexander Duff stressing English. This difference paralleled debates in British administrative circles, and British officials ultimately settled on English as the primary language of instruction in 1835. Christian missions remained ambivalent on the language question for decades, given the view that conversions occurred more frequently if missions adopted South Asian languages, but they ultimately followed colonial policy.[31] In Punjab the American Presbyterians, despite reservations, accepted British educational grant-in-aids for their schools, and others followed: Christian missionaries ran thirty of thirty-one government-aided secondary schools in Punjab by the 1880s.[32] While many Punjabi residents sent their children to mission schools, controversies arose when students converted to Christianity.

Christianity expanded at a slow pace in Punjab until the last decades of the nineteenth century. Most missionary societies placed significance on baptism as the event marking conversion; the American Presbyterians believed, for example, that conversion was the work of the Holy Spirit and that baptism should wait until after that moment.[33] Accepting Christianity meant severing ties with one's family and kin, if they were not Christians, and participating in new rituals and activities. In the early decades conversions occurred in towns where mission schools attracted diverse social groups: these new Christians became public figures making a case for conversion as a matter of personal conscience.[34] Christianity remained an urban religion in Punjab until landless groups in rural areas of the central *doabs* became Christians in the late nineteenth century. Small groups of pioneering converts organized others, and it became a mass movement in the 1880s among social groups now known as Dalits. Interpreting teachings about the Day of Judgment as their vindication for centuries of oppression, these new Christians integrated their own ideas about ritual practices and beliefs into the communities they formed. At the turn of the nineteenth century the Punjabi Christian community had become associated with the rural poor.[35]

Christian proselytism altered the religious landscape in nineteenth-century Punjab. Interpreting the changes in terms of a marketplace, the Christian missionaries brought new products, such as Christian rituals and beliefs, and services, such as Anglo-vernacular education, and pushed an understanding of conversion as a matter of personal conscience and individual choice. They developed marketing strategies to promote these products and services through the lithographic press and to disseminate them in a religious network of chapels, schools, and orphanages. Christian missionaries proved adept at sensing changes in market demand: they initially targeted urban contexts but then switched to cater to rural consumers in the 1880s as the landless embraced their products and services. Christian missionaries, of course, were not crudely marketing themselves; religious commitment was the primary concern of both missionaries and converts. The market perspective merely illuminates how Christian missionaries introduced novel features to a pluralistic religious context. In urban areas these practices were adopted by new Hindu and Sikh religious reform movements forming in the late nineteenth century.

Hindu and Sikh Reform Movements

Several Hindu and Sikh reform movements arose in late nineteenth-century Punjab. The first was the Brahmo Samaj, "Society for the Transcendent Deity," opened in Lahore in 1863. It was a branch of the broader movement inspired by the early nineteenth-century South Asian intellectual Rammohun Roy and shaped by Debendranath Tagore and his son, Hemendranath Tagore. Roy's Hindu unitarianism was articulated in *The Precepts of Jesus*, a book that accepted Jesus' moral vision but not his status as a deity, and Debendranath Tagore centered the movement on the interpretation of the Vedas free from Brahman influences, with his son adding a guide illuminating the Brahmo Samaj path of individual spirituality shorn of many Hindu rituals and including social reformism, such as the rejection of purity restrictions. The Brahmo Samaj branch in Lahore purchased a lithographic press, the first in Punjab not operated by either Christian missionaries or the colonial government, and propagated a reformist Hindu message. The Brahmo Samaj did not recruit many Punjabi residents, but it was an influential example of a South Asian movement adopting Christian missionary techniques.[36]

The Arya Samaj, or "Noble Society," gained a much larger following in Punjab.[37] The founder of this movement was Dayananda Saraswati, a member of a Gujarati Brahman family who left his family, lived as an ascetic, and studied with others before building his own network of Vedic schools in the 1860s. Dayananda's interaction with the Brahmo Samaj, after his schools collapsed, convinced him to alter his approach, and he published *The Light of Truth*,[38] articulating a reformed Hinduism as a monism based on the Vedas and cleansed of customs, such as sati, ritual restrictions, pilgrimages, and other popular rituals. Dayananda founded the first Arya Samaj in Bombay in 1875, and in 1877 Punjab's new elite opened a branch in Lahore during Dayananda's visit. The Lahore branch defined ten principles that others accepted as a universal Arya Samaj creed. It also founded the Dayananda Anglo-Vedic Trust and Management Society in 1886 to open and run the Anglo-Vedic College in Lahore. This effort divided the Arya Samaj, however, between those promoting Sanskrit and those who wanted an English-language institution free from non-Hindu influences. After Dayananda's death in 1883 the disagreement split the movement between a small group running the English-language institution and a majority emphasizing Dayananda as an enlightened prophet whose writings provided an infallible guide to reformed Hinduism.

The religious wing of the Arya Samaj engaged in a campaign to convert others in Punjab. Led by Guru Datta, and then Lala Munshi Ram and Lekh Ram after Datta's death in 1890, these leaders appropriated and modified aspects of Christian missionary practices. They divided Punjab into circuits where they sent members to convert new followers into the movement. The initial emphasis was on individual conversions, but the Arya Samaj eventually concentrated on group conversion rituals known as *shuddhi* for those who wished to return to Hinduism from other religious communities. The activities of the Arya Samaj increased tensions with Muslims, particularly as Lekh Ram had been educated by Muslim scholars in his youth and used this knowledge to make negative comparisons between Islam and Arya Samaj in public debates and more than two dozen books. Ghulam Ahmad would become one of Lekh Ram's many opponents in the late nineteenth century.

In the Sikh tradition several reform movements emerged in the late nineteenth century.[39] One was the Singh Sabha organized in 1875 at Amritsar, home to the Great Temple. Its members sought to defend Sikhism from the perceived assaults it weathered under British rule and was a broad coalition representing a diversity of Sikh practices. In 1879 another group formed in Lahore among members of the new elite committed to reforming Sikh practices along the lines of *khalsa* discipline: calling themselves the Tat Khalsa, or "True Khalsa," these reformers stressed a homogeneous Sikhism. These two groups engaged in a vigorous contestation in the late nineteenth century. The Amritsar movement reflected the consensus that had emerged in the early nineteenth century, but the circumstances of the late nineteenth century favored the Lahore group: rigid colonial categorizations encouraged clear definitions of religious identity, and the Tat Khalsa effectively used the printing press to produce an extensive literature that appealed to those attending English-language schools. The Tat Khalsa's religious practices, including a specific physical presentation in addition to ritual activities, ultimately came to define Sikhism in the twentieth century.

Sikh and Hindu reform movements emerged in the competitive religious context of late nineteenth-century Punjab. They initially recruited among the new elite in towns, and over time internal issues divided them. The Tat Khalsa mastered the strategies of the Christian missionaries more effectively than the Singh Sabha based in Amritsar and captured Sikh market share through a media campaign backed by an effective organization. The religious faction dominating the Arya Samaj similarly adopted Christian strategies to disseminate the writings of its founder and to develop a conversion ritual to attract rural consumers. The religious marketplace metaphor has limits, but it underscores how some Hindu and Sikh reformers were successful in building new religious movements in Punjab.

Muslims in the Religious Marketplace

Muslim reform movements first emerged in the Ganga plains to the east of Punjab. This region, the former Mughal imperial heartland, experienced British rule and Christian missionary activity much earlier than in Punjab. The 1857 revolt also shaped the experiences of these Muslims more profoundly than those in Punjab, who did not participate in it. Muslim reformers in the Ganga plains promoted standardized Muslim practices and the removal of custom, but they disagreed on other issues in heated debates.[40] Some Muslim reformers gained supporters in Punjab, but Sufi *pirs* and *sajjada nishin* still held sway, especially in rural areas. The authority of these Sufi figures was enhanced by British efforts to incorporate them at the lowest ranks of the colonial administrative apparatus.[41] The Ahmadiyya emerged in a context in which Sufism dominated the Muslim sphere, reform movements were gaining followers among Hindus and Sikhs, and Christian missionaries were influential. This section reviews the Muslim reform movements in the Ganga plains before turning to the Ahmadiyya.

Muslim Reformism

Sayyid Ahmad Khan was the most prominent Muslim reformer of nineteenth-century British India. Son of a noble Mughal family, Sayyid Ahmad Khan served as a Muslim judge for the British East India Company and acted to protect British officials during the 1857 revolt. Sayyid Ahmad Khan condemned the aggressive preaching style of Christian missionaries, and he encouraged Muslims to learn English, translate English works into Urdu, and embrace science education. The 1875 founding of the Anglo-Oriental College at Aligarh was an expression of these values: it was organized on the English public school model and received partial colonial financial support. Similar schools followed, and the effort gained an informal name, the Aligarh movement.[42] Advocates of the Aligarh movement established a society in Lahore, the Anjuman-i-Himyat-i-Islam, and opened a college in 1892. The Aligarh movement attracted support from elite Muslim families in Lahore, and it stressed a standard practice of Islam far removed from the mediatory practices of *pirs* and *sajjada nishin* of Punjab.

Another major Muslim reformist stream emerged in Deoband, a small town in the Ganga plains where some *ulama* had moved from Delhi in the early nineteenth century and opened a madrasa or advanced Islamic school in 1867. Known as the *dar al-ulum* or "house of knowledge," the Deoband madrasa became the model for Islamic schools in an expanding network throughout the Ganga plains in the late nineteenth century. Eschewing colonial financial assistance as well as the teaching of English, Muslim scholars at Deoband accepted subscriptions and donations from supporters to keep their schools free from state support and control. Deobandi *ulama* stressed fidelity to Muslim law and inculcated a sense of individual responsibility among its students. Deobandi *ulama* used the lithographic press to produce Urdu translations of classical Islamic works and original religious works of their own. The donors of the Deoband network of schools tended to be high-status urban Muslims working in the colonial bureaucracy or in commerce. A few early donors were from Punjab, but schools in the Deoband network did not open in Punjab until the early twentieth century.[43]

Other reform movements followed the teachings of the eighteenth-century Muslim scholar Shah Waliullah. The most influential movement in this tradition was the Ahl-i-Hadith, "the People of the Traditions," named because its *ulama* rejected the classical legal tradition studied in the Deobandi schools in favor of Shah Waliullah's advocacy of independent legal opinions based on reading the *ahadith*. The leading figure in this movement was Maulana Sayyid Nazir Husain, a scholar who studied with many prominent South Asian *ulama* before launching his own career as a teacher at Delhi in 1826. The Ahl-i-Hadith was a movement among *ulama*, and Nazir Husain had a small following in the eastern Ganga plains and Punjab. His former student, commonly known as Ustad-I Punjab or "Professor of the Punjab," established a school in western Punjab, and another supporter, Muhammad Husain Batalawi, published an Urdu newspaper at Batala in central Punjab. Members of the Ahl-i-Hadith confronted other Muslims, including *pirs*, whom they accused of inappropriate mediatory activities, and Deobandi scholars, whose legal approach they rejected. Ahl-i-Hadith scholars followed the other Muslim reformist movements in using Urdu print publications to disseminate their views.[44]

These Muslim reform movements did not exert much influence in nineteenth-century Punjab. The Aligarh movement and the Ahl-i-Hadith only had a presence in urban areas and left rural areas to *pirs*, *sajjada nishin*, and advocates of other religious traditions. Defenders of Sufism existed elsewhere in north India: the most influential was led by Sayyid Ahmad Barelwi of Rai Bareilly, a town near Lucknow in northern India, and the Barelwi movement gained supporters in reaction to the attacks on Sufism.[45] Despite this defense, rural Muslims were aware of the reformist criticism of Sufi eclecticism, and many were attracted to English-language education and standard norms for Muslim practice. The rural religious marketplace was open to a Muslim reformer bringing new strategies and organizational forms while retaining elements of mediatory religious expressions. The Ahmadiyya entered that market niche in Punjab.

Ghulam Ahmad and the Ahmadiyya

The Ahmadiyya has its genesis in the preaching of Ghulam Ahmad of Qadian, a village seventy miles north of Lahore in rural Gurdaspur district. The Ahmadiyya offered a distinctive path among Muslim reformist movements in British India: it sought engagement with the colonial milieu and removal of custom from Muslim practice through individual responsibility, but it also stressed Ghulam Ahmad's role as the recipient of divine guidance as the Mahdi and Messiah. Sufi influences are apparent in Ghulam Ahmad's writings and the ways he inaugurated the Ahmadiyya through oaths in face-to-face interactions with his followers. Ghulam Ahmad was not a Sufi, however, and he preached against the superstitious beliefs associated with *pirs* and *sajjada nishin*, demanding that his followers foreswear allegiance to them, accept individual responsibility, and improve their lives through education. Ghulam Ahmad offered a unique combination of mysticism and reformism, mediatory revelations and self-improvement. His followers included both rural and urban residents, members of landed families and the poor.[46] Ghulam Ahmad led a complex religious movement in a competitive religious marketplace.

Ghulam Ahmad's was born around 1835 to a noble Muslim family in Qadian. He held the title of *mirza*, or "prince," owing to the stature of his Central Asian ancestors who arrived at the inception of the Mughal Empire: his family received rights to collect revenues from numerous plots in Gurdaspur. With the eighteenth-century Mughal collapse and the rise of Khalsa Sikh polities, they lost their holdings and left Qadian, only to return after Ghulam Ahmad's father, Murtada Ahmad, joined Ranjit Singh's army and reclaimed a portion of the former rights to collect revenues. Ghulam Ahmad was the younger of two sons surviving into adulthood, and he received an Islamic education through tutorial sessions at home and at the residences of several Muslim scholars. Religious issues attracted Ghulam Ahmad, but his father demanded that he serve as a reader in a law court in the town of Sialkot. Ghulam Ahmad encountered Christians, including a Scottish missionary and a South Asian convert heading a mission school, before returning to Qadian in 1868. After his father's death, Ghulam Ahmad devoted himself primarily to a religious career in Qadian.[47]

Advocacy for Islam and following the Quran was at the heart of Ghulam Ahmad's religious mission. At first he published letters and short tracts in several Urdu newspapers asserting the Quran's superiority over other scriptures. He later wrote a major treatise, *Proofs of the Ahmadiyya*,[48] a multivolume work published in the early 1880s that presented Islam's principles and dismissed critics, such as Christian missionaries, the Arya Samaj, and others. *Proofs of the Ahmadiyya* received a positive reception from Muslims, but others attacked it, including Christians and members of the Arya Samaj, such as Lekh Ram, who wrote an inflammatory rebuttal that deeply offended Muslims. Ghulam Ahmad also participated in public debates, adopting a vigorous style that was notable, even in the competitive religious context of Punjab: Ghulam Ahmad occasionally invoked *mobahala*, a predebate challenge acknowledging God's disapproval of liars that opened participants to humiliation or even death. Heated controversies arose over disputed fulfillment of *mobahala*, and British officials halted these practices in the late 1890s. Thereafter Ghulam Ahmad turned his attentions to John Dowie, a Scottish-born evangelist who claimed to be the returned Elijah and founded a utopian community named Zion north of Chicago in the United States. Dowie eventually was exposed as a fraud and died shortly after engaging Ghulam Ahmad. Throughout this period of debates and confrontations, Ghulam Ahmad continued to write, authoring more than eighty books in Arabic, Persian, and Urdu.

Propelling Ghulam Ahmad forward was a growing sense that he was receiving guidance from God. Muslims accept a long line of divine revelation beginning with Jewish prophets and culminating in the Prophet Muhammad. The Quran refers to Muhammad as the *khatam an-nabiyyin*, or "seal of the prophets," and the widespread Muslim scholarly interpretation is that revelation ended with him. Some Muslim scholars disagreed—notably, Ibn Arabi in the eleventh century, who argued that divine prophesy continued until the end of time, even though scriptural or "legislative" revelation ended in the Quran. Ibn Arabi's interpretation influenced subsequent Muslims who believed that visions and dreams were forms of revelation open to the spiritually inclined, such as Sufi *pirs*. Ghulam Ahmad drew on these understandings, claiming to be not a Sufi guide but the Mahdi and the Messiah. These communications occurred over Ghulam Ahmad's lifetime, and in 1902 he claimed to be a prophet in the reflection of Muhammad but not in his capacity as a recipient of scripture. Ghulam Ahmad noted that 1,400 years separated the lawgiving Moses and the appearance of Jesus, whose teachings ended prophesy in the Jewish line, and 1,400 years also was the span between the lawgiving Muhammad and Ghulam Ahmad's lifetime.[49]

Ghulam Ahmad reportedly received his first divine revelation when he was in his early thirties, and they increased in frequency and intensity over the years.[50] The Prophet Muhammad sometimes appeared to him, an experience Sufi *pirs* seek to attain. An early encounter involved a text written by Ghulam Ahmad that became "beautiful fruit" in Muhammad's hands, a transformation interpreted as foretelling the success of *Proofs of the Ahmadiyya*.[51] Another encounter occurred in 1881, when Muhammad appeared to Ghulam Ahmad in his sleep, embraced him, and told him, "Oh, Ahmad, God has blessed thee. . . . Tell the people you have been called to a Divine Mission and that you are yourself the first to believe in that mission."[52] In 1883 Ghulam Ahmad proclaimed that this revelation meant that he was the *mujaddid*, the reformer whom some Muslims believe appears every hundred years to revive Islam. Revelations kept coming, including communications in the form of verses from the Quran, the renewed revelation of which Ghulam Ahmad interpreted to underscore their relevance to the contemporary era: the continued receipt of verses from the Quran led him to form the Ahmadiyya in 1889.[53] Clarifying his role in the movement was God's direct statement to Ghulam Ahmad in 1891: "The Messiah, son of Mary, Prophet of God is dead. It is thou who has appeared in his spirit, according to the promise. And the promise of God is ever fulfilled."[54] With this revelation Ghulam Ahmad came to understand the communications as guidance offered by God to him in his role as the Messiah. These divine revelations continued unabated throughout Ghulam Ahmad's later years.

The assertion that Jesus died challenged both Christian and Muslim teachings. In Christianity Jesus is the son of God who was crucified, died, and was resurrected by God to heaven; Christian missionaries have contrasted the living Jesus and his expected return with the death of the Prophet Muhammad to assert the superiority of Christianity over Islam. For Muslims Jesus is a prophet who was not crucified but taken alive by God to heaven; popular beliefs associated Jesus' return with the End Times as the Day of Judgment approaches. Ghulam Ahmad, moved by the 1891 revelation, engaged in close analysis of the Quran as well as accounts of Jewish travelers in India to argue that Jesus survived the crucifixion, embarked on a religious mission to Central Asia, and died in India, where he was buried in the Kashmiri town of Srinagar (see figure 10). He was not alone in discussing traditions of the Central Asian travels of Jesus: the late nineteenth-century Russian journalist Nicholas Notovich independently wrote a book based on these accounts, which was published in English as *The Unknown Life of Christ* in 1890. Ghulam Ahmad's revelation about his spiritual role as the Messiah led him to assert through theological and historical argumentation that Jesus had died, and in the process he received criticisms from both Christians and Muslims.

Ghulam Ahmad invoked other Islamic eschatological figures, such as the Mahdi, whom many Muslims believe will precede the arrival of the returned Jesus. The Quran provides ample discussion of the End Times with specific references to an apocalypse, the resurrection of humans for a Day of Judgment, and the pleasures of paradise and tortures of hell.[55] Some *ahadith* mention the Mahdi, or "Guided One," whose appearance prepares the way for the return of the Messiah. A popular view is that the Mahdi, arriving at a time of moral degradation and strife, would reestablish a just and unified Muslim community through warfare against unbelievers, a belief that influenced several militant, anti-colonial movements in various late nineteenth-century contexts.[56] Ghulam Ahmad claimed to serve in the role of the Mahdi but combined it with his role as the Messiah and insisted that it coincided with a peaceful era. He cited *ahadith* from classical scholars, such al-Bukhari's report that "the Mahdi is none other than the Messiah,"[57] and others who stated that the Messiah's arrival led to the cessation of wars.[58] Ghulam Ahmad reinforced the eschatological dimensions of his religious role by serving as both the Mahdi and the Messiah: he prophesized that the late nineteenth century was the dawn of a new religious era during which true believers would join the Muslim community under his leadership.

This eschatological emphasis on a peaceful era not only challenged conventional understandings of a violent Mahdi but led Ghulam Ahmad to interpret the Islamic concept of jihad as nonviolent efforts to advance Islam. Muslims understand jihad to refer to activities ranging from nonviolent religious advocacy to defensive warfare against unbelievers. The diversity of textual references to jihad in the Quran led classical Muslim scholars to invoke the concept of *naskh*, or "abrogation," of earlier passages by later revelations to resolve what appeared to be contradictory statements.[59] Classical Muslim scholars reached consensus by invoking *naskh* to place less emphasis on the peaceful activities associated with jihad early in Muhammad's prophetic career and to stress forceful retaliation against enemies when Muhammad defeated his opponents at Mecca from a base in Medina as the enduring scriptural recommendation. Ghulam Ahmad argued that the Quran was a complete revelation without contradiction; noting that the Quran's lone reference to *naskh* pertained only to revelations in the Jewish line, Ghulam Ahmad refused to use *naskh* in his analysis of jihad.[60] He reversed the interpretations of classical Muslim scholars by insisting that warfare was exceptional, confined to Muhammad's defensive campaigns, and by accepting the verses regarding peaceful practices in Mecca as the enduring recommendation. Ghulam Ahmad joined several nineteenth-century South Asian Muslim scholars in refusing to endorse Muslim military action against the British colonial presence, but he alone tied it to a reinterpretation of the classical tradition.[61] For Ghulam Ahmad his appearance as the Messiah meant the dawning of a new religious era in which only the nonviolent dimensions of jihad were appropriate.[62]

Ghulam Ahmad's claims about his status as the Messiah, the death of Jesus, and jihad constituted a break from widely held Muslim interpretations and brought sharp criticisms. Muhammad Husain, a member of the Ahl-i-Hadith in Batala who had published extracts of *Proofs of the Ahmadiyya* in his newspaper, became a bitter opponent of Ghulam Ahmad in the 1890s. Ghulam Ahmad also engaged with the *ulama* in the Ganga plains, traveling to Delhi and debating Muhammad Bashir, a Muslim scholar from Bhopal, on the death of Jesus. In these encounters Ghulam Ahmad remained resolute in his views, and then, in 1902, he added his claim of prophetic status. This proclamation offended many Muslims, some of whom made unsavory allegations about Ghulam Ahmad's mental state and motivations. Similar allegations also were made by Christians and members of the Arya Samaj.

Some viewed Ghulam Ahmad as an honorable opponent. Dr. Hervey D. Griswold, an American Presbyterian teacher posted to a missionary college in Lahore and known for his forceful defense of Christianity from Muslim polemics, met Ghulam Ahmad and read his works. Griswold was not convinced by his arguments, but he concluded that Ghulam Ahmad was neither a charlatan nor insane but someone who honestly convinced himself that he was receiving divine revelation: "So far as I am able to judge, his writings have a ring of sincerity. His persistence in affirming his claims in the face of the most intense and bitter opposition is magnificent. He is willing to *suffer* on behalf of his claims."[63] It is notable that a competitor in the Punjabi religious marketplace respected Ghulam Ahmad as a sincere advocate of his ideas. Ghulam Ahmad's followers most certainly did, as they swore allegiance to him and joined the Ahmadiyya in the late nineteenth century.

The Ahmadiyya

Ghulam Ahmad launched the Ahmadiyya in 1889 at Ludhiana, a large town about a hundred miles south of Qadian where the American Presbyterians had founded the first Christian mission in the region in 1834. There he accepted the oaths of a hundred or so followers, including the Muslim scholar Nur ud-Din, an Arab who had moved to Central Asia, studied with prominent South Asian *ulama*, and established himself in Kashmir before moving to Qadian and becoming one of Ghulam Ahmad's most devoted followers. The Ahmadiyya drew followers from the central *doabs* of Punjab in the years that followed, and Ghulam Ahmad, facing increasing opposition from other Muslims, published a formal public statement (*ishtihar*) announcing the Ahmadiyya as a new movement (a sect, in British colonial terms) within Islam in 1900.[64] Its membership grew slowly at first, but it gained the support of over a thousand followers by the time of Ghulam Ahmad's death in 1908. The Ahmadiyya expanded thereafter to nearly twenty thousand in 1911 and to nearly thirty thousand in 1921.[65] Changes occurred as the movement grew, but Ghulam Ahmad's writings remained central to the Ahmadiyya.

The oath of allegiance (*bayat*) to Ghulam Ahmad was the first step in joining the Ahmadiyya. At the initial public acceptance of oaths, Ghulam Ahmad demanded that followers pledge to fulfill ten conditions, including diligent performance of Muslim rituals such as performing *salat* five times a day and relying on the Quran and *ahadith* as guiding religious principles. The tenth condition was a statement of allegiance to Ghulam Ahmad; it required the oath taker to "establish a brotherhood with me (Ahmad) on condition of obeying me in everything good, and maintain it to the day of his death; and this relationship shall be of such a high order that its example shall not be found in any worldly relationship either of blood relations or of servant and master."⁶⁶ The *bayat* was not equivalent to Christian baptism, but it was a public affirmation of individual commitment that would stand as the inflection point for a transformed religious life. The *bayat* was, in the words of Ghulam Ahmad's biographer, "a most solemn covenant with God through the leader."⁶⁷ The emphasis on obeying Ghulam Ahmad and the personal nature of the bond was reminiscent of the kind of spiritual relationship that a Sufi *pir* established with each disciple, but in the Ahmadiyya case the focus was not on the ritual activities associated with Sufism but on the reformed individual life of a Muslim who was committing to serve Ghulam Ahmad. In 1891 when Ghulam Ahmad announced the revelation that he was the Messiah, this *bayat* became a direct, personal tie to a religious leader on a mission from God.

Qadian was the center of the Ahmadiyya movement. In December 1891, shortly after Ghulam Ahmad publicly announced his status as the Messiah, he convened his followers at Qadian for reflection and fellowship, and this meeting became an annual event, known as the *jalsa salana*, or "annual convention." Qadian had fewer than a thousand residents in the late nineteenth century, and this meeting would increase its residents in December; Ghulam Ahmad eventually expanded the mosque to accommodate those attending the *jalsa salana* as well as the increasing flow of visitors coming at other times of the year.⁶⁸ Qadian had a Muslim school teaching Arabic, Persian, and Islamic topics, and Ghulam Ahmad opened an English-language middle school in the late nineteenth century.⁶⁹ Qadian also became an active publishing center after the acquisition of a printing press. The Ahmadiyya launched a weekly Urdu newspaper, *al-Hakam*, in 1897, and it followed in 1902 with two other periodicals: *al-Badr*, an irregularly published Urdu paper, and the *Review of Religions*, a monthly journal in both English and Urdu.⁷⁰ Ghulam Ahmad headed a religious organization that provided education and an active new media presence as well as fellowship to those who had accepted *bayat*. He traveled to debate, seek medical attention, and conduct other business in towns, but otherwise Qadian remained Ghulam Ahmad's residence for the rest of his life.

The Ahmadiyya attracted most of its support from rural areas near Qadian, but some followers resided in Lahore, Amritsar, Sialkot, and other towns in central Punjab. In these contexts the Ahmadiyya competed directly with Christian missions, the Arya Samaj, and other South Asian religious movements. The editing of Ahmadiyya publications depended on urban followers, some of whom relocated to Qadian in the 1890s. *Al-Hakam*, for example, was edited by a follower who had experience working at a newspaper published at Amritsar, and *al-Badr* similarly was edited by two former residents of Amritsar. The *Review of Religions* initially was coedited by two members of the new elite, the lawyer Khwaja Kamal ud-Din and Muhammad Ali, who had a master's degree in English. *Review of Religions*, with its English language articles and well-educated editors, made the case for a modern Muslim movement in colonial India and other Anglophone contexts as it began to circulate more widely in the British imperial sphere. The Ahmadiyya, with its emphasis on education and new media, appealed to the new elite as well as its rural constituency.

Diverse groups joined the Ahmadiyya in its early years. Kenneth W. Jones described it as a bipolar movement attracting "middle-class, literate Muslims" in towns and "members from the less educated, poorer rural classes."[71] But Spencer Lavan noted that the British colonial *Gazeteer* for Gurdaspur district stated in 1891 that Ghulam Ahmad "had a special mission to the sweepers, who flocked to him in crowds."[72] "Sweepers" was a reference to landless farmworkers and village residents, referenced in some circles at the time as "untouchables." This statement prompted a sharp rebuttal from Ghulam Ahmad, who denied the allegation, and Lavan took from this response, combined with an analysis of the published list of initial Ahmadi members, that the Ahmadiyya concentrated on attracting the rural middle class.[73] Nonetheless Ghulam Ahmad frequently made positive references to the poor, and he was a *mirza* living in Gurdaspur, where his family had elevated status: the Ahmadiyya likely attracted followers from landless residents in Qadian and other villages. Avril Ann Powell observed that the Ahmadiyya offered social mobility and attracted a segment of the poor who, within two generations, joined the ranks of a "highly-educated, ambitious community."[74] Ghulam Ahmad's followers were diverse, including rural and urban middle classes and rural poor, with all groups valuing educational achievement and the inspired leadership of the Messiah.

Ghulam Ahmad received revelations about his approaching death and wrote *al-wasiyah*, or *The Will*, in 1905, and added an addendum in 1906. *The Will* called for an *anjuman*, or council, to provide for a cemetery in Qadian where Ghulam Ahmad would be buried. It also named Nur ud-Din, Ghulam Ahmad's trusted companion, to head the council. The cemetery was to be open to "true and sincere" Muslims who provided funds to be used by the *anjuman* "for the propagation of Islam and the Unity of God."[75] Those wishing burial were asked to bequeath at least a tenth of their estate to the *anjuman*, although pious Muslims without property could be buried without such a contribution. The Sadr Anjuman-i-Ahmadiyya, or Supreme Council of the Ahmadiyya, was founded in 1906 with Nur ud-Din at its head and Muhammad Ali, one of the *Review of Religions* editors, as its secretary. *The Will* also announced the revelation that divine guidance would be provided to a descendant of Ghulam Ahmad. No specific descendant was mentioned, but Ghulam Ahmad's eldest surviving son, Bashir ud-Din Mahmud Ahmad, who was in his midteens at the time, came to the mind of many followers.

Ahmadiyya Succession and the Split of 1914

Ghulam Ahmad died on May 26, 1908. His will provided for the future, but it did not specify a successor, mentioning both Nur ud-Din, his trusted companion, and his son, Bashir ud-Din Mahmud Ahmad. Ahmadi elders consulted and chose Nur ud-Din to become the first *khalifatul masih*. Nur ud-Din was nearly the same age as Ghulam Ahmad, had attended the initial oath taking at Ludhiana in 1889 and headed the Sadr Anjuman, as *The Will* proscribed. Khalifatul Masih Nur ud-Din commanded the loyalties of Ahmadiyya followers, and his leadership helped the movement endure a critical transition, but he did not resolve conflicting views of the nature of leadership in the Ahmadiyya. One perspective stressed divine guidance and the position of the *khalifatul masih*; this view was championed by Ghulam Ahmad's son, Bashir ud-Din Mahmud Ahmad. Another emphasized the leadership of the Sadr Anjuman; this view was advocated by Ahmadi Muslims in Lahore, including Muhammad Ali and Kamal ud-Din, initial editors of *Review of Religions*. These differences proved irreconcilable, and tensions increased in the years following Ghulam Ahmad's death.[76]

The breach opened with Khalifatul Masih Nur ud-Din's death in 1914. Muhammad Ali proposed waiting to name a successor until after agreement was reached on the division of authority between the Sadr Anjuman and the *khalifatul masih*, but the majority present at Qadian did not want to delay and selected Bashir ud-Din Mahmud Ahmad as second successor. At a public oath-taking ceremony at Qadian, fifty followers refused to pledge allegiance to Khalifatul Masih Bashir ud-Din Mahmud Ahmad, whereas the remaining group, perhaps fifteen hundred strong, took the oath.[77] The split reflected different perspectives on the meaning of Ghulam Ahmad's last wishes and the role of the Sadr Anjuman. Muhammad Ali wanted to consolidate the power of the council and limit the influence of the second successor, but others did not agree, given that a *khalifatul masih* had been named once and the council's authority was unclear.

The split expressed other differences. One was the issue of prophecy. Muhammad Ali and Kamal ud-Din placed less emphasis on Ghulam Ahmad's prophetic role after the split. Yohanan Friedmann argued that these two accepted Ghulam Ahmad's prophetic claims before 1914, but one wonders whether Bashir ud-Din Mahmud Ahmad, attentive to his father's legacy, detected hints of their evolving position.[78] Spencer Lavan added that a personality conflict fostered animosity between Mahmud Ahmad, a young man in his midtwenties with only a secondary school education, and Kamal ud-Din and Muhammad Ali, both of whom were in their forties and "thinkers, reformers, writers and leaders in their own right."[79] Reinforcing these personal differences was the chasm between the rural ethos of Qadian, where Mahmud Ahmad resided, and worldly Lahore, where those who broke primarily resided. Whatever the causes of the split, Muhammad

Ali and Kamal ud-Din left and founded the Ahmadiyya Anjuman Isha'at Islam in Lahore. They promoted the ideas of Ghulam Ahmad and sought reconciliation with other Muslims. The main Ahmadiyya stream stressed the receipt of divine guidance by Ghulam Ahmad and his successors.

The leadership dispute mirrored differences in Ahmadiyya constituencies. Spencer Lavan argued that the Ahmadiyya split divided two groups, one based in Lahore and desirous of "a new Islamic outlook," and another based in smaller towns and Punjabi rural areas, composed of members of the landed elite and merchants who were willing to accept "the authoritarian leadership and charismatic programme of a Promised Messiah."[80] Avril Ann Powell perceptively added another rural constituency, aspirational poorer members who hoped for social mobility.[81] This group likely had been involved in Sufism, and the presence of those engaging in those activities is evident in the *bayat*'s first condition, an affirmation to "abstain from *shirk* (idolatry):" Ghulam Ahmad was demanding that his followers stop those esoteric practices.[82] Past association with *pirs* and *sajjada nishin*, however, meant that these rural followers could accept spiritual leadership from someone claiming to receive divine guidance as the Mahdi and Messiah. In 1914 they joined the majority in accepting Ghulam Ahmad's son as a successor who would continue to receive prophesies.

Consolidation under Khalifatul Masih Bashir ud-Din Mahmud Ahmad

Bashir ud-Din Mahmud Ahmad was twenty-five years old when he was appointed the second *khalifatul masih*, and he served for fifty-one years until his death in 1965. This long tenure allowed him to put the movement on a firm organizational basis: initial steps were taken immediately after the split, and others were implemented over the decades.[83] He also provided a direct link to his father, Ghulam Ahmad: Mahmud Ahmad routinized charisma in the position of *khalifatul masih*. All subsequent successors have been Ghulam Ahmad's direct descendants who claimed to receive divine guidance through visions and dreams. In his personal ties to Ghulam Ahmad and in his actions, Mahmud Ahmad ensured that the Ahmadiyya branch based in Qadian survived the division of 1914 and moved in new directions.

Consolidation of Bashir ud-Din Mahmud Ahmad's position followed quickly after his appointment. Less than a month after the oath swearing, some two hundred delegates passed a resolution affirming Mahmud Ahmad as successor and stating that his "orders . . . shall be final and conclusive" for all committees of the Ahmadiyya, including the Sadr Anjuman.[84] The statement unambiguously clarified Mahmud Ahmad's authority as the *khalifatul masih* in relation to the

Sadr Anjuman. In the decade that followed Mahmud Ahmad oversaw the Sadr Anjuman's reconstitution and the addition of other bodies: he created an administrative apparatus directed by the *khalifatul masih* and appointed lieutenants reporting to him. The Sadr Anjuman included heads responsible for the treasury, community discipline, education, missionary work, publications, hospitality, and affairs with the British colonial administration, and it was run by a senior secretary who served as its president and consulted closely with Mahmud Ahmad. A new body known as the Advisory Council was added, too, with more than five hundred elected and appointed delegates who reviewed and approved of the activities of the Sadr Anjuman; their decisions were advisory, with the *khalifatul masih* making the final decision.[85] These measures broadened participation and added administrative order as well as a clear line of authority from the successor to the subsidiary organs of the Ahmadiyya.

The *bayat* remained central to the Ahmadiyya. In May 1915 a new formulation of the "Conditions of Bayat" appeared to reiterate the original ten conditions demanded by Ghulam Ahmad and to add new "duties." One duty was to "pray under the leadership of Ahmadi imams only," with the caveat that praying alone was admissible when away from the community. Another was that Ahmadi Muslims should marry within the community and could not attend the funeral services those outside the community.[86] These new duties signaled that the Ahmadiyya was an exclusive religious movement. The severing of ritual and kinship ties was similar to the demands of Christian missions and other reformist religious movements. These changes were the natural outgrowth of the 1900 *ishtihar* announcing the Ahmadiyya as a new movement: thereafter it appeared as a distinct religious category in the British colonial census. The new *bayat* reinforced the religious boundary that Ghulam Ahmad had begun to construct in 1900 by adding clarity to the duties of Ahmadi Muslims.

Qadian remained the center of the Ahmadiyya in British India. The cemetery where Ghulam Ahmad was buried was a site of visitation, and Khalifatul Masih Bashir ud-Din Mahmud Ahmad made Qadian his residence until the partition of India in 1947, when he moved to Rabwah in Pakistan, leaving a few Ahmadi Muslims to guard the cemetery. Qadian served as an Ahmadiyya educational center through the founding of a theological seminary for training Ahmadi missionaries. Publishing also continued at Qadian: Bashir ud-Din Mahmud Ahmad maintained the *Review of Religions* as the primary English-language publication, expanded the Urdu weekly *al-Fazl* into a thrice-weekly publication, and started a new monthly publication in Urdu, *Tashhīdh al-adhlān*, "Sharpening of Minds."[87] Muhammad Ali had begun to translate the Quran into English, and Khalifatul Masih Mahmud Ahmad launched a separate effort to translate the Quran and *ahadith* into both English and Urdu.[88]

The Ahmadiyya established a missionary organization immediately after Bashir ud-Din Mahmud Ahmad's succession. The Anjuman-i-Taraqqi-Islam, "Council for the Propagation of Islam," was founded in 1914 to spread the word of the Ahmadiyya. It had five units. Two were concerned with the provision of education and other services: one focused on religious and secular education for Ahmadi Muslims and the other sought to rehabilitate groups categorized by the British officials as "criminal tribes." These two units obtained British colonial government grants to support their efforts. The other three units were more directly involved in Ahmadi proselytism: one was tasked with training missionaries at a seminary established at Qadian, another was devoted to the publication and distribution of books and other religious materials in English and Indian languages (including a project to translate the Quran into English as well as to develop religious pamphlets for use by missionaries), and the third responded to letters and other inquiries in a sustained correspondence with interested religious seekers. These units worked together, so that missionaries abroad drew on the expertise of the educational wing as they founded Ahmadi schools outside British India.[89]

This Ahmadiyya missionary effort was most successful in British India. Census figures show a 50 percent increase in Ahmadi Muslims in India from 1911 to 1921, and growth continued thereafter at a slower but steady rate.[90] The Anjuman-i-Taraqqi-Islam's success was in part its adoption of strategies from Christian missions, the Arya Samaj, and the Tat Khalsa. It also targeted Anglophone contexts abroad. The first Ahmadi missionaries went to Britain, Ceylon, and Mauritius in the mid-1910s. Then efforts expanded to the Arab world, Indonesia, North America, and West Africa in the 1920s. Ahmadi proselytism abroad followed its own trajectory. When successful, the missionaries created an Ahmadiyya branch headed by a missionary-in-charge who reported to the Anjuman-i-Taraqqi-Islam and ultimately the *khalifatul masih*. Converts served as local leaders in a hierarchical structure with regional leaders, an overall head, and a council advising the missionary-in-charge. They also established Ahmadi institutions such as mission houses and schools.

Khalifatul Masih Bashir ud-Din Mahmud Ahmad led the Ahmadiyya Muslim community as it emerged from a divisive succession dispute. Over the decades the Ahmadiyya developed into a mass organization with an extensive bureaucracy that provided social services to its members. In terms of theology Mahmud Ahmad stressed the distinctive identity of Ahmadi Muslims as a sect within Islam, ever hopeful of bringing others into the movement but often experiencing heated opposition from other Muslims. By the 1940s Ahmadi Muslims had become an aspirational, well-educated community, one that would survive the partition of India as its headquarters moved to Pakistan. The global reach of the Ahmadiyya expanded in the postcolonial era with new initiatives and activities.

Conclusion

Ghulam Ahmad founded the Ahmadiyya in the competitive religious marketplace of late nineteenth-century Punjab. Christian missionaries had engaged in an "ecclesiastical conquest," and reform movements arose in local religious communities. The Ahmadiyya followed a reformist path by offering educational and other social services to its growing membership of urban middle classes, rural landlords, and the poor. And it also offered a distinctive message regarding Ghulam Ahmad's mediatory religious roles as the Mahdi and Messiah. The Ahmadiyya's doctrinal and social complexity did not survive the founder's death, and it split into two movements, primarily along the sociological divide between urban and rural groups. A minority based in Lahore adopted a council and denied continued prophesy in the Ahmadiyya movement. The majority branch, the Ahmadiyya Muslim Community, was based primarily in rural areas and accepted the leadership of Ghulam Ahmad's son as his inspired successor.

Both Ahmadiyya branches aspired to take Ghulam Ahmad's message abroad. Shortly after Ghulam Ahmad died in 1908, the Sadr Anjuman met to discuss the future of the movement. One of its members, Rashid ud-Din, argued for Muslim missionary endeavors. Noting that "English was becoming the lingua franca of the whole world," Rashid ud-Din credited Ghulam Ahmad with spiritual sagacity for having an English-language publication to spread the message globally. He continued: "what was really required was a number of Muhammadan missionaries who should serve as models of the moral and spiritual elevation to which Islam could raise humanity."[91] Thereafter Ahmadi Muslims evangelized the movement informally as they traveled abroad for study or business. Khalifatul Masih Bashir ud-Din Mahmud Ahmad consolidated this effort through the creation of a missionary organization that engaged in activities abroad. This effort took Ahmadi missionaries to London, where they made contact with West African Muslims from Lagos, as the next chapter discusses.

Notes

1. Muhammad Zafrullah Khan, trans., *Tadhkirah: English Rendering of the Divine Revelation, Dreams, and Visions Vouchsafed to Hazrat Mirza Ghulam Ahmad of Qadian, The Promised Messiah and Mahdi, On Whom Be Peace*, rev. ed. (Tilford, UK: Islam International Publications, 2009).
2. Andrea Latham, "The Relativity of Categorizing in the Context of the Ahmadiyya," *Die Welt des Islams* 48 (2008), 372–393.
3. Those emphasizing Sufi aspects of the Ahmadiyya include Friedmann, *Prophesy Continuous*; Khan, *From Sufism to Ahmadiyya*; Lavan, *Ahmadiyyah Movement*, 38, 47–49; Annemarie Schimmel, *Islam in the Indian Subcontinent* (Leiden: Brill, 1980), 212; William Cantwell Smith, "Ahmadiyyah," *Encyclopaedia of Islam*, 2nd ed. (Leiden: Brill, 1960), 301–303.

Those emphasizing reformist aspects of the Ahmadiyya include Kenneth W. Jones, *The New Cambridge History of India: Socio-Religious Reform Movements in British India*, vol. 3, no. 1 (Cambridge: Cambridge University Press, 1989); and Bob van der Linden, *Moral Languages from Colonial Punjab* (New Delhi: Manohar, 2008).

4. Edward Simpson and Kai Kress, "Cosmopolitanism Contested: Anthropology and History in the Western Indian Ocean," in *Struggling with History: Islam and Cosmopolitanism in the Western Indian Ocean*, ed. Edward Simpson and Kai Kresse (London: Hurst and Company, 2007), 26.

5. Punjab's geographical definition changed under different political administrations: under British colonial rule it included lands extending well west of the Sutlej River, including Delhi, but in 1911 Delhi was removed from Punjab when it became the new colonial capital.

6. Romila Thapar, *Early India: From the Origins to AD 1300* (Berkeley: University of California Press, 2002).

7. John Keay, *India: A History*, rev. and expanded ed. (New York: Grove Press, 2010).

8. Kin-based groups were called *jāti* and *birādarī*, the former term associated with the South Asian "caste" system and the latter term derived from *barādar*, the Persian word for "brother." Mapping religious meanings onto these categories would not reflect the social complexities within the various *doabs* of Punjab.

9. Kenneth W. Jones, *Arya Dharma: Hindu Consciousness in Nineteenth-Century Punjab* (Berkeley: University of California Press, 1976), 1–29.

10. David Gilmartin and Bruce B. Lawrence, eds., *Beyond Turk and Hindu: Rethinking Religious Identities in Islamicate South Asia* (Gainesville: University Press of Florida, 2000).

11. David Gilmartin, *Empire and Islam: Punjab and the Making of Pakistan* (Oxford: Oxford University Press, 1989), 40–46.

12. Harjot Oberoi, *The Construction of Religious Boundaries: Culture, Identity, and Diversity in the Sikh Tradition* (Chicago: University of Chicago Press, 1994), 207–257.

13. John C. B. Webster, *The Nirankari Sikhs* (New Delhi: Macmillan, 1979).

14. For rural Punjab's "enchanted universe," see Oberoi, *Construction of Religious Boundaries*, 139–203.

15. Cox, *Imperial Fault Lines*, 21.

16. Jones, *Socio-Religious Reform Movements*, 120.

17. Ibid., 3.

18. Gilmartin, *Empire and Islam*; and Ian Talbot, *Punjab and the Raj, 1849–1947* (Riverdale, MD: Riverdale Company, 1988).

19. For the use of "new elite" to describe this group, see Oberoi, *Construction of Religious Boundaries*, 262.

20. Van der Linden, *Moral Languages*, 84.

21. John C. B. Webster, *The Christian Community and Change in Nineteenth Century North India* (New Delhi: Macmillan, 1976).

22. Emiko Sunaga, "A Study of Urdu Print Culture of South Asia since the Eighteenth Century, *Kyoto Bulletin of Islamic Area Studies* 6 (2013), 138.

23. Farina Mir, *The Social Space of Language: Vernacular Culture in British Colonial Punjab* (Berkeley: University of California Press, 2010), 39–40.

24. Webster, *Christian Community and Change*, 5:14–15.

25. Cox, *Imperial Fault Lines*, 23; John C. B. Webster, *A Social History of Christianity: North-West India since 1800* (Oxford: Oxford University Press, 2007).

26. Geoffrey A. Oddie, *Imagined Hinduism: British Protestant Missionary Constructions of Hinduism* (New Delhi: Sage, 2006); Brian Pennington, *Was Hinduism Invented? Britons,*

Indians, and the Colonial Construction of Religion (Oxford: Oxford University Press, 2005); Webster, *Social History of Christianity*, 48–62, 75–82.

27. Avril Ann Powell, *Muslims and Missionaries in Pre-Mutiny India* (Surrey, UK: Curzon, 1993).

28. For an English translation of Sayyid Ahmad Khan's Urdu text, see Van der Linden, *Moral Languages*, 74.

29. Webster, *Social History of Christianity*, 44–47.

30. Cox, *Imperial Fault Lines*, 190–194; Van der Linden, *Moral Languages*, 76–78; Webster, *Christian Community*, 154, 168.

31. Porter, *Religion versus Empire?*, 106–109.

32. Stanley E. Brush, "Protestants in the Punjab: Religion and Social Change in an Indian Province in the Nineteenth Century," PhD diss., Stanford University, 1971, 251, cited in Van der Linden, *Moral Languages*, 77n32.

33. Webster, *Christian Community*, 54.

34. Webster, *Social History of Christianity*, 118–126.

35. Christopher Harding, *Religious Transformation in South Asia: The Meanings of Conversion in Colonial Punjab* (Oxford: Oxford University Press, 2008); John C. B. Webster, *A History of Dalit Christians in India* (San Francisco: Mellen Research University Press, 1992); Webster, *Social History of Christianity*, 167–182.

36. Jones, *Socio-Religious Reform Movements*, 30–39.

37. For the Arya Samaj, I draw on Jones, *Arya Dharm*.

38. *Satyārth Prakāsh*.

39. Oberoi, *Construction of Religious Boundaries*, 258–377; and Tony Ballantine, "Looking Back, Looking Forward: The Historiography of Sikhism," *New Zealand Journal of Asian Studies* 4, no. 1 (2002), 5–29.

40. Barbara Daly Metcalf, *Islamic Revival in British India: Deoband, 1860–1900* (Princeton, NJ: Princeton University Press, 1982), 63.

41. For Sufis and the British colonial administration, see Gilmartin, *Empire and Islam*.

42. David Lelyveld, *Aligarh's First Generation: Muslim Solidarity in British India* (Princeton, NJ: Princeton University Press, 1978).

43. Metcalf, *Islamic Revival*, 87–260.

44. Ibid., 268–296.

45. Ibid., 296–313.

46. For an insightful analysis of sociology of the early Ahmadiyya community, see Powell, "Duties."

47. For an Ahmadi view of the early years of Ghulam Ahmad's life, see Abdul Rahim Dard, *Life of Ahmad, Founder of the Ahmadiyya Movement* (Tilford, UK: Islam International Publications, 2008).

48. *Barahīn-i-Ahmadīyya*.

49. Friedmann, *Prophesy Continuous*, 133.

50. *Tadhkirah*.

51. Dard, *Life of Ahmad*, 70.

52. Francis Robinson, "Ahmad and the Ahmadiyya," *History Today* 40, no. 6 (1990), 42.

53. For an Ahmadi view of the founding of the Ahmadiyya, see Dard, *Life of Ahmad*, 151–159.

54. Robinson, "Ahmad and the Ahmadiyya," 42.

55. Thomas O'Shaughnessy, *Eschatological Themes in the Quran* (Manila: Ateneo de Manila University, 1986).

56. Hodgkin, "Mahdism, Messianism, and Marxism."

57. Ghulam Ahmad, *British Government and Jihad*, 10, 17; Tayyba Seema Ahmad, *Ghulam Ahmad's Exposition of Jihad* (Tilford, UK: Islam International Publications, 1993), 26.

58. Ghulam Ahmad drew on Ibn Hanbal's *Musnad* and Ibn Maja's *Sunan*. Friedmann, *Prophecy Continuous*, 167–168.

59. John Burton, *The Sources of Islamic Law: Islamic Theories of Abrogation* (Edinburgh: Edinburgh University Press, 1990).

60. T. S. Ahmad, *Ghulam Ahmad's Exposition of Jihad*, 26–28; and Friedmann, *Prophecy Continuous*, 174–175.

61. Ghulam Ahmad, *British Government and Jihad*, 5–7, 10–13, 17. For elaboration of these views, see T. S. Ahmad, *Exposition of Jihad*, 28–33; and Friedmann, *Prophecy Continuous*, 172–180.

62. Ghulam Ahmad, *British Government and Jihad*, 9, 11, 18–20.

63. H. D. Griswold, *Mirza Ghulam Ahmad, the Mehdi Messiah of Qadian* (Ludhiana: 1902), quoted in Howard A. Walter, *The Ahmadiya Movement* (London: Oxford University Press, 1918), 21.

64. Lavan, *Ahmadiyyah Movement*, 93.

65. Powell, "Duties," 129.

66. Dard, *Life of Ahmad*, 153.

67. Ibid., 155.

68. Ibid., 92–93.

69. Lavan, *Ahmadiyyah Movement*, 96.

70. Ibid., 96.

71. Jones, *Socio-Religious Reform Movements*, 119.

72. Lavan, *Ahmadiyyah Movement*, 93.

73. Ibid., 94–95.

74. Powell, "Duties," 134.

75. Ghulam Ahmad, *The Will* (Tilford, UK: Islam International Publications, 2005), 26–27.

76. For the Ahmadiyya split, see Lavan, *Ahmadiyyah Movement*, 98–114; Friedmann, *Prophesy Continuous*, 16–22; and Khan, *From Sufism to Ahmadiyya*, 64–78.

77. Lavan, *Ahmadiyyah*, 111.

78. Friedmann, *Prophesy Continuous*, 16–18.

79. Lavan, *Ahmadiyyah Movement*, 99

80. Ibid., 98–99.

81. Powell, "Duties,"132–134.

82. Dard, *Life of Ahmad*, 152.

83. Khan, *From Sufism to Ahmadiyya*, 78–90.

84. "Islam in England," *RR* 13, no. 4 (April 1914); Friedmann, *Prophesy Continuous*, 22–23; Lavan, *Ahmadiyyah Movement*, 112–113.

85. Lavan, *Ahmadiyya Movement*, 114–117.

86. Ibid., 113–114.

87. Friedmann, *Prophesy Continuous*, 22–23.

88. Lavan, *Ahmadiyyah Movement*, 113.

89. The genesis and consolidation of the Ahmadiyya missionary organization is not developed in the existing literature: I draw here on information obtained from *RR* in the 1910s and 1920s as well as my research on the Ahmadiyya mission in the Gold Coast.

90. Powell, "Duties," 129.

91. "The Propagation of Islam in English-Speaking Countries," *RR* 8, no. 3 (March 1909), 97–105.

4 Ahmadiyya Expansion to London and Lagos

ATLANTIC CONNECTIONS CARRIED the Ahmadiyya to West Africa. The Ahmadiyya Muslim Community founded a mission in London in 1914 to take its message to Britain, and its missionaries came into contact with two Africans, Dusé Mohamed Ali and Muhammad Lawal Basil Agusto. Dusé Mohamed Ali, a pan-Africanist intellectual claiming roots in northeastern Africa, edited the *African Times and Orient Review* from London during the 1910s before moving to the United States and then settling permanently in Lagos, Nigeria; M. L. B. Agusto, an Afro-Brazilian Muslim at Lagos, founded an English-language Muslim school during the 1910s and later studied law in London during the early 1920s. Before Agusto arrived in London, Dusé Mohamed Ali had put West African visitors to London in touch with Ahmadi Muslims: one of Ali's contacts returned to Lagos with Ahmadi publications and gave one to Agusto. Dusé Mohamed Ali never became an Ahmadi Muslim, but Agusto did. He was the first to send in his membership application from Lagos in 1916, but he later broke from the Ahmadiyya to found his own Muslim movement at Lagos during the mid-1920s. Nevertheless, Agusto and Ali had an enduring influence on the Ahmadiyya in West Africa. Dusé Mohamed Ali's pan-Africanist ideas shaped Ahmadi missionary views of Africans, and one of Agusto's fellow Afro-Brazilian Muslims, Amadu Ramanu Pedro, accepted the Ahmadiyya and proselytized the movement in the Gold Coast.

The early history of the Ahmadiyya at Lagos is well-traveled terrain, but the Atlantic connections are not developed. Humphrey Fisher discussed the Ahmadiyya arrival at Lagos in the 1910s and its subsequent fragmentation in the decades that followed.[1] Stephan Reichmuth situated the movement among wider patterns of Muslim religious change in early twentieth-century Lagos.[2] They overlooked the influential roles of Dusé Mohamed Ali and M. L. B. Agusto as well as the activities of the Ahmadiyya Muslim Community mission in London. The historical literature on the Ahmadiyya also neglects the early missionary efforts of the majority branch and focuses instead on the global activities of the Lahori branch.[3] This chapter discusses that early history in London and the Afro-Brazilian connections involved in the expansion to West Africa. It begins with the Ahmadiyya Muslim Community mission in London and discusses the influence of Dusé Mohamed Ali on Ahmadi missionaries. The next section provides background on Lagos and its Muslim communities before discussing the early years of the Ahmadiyya at Lagos, drawing on contemporaneous materials that Fisher did not consult and illuminating a broader range of African initiatives. The final section examines Maulvi Nayyar's visit to Lagos and the fragmentation of the movement after Agusto's return from London, when successive waves of Afro-Brazilian Muslims left to found competing Muslim movements.

Ahmadiyya in London

Ghulam Ahmad never traveled to London, but he had a vision about preaching at the center of the British Empire shortly after announcing the founding of the Ahmadiyya. The vision included white birds on the branches of trees, which Ghulam Ahmad interpreted to mean that, although he might never visit London, his "writings would be published among those people" and that many "would realize the truth."[4] Ahmadi Muslims invoked Ghulam Ahmad's revelation as they began to proselytize in London during the 1910s. Mr. Bird and Mr. Sparrow were among the first British converts, proclaimed the Ahmadiyya monthly *Review of Religions*.[5] The vision of "white birds" and the allusion to Bird and Sparrow underscored the desire of Ahmadi Muslims to take the Ahmadiyya message to the home of Christian missionary societies that had proselytized in Punjab. The focus on converting British Christians continued, but the missionaries' experiences in London contributed to a broadening of the effort in the Atlantic world, especially to West Africa and African diaspora communities in the United States.

Ahmadi Muslims joined other Muslims residing in early twentieth-century Britain.[6] Thousands of immigrant Muslim sailors and other workers from Africa and Asia resided in several port cities. Smaller numbers of Muslim students from British colonies also were present for extended periods, as were Muslim lawyers presenting cases before the Privy Council. Muslim networks emerged, especially among lawyers and other professionals as they sought to advance individual and communal interests in politics, religious affairs, and occupational pursuits.[7] African-diaspora Muslims also had their own networks.[8] Adding to these immigrant Muslims were a small but growing number of British converts to Islam. One prominent British Muslim was Abdullah Quilliam, the son of a British merchant, who became Muslim during a residence in Morocco. Quilliam established a mosque and Muslim society at Liverpool in the late nineteenth century and also toured West Africa as a representative of the Ottoman sultan.[9] The first Ahmadi Muslims arrived in London in the 1910s. One was Muhammad Zafarulllah Khan (1893–1985), who studied at King's College and Lincoln's Inn from 1911 to 1914. He used his vacations to travel in Europe and promote the Ahmadiyya before returning to India to practice law. Another was Khwaja Kamal ud-Din (1870–1932), a lawyer from Lahore who traveled to London to present a case in 1912, stayed two years, and returned for several other visits over the following two decades: he discovered an ability to convince Christians to accept Islam by drawing his knowledge of the Bible gained at Christian mission schools in India. Kamal ud-Din joined with other Indian Muslims to establish the Woking Muslim Trust, which took control of an abandoned mosque built by the Orientalist scholar William Leitner. Kamal ud-Din discovered the mosque at Woking, a small town twenty miles southwest of London, and organized the effort to reclaim it; he used it as a center to publish *Islamic Review*, a monthly periodical promoting a nonsectarian, assimilationist approach to Islam.[10]

Khwaja Kamal ud-Din's initial activities in London occurred as the Ahmadiyya split into two movements. He reported on his activities to the Khalifatul Masih Nur ud-Din, writing to describe the Woking mosque and his efforts to reopen it.[11] But Kamal ud-Din's involvement with non-Ahmadi Muslims in forming the Woking Trust and the nonsectarian nature of the *Islamic Review* contrasted with the views of Ghulam Ahmad's son, Bashir ud-Din Mahmud Ahmad, who emphasized the distinctive claims of Ghulam Ahmad and sought to increase the size of the Ahmadiyya Muslim community when he became successor of the movement in 1914. Kamal ud-Din allied with the group that broke from the main movement: he was a vocal partisan for the Lahori branch when he was in India, but he did not dwell on the internal dispute in Britain, until it surfaced in the mid-1920s as both branches sought to expand their presence in London.

The Ahmadiyya Muslim Community formally launched its missionary efforts in London after the internal split in 1914. The first missionary was Muhammad Fateh Sayal, a young Ahmadi Muslim who had arrived from India in late 1913 to assist with Khwaja Kamal ud-Din's activities at Woking. Sayal swore loyalty to Khalifatul Masih Bashir ud-Din Mahud Ahmad in 1914 and left Woking to establish an Ahmadiyya Muslim Community mission in central London.[12] The mission occupied rental spaces and shifted several times during its first years of operations. Several missionaries worked in London in this early era. Two long-serving missionaries were Qasim Abdullah, who was a classmate of Sayal, and Mufti Muhammad Sadiq, who took Sayal's place when he went on leave to India in 1916. Qasim Abdullah returned to India in 1919 and was replaced by Maulvi Abdul Rahim Nayyar. When Mufti Sadiq went to the United States, Sayal returned to take his place in London.[13] Sayal's major task of his second tour was acquiring land for a permanent Ahmadi mission: he found a site in Southfields, a suburb of London, and converted a building on the property into a mission house. The central London mission remained active, but the Southfields location became the primary locale for operations in London in the 1920s. Abdul Rahim Dard, the personal secretary of Khalifatul Masih Bashir ud-Din Mahmud Ahmad, began a long tour of duty at Southfields in 1924: one of his first major acts was hosting Mahmud Ahmad as he laid the cornerstone for the first Ahmadi mosque in Britain.[14]

The first decade of Ahmadiyya Muslim Community missionary presence in London was filled with diverse initiatives. London was only one focus, as the missionaries took several tours of the countryside to give lectures, distribute Ahmadi pamphlets, and win a few members to the Ahmadiyya. They also wrote several letters to the editor. Mufti Muhammad Sadiq became the public face of the Ahmadiyya during his nearly half decade in Britain: he wore a green turban in photographs that appeared in national newspapers and gained a reputation for making the Ahmadi case that Jesus had died at Srinagar, Kashmir (see figure 10).[15] Mufti Sadiq had been the personal secretary of Ghulam Ahmad from 1905 until his death in 1908 and served as editor of *Al-Badr* from 1905 to 1915. In Britain Mufti Sadiq proved adept at convincing Christians to accept the Ahmadiyya: one of his many converts wrote that "It was just as though we had known him for years. He led prayers in Arabic and we did enjoy it, and he read to us in Arabic and showed us the Holy Book and made things plain to us."[16] Mufti Sadiq turned to new missionary horizons in 1920, leaving London for the United States. A year later Maulvi Abdul Rahim Nayyar traveled from London to West Africa on a two-year tour. This move outward from London into the Atlantic world was due in part to the influence of pan-Africanism on the Ahmadiyya.

Dusé Mohamed Ali, Pan-Africanism, and the Ahmadiyya

Dusé Mohamed Ali was one of the most prominent pan-Africanists of the first decades of the twentieth century. In his biography Dusé Mohamed Ali claimed to be the son of an Egyptian army officer and a Sudanese woman, and he arrived in Britain as a youth in the company of a French man, known only by his surname, Dusé, which Ali took as part of his name. Once he moved to London, Ali gained notice for his acting from a group of young intellectuals, and he launched a literary career in *New Age*, an influential literary journal, in which he published articles that denounced British imperialism. By 1912 Dusé Mohamed Ali was editing his own journal, *African Times and Orient Review*, from an office on Fleet Street at the center of the British publishing industry. This journal, owned by the pan-Africanist Sierra Leonean businessman John Eldred Taylor and then taken over by a consortium of pan-Africanists from Lagos and the Gold Coast, circulated widely in Africa, Asia, and North America. Ali's publishing efforts attracted Marcus Garvey, who worked at a low level position in his youth.[17] The *African Times and Orient Review*'s strident expression of pan-Africanism and pan-Islamism drew official scrutiny and bans during the First World War, when the *African Times and Orient Review* was published only intermittently. After the war it continued to give a voice to pan-Africanist and pan-Islamic concerns, but in 1920 it ceased publication when Dusé Mohamed Ali left Britain. He toured West Africa, sailed for an extended residence in the United States, and finally moved in Nigeria in 1931, where Ali served as an editor of the *Daily Times* and wrote creative works until he died in 1945.[18]

Khwaja Kamal ud-Din came into Dusé Mohamed Ali's orbit through Abu Majid, a London-based Indian lawyer who contributed several articles to *African Times and Orient Review*. Kamal ud-Din and Dusé Mohamed Ali never were close friends, and they differed on many political issues, as Kamal ud-Din was concerned about not eroding ties with the British upper class. Nevertheless, they worked together on finding a place for *salat* at Caxton Hall in London and contributed articles to each other's journals, the *Islamic Review* and *African Times and Orient Review*. They also wrote a collaborative piece to *The Times* of London in 1914: the letter expressed opposition to Christian missionary proselytism in Africa, commenting on disparaging remarks about Africans at a missionary conference in East Africa. This joint letter reveals how Dusé Mohamed Ali's pan-Africanism, detached from European political issues, could gain Kamal ud-Din's public support.[19] Ali's ideas influenced the Ahmadiyya well beyond his personal contact with Kamal ud-Din, and other Ahmadi Muslims came to espouse pan-Africanist ideas.

Ahmadi Muslim ambitions to compete with Christian missionaries were compatible with Dusé Mohamed Ali's pan-Africanism. Already in 1908, immediately after Ghulam Ahmad's death, the Ahmadiyya targeted the global English-speaking world for proselytism.[20] Thereafter the *Review of Religions* published a series of reports about receptivity to Islam in other regions, including sub-Saharan Africa. It published a note in 1910 about an article in the *Truth Seeker*, a Christian missionary journal, describing Christian alarm about the expansion of Islam in Africa.[21] It followed in 1913 with an article quoting from the *Courier Journal* in Louisville, Kentucky, in the United States: "The faith of Islam is now sweeping over Africa like a prairie fire over the Western plains."[22] The second article appeared as Kamal ud-Din was coming into contact with Dusé Mohamed Ali, suggesting him as a possible source. More important, these articles pointed to Ahmadiyya receptivity to opening a new missionary field in Africa. Kamal ud-Din was not a formal missionary, but his collaborative letter with Ali, discussed earlier, reveals how Africa was becoming a region of interest for Ahmadi Muslims.

The Ahmadiyya began to combine issues of race, slavery, and Christian expansion in Africa as its members read Dusé Mohamed Ali's writings. A *Review of Religions* article in 1914 reports on an *African Times and Orient Review* account of a wife of a European Methodist missionary who took exception to an African sitting in the church's front pew, even though she was the wife of an African Methodist minister. The article, "Colour Distinctions in Christian Churches," was the first mention of race in the *Review of Religions*, and the article concluded with a statement about Islam's egalitarianism: "a peasant may stand next to a prince in a mosque, a pauper next to a millionaire."[23] Similar articles appeared in *Review of Religions* in the years ahead, pairing pan-Africanist and pan-Islamist sentiments about the lack of racial distinctions in Islam. The first Ahmadi missionary in the Gold Coast, Maulvi Nayyar, stressed the common bonds that Africans and Asians had as British colonial subjects.[24] The first residential Ahmadi missionary at Saltpond, Maulvi Hakeem, wrote letters to Gold Coast newspapers in the mid-1920s about the evils of the European slave trade in rebuttal to Christian assertions that Muslims introduced the idea of slavery to Africans in the Gold Coast.[25]

The history of the European slave trade in Africa remained a topic in official Ahmadiyya works in the years that followed. A notable example is the 1961 lecture on "Islam in Africa" written by Mubarak Ahmad, the secretary of the Ahmadiyya Foreign Missions Office. Translated into English and distributed globally, this lecture extolled the "civilized" states established by West Africans and responded, as Maulvi Hakeem did, to Christian allegations that Muslims introduced slavery into Africa. Mubarak Ali asserted that "Christianity has played an important role in spreading Slavery in Africa" and added that "the material progress and prosperity which Christian nations flaunt in the face of the world . . . is the fruit of the labour extracted from helpless slaves in the most inhuman manner." Mubarak Ahmad concluded that slavery's legacy remained and cited "colour prejudice" in the United States as his example.[26] This exposition, while not quoting pan-Africanists directly, reflected the influence these ideas continued to have in the Ahmadiyya missionary organization four decades after Ahmadi missionaries interacted with Dusé Mohamed Ali in London.

Dusé Mohamed Ali's influence on the Ahmadiyya included personal contacts from his vast pan-Africanist network. One was Dr. Orisha Sapara, a member of a prominent Christian family at Lagos.[27] Sapara was a reader of Ali's *African Times and Orient Review* and wanted to make contact with Khwaja Kamal ud-Din, whose articles on the shared Abrahamic traditions of Islam and Christianity interested him. Sapara made a point of visiting Dusé Mohamed Ali's Fleet Street offices during a trip to London in 1913, and Ali connected him to Kamal ud-Din. Sapara arrived at a propitious moment, when *Islamic Review* was first being published, and Kamal ud-Din gave him copies of his journal and perhaps other Ahmadi publications to take to Lagos.[28] One of the recipients of these materials was M. L. B. Agusto, a young Afro-Brazilian Muslim who shared Sapara's ecumenical approach to Islam. Agusto, as discussed in the next section, contacted the Ahmadiyya and established a branch at Lagos. Agusto was in Dusé Mohamed Ali's network and resided with him for six months when he first arrived at London to study for a law degree in the early 1920s. Agusto also interacted with Ahmadiyya missionaries at Southfields and Kamal ud-Din at Woking.²⁹ Dusé Mohamed Ali's influence on the Ahmadiyya extended to the United States, where Mufti Muhammad Sadiq, the first Ahmadi missionary in the United States, concentrated his efforts on African Americans in several northern cities, most likely through Ali's contacts.³⁰ Dusé Mohamed Ali eventually made Lagos his permanent residence, and although he was not an Ahmadi Muslim, he could take heart in the knowledge that he helped the Ahmadiyya Muslim Community found a branch at Lagos.

Ahmadi missionaries in London were influenced primarily by the teachings of Ghulam Ahmad, and their service to the Ahmadiyya Muslim Community expressed their loyalty to Khalifatul Masih Bashir-ud-Din Mahmud Ahmad. Most Ahmadi missionaries served in several postings over their lifetimes, and their personal perspectives reflected this history of religious engagement.³¹ Dusé Mohamed Ali's influence was a momentary one, but it occurred at a crucial time in the history of the movement. In the immediate aftermath of the succession crisis, Khalifatul Masih Mahmud Ahmad moved to bolster the movement's presence in London by securing the loyalty and service of Muhammad Fateh Sayal, who had been an assistant to Kamal ud-Din. The latter had made the initial connection to Dusé Mohamed Ali, but Sayal and others maintained those relations. One cannot argue that the Ahmadiyya proselytized in West Africa because of Dusé Mohamed Ali, but his connections aided the process and his ideas shaped their perspectives as they interacted with Africans.

Muslims in Early Twentieth-Century Lagos

Early twentieth-century Lagos was the administrative and economic center of southern Nigeria, a British colonial territory acquired through treaty making and military conquest during the last two decades of the nineteenth century. Southern Nigeria's palm oil, which was particularly suited to industrial usage in Europe, enticed British imperial expansion in two thrusts. From Lagos British colonial armies fought a series of wars to expand its control over the palm oil groves of southwestern Nigeria. From the Niger River basin in southeastern Nigeria, the Royal Niger Company established control of the river before handing its new possessions to the British government. Lagos grew rapidly as a capital of both regions, once combined under British colonial rule, and British officials relied on Africans with English-language education to staff the lower levels of their growing bureaucratic apparatus. This employment of Africans came, however, as overt and pervasive racial discrimination increased in the late nineteenth century, a development that stimulated assertions of African cultural nationalism. Pan-Africanism was one expression among many in this intellectual efflorescence as Africans drew on diverse cultural heritages to contest the British colonial division between black and white.³² African and Atlantic ideas mingled at Lagos, as they had for decades, but with new intensity as voluntary associations formed to engage with others and promote common interests.³³

The Muslim communities of Lagos grew in size and diversity in this era. Muslims reportedly constituted less than a thousand residents in the early 1860s, but by the 1891 colonial census, more than fourteen thousand Muslims resided at Lagos, nearly 45 percent of the population at the time; a decade later Muslims passed the 50 percent threshold, with more than twenty-two thousand residents at Lagos in 1901.³⁴ This half century of Muslim expansion arose from migrations and conversions alike. The immigrants included the continuing flow of African Muslims from Freetown and Brazil.³⁵ Other immigrants were Yoruba-speaking Muslims from the interior: the growth of Islam in many Yoruba states mirrored the upward trend at Lagos in this era.³⁶ This expansion was in part the influence of itinerant Yoruba Muslims from Ilorin, a Muslim state in the hinterland of Lagos and regional center of Muslim scholarship.³⁷ Several Yoruba political leaders at Lagos and in the hinterland Yoruba states became Muslims, encouraging the conversion to Islam of their subjects. Muslim scholars from the Arab world began to visit Lagos in the early twentieth century due to the rising Muslim presence. These developments produced a diverse Muslim community, not only in terms of ethnic heritage but also in terms of their responses to political and religious issues. Muslims began to engage in internal debates, initially over political responses to a colonial water rate hike in 1908 and then after 1915 over control of the central mosque, a dispute that only was resolved in 1947.³⁸

Christians educated in mission schools had an advantage over Muslims in gaining employment in Lagos's expanding colonial bureaucracy. The British administration, which declared English the official language in the colony in 1882, addressed the disproportionate Christian presence in the colonial service by establishing English-language Muslim schools in the 1890s. This effort had its roots in the British experience in Sierra Leone, where hostile relations with Muslims in the early nineteenth century had given way to more constructive relations and the founding of English-language Muslim schools by the colonial administration.³⁹ British officials in Lagos turned to Edmund Blyden, an Afro-Caribbean Christian scholar who learned Arabic and was involved in pedagogical engagement with the Muslim community in late nineteenth-century Sierra Leone and Liberia. Blyden, employed for a brief period in Lagos, convinced Muslim leaders to agree to the opening of a government Muslim school offering an English-language education in 1896.⁴⁰ The school led to several others in the years that followed, and they produced a small number of graduates. But most Muslims emphasized Arabic-language education as a priority. New Arabic-language schools were founded in the 1910s, including one by Muhammad Shitta's son who had studied at al-Azhar in Cairo. These Arabic-language Muslim schools rose in stature at the expense of English-language Muslim schools in Lagos.[41]

Interest in English-language education nevertheless did not dissipate among Muslims at Lagos. Some young Muslims formed an association named after Abdullah Quilliam, a British Muslim who visited Lagos during the Shitta Bey mosque's inauguration in 1894.[42] This association promoted reforms in Muslim life, including the expansion of English-language education. These Muslims included graduates of the colonial Muslim school and Muslim readers of Dusé Mohamed Ali's *African Times and Orient Review*.[43] One of those readers was Salihu Mohammed, a Muslim from Lagos, who wrote a letter to the editor in 1913 to inform *African Times and Orient Review* readers about the state of Muslim education at Lagos:

> [The Muslims of Lagos] have no school of their own, and the one they could boast of was erected and maintained from the Public Fund of the Colony by the Government. In spite of the aristocratic class among them, they have little care of their children: what they do care for, is to collect wealth and not to use it for the welfare of the children, but to keep it during their lifetime, and then, when the time of demise arises, the children to inherit it, and, in the course of a few years, to devastate the whole thing. They have not learned that maxim of educating their children, which is the highest legacy that can be left to children. Fortunately for them, an intelligent Indian, whose name, Ahmad Deen, Clerk to the Director of Railways . . . urges on the Muslim elements the importance of establishing a school of their own, where good knowledge of both English and Arabic should be imparted, and the people seemed pleased at the project.[44]

The passage points to the growing divide over Muslim education. Salihu expected the Muslim community to provide for its own education and not rely on the colonial Muslim English-language school. Salihu disparaged the Muslim community of Lagos, especially the "aristocratic class" that did not invest its fund in education. Significant, too, is the openness to Muslim reformism advocated by Indian Muslims: Ahmad Deen likely was a member of the Aligargh movement in India before serving in West Africa. The letter illustrates the reading and writing practices of Muslims at Lagos, who engaged in contemporary issues. This dynamism was evident in the founding of the Ahmadiyya at Lagos.

The Founding of an Ahmadiyya Branch at Lagos

Muslims founded a branch of the Ahmadiyya at Lagos in 1916. Muhammad Lawal Basil Agusto, an Afro-Brazilian Muslim who headed of the Muslim Literary Society and founded a Muslim school in 1916, took an interest in the Ahmadiyya after reading Ahmadi publications that Dr. Orisha Sapara brought back from

London.⁴⁵ Agusto corresponded with the Ahmadiyya headquarters in Qadian and eventually sent in his application form, the acceptance of which was announced in the *Review of Religions* in June 2016.⁴⁶ Agusto convinced twenty others to join and informed the Ahmadiyya headquarters that the commitment occurred after great deliberation and "prayerful cogitation over the subject of the Ahmadiyya Movement."⁴⁷ This initial group included many Afro-Brazilian Muslims who were members of the Muslim Literary Society and Muslim Juvenile Society at Lagos. They were students and teachers in the government Muslim school and Christian missionary schools, and others worked as clerks, draftsmen, and telegraph operators in the colonial service. Fourteen more joined the Lagos branch of the Ahmadiyya Muslim Community within half-a-year of its founding, and the branch grew to sixty members by 1919.⁴⁸ Included in the second wave were members of the Pedro family, Afro-Brazilians from Lagos; one member, Amadu Ramanu Pedro, subsequently left Lagos to start a business in the Gold Coast.

Ahmadiyya proselytism in the early years at Lagos was in the hands of its lay members. M. L. B. Agusto requested and received Ahmadiyya pamphlets from Qadian for distribution. He also wrote and published his own pamphlets. A glimpse into those initial years is provided in a letter from an Ahmadi Muslim in Lagos, reproduced as mission news in the *Review of Religions*:

> It is hardly necessary for me to mention that the Muslim inhabitants are disadvantageously situated in a place like Lagos where the majority of them are unlettered and corrupted by all bad actions which are derogatory to Islam; and where Christian influence is greater despite the fact that the Muhammadan population is nearly double that of the Christians and heathens put together. The Lagos Muslims know nothing of their own religion and this may be attributed to the fact that those among whom the religion was first introduced allowed the native customs, habits and ideas to creep in.
>
> The Holy Koran being only learnt by rote, we have not sufficient knowledge of Islam to meet with the opposition of our Christian compatriots who have made Islam their target of attack. I must thank God that since the advent of the Ahmadia Movement amongst us and with the very scanty knowledge we have got from your books, no Christian ever opposed an Ahmadi without discomfiture.⁴⁹

The competition with Christians mirrored the Ahmadiyya context in Punjab. Ahmadi Muslims at Lagos also faced opposition from other Muslims: another early letter from Lagos reports that the "so-called orthodox Muhammadans of Lagos are persecuting us from sheer ignorance."⁵⁰

The Lagos branch of the Ahmadiyya Muslim Community adopted measures to reform Muslim practices. In 1918 they convened a general meeting of the Nigerian branch in which seven resolutions were passed: they affirmed that the Ahmadiyya was a Muslim religious organization that was founded by Ghulam Ahmad, rejected violence, and was loyal to the British.[51] The branch added nine clauses to the general Ahmadiyya oath. These additions included prohibitions against the consumption of alcohol and fraternization of married men with unmarried women. They also included prohibitions specific to the Nigerian context, such as forbidding several activities: dancing at ceremonies with drumming, wearing masks, attending the funerals of non-Muslims, wearing the customary black mourning cloth, and prostrating before political elites. Some restrictions related to local Muslim practices, such as preparing food for *mallams* in exchange for amulets.[52] These initiatives were elaborations of Ahmadiyya Muslim reformism drawn from reading the movement's literature.

Ahmadi Muslims at Lagos pressed for a visit from an Ahmadi missionary. M. L. B. Agusto made clear in September 1916 that the group desired a missionary to provide training. He offered to study at Qadian but lamented that his responsibilities at his Muslim school did not allow him to leave Lagos. Agusto implied that an Ahmadi missionary was needed to teach those who promised "to give themselves up to be trained for Missionary work, either entirely or in conjunction with whatever may be their vocations in life."[53] Requests for an Ahmadi missionary continued in the years ahead, and they grew more urgent after Agusto's Muslim school closed: the request was transformed into an appeal to help found a new school on firmer foundations. The Ahmadiyya did not send a missionary immediately because of travel difficulties created by the First World War.[54] Some could not wait: Abdul Rahim Smith, a convert from Christianity and likely a member of the Saro community of Lagos, paid his own transport to Qadian to become a missionary.[55] Ahmadi Muslims at Lagos collected funds to pay the transportation costs for an Ahmadi missionary as an affirmation of their interest in founding an Ahmadiyya school.[56] Mufti Muhammad Sadiq initially was scheduled to travel to West Africa, but Khalifatul Masih Bashir ud-Din Mahmud Ahmad's decision to send him to the United States instead meant that Maulvi Nayyar took his place in fulfilling the Lagos branch's long-held desires for a visit from an Ahmadi missionary. Maulvi Nayyar departed for West Africa in 1921.[57]

Maulvi Abdul Rahman Nayyar's Visit to Lagos and Its Aftermath

Memories of Maulvi Nayyar's visit to Nigeria remained strong well into the late 1950s, nearly forty years after his trip. Humphrey Fisher interviewed pioneering Ahmadi Muslims who described Nayyar as open, gentle, and unassuming in both personal interactions and theological discussions.[58] Maulvi Nayyar broke from Muslim practice at Lagos by preaching on religious topics in English, not Arabic, and by having Africans translate his statements into Yoruba for his audiences. He also spoke in open-air venues and not just on Fridays at the mosque.

His first occasion to introduce this new preaching style was two days after his arrival at the Shitta Bey mosque in central Lagos. This mosque had been funded by the late Muhammad Shitta, a Saro Muslim merchant and philanthropist, and those in attendance, Saro Muslims and others, were polite but largely unmoved by his preaching. This initial effort was followed with other public presentations, in which Nayyar preached about the Messiah and the need to reform local Muslim practices. At the same time Maulvi Nayyar encouraged what were seen as novel expressions, such as allowing Muslims to perform *salat* in European clothing and admitting Muslim girls and women into mosques for Friday communal prayers.

Some Muslims were convinced to join the Ahmadiyya movement during Maulvi Nayyar's residence. Additional young Muslims who had been educated in English-language schools joined, but the largest group was the Alakurani or "Quranic People" based in the Aroloya neighborhood of Lagos. The Alakurani were Yoruba Muslims who broke from other Muslims in the 1870s by insisting on the Quran as the only authoritative Islamic text. It lost members over the years, but regained energy in the mid-1910s with the selection of a new leader, Dabiri, a young man. Dabiri met with Maulvi Nayyar and decided to accept the Ahmadiyya, convincing forty elders to join him in a public acceptance at the end of Ramadan in 1921, echoing the founding of the Alakurani community during Ramadan more than a half century earlier. Thereafter, several thousand more members of the Alakurani accepted the Ahmadiyya.[59]

The Ahmadiyya at Lagos no longer was a small community of young male members and had become a sizable movement dominated by former members of the Alakurani and their families. The inclusion of a dissident Muslim community within the Ahmadiyya ranks may have stunned those in the initial group who had sent in their membership forms. Maulvi Nayyar finessed the incorporation of the two groups by creating a new administrative structure for the Ahmadiyya branch: the original group of young men controlled the managing executive committee and the former members of the Alakurani dominated the advising council of elders, an arrangement that gave the former Alakurani a formal mechanism for providing input but retained the influence of the initial, younger generation in making final decisions for the branch.[60] Expansion was a goal of the Ahmadiyya headquarters in India, and Maulvi Nayyar tried to ensure that the initial group was not overwhelmed and sidelined by the addition of new members.

Maulvi Nayyar moved quickly to found an Ahmadiyya school at Lagos and fulfill the local request for assistance. Immediately upon his arrival Maulvi Nayyar opened a small Ahmadiyya school at the Alakurani mosque in Aroloya, but he took steps simultaneously to establish a permanent school, one that could attract British colonial support. His first step was building a structure in the

Elegbata neighborhood of Lagos. Maulvi Nayyar financed the initiative with various revenue streams: the original group of young Ahmadi Muslims had collected £60 for the school, the Alakurani treasure provided additional funds, but the vast majority came from monthly financial contributions to the Ahmadiyya from local members; within a year Maulvi Nayyar had more than £600 for the school. He was able to open it just before returning to London in 1922, and it received local Ahmadi financial support and leadership as it made its way onto the list of schools supported by the British colonial government.

The establishment of the Ahmadi primary school and its financial requirements posed a challenge to former members of the Alakurani. The targeting of funds to support a school went against the usual Alakurani practice of giving charity to the needy; it also diverted cash that had supported Alakurani leaders. Adding to these issues were two other concerns. One related to Ahmadiyya theology and how it fit with the Alakurani emphasis on a literalist reading of the Quran and *ahadith*. The second was their fear that the organizational structure ceded too much influence to the younger, original Ahmadi Muslims. These issues proved too formidable and led to a rupture. During Ramadan in 1922, literally a year after the initial group of Alakurani had joined the Ahmadiyya, a large number broke from the movement in a dramatic gathering at the Okepopo mosque.[61] Maulvi Nayyar's effort to expand the movement, and the difficulties in bringing two different groups of Muslims at Lagos into one community led to the first split in the Ahmadiyya community at Lagos.

Local Muslim criticism of the Ahmadiyya also increased during Maulvi Nayyar's residence at Lagos. In September 1922 the *Times of Nigeria* published in its Yoruba-language column an article that opposed the Ahmadiyya in uncompromising terms, bringing to public attention a growing effort to confront the new style of Ahmadiyya proselytism fostered by Maulvi Nayyar and the young leadership of the executive committee.[62] An atmosphere of hostility turned to outright physical intimidation in November of that year, when non-Ahmadi Muslims assaulted a group of Ahmadi Muslims holding a prayer meeting at Balogun Square, a prominent public place in Lagos. Accusations for writing the column and encouraging the assault fell on Mustapha Adamu Animashaun, educated in the government Muslim school. The school's headmaster, Alfa Idris Animashaun, gave Adamu, his manumitted slave, an education and then funded his Muslim printing press. Adamu Animashaun may not have written the column or organized the attack, but his opposition to the Ahmadiyya was known throughout Lagos and convinced British authorities to put Adamu and some of his close associates in prison for three months as punishment for the actions against the Ahmadiyya. Although the British action halted the overt physical threats against Ahmadi Muslims, the incident revealed the depth of opposition to the Ahmadiyya. Adamu Animashaun, a respected leader of the Muslim community of Lagos, challenged the proselytism of the Ahmadiyya, a movement brought by young Muslims whose approach to religious matters stretched beyond what the Muslim establishment was willing to accept.[63]

M. L. B. Agusto's return to Lagos from London produced another rupture in the Ahmadiyya community. Immediately upon arriving, Agusto broke publicly from the Ahmadiyya and founded a new Muslim movement, the Jama'at-ul Islamiyya.[64] This breach occurred despite Agusto's involvement with the Ahmadi mission in London, which received favorable mention in the *Review of Religions* in the early 1920s.[65] Agusto later told Humphrey Fisher that he changed his opinion because Maulvi Nayyar expanded membership after having reassured Agusto that the only goal for his Lagos visit was founding an Ahmadiyya school. Fisher concluded that Agusto's explanation probably was "a reflection of Agusto's unwillingness to see the Nigerian initiative pass from his hands, or to pay the price in doctrine and practice which the Indians demanded for their help in education."[66] The dispute may have had personal dimensions: when Agusto was in London, Jibril Martin, another Afro-Brazilian Muslim a few years his junior, had come to prominence in the Lagos branch in his absence. Whatever the actual issues or motivation, Agusto left the Ahmadiyya in 1924 and founded the Jama'at-ul Islamiyya, an organization devoted to an "enlightened" interpretation of Islam and the promotion of English-language education for Muslims.[67] This new movement attracted many Afro-Brazilian and Saro Muslims, some who had joined the Ahmadiyya and now followed Agusto in leaving. This second split did not produce much acrimony, but the departure of Agusto and many Afro-Brazilian Muslims was a loss of energetic young Muslims less than a decade after that group had founded the first Ahmadiyya community in West Africa.

Jibril Martin remained an influential Ahmadi Muslim for several years, but he also broke from the Ahmadiyya in the late 1930s. Martin was a member of a prominent Afro-Brazilian family that included both Muslims and Catholics; he was Muslim but attended the English-language Catholic school as a youth.[68] Martin later studied law in London, arriving shortly after Agusto completed his studies, and he became immersed in the activities of the Ahmadi mission in London. Martin engaged in Ahmadi missionary activities and wrote an article for the *Review of Religions*, "The Religion of Humanity," extolling the virtues of the Ahmadiyya.[69] When Martin completed his studies, the London mission gave him a lengthy tribute. It acknowledged Martin's contributions and spoke about the bonds that transcended "all barriers of race, and nationality" and were personal: "God has welded us into a family constituted of members representing all nations and peoples of the earth."[70] Back at Lagos Martin remained devoted to the Ahmadiyya for a decade. But he left in 1939 to found the rival Ahmadiyya Movement in Nigeria, a Muslim organization that did not acknowledge leadership from Qadian.[71] Martin made the decision after the arrival of Maulvi Hakeem, the long-serving residential Ahmadi missionary to the Gold Coast, who sought to increase discipline and fidelity to Ahmadiyya practices in Lagos.[72] Martin led several other pioneering Ahmadi Muslims in breaking away. Combined with the previous losses when Agusto formed the Jama'at-ul-Islamia, the Ahmadiyya Muslim Community had lost many of the Afro-Brazilian Muslims who first had read Ahmadi publications and formed a branch in the mid-1910s.

The history of the Lagos branch reveals the opportunities and challenges that the Ahmadiyya confronted as it expanded from London to Lagos. Ahmadiyya publications spread the word in advance of active proselytism, and Muslims with an English-language education were open to the movement and its efforts to establish schools. The network that first brought Ahmadiyya materials to Lagos, however, was an element of the broader pan-Africanist movement that was gaining momentum in West Africa and the African diaspora. M. L. B. Agusto concluded that the Ahmadiyya, even though its missionaries were open to these ideas, still thwarted African aims and founded his own organization in 1924. Jibril Martin similarly departed when an Ahmadi missionary arrived and imposed a different regime on the branch. Agusto and Martin might not have been as stridently pan-Africanist as some West Africans of the era, but they did not want to cede control to South Asian Ahmadi missionaries.

Conclusion

The split within the Ahmadiyya in 1914 produced two branches, both of which pursued global evangelism. The branch in Lahore benefited from the initiatives of Khwaja Kamal ud-Din, whose residence in London led to the founding of an ecumenical Woking mosque. The London mission of the Ahmadiyya Muslim Community also was active, initially focused on Britain, but it eventually expanded to West Africa and the African diaspora in the Americas. Dusé Mohamed Ali was a decisive influence on this development, and his pan-Africanism shaped the views of Ahmadi missionaries as they proselytized in West Africa.

The Ahmadiyya arrival in West Africa, nonetheless, was an expression of African initiative. M. L. B. Agusto and others formed an Ahmadi Muslim community at Lagos through correspondence with the Ahmadiyya headquarters in 1916. The local movement expanded its members in the half decade before an Ahmadi missionary arrived for a visit. Maulvi Nayyar provided tangible support by helping establish an English-language Muslim school, but he also expressed the Ahmadiyya ambition of expanding membership. Agusto, dissatisfied with the direction of the Ahmadiyya, founded his own movement in 1924. The Ahmadiyya's initial success was followed with fissure, as the aspirations of a large and diverse membership in a major West African colonial capital did not fit the religious vision of the South Asian Ahmadi missionaries.

The story of the Ahmadiyya in West Africa did not end at Lagos. Amadu Ramanu Pedro brought news of the Ahmadiyya to Fante Muslims in the Gold Coast in the late 1910s. Fante Muslims expressed interest and contributed funds so that Maulvi Nayyar would stop over on his way to Lagos. The next chapter turns to the Ahmadiyya arrival in the Gold Coast.

Notes

1. Humphrey J. Fisher, "The Ahmadiyya Movement in Nigeria," in *African Affairs*, ed. Kenneth Kirkwood (Carbondale: Southern Illinois University Press, 1961), 60–88; id., *Ahmadiyyah*, 91–116.
2. Stefan Reichmuth, "Education and the Growth of Religious Associations among Yoruba Muslims: the Ansar-Ud-Deen Society of Nigeria," *JRA* 26, no. 4 (1996), 365–405.
3. Ansari, "Woking Mosque"; Germain, "Ahmadi-Lahore Networks in the Inter-War Period"; Jonker, "A Laboratory of Modernity"; Salmat, *Miracle at Woking*. The Ahmadiyya Muslim Community's early mission in London is mentioned in passing in Moles, "Evolution of the Ahmadiyya Community in the UK."
4. Ghulam Ahmad, "The Removal of Misconceptions," English translation of *Izala-e-Auham*, 515–516.
5. "Ahmadiyya Mission News: England," *RR* 16, no. 6 (June 1917), 227. Earlier Kamal ud-Din made a reference to Ghulam Ahmad's "white birds" revelation when announcing British conversions to Islam in "Islam in England," *RR* 13, no. 4 (1914), 154–155.
6. K. Humayun Ansari, *The Infidel Within: Muslims in Britain Since 1800* (London: Hurst & Company, 2004).
7. K. Humayun Ansari, "Making Transnational Connections: Muslim Networks in Early Twentieth-Century Britain," in *Islam in Inter-War Europe*, ed. Nathalie Clayer and Eric Germain (London: Hurst and Company, 2008), 31–63.
8. Gilroy, *Black Atlantic*, discusses the general context.
9. Ron Geaves, *Islam in Victorian Britain: The Life and Times of Abdullah Quilliam* (London: Kube Publishing, 2010).
10. Ansari, "Woking Mosque"; Salmat, *Miracle at Woking*.
11. Kamal ud-Din to Khalifatul Masih Nur ud-Din, translated in Salmat, *Miracle at Woking*, 24–26.
12. Muhammad Fateh Sayal moved from Woking, where he assisted Kamal ud-Din, to central London, where he worked under orders from Qadian, in mid-1914. See "Christian and Islamic Ideals," *RR* 13, no. 7 (1914), 266–267.
13. *RR* is my source for the arrivals and departures of missionaries at London. Two served together most of the time, but occasionally one was alone for months. A particularly detailed description is "Ahmadiyya Mission News: England," *RR* 18, nos. 8–9 (1919), 282.
14. Marzia Balzani, "A Tale of Two Ahmadiyya Mosques: Religion, Ethnic Politics, and Urban Planning in London," *Laboratorium* 7, no. 3 (2015), 49–71; Asif M. Basit, "London's First Mosque: A Study in History and Mystery, Part One," *RR* 107, no. 6 (2012), 30–46; id., "London's First Mosque: A Study in History and Mystery, Part Two," *RR* 111 107, no. 7 (2012), 44–57; Simon Naylor and James Ryan, "The Mosque in the Suburbs: Negotiating Religion and Ethnicity in South London," *Social and Cultural Geography* 3, no. 1 (2002), 39–59.
15. "Ahmadiyya Mission News: England," *RR* 17, nos. 11–12 (1918), 433–434.
16. "Ahmadiyya Mission News: England," *RR* 16, nos. 10–11 (1917), 393–394.

17. Michael A. Gomez, *Black Crescent: The Experience and Legacy of African Muslims in the Americas* (Cambridge: Cambridge University Press, 2005), 259.
18. For Dusé Mohamed Ali's autobiography, see "Scenes from an Active Life," *The Comet* (Lagos, Nigeria), 12 July 1937–5 March 1938.
19. Abu Majid reportedly betrayed Ali by informing on his activities to British officials. Ian Duffield, "Dusé Mohamed Ali, Afro-Asian Solidarity and Pan-Africanism in Early Twentieth Century London," in *Essays on the History of Blacks in Britain*, ed. J. S. Gundara and Ian Duffield (Aldershot, UK: Avebury, 1992), 134.
20. "The Propagation of Islam in English-speaking Countries," *RR* 8, no. 3 (1909), 97–105.
21. "Notes and Comments: The Spread of Islam in Africa," *RR* 9, no. 10 (1910), 437–438.
22. "Progress of Islam in Africa," *RR* 12, no. 4 (1913), 172–173.
23. "Colour Distinctions in Christian Churches," *RR* 13, no. 8 (1914), 311.
24. Maulvi Nayyar reportedly told a group in Saltpond shortly after his arrival that "the coloured races of Islamic faith would soon be able to take world power and exercise it." PRAAD, Cape Coast: ADM 1/23/353: 3 March 1921, Saltpond DC to CCCP.
25. Maulvi Hakeem's letter appeared on 30 January 1926 in the *Gold Coast Times* (Cape Coast) in response to Reverend W. T. Balmer. See "Mission News: Gold Coast," *RR* 25, no. 3 (1926), 20–22.
26. Mubarak Ahmad, *Islam in Africa* (Rabwah: Ahmadiyya Foreign Missions Office, 1962), 2, 4, and 7.
27. Dr. Sapara was known familiarly as Oguntola Odunmbaku. For the Sapara family and its role in Lagos, see "Christopher Alexander Sapara-Williams, Nigeria's First Lawyer," at http://www.nairaland.com/1304986/christopher-alexander-sapara-williams-nigerias-first (accessed 10 June 2014).
28. It is unclear if Sapara returned with *Review of Religions* and *Islamic Review* or only the latter. Ian Duffield interviewed Agusto in 1967 and heard him recount that Sapara returned with copies of *Islamic Review*, but local memories insist it was copies of *RR* that first arrived at Lagos. Given Agusto's later break from the Ahmadiyya, he may have referenced Kamal ud-Din's journal in his Duffield interview to diminish the influence of the *RR*. But Kamal ud-Din likely would not have connected Agusto to Qadian, where Agusto sent his Ahmadiyya membership forms, so Sapara may have returned with a copy of the *RR*. See for Agusto's memories of Sapara returning from London with Ahmadi materials: Duffield, "Dusé Mohamed Ali," 558.
29. Duffield, "Dusé Mohamed Ali," 408.
30. Ibid., 679.
31. The biographies of these pioneering Ahmadiyya Muslim Community missionaries are narrated in Urdu as part of a series on Muslim Television-Ahmadiyya.
32. J. F. A. Ajayi, "Nineteenth-Century Origins of Nigerian Nationalism," *Journal of the Historical Society of Nigeria* 2, no. 2 (1961), 196–210.
33. Zachernuk, *Colonial Subjects*; Nozomi Sawada, "The Educated Elite and Associational Life in Early Lagos Newspapers: In Search of Unity for the Progress of Society," PhD diss., University of Birmingham, 2013.
34. Gbadamosi, *Growth of Islam*, 51, 98.
35. Cole, *Krio of West Africa*, 132–146; Kopytoff, *Preface*, 245–249; Lindsay, "'To Return to the Bosom of their Fatherland'"; Olatunji, "Afro-Brazilians in Lagos."
36. Gbadamosi, *Growth of Islam*, 49–83; Peel, *Religious Encounter*, 187–214; Ryan, *Imale*.
37. Gbadamosi, *Growth of Islam*, 10–13, 34, 63–64, 86, 200, 214–215; Stefan Reichmuth, *Islamische bildung Und soziale Integration in Ilorin* (Munster: Lit. Verlag, 1998).
38. Danmole, "Crisis of the Lagos Muslim Community"; Lawal, "Islam and Colonial Rule in Lagos."

39. Skinner, "Muslim Elites." British officials at Lagos withdrew colonial support for the English-language Muslim schools in 1926.
40. Euba, "Muhammad Shitta Bey"; Gbadamosi, *Growth of Islam*, 164–177.
41. Abubakre and Reichmuth, "Arabic Writing."
42. Brent D. Singleton, "'That Ye May Know Each Other': Late Victorian Interactions between British and West African Muslims," *Journal of Muslim Minority Affairs* 29, no. 3 (2009), 369–385.
43. Stefan Reichmuth, "Ansar-Ud-Deen Society of Nigeria," *JRA* 26, no. 4 (1996), 365–405.
44. *The African Times and Orient Review*, November–December 1913, 256.
45. Several claim to have been the first to read Ahmadi publications at Lagos, but Agusto was the first to send in his application form, according to "Ahmadiyya Mission News: Nigeria," *RR* 15, no. 6 (1916), 226. For other claims, see Ahmad Olayiwola Jegede, "History of the Ahmadiyyat in Nigeria," *RR* 88, no. 1 (1989), 20; H. A. B. Fashinro, *Ahmadiyya As I See It* (Lagos: Irede Printers, 1995); Saheed Oluron Timehin, "Achievements of the Ahmadiyya Muslim Jama'at in Nigeria"; and "Ahmadiyya Muslim Jama'at in Nigeria: How Ahmadiyya Was Introduced in Nigeria," online publications of the Ahmadiyya Muslim Community in Nigeria (http://www.ahmadiyyang.org). For Agusto's memories, see Duffield, "Dusé Mohamed Ali," 558.
46. "Ahmadiyya Mission News: Nigeria," *RR* 15, no. 6 (1916), 226.
47. "Ahmadiyya Mission News: Africa," *RR* 15, no. 11 (1916), 434–436.
48. "Ahmadiyya Mission News: Nigeria," *RR* 16, no. 1 (1917), 41.
49. "Ahmadiyya Mission News: Nigeria," *RR* 17, no. 1 (1918), 40.
50. "Ahmadiyya Mission News: Nigeria," *RR* 17, nos. 11–12 (1918), 434.
51. "Ahmadiyya Mission News: Nigeria," *RR* 17, nos. 11–2 (1918), 435–436.
52. "Ahmadiyya Mission News: Nigeria," *RR* 18, nos. 1 & 2 (1919), 60–61.
53. "Ahmadiyya Mission News: Africa," *RR* 15, no 11 (1916), 434–436.
54. "Ahmadiyya Mission News: Miscellaneous," *RR* 17, no. 2 (1918), 78.
55. "Ahmadiyya Mission News: Nigeria," *RR* 18, nos. 8–9 (1919), 282–283; "Ahmadiyya Mission News: West Africa," *RR* 19, no. 7 (1920), 247. His return is never reported.
56. "Ahmadiyya Mission News: England," *RR* 18, nos. 8–9 (1919), 282 (the reference to funds from Nigeria appears at the end).
57. For the change in Mufti Sadiq's missionary charge, see "Ahmadiyya Mission News: England," *RR* 18, nos. 8–9 (1919), 282; "Ahmadiyya Mission for America," *RR* 18, no. 12 (1919), 405–406.
58. Fisher, *Ahmadiyyah*, 98. N. M. Saifi, an Indian Ahmadi missionary at Lagos, reportedly published a pamphlet about Maulvi Nayyar in the 1940s. See Jegede, "History of the Ahmadiyya in Nigeria," 21.
59. Fisher, *Ahmadiyyah*, 99–101. Maulvi Nayyar reported that more than ten thousand joined: "News and Notes: West Africa," *RR* 20, no. 4 (1921), 158.
60. Fisher, *Ahmadiyyah*, 101.
61. Ibid., 101–102.
62. *The Times of Nigeria*, 26 September 1922.
63. H. O. Danmole, "A Visionary of the Lagos Muslim Community: Mustapha Adamu Animashaun, 1885–1968," *Lagos Historical Review* 5 (2005), 22–48.
64. Aliu Babs Fafunwa, *Jama-at-ul Islamiyya of Nigeria at 60* (Lagos: n.p., 1984); Fisher, *Ahmadiyyah*, 104–105; Reichmuth, "Ansar-Ud-Deen Society of Nigeria," 372.
65. "Our Mission Notes: England," *RR* 21, nos. 3–5 (1922), 186, and "London Mission," *RR* 21, nos. 6–8 (1922), 197.
66. Fisher, "Ahmadiyya Movement in Nigeria," 73.

67. Fafunwa, *Jama-at-ul Islamiyya of Nigeria at 60*, 8.
68. A. B. Laotan, *The Torch Bearers, or Old Brazilian Colony in Lagos* (Lagos: Ile-Olu Printing Works, 1943), 17.
69. Jibril Martin, "The Religion of Humanity," *RR* 25, no. 1 (1926), 28–30.
70. "Farewell Address Given to Jibril Martin, Esq., LL.B." *RR* 26, no. 1 (1927), 15–16.
71. Fisher, *Ahmadiyyah*, 112–113.
72. B. B. Salami, "Ahmadiyya Movement in West Africa," *RR* 34, no. 6 (1935), 232–236.

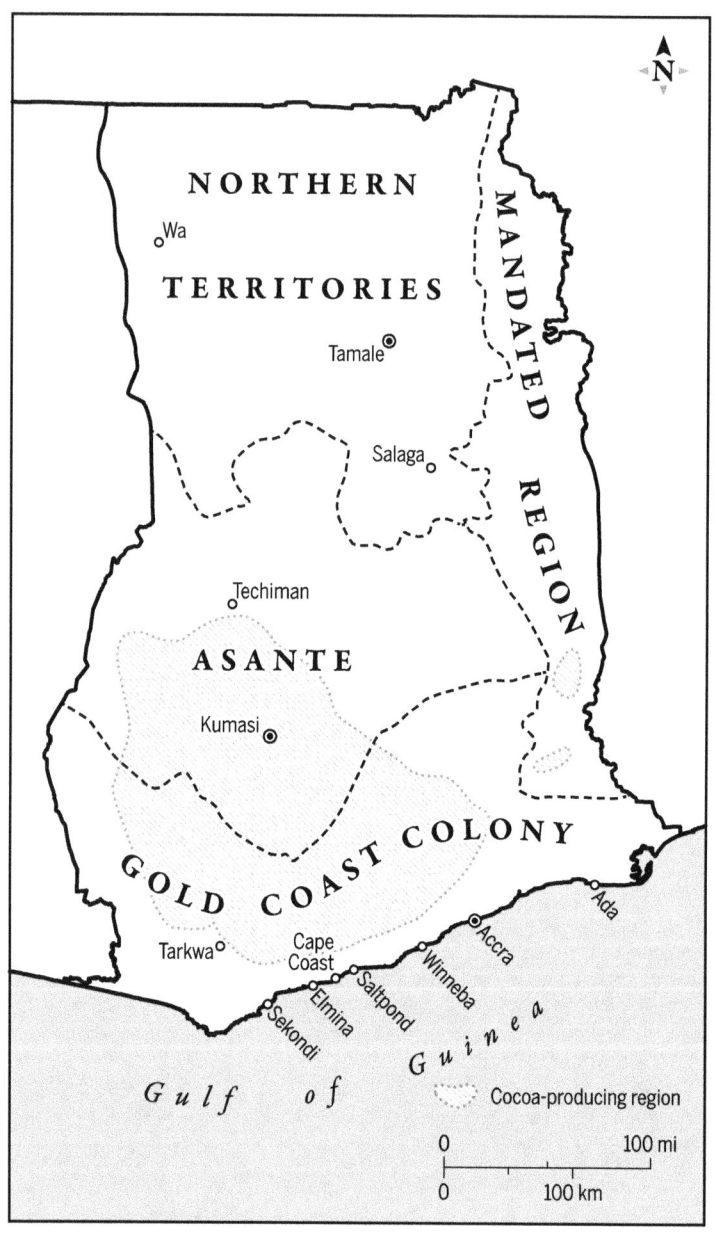

Map 1. British Gold Coast, early twentieth century

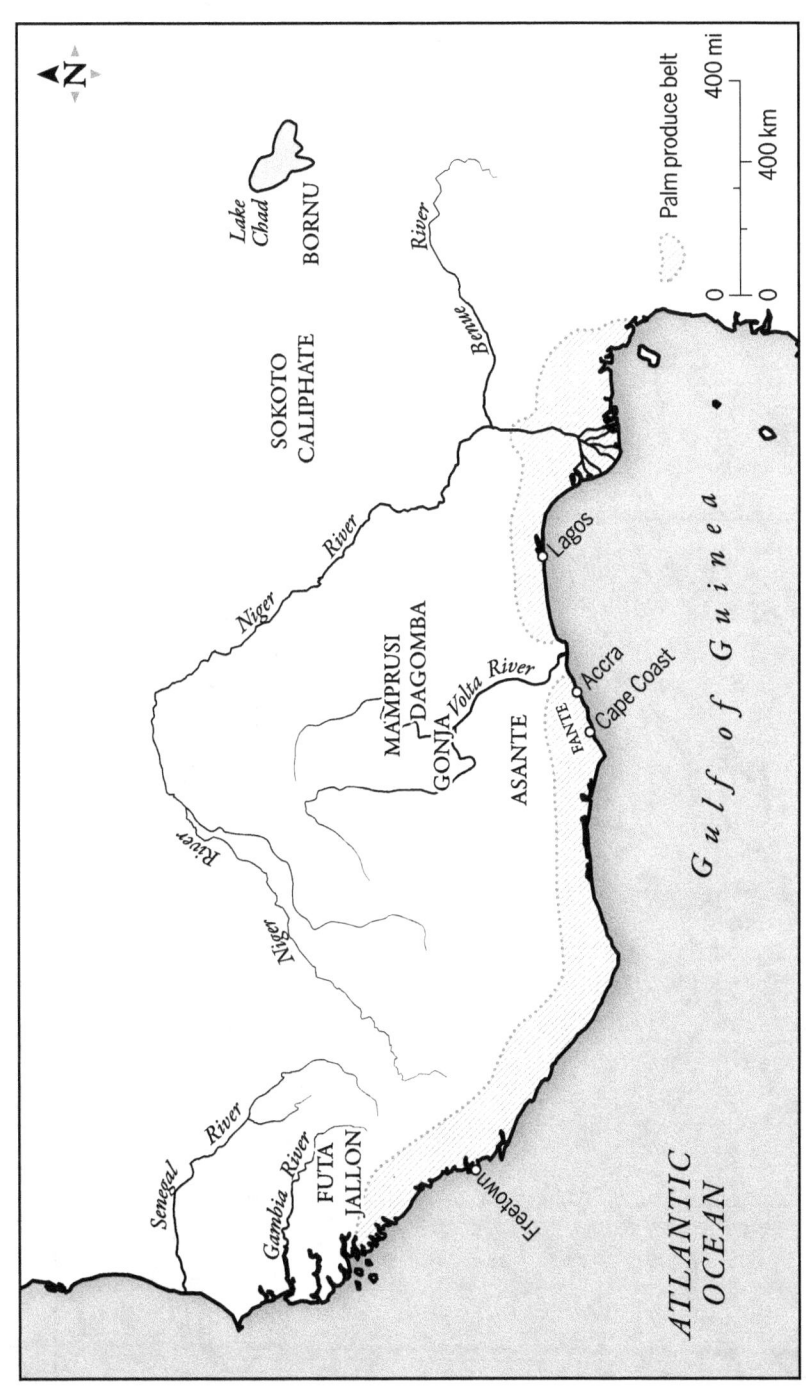

Map 2. West Africa in the mid-nineteenth century

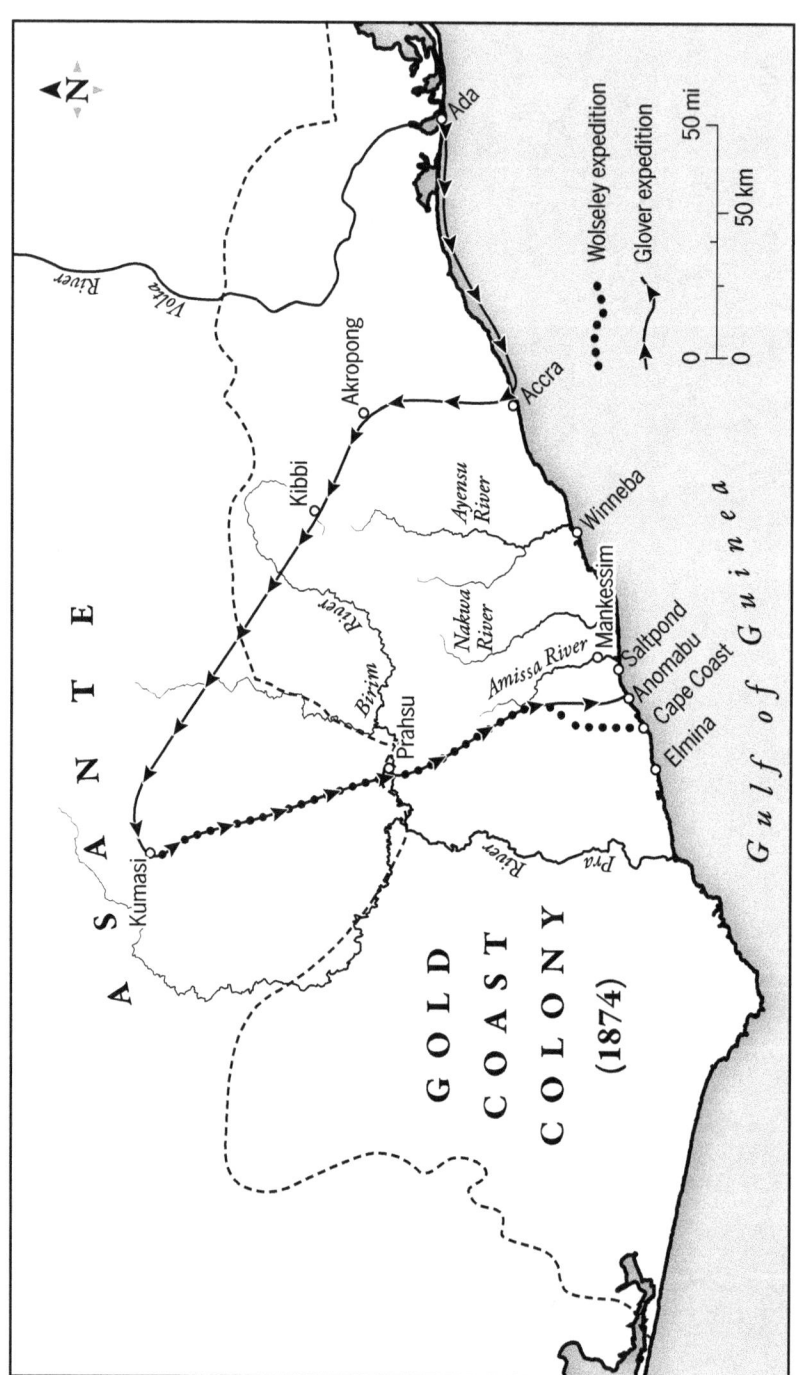

Map 3. British invasion of Asante, 1873–1874

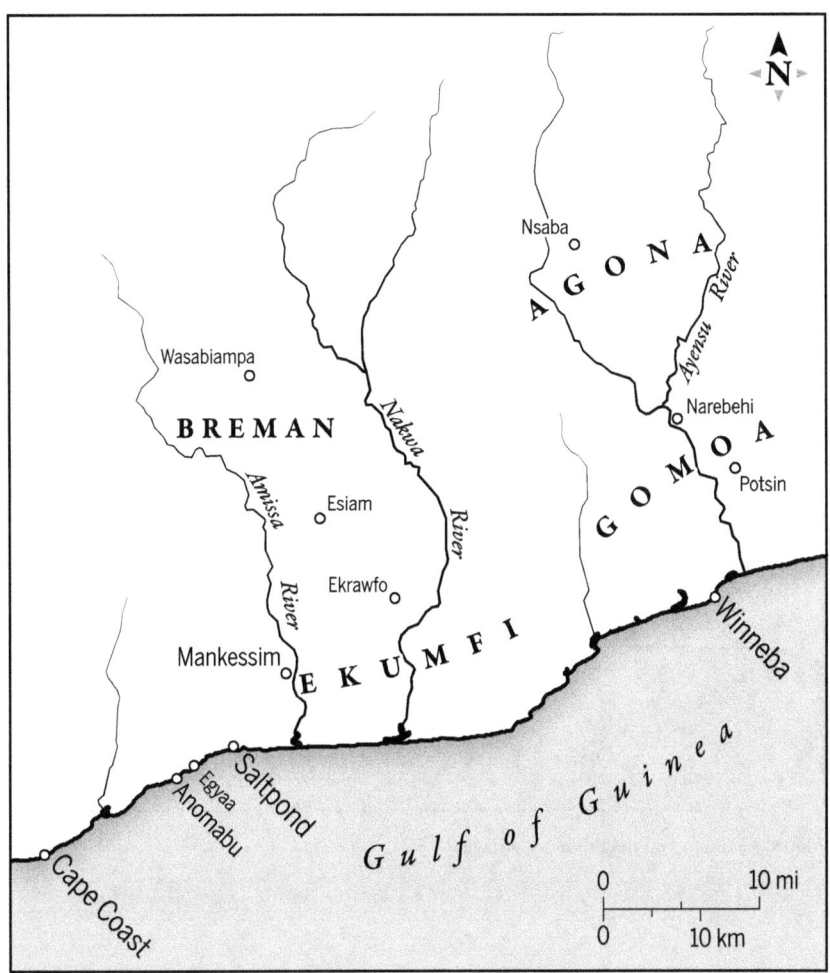

Map 4. Ekumfi and neighboring regions

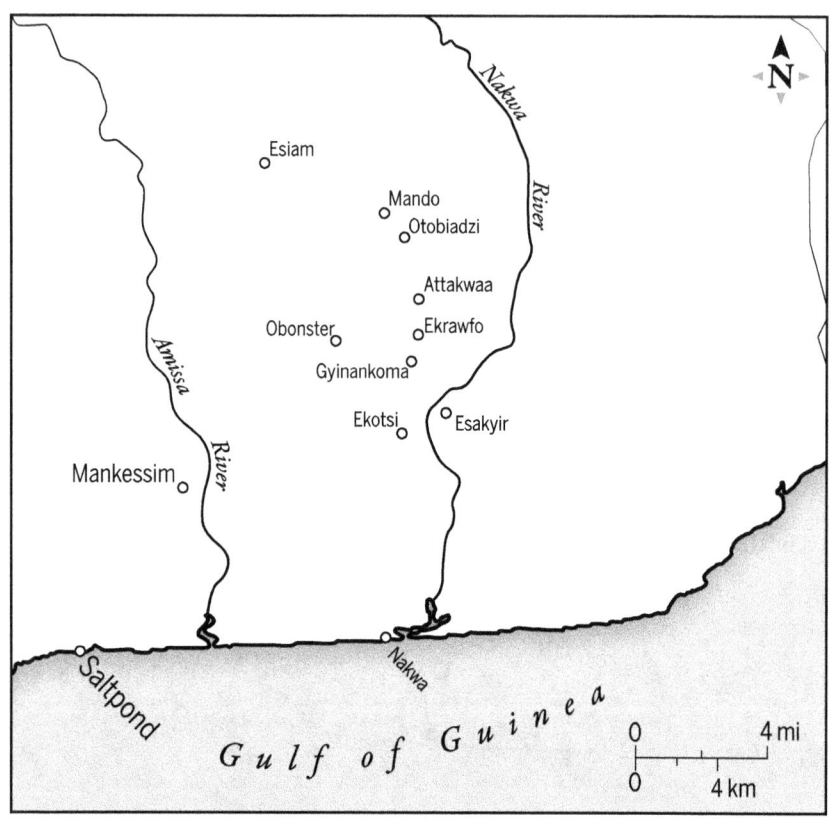

Map 5. Ekrawfo and neighboring villages

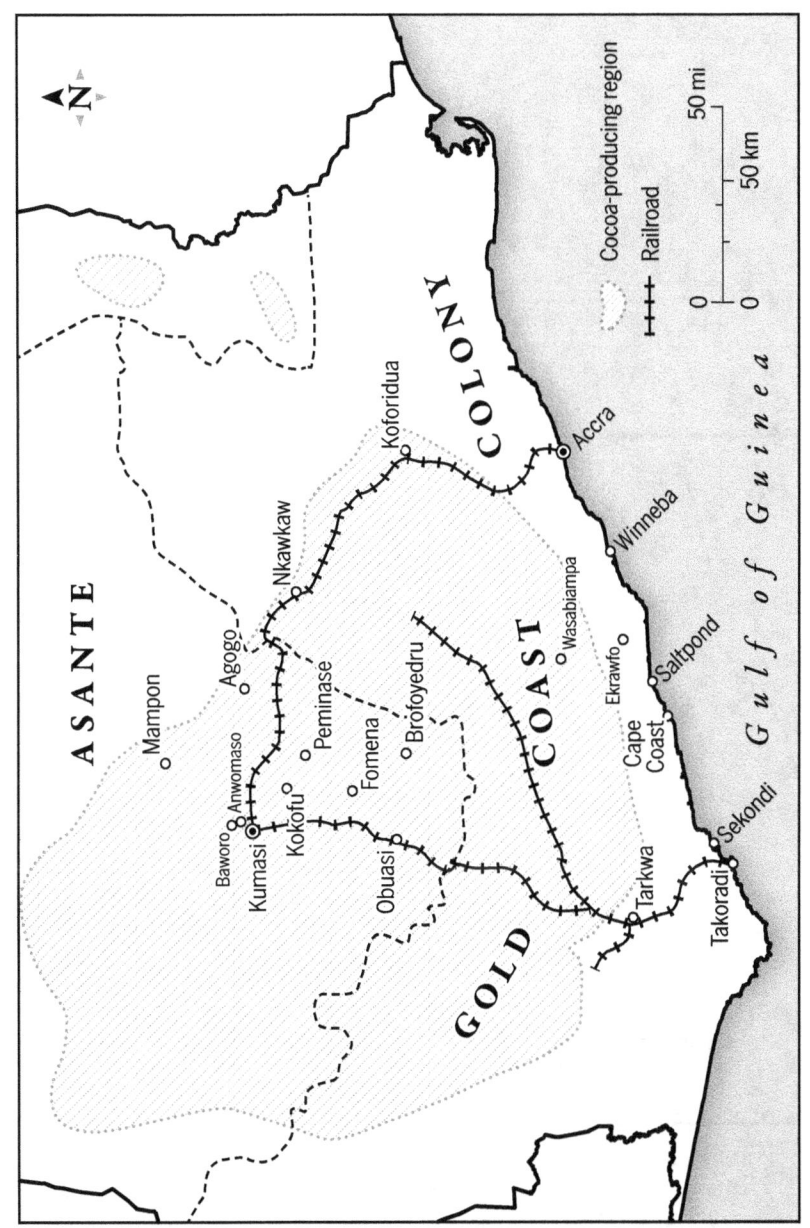

Map 6. Cocoa production in the Gold Coast

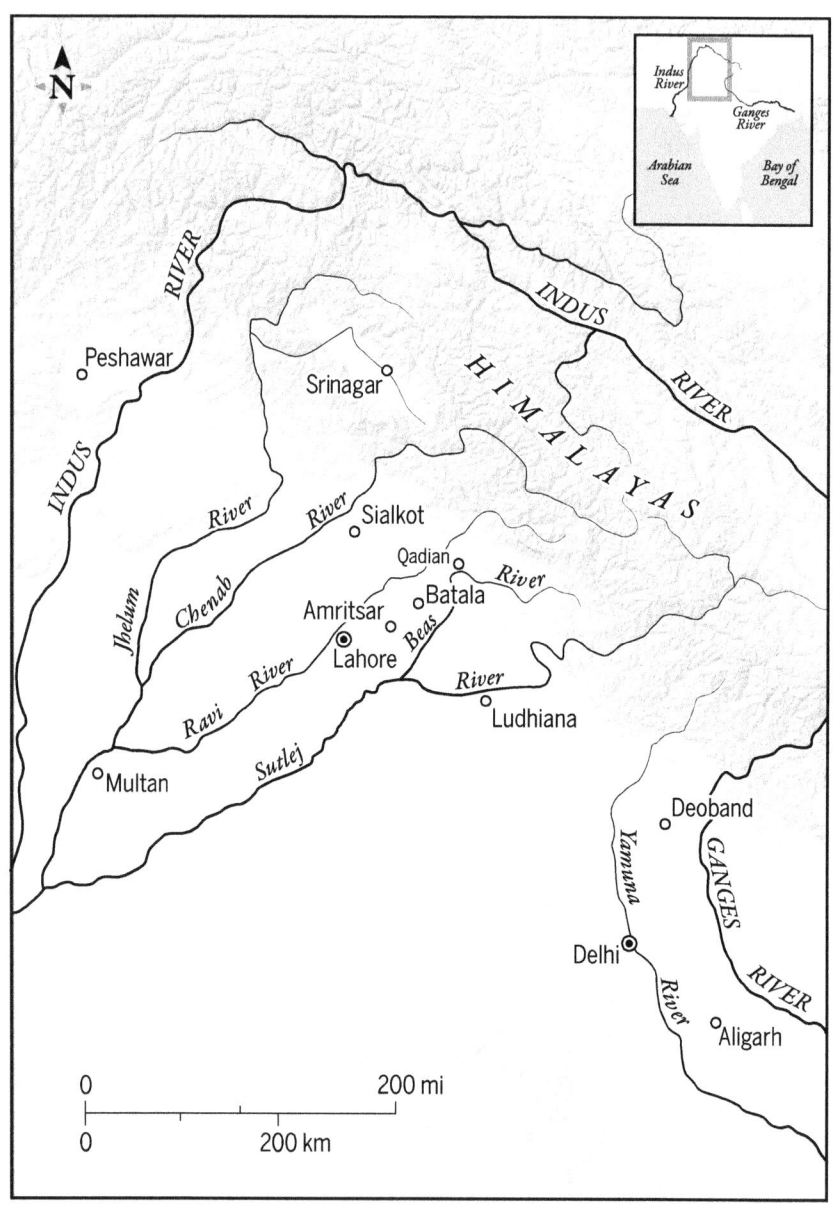

Map 7. British Punjab

Figure 1. Maulvi Hakeem with teachers and students at Talim-ul-Islam School, 1924
Source: "Talimul Islam High School, Saltpond, Gold Coast," *Review of Religions* 24, no. 6 (1925), frontispiece. Photo courtesy of the Ahmadiyya Muslim Community, United Kingdom, and the School of Oriental and African Studies Library, University of London, United Kingdom.

Figure 2. Khalifatul Masih Masroor Ahmad and Ameer Maulvi A. Wahab Adam (second from left) at Mahdi Appah's Grave, Ekrawfo, Ghana, 2008
Source: Photo courtesy of Ahmadiyya Muslim Community, London, United Kingdom.

Figure 3. Soldier and *mallam*, late nineteenth-century southern Nigeria
Source: Seymour Vandeleur, "Nupe and Ilorin," *Geographical Journal* 10 (1897), 367.

Figure 4. The Hausa Force, with Captain Glover, c. 1873 Gold Coast
Source: Elizabeth R. S. Glover, "An Imperial Pioneer: Close of the Ashanti Campaign and a Touching Farewell," *West Africa* (16 June 1917), 339. Photo courtesy of The British Library Board.

Figure 5. Gold Coast Constabulary *mallam*, late nineteenth-century Elmina
Source: PRO: CO 1069/32, 21a. Photo courtesy of The National Archives, United Kingdom.

Figure 6. Gold Coast Constabulary mosque, late nineteenth-century Elmina
Source: PRO: CO 1069/34 part 1, 36. Photo courtesy of The National Archives, United Kingdom.

Figure 7. Methodist church, late nineteenth-century Anomabu
Source: PRO: 1069/34, part 1, 51. Photo courtesy of The National Archives, United Kingdom.

Figure 8. Ahmadiyya mosque, Ekrawfo, 2005
Source: Photo courtesy of the author.

Figure 9. Mahdi Appah's mosque, Wasabiampa, 2005
Source: Photo courtesy of the author.

Figure 10. Mufti Sadiq at tomb in Srinagar, Kashmir, where Jesus is said to have been buried, mid-1920s
Source: "The Tomb of Jesus Christ, Siringar, [*sic*] Kashmir with Dr. M. M. Sadiq of Chicago in Centre," *Review of Religions* 24, no. 11 (1925), frontispiece. Photo courtesy of the Ahmadiyya Muslim Community, United Kingdom, and the Bodleian Libraries, the University of Oxford, United Kingdom, shelfmark Per. 943 d.56.

Figure 11. Maulvi Hakeem and Binyameen Keelson welcoming Maulvi Ali, 1929
Source: "Maulvi F. R. Hakeem (third from right), in charge of the Ahmadiyya Movement, Gold Coast, West Africa, with a group of friends, prior to his departure for India after six years' service in Africa," *Review of Religions* 28, nos. 11–12 (1929), frontispiece. Photo courtesy of the Ahmadiyya Muslim Community, United Kingdom, and the Bodleian Libraries, the University of Oxford, United Kingdom, shelfmark Per. 943 d.56.

Figure 12. Governor's visit to Talim-ul-Islam School, 1928
Source: "The Staff and Students at Talim-ul-Islam Ahmadiyya School, Saltpond, Bidding God-speed to H.E. the Governor of Gold Coast . . . on December 11th, 1928," *Review of Religions* 28, no. 2 (1929), frontispiece. Photo courtesy of the Ahmadiyya Muslim Community, United Kingdom, and the Bodleian Libraries, the University of Oxford, United Kingdom, shelfmark Per. 943 d.56.

Figure 13. Ahmadiyya stamp, late 1920s
Source: Author's collection.

Figure 14. Maulvi Ali at Tamale, 1931
Source: "Members of the Ahmadiyya Community in Tamale (Br. West Africa) with Mr. Nasir Ahmad [Ali], the Ahmadiyya Missionary in Africa," *Review of Religions* 30, no. 9 (1931), frontispiece. Photo courtesy of the Ahmadiyya Muslim Community, United Kingdom, and the Bodleian Libraries, the University of Oxford, United Kingdom, shelfmark Per. 943 d.56.

PART III

Ahmadiyya Arrival and Consolidation in the Gold Coast

5   Ahmadiyya Arrival in the Gold Coast

YUSUF NYARKO, Binyameen Sam's relative, reportedly had a dream that led the Fante Muslim community to invite the Ahmadiyya to the Gold Coast.[1] Memories of Nyarko's dream are recounted in a pamphlet commemorating the fortieth anniversary of the Ahmadiyya in Ghana. The pamphlet states that Nyarko

> dreamt that he was praying with white men. He informed one Mr. Abdul Rahman Pedro, a Nigerian who was residing at Saltpond, six miles from Mankessim. On hearing this he [Pedro] told Mr. Yusuf Nyarku [sic] that he had read about a Muslim Mission in India with a branch in London. . . . Yusuf Nyarku informed also Chief Mahdi Appah, who was then at Bedum, about his dream. On hearing this he [Appah] sent some people to the towns and villages . . . [calling a meeting of] all the Fante Muslims. . . . They all assembled at Mankessim and decided that a letter should be written to Qadian . . . asking for an Indian Muslim missionary to be sent to Ghana.[2]

This dream was not as detailed in its content as the visions reportedly associated with Binyameen Sam, but it similarly produced religious change in the Gold Coast. After Sam's death, the Fante Muslim community was adrift, and West African *mallams* from the savanna came to reside at Ekrawfo, the center of the Fante Muslim community. These *mallams* taught Arabic and encouraged Fante Muslims to adopt savanna norms over the practices that Sam had advocated. Nyarko's dream, as Fante Muslim elders interpreted it, pointed auspiciously to the Ahmadiyya. Fante Muslims acted on the dream; Maulvi Nayyar stopped in the Gold Coast on his way to Lagos in 1921; and Fante Muslims joined the Ahmadiyya and supported the residence of a South Asian Ahmadi missionary at Saltpond.

Memories convey only part of the complex story leading to the arrival of the Ahmadiyya in the Gold Coast. Unstated is that Yusuf Nyarko's dream occurred in the aftermath of the 1918 global influenza pandemic, an event that killed nearly one hundred thousand people in the Gold Coast alone.[3] New Christian movements arose, claiming followers with emphases on spiritual healing that established Christian missions did not offer.[4] Amadu Ramanu Pedro, an Afro-Brazilian Muslim from Lagos, was an Ahmadi Muslim who, I contend, evangelized the Ahmadiyya's End Times message in this era of religious questioning and influenced Nyarko's dream. Mahdi Appah, who had been absent from Ekrawfo for decades as he farmed cocoa near Bedum, was moved by the Ahmadiyya message and used Nyarko's dream to reassert his authority; he pushed Fante Muslims to explore the Ahmadiyya as an alternative to the rising influence of savanna Muslim norms at Ekrawfo and contributed his own funds to support Maulvi Nayyar's stopover. After Fante Muslims accepted the Ahmadiyya, Mahdi Appah capped his renewed leadership of the Fante Muslim community by negotiating to receive assurances from Maulvi Nayyar that financial contributions would be used to open English-language and Arabic schools in the Gold Coast.

Humphrey Fisher mentioned Yusuf Nyarko's dream, but only in passing, and he did not probe contemporaneous materials to anchor events in the era of religious questioning after the 1918 influenza pandemic. This chapter places the Ahmadiyya arrival in that altered religious marketplace and illustrates the key roles of Amadu Ramanu Pedro and Mahdi Appah, as well as others, in events. The chapter begins with the British colonial consolidation and transformations in the Gold Coast religious marketplace. It then turns to Ahmadiyya proselytism, accounts of Nyarko's dream, and the decision to invite the Ahmadiyya to the Gold Coast. The final section examines Maulvi Nayyar's visit and the negotiation of the terms of the Ahmadiyya arrival.

British Colonial Rule in Early Twentieth-Century Gold Coast

British colonial rule influenced power and authority at all levels of society in the Gold Coast. African political leaders, *chiefs* in the colonial lexicon, experienced significant changes in the early colonial era as the British administration imposed policies limiting their authority. The Native Jurisdiction Ordinance of 1878 initially weakened the authority of African political elites by defining a form of direct rule in the hands of British officials. But a subsequent colonial ordinance in 1883 repealed some of the previous measures, and for several decades local political elites had relative autonomy over most local affairs. In 1902 British officials reestablished a form of direct rule through the establishment of the Secretariat of Native Affairs to supervise local political leaders. The changes intended with the creation of the secretariat never completely eroded the authority of African political elites, especially in rural areas, and in the early 1930s British officials adopted another variant of indirect rule that granted political elites much more local autonomy. Throughout these changes African political elites represented themselves as protectors of "tradition" against those with English-language education who were emerging as rival leaders.[5]

The colonial administrative apparatus and British firms relied on Africans to staff the lower levels of their organizations. This development merely increased demand for English-speaking Africans that had started in the mid-nineteenth century, when British firms first started operating in the Gold Coast. By the early twentieth century the Gold Coast administration had 800 positions in its lower ranks, and it continued to recruit Africans over the following decades. Most members of the new elite were educated in English-language schools run by Christian missionaries: the colonial government operated a few schools to educate the sons of local political elites, but the overwhelming majority of English-language schools were run by missions. These schools received supplemental government grants for teaching an approved curriculum and meeting educational standards. The number of government-assisted schools increased dramatically in the early colonial era, nearly 90 percent, from 74 to 138 schools in the period between 1891 and 1900, and continued to expand over the course of the colonial era.[6]

Significant transformations also occurred in the economic domain. The last two decades of the nineteenth century witnessed the rise of a small group of African merchants investing in new export-oriented activities, such as intensive gold mining, rubber collecting, and timber harvesting. These merchants, drawing on entrepreneurial talents and connections developed during the mid-nineteenth century economic expansion, made considerable wealth in the late nineteenth century, but British firms eventually came to dominate these activities as colonial consolidation limited the export activities of Africans.[7] Other economic opportunities remained open to Africans. Cocoa production, for example, emerged as a major African activity in the late nineteenth century (see map 6). Entrepreneurial African families acquired virgin forest lands for new cocoa farms, most notably Akuapem residents who moved into neighboring Akyem Abuakwa. But several others participated, notably Asante and Fante farmers who worked land suitable for cocoa cultivation. Cocoa trees grew best in newly cleared forest, and it took years after planting before mature trees could be harvested for their pods. The initial investments occurred in families, which acquired land from local authorities and relied on household labor as the trees developed. They later added wage labor to carry loads when they could afford such outlays.[8] By 1911 Ghana was the largest exporter of cocoa globally, contributing more than 80 percent of the Gold Coast colony's export earnings by 1920. Although cocoa prices fell in 1921, many African families already had acquired great wealth in the previous decades, and despite the decline cocoa farming remained a major economic activity for the entire colonial period.[9]

Changes in transportation infrastructure and other technologies supported the creation of an export-oriented economy in the Gold Coast. British officials built a railroad from the coast to Asante to facilitate the export of cocoa, gold, timber, and other resources. The British administration later extended motor roads into the Northern Territories to encourage labor migration to the gold mines and cocoa farms. The coast had no natural ports, and surf boats carried products to ocean steamers anchored outside Saltpond, Winneba, and other coastal towns until the harbor at Takoradi was expanded into a major port. Communications technologies also linked regions in a network of telegraph lines. Christian missionaries introduced the lithographic press, and various missionary and secular newspapers were published. In contrast to British India, the new print media did not spark heated religious debates, as neither Muslims nor indigenous religious specialists embraced the press. But the religious marketplace in the Gold Coast underwent other changes.

Transformations in the Gold Coast Religious Marketplace

The British colonial consolidation encouraged changes in the Gold Coast religious marketplace. While official policy affirmed religious liberty, colonial officials moved to restrict indigenous religious expressions, such as movements identifying asocial behavior and providing mechanisms to address social tensions.[10] These restrictions expressed the British "civilizing mission," and Christian missionaries joined the effort by providing moral teaching at Sunday services and in English-language schools. Some missionaries were Africans, but most mission leaders were from Europe and North America, having pushed Africans out of positions that some had held in the nineteenth century. While Africans still found ways to take initiatives in mission churches,[11] some founded independent churches and others joined prophetic movements that allowed for African expressions that expatriate missionaries did not tolerate. Muslims also arrived in the southern regions of the Gold Coast. These movements provided more choices in the Gold Coast religious marketplace.

Many new religious movements were led by African prophets claiming divine inspiration. These leaders often had been involved with Christian missions and drew on visionary experiences to articulate a religious message integrating aspects of local culture with Christian teachings. One of the first movements came from outside the Gold Coast: William Wadé Harris brought his prophetic movement during travels as an itinerant preacher in 1913–1914, inspiring the creation of autonomous "Harrist" churches. Another movement sprang from within the Methodist congregation in the Gold Coast: Joseph William Egyanka Appiah formed a Methodist prayer group in 1919, but its emphasis on healing, speaking in tongues, and prophesizing led to its expulsion in 1922 and continued activity as the Musama Disco Christo Church. These two were only some of the many examples of local initiative in religious affairs emerging in the Gold Coast religious marketplace of the early twentieth century.[12]

Other new suppliers were Muslim scholars who moved to the towns of the Gold Coast from the savanna in the late nineteenth and early twentieth centuries. Colonial officials noted increasing Muslim settlement in the coastal towns beginning in the 1890s, and memories in the Hausa community point to a "revolutionary era" of large-scale immigration from the savanna to permanent Muslim neighborhoods, or *zongos*, in coastal towns.[13] Initially only itinerant Muslim traders arrived for short visits to the coast after the lifting of the Asante travel ban in the 1870s, but economic change and the exodus from the Muslim trading town of Salaga, which suffered a civil war in the early 1890s, increased the numbers of Muslims in *zongos*. Savanna *mallams* increased the supply of esoteric healers along the coast, and some collaborated with British-recognized "headmen" to enforce Muslim norms in the *zongo*. These Muslim scholars looked askance at Fante Muslim practices. The headman of the *zongo* in Winneba, for example, told the British that Hausa Muslim scholars were doing their best to teach Fante Muslims "how to be proper Muslims."[14] The Basel missionary A. J. Lochmann added that Hausa Muslims did not recognize Fante Muslims as "Mohamedans of equal rank."[15] As discussed in chapter 2, the criticisms of savanna Muslim scholars won over some members of the younger generation. But before savanna Muslims could consolidate their position, the influenza pandemic of 1918 produced a devastating human toll that raised questions about the efficacy of esoteric healing provided by *mallams*.

The Influenza Pandemic and the Religious Marketplace

The global influenza epidemic of 1918–1919 altered the religious marketplace in the Gold Coast. This outbreak was the most devastating global pandemic since the medieval Black Death, killing more than fifty million people worldwide in just two years.[16] In the Gold Coast, it produced the most acute demographic disaster of the twentieth century, claiming approximately one hundred thousand in the last three months of 1918. The trajectory of transmission went from the coast to the interior: railroads and lorry routes associated with gold mining and cocoa farming became routes of disease transmission. The colonial medical corps could not meet this challenge, as they were unprepared to treat the infected and understaffed, as many doctors were serving in Europe during the First World War.[17] The general failure of biomedical responses to address the pandemic meant that Africans turned to other sources to provide relief and meaning. This questioning introduced new demand in the religious marketplace, leading to the emergence of new providers of religious services.

African Christian religious movements filled a gap left by biomedicine and mission churches in the Gold Coast. Many established Christian missions were closed by the Gold Coast government in their effort to prevent disease transmission at services.[18] In any case mission churches offered few practical remedial services to address the influenza pandemic.[19] New prophetic Christian movements, in contrast, offered the promise of spiritual healing and adopted cultural forms that Africans found more comforting than Christian mission expressions.[20] The Faith Tabernacle Congregation, a local branch of a Philadelphia-based church, for example, launched itself as a new religious provider in the Gold Coast through spiritual healing in the wake of the epidemic: its African leaders took the ill to the movement's divine healing center, called their "Faith Home," where the ill rested and nonafflicted members prayed for their recovery. Survivors became avid members and promoted the Faith Tabernacle Congregation with claims of having been cured by miracles.[21] Other prophetic movements supplied similar assistance. The first meetings of the Methodist prayer group led by Joseph William Egyanka Appiah occurred in 1919, for example, and his spiritual services probably reflected a turn to new expressions of spirituality in the wake of the influenza epidemic. Amadu Ramanu Pedro was proselytizing the Ahmadiyya in this era. The Ahmadiyya did not offer spiritual healing, but it had an explanation for the calamity in Ghulam Ahmad's End Times preaching and the hopeful news that the Mahdi and the Messiah had appeared in the East.

Ahmadiyya Proselytism and Dreams of Foreigners in the Gold Coast

Ahmadi memories mention, only in passing, the involvement of Amadu Ramanu Pedro, an Afro-Brazilian Muslim from Lagos who had a business at Saltpond. Pedro's role is secondary in most accounts, merely serving to convey knowledge of the Ahmadiyya to Fante Muslims. I contend that Pedro's involvement was more extensive. He was an Ahmadi Muslim who proselytized the movement in the late 1910s, perhaps meeting Yusuf Nyarko before his dream. Pedro also was a cultural broker as Fante Muslims interpreted the dream and negotiated their involvement with the Ahmadiyya during Maulvi Nayyar's residences in the Gold Coast. These activities are lost in local memories because Pedro subsequently left the Ahmadiyya, as did many Afro-Brazilians in the mid-1920s, including members of the Pedro family in Lagos, who joined Muhammad Lawal Basil Agusto's Muslim movement.[22] Contemporaneous written materials help recover Amadu Ramanu Pedro's role as an Ahmadi Muslim who facilitated contacts between the Fante Muslim community and both the Ahmadiyya headquarters in Qadian and Maulvi Nayyar when he visited the Gold Coast in 1921.

Amadu Ramadu Pedro accepted the Ahmadiyya just before he left Lagos to establish a business at Saltpond.[23] Pedro joined during the second wave of Lagosian members in the months after the initial group of twenty-one had sent in their membership applications.[24] Pedro then moved to the Gold Coast to launch a commercial career, possibly with funds that he had earned serving with the British military.[25] He initially was involved in the kola nut trade between the Gold Coast and Lagos and later added other commercial ventures, ultimately moving business operations to Cape Coast.[26] Amadu Ramanu Pedro's 1917 arrival in the Gold Coast is reported in the *Review of Religions*, not as a career decision, but as the founding a new Ahmadiyya branch.[27] This reference is aspirational, as widespread acceptance of the Ahmadiyya never came; the *Review of Religions* dropped its references to the Gold Coast after 1917 until Maulvi Nayyar's arrival in 1921. Pedro nonetheless continued his informal proselytism as he operated in commercial networks that took him from Saltpond to Mankessim and other interior trading towns. After the 1918 influenza pandemic, Pedro's evangelism about Ghulam Ahmad's claims to be the Messiah took on greater relevance. Fante Ahmadi Muslim memories do not mention Pedro's proselytism. Nor do their memories make reference to the 1918 influenza pandemic. They focus instead on the dream of Yusuf Nyarko, Binyameen Sam's relative.

Memories of Yusuf Nyarko's dream have circulated for at least half a century and probably for much longer. Numerous versions exist, such as the account in the Ahmadiyya pamphlet quoted in the chapter introduction. The content of Yusuf Nyarko's dream in all accounts is that he was performing *salat* with foreign Muslims. The conventional translation is "white men," but the Fante term is *aburofoo kokoo*, a reference to lightly pigmented or "red" foreigners from outside West Africa.[28] Humphrey Fisher suggested the dream had salience because "the Christian mocked the Muslims for having no white man."[29] I argue that Fante Muslims valued Muslims from abroad as a counterweight to savanna *mallams*: their appeal as authoritative Muslim outsiders figured more centrally than colonial racial politics or competition with Christian missions. Nyarko's dream also occurred after the 1918 influenza pandemic, when the efficacy of amulets produced by savanna Muslim scholars was open to public questioning. Nyarko's dream may have been compelling, too, because it echoed the conversion narratives suggesting that Sam had visions of Muslims before he accepted Islam and founded the Fante Muslim community. But Nyarko's dream came from an era when Fante Muslims were more knowledgeable about Islam: the focus was not on the attire of *mallams* but on Muslim practices such as *salat*.

Local memories identify two persons influencing the interpretation of Yusuf Nyarko's dream. In most accounts, Nyarko made contact with Amadu Ramanu Pedro after his dream and then informed Mahdi Appah; in others Nyarko recounted his dream first to Appah, who then interacted with Pedro. Although the precise sequence of action is unclear, the narrative thread in all memories connects Appah and Pedro to the interpretive process. Pedro's role may well have been more pronounced than current memories allow, such as proselytizing the Ahmadiyya to Nyarko before he had his dream. Whatever Pedro's specific involvement with Nyarko, he passed information to Appah, who was central to interpreting Nyarko's dream for the Fante Muslim community. Appah had been a personal friend of Binyameen Sam and a leader of the Fante Muslim community, but at the time of Nyarko's dream, Appah resided in Bedum near his cocoa farm where he had been for nearly two decades. When Lochmann visited Ekrawfo in 1913, he still referred to Appah as the leader of Fante Muslims, but Lochmann also mentioned others, including Musa, a Hausa *mallam* teaching Arabic and leading Friday communal prayers at Ekrawfo.[30] Mahdi Appah was an absent leader, one who allowed Musa and other savanna Muslim scholars to assume authority at Ekrawfo. Memories do not refer to the erosion of Mahdi Appah's status because reports of Nyarko's dream opened the way for Appah to return to an active leadership position in the Fante Muslim community.

Mahdi Appah used Yusuf Nyarko's dream to reassert his authority over Fante Muslims. He did so in part by calling a meeting of Fante Muslims at Mankessim. This town had been the center of an eighteenth-century Fante political coalition and, more recently, the site where late nineteenth-century political activists met to form the Fante Confederation on the eve of the British declaration of the Gold Coast colony. Meeting at Mankessim marked the significance of the meeting. It also avoided Ekrawfo, the historical base of the movement, and enabled Mahdi Appah and Fante Muslims to discuss the Ahmadiyya in isolation from Yakubu, the savanna Muslim scholar who ran the Arabic school at Ekrawfo in the late 1910s. Appah could focus attention on the dream and not on issues of Muslim practice that divided the community. In 1919 Mahdi Appah was a newly engaged leader who used his influence to facilitate a meeting, explicitly to discuss a dream but perhaps implicitly to reconcile divisions in the Fante Muslim community created by the criticism of savanna Muslim scholars.

Details of the Fante Muslim meeting at Mankessim are sketchy. Memories focus on a copy of the *Review of Religions*, which Mahdi Appah received from Amadu Ramanu Pedro; Appah reportedly needed it to find an address for the Ahmadiyya in India. Evidence suggests that Pedro was more consequential than as a source of information; at the very least, he and not Appah wrote to the Ahmadiyya to arrange the Gold Coast stopover.[31] Pedro also may have addressed the assembled Fante Muslims to convey the Ahmadiyya's message. In addition to the End Times claims, Pedro's address might have referenced aspects of Ahmadiyya reformism, such as its educational initiative and its criticism of amulets and esoteric healing. Whether Pedro presented or not, the outcome of the Mankessim meeting hinged on Mahdi Appah's views. Only a general memory of what Appah communicated endures. Appah may well have argued for Ahmadiyya schools: he had had helped Sam found schools in the 1890s, including one near his cocoa farm in Bedum, and two decades later likely advocated forcefully for another Muslim educational initiative to teach both English and Arabic. What is remembered is Appah's offer to contribute his own funds to defray some of the Ahmadi missionary's travel costs. This gesture convinced others with wealth from the cocoa boom to contribute. It was not a commitment to join the Ahmadiyya, merely a decision to explore a new movement that promised Muslim reformism, English-language education, and inspired leadership associated with the Mahdi and Messiah. After this meeting Pedro sent £150 to Qadian to support the visit of an Ahmadi missionary to West Africa.[32]

The Ahmadiyya Muslim Community in Qadian, once it received Amadu Ramanu Pedro's letter with the funds for the missionary's transport, made plans to send a missionary to West Africa. Several options were explored, and eventually Maulvi Abdul Rahman Nayyar, recently arrived as an Ahmadi missionary in London, traveled to West Africa.[33] The tour included a brief stop in Freetown, a layover in Saltpond, and an extended residence in Lagos. Maulvi Nayyar had stationary both announcing his title as "Ahmadi Muslim Missioner, West Africa" and giving addresses in Qadian and London and contact information for Freetown, Saltpond, and Lagos.[34] Nigeria was the focus of Maulvi Nayyar's visit: when he arrived at Saltpond, he told the British district commissioner that he had been "invited by the Nigerian branch of the Ahmadia" and did not mention either Amadu Ramanu Pedro or Fante Muslims. Maulvi Nayyar made passing reference to his hopes of engaging "Wesleyan and other Christian-taught youths, ripe for Islam," perhaps an oblique reference to the Methodist background of most Fante Muslims.[35] Maulvi Nayyar was unprepared for the enthusiastic reception he received at Ekrawfo.

Maulvi Nayyar's Gold Coast Visits

Maulvi Abdul Rahim Nayyar first arrived in the Gold Coast on February 28, 1921. He was thirty-seven years old and bolstered by two years of experience as an Ahmadi missionary in London. On the ocean voyage he conversed with passengers, gaining confidence in his ability to evangelize Africans.[36] As Maulvi Nayyar disembarked from the commercial steamer at Saltpond, his distinctive green turban attracted the attention of the harbor police, who promptly took him to see the British district commissioner. Maulvi Nayyar stressed that the Ahmadiyya "does not believe in a deliverer to come with the sword to wage war on infidels" in his testimony to the district commissioner, who found Maulvi Nayyar to be "affable" and allowed him to stay in the Gold Coast. British officials nonetheless warned Muslim leaders and Christian missionaries to be on guard for "charlatanism and seditious talk."[37] The colonial administration also kept an eye on Maulvi Nayyar's movements: they had Muslims in the police force attend his meetings in plain clothes and report on his conversations with Muslims in the *zongos*. In the middle of his trip, they asked Maulvi Nayyar to produce his travel papers for reexamination.[38] This surveillance and subtle intimidation did not provoke Maulvi Nayyar, who repeatedly reaffirmed his loyalty to the British.

Maulvi Nayyar's primary residence in the Gold Coast was Saltpond, where he was hosted by Amadu Ramanu Pedro, likely the only other Ahmadi Muslim in the Gold Coast at the time. Maulvi Nayyar's visit to Ekrawfo was the main event of his stopover in the Gold Coast. This trip escaped British attention, in contrast to Maulvi Nayyar's subsequent travels to coastal towns, but local memories concentrate on Maulvi Nayyar's visit to the center of the Fante Muslim community. Maulvi Nayyar reportedly was carried in a hammock in the style of local political leaders, with the entourage singing the entire way about the arrival of the Mahdi. At Ekrawfo Mahdi Appah received Maulvi Nayyar and engaged him in discussions. The details of their meeting are not remembered, but they no doubt included Amadu Ramanu Pedro as a facilitator and focused on both spiritual and practical matters, such as the desire for English- and Arabic-language education. The meeting produced an agreement, as memories stress what happened next: a large assembly of Fante Muslims, led by Mahdi Appah, accepted membership in the Ahmadiyya and swore *bayat* in the presence of Maulvi Nayyar.[39] On his return to Saltpond, Maulvi Nayyar cabled London and exclaimed that thousands Fante Muslims just had joined the Ahmadiyya.[40] The initial group of Fante Ahmadi Muslims probably was in the hundreds, but whatever the exact number, the enthusiastic reception left an impression on Maulvi Nayyar.[41]

Maulvi Nayyar met others in the weeks that followed. He visited the *zongo* community at Saltpond and traveled to Sraha, a commercial town in Gomoa, to visit another *zongo*. The Hausa headman in Sraha did not accommodate Maulvi Nayyar overnight, as would have been expected, and Nayyar stayed in the home of a Fante Muslim instead. Both Hausa headmen complained to British officials that Maulvi Nayyar had not been appropriately deferential. One Muslim leader in the Saltpond *zongo* expressed a religious concern that Nayyar encouraged "innovations," a reference to the Arabic term, *bida*. These statements, as well as information gathered from spies following Maulvi Nayyar during his meetings with Hausa leaders, led British officials to conclude that "a normal Mohammedan would achieve more on a mission" than Maulvi Nayyar had. As Maulvi Nayyar departed Saltpond for Lagos in early April, 1921, the district commissioner wrote dismissively in his report: "If Nayyar is not a propagandist under religious guise, then he is a misguided zealot of a new sect. . . . Personally I think he is somewhat of a charlatan."[42] Unknown to the British officials, hundreds of Fante Muslims had accepted the Ahmadiyya, and Maulvi Nayyar altered his plans and would return to the Gold Coast in late 1921.

During Maulvi Nayyar's absence in the middle of 1921, the Fante Muslim community collected funds to support a residential Ahmadi missionary. Mahdi Appah led the effort, but Amadu Ramanu Pedro was in charge of depositing the money in the Saltpond branch of the Bank of West Africa. This accumulation depended on the generosity of Mahdi Appah and other wealthy cocoa farmers, but others also contributed, including members of Fante fishing communities along the coast. Stories of Maulvi Nayyar's arrival and the assembly at Ekrawfo probably worked to convince a broad cross section of new Ahmadi Muslims to provide financial support. This extensive collection precipitated rumors of misdeeds. One allegation was that Maulvi Nayyar had absconded with £1,500. Another was that Nayyar promised to pay more for cocoa than the British paid, which caused some farmers to hold back cocoa in 1921. These rumors were false, and any holdbacks reflected the dramatic fall in cocoa prices that year.[43] Reference to cocoa farmers, however, suggests that Mahdi Appah may have worked to expand the network of Ahmadi Muslims among his fellow cocoa entrepreneurs, some of whom might not have attended the assembly at Ekrawfo. The collection was based on the trust and self-sufficiency of Fante Muslims. It also communicated to Maulvi Nayyar, then in Lagos, that Fante Muslims were honoring their commitments and that he needed to return to prepare for the founding of a new mission in the Gold Coast.[44]

On his return Maulvi Nayyar put the Ahmadiyya branch in the Gold Coast on a firm organizational foundation. During the four months of his second residence, he produced two documents to define the Ahmadiyya. The first was a short statement of general principles, titled "Resolutions," which Maulvi Nayyar presented to Fante Muslims shortly after his return from Lagos. Three months later Fante Muslims agreed to a second document, "Rules and Regulations," which defined the organizational structure and operations of the Ahmadiyya in the Gold Coast. "Resolutions" was a copy of the printed document adopted by the Nigerian branch: its first line had "Nigeria" crossed out and "Gold Coast" added in handwriting.[45] This document confirms that Maulvi Nayyar's primary focus had been the Lagos branch and how his visit to Ekrawfo had altered his plans. "Rules and Regulations" was typed and not printed, and it had "Gold Coast" in its title line with no erasures: it was produced for Fante Muslims who accepted the Ahmadiyya.[46] The document included general points relevant to any Ahmadiyya branch, but added provisions only relevant to the Gold Coast. "Rules and Regulations," I contend, reflected the outcome of discussions involving Maulvi Nayyar, Mahdi Appah, and other Fante Muslim elders over the course of late 1921.

"Resolutions" expressed fundamental Ahmadiyya teachings and positions. The first was that the Ahmadiyya was a "purely religious Revival started by the late Mirza Ghulam Ahmad of Qadian, the Promised Messiah and Mahdi and the Divine Messenger of the latter days who was raised for the regeneration of mankind and the renewal of faith in the only living religion of Allah, Islam." It added that the Ahmadiyya was not in conflict with the Quran or the "real teachings and practices of the Holy Prophet Muhammad." The next point pertained to Ahmadiyya loyalty to any constituted political authority and explicitly to the British. The third resolution added the verse from the Quran regarding no compulsion in religion and stated that the movement did not belief in warfare: only "the pen and the tongue and the heavenly signs" would be used in the promotion of Islam. The fourth resolution was that the movement did not believe in a "warrior Mahdi," and the fifth added that military jihad was unlawful according to the teachings of the Quran. The sixth noted that the Ahmadiyya distinguished between the activities of Christian missionaries and the British government, and the last resolution prayed for success in the war of humanity against barbarism. Published in English and sent to the Saltpond district commissioner, the resolution functioned less as resolutions for members to adopt and more as an affirmation of loyalty in the colonial context. Amadu Ramanu Pedro signed the document in his capacity as secretary of the Gold Coast branch of the Ahmadiyya.

"Rules and Regulations" had twenty-six points pertaining to the organization of the local Ahmadiyya branch as well as to expectations for personal and community conduct. The rules and regulations fell into three categories. Nine defined the administration of the branch, including the Ahmadiyya's overall mission hierarchy descending from the *khalifatul masih*, through the residential missionary-in-charge in the Gold Coast, to African missionaries and lay leaders working under the missionary's direction. Local deliberative processes involved village committees of three to five persons and an overarching council of elders of twelve to forty members who would meet at least twice a year to elect members, settle any disputes, and discuss important issues. The branch also had chiefs, treasurers, and secretaries in villages, where the regular collection of financial contributions was recorded before being sent to the missionary-in-charge. At the top, but under the missionary-in-charge, were two local leaders, the head or ameer and the general secretary. These organizational arrangements were standard features of local Ahmadiyya branches, but Gold Coast rules added the proviso that regular financial contributions, a portion of which usually was sent to Qadian for missionary work under the direction of the *khalifatul masih*, would be "used for Gold Coast activities only; to pay for the preaching, teaching, and maintenance of the Missionary." The duration of this targeting of funds for local use was not specified, but the location of the deposit was noted as the Saltpond Bank, where the initial contributions had been accumulated.

The provision of education was defined in the "Rules and Regulations." Six rules stated the Ahmadiyya intent to establish both primary schools and a missionary training center in Gold Coast. Two rules involved missionary training. One was that it was to begin "soon" at Saltpond; and the other was that the school would be raised to a "college with both secular and religious education." The intention, expressed in a separate proviso, was to train "African missionaries" who would found new missions under the supervision of the missionary-in-charge. Three other rules concerned English-language primary schools: a "large number" were projected to be opened under the management of "local committees controlled by the Missionary through his representatives," and "every important place wanting a school needs to apply to the Missionary and agree to provide some funds for the school." Finally, a rule expressed the expectation that members "preach Islam and devote their leisure hours to the study of English and Arabic." These provisions resolved any concerns over English versus Arabic by stating an expectation that every member study both languages and by offering English-language instruction in primary schools and Arabic to those wishing to be missionaries. The effort to establish primary schools represented a return to the aborted initiative of Binyameen Sam's era.

Individual and community conduct was the final set of concerns addressed in the "Rules and Regulations." One of the eleven expressed the general Ahmadiyya position regarding loyalty to the British government, and two more specifically forbade what it defined as Hausa practices, namely calling Christians "Nasrani" and referring to the Ottoman sultan in sermons at mosques. Two related to funeral practices, which often commanded a considerable outlay of Fante family resources: one prohibited funeral services for "drunkards, adulterers, or non-observers of prayer unless they repent and pay repentance offering," and the other forbade paying "unnecessary expenses" and recommended saving the funds for "missionary work." Related to funerals was the rule about inheritance, which prohibited matrilineal preferences widely practiced among Akan speakers: children usually inherited from their mother's brothers and not their fathers, and the rule affirmed the need to follow Islamic practice of fathers providing for their wives and children directly. It also added the recommendation to write a will and to consider a donation of a tenth of the estate to the Ahmadiyya community in Qadian. The scarification of children was forbidden, girls were advised to cover their breasts, and boys were required to be circumcised. Three more rules related to religious practice: the Muslim greeting of "peace upon you" should be used with other Muslims, and dirty sheepskins should be removed from mosques and replaced with clean mats. The third religious rule was that esoteric or "magical" Muslim practices were completely forbidden: the faithful were instructed to pray directly to God in their own language and not rely on Arabic-speaking intermediaries who made appeals on their behalf.

Adhering to these "Rules and Regulations" removed Fante Muslims further from savanna Muslim norms. Several rules explicitly referred to "Hausa" Muslim practices that should be avoided. The most serious challenge applied to all *mallams* in the savanna Muslim tradition: their esoteric services were deemed "magical" and without religious merit. Other differences, not stated in the rules, also marked Ahmadi Muslims from others Hausa and other Muslims in West Africa. One was the requirement to only perform *salat* with Ahmadi Muslims and never to pray behind leaders of other Muslim communities. Another was to perform *salat* with arms crossed as opposed to the Maliki practice of relaxed arms at one's side. Eventually, too, Fante Muslims began to purchase prayer rugs instead of using cured sheepskins. An emphasis on Ahmadiyya distinctiveness resonated with Fante Muslims who had resisted pressures from savanna Muslim scholars to conform to their norms. But they joined a movement that demanded fidelity to its understanding of reformed Islam, and thus some of Binyameen Sam's practices no longer were accepted.

Memories of the early years point to hesitation before a few Fante Muslims agreed to join the Ahmadiyya. M. A. Ishaque, a young Fante Muslim, reportedly had private conversations with Maulvi Nayyar before accepting the Ahmadiyya. Ishaque had acquired fluency in Arabic from savanna Muslim scholars teaching at Ekrawfo during the 1910s. He conversed with Maulvi Nayyar in Arabic, and only after a lengthy exchange on various topics was he convinced to join the Ahmadiyya.[47] This story of hesitancy and questioning is celebrated in Ahmadi memories because Ishaque decided to become an Ahmadi Muslim. To historians it points to serious deliberations among young Fante Muslims. One imagines that several others had similar conversations with Maulvi Nayyar or Ishaque after his meeting with Nayyar. Their acceptance of the Ahmadiyya, occurring after careful consideration and not at the mass meeting at Ekrawfo, underscores the generational divisions within the Fante Muslim community. Maulvi Nayyar's ability to engage in Arabic was critical to convincing those who had attended the Arabic school at Ekrawfo.

Maulvi Nayyar returned to Lagos in late November 1921. The Ahmadiyya "Resolutions" and "Rules and Regulations" were in place, so Maulvi Nayyar could devote the remaining twelve months of his West African residence to the Ahmadiyya community in Lagos. Given that Fante Muslims had made financial contributions to found an Ahmadiyya mission at Saltpond, Maulvi Nayyar knew that his work would continue. Maulvi Nayyar informed British officials at Saltpond, as he returned to Lagos, that Amadu Ramanu Pedro was the "secretary of the movement and my representative till reinforcement."[48]

The Split among Fante Muslims after the Arrival of the Ahmadiyya

Not all Fante Muslims joined the Ahmadiyya. Among those who did not were those who remained loyal to Mallam Yakubu, the Hausa Muslim scholar who taught at Ekrawfo in the late 1910s and early 1920s. Memories of the divide are not extensive and focus on a symbolic act: Maulvi Nayyar refused to perform *salat* behind Mallam Yakubu at Ekrawfo's mosque. The issue resonated with significance on both sides: Ahmadi Muslims were following exclusive practices, from the perspective of those who did not join, and for Ahmadi Muslims Mallam Yakubu was not recognizing the Ahmadiyya. Whether or not the event happened as recounted, it stands in the public memory of Fante Muslims who did not accept the Ahmadiyya and moved their center to the village of Obonster. This village was northwest of Ekrawfo in Enyan, where Nana Kwamosa, a member of the royal family, welcomed the dissenters. Mallam Yakubu joined the Fante Muslims there, but left shortly thereafter. The leadership of the Obonster Muslim community fell to Hamidu, son of Nana Kwamosa and one of Mallam Yakubu's best students; Hamidu was a member of the second generation of Fante Muslims, similar in age to M. A. Ishaque, but someone from the younger generation who came to a different conclusion about the merits of the Ahmadiyya.[49]

Those who rejected the Ahmadiyya had concerns with its message, the demands it placed on individuals and the community, and English-language education. Hausa Muslim scholars concluded that Ghulam Ahmad's teachings were unacceptable innovations, and those accepting Mallam Yakubu's leadership likely heard him express similar opinions and came to the same conclusion. The new organizational arrangements of the Ahmadiyya were not immediately apparent, but the 1921 collection of funds to support a missionary mirrored what was to come: a movement led by an outsider supported by local funds. British canvassing of information about the Ahmadiyya uncovered testimony that some Fante Muslims refused to make contributions.[50] This resistance tapped a deep strand in the Fante Muslim community, given Binyameen Sam's views on Methodist "ticket money." The desire to receive Muslim esoteric healing also may have been another reason some followed Mallam Yakubu and moved to Obonster. Reintroduction of English-language schools under the Ahmadiyya also encouraged the split. Fante Muslims disagreed about the merits of English-language schools at the turn of the nineteenth century, and many still remained opposed. Hamidu, the Fante Muslim who eventually led the Obonster Muslim community, was Mallam Yakubu's student and had personal interests in pedagogical continuity. It was only a small group, however, that moved to Obonster. Most followed the example of M. A. Ishaque. He eventually taught Arabic at the Ahmadiyya mission at Saltpond: the vexing issue of education that divided the Fante Muslim community was not as divisive with both Arabic- and English-language instruction encouraged by the Ahmadiyya.

The new Fante Muslim center at Obonster was a creation of the split, and other Fante Muslims, outside those who assembled at Ekrawfo, existed in the Gold Coast in the early twentieth century. These communities had not been a part of the Fante Muslim network created by Binyameen Sam and Mahdi Appah.[51] The arrival of Hausa and other Muslims at the coastal town of Winneba, east of Saltpond and a major center for commerce, produced Fante conversions to Islam in the early twentieth century. Some of these Fante Muslims joined the Ahmadiyya in the years ahead, but others did not. The Fante Muslims who did not accept the Ahmadiyya, including the community at Obonster, largely were tolerant of others who joined the movement. This experience contrasts with developments in Lagos, where Maulvi Nayyar's visit had great initial success but was followed by several waves of acrimonious fission after his departure.

Conclusion

Maulvi Nayyar did not expect much from his stop at Saltpond on his way to Lagos. Upon arrival he told the British district commissioner that he hoped to convince a few "Wesleyan and other Christian-taught youths" to accept the Ahmadiyya, but instead he won over several hundred Fante Muslims, including the influential leader Mahdi Appah. These new members pressed Maulvi Nayyar to return, and during that second visit Maulvi Nayyar and Mahdi Appah negotiated the terms of Ahmadi missionary activities in a document known as "Rules and Regulations." It was a contract pledging future contributions from Fante Muslims to support a residential missionary, who in turn agreed to build schools and provide religious leadership. British officials, unaware of these developments and learning about Maulvi Nayyar's activities from Hausa Muslim leaders, were not favorably disposed, but saw little harm or prospect for expansion. But the Ahmadiyya grew in the Gold Coast, as local Ahmadi Muslims collaborated with a series of Ahmadi residential missionaries to make Saltpond the headquarters of an expanding movement, as the next chapter discusses.

Notes

1. Fisher identified Nyarko as Sam's cousin in *Ahmadiyyah*, 118, but oral testimony from the late 1950s stated that Nyarko was Sam's nephew. See Debrunner, Fisher, and Fisher, "Early Fante Islam [continued]," *GBT* 1, no. 8 (1960), 28. I also heard memories that Nyarko was Sam's nephew: Hanson interview at Ekrawfo: Hakeem Kofi Yamoah, 1 June 2005. No definitive conclusions on Nyarko's background are in Guar-Gorman, "Islam in Fantiland," 67–68.
2. *Ahmadiyya Movement in Ghana*, 2.
3. Patterson, "The Influenza Epidemic." This pandemic occurred after the transformations associated with the First World War in the Gold Coast. See David Killingray, "Repercussions of World War I in the Gold Coast," *JAH* 19, no.1 (1978), 39–59.
4. The impact of the influenza epidemic on new religious expressions is detailed in Adam Mohr, "Capitalism, Chaos, and Christian Healing: Faith Tabernacle Congregation in Southern Colonial Ghana, 1918–26," *JAH* 51, no. 1 (2011), 70–71. Also see Mohr, *Enchanted Calvinism: Labor Migration, Afflicted Spirits, and Christian Therapy in a Presbyterian Church* (Rochester, NY: University of Rochester Press, 2013), 61.
5. Gocking, *Facing Two Ways*; Parker, *Making the Town*.
6. The annual listing of schools are in colonial Blue Books in PRO CO 100/49–61.
7. G.B. Kay, *The Political Economy of the Colonialism in Ghana* (Cambridge: Cambridge University Press, 1972).
8. Gareth Austin, *Labor, Land, and Capital in Ghana: From Slavery to Free Labor in Asante, 1807–1956* (Rochester, NY: University of Rochester Press, 2005); Hill, *Migrant Cocoa Farmers*.
9. Kay, *Political Economy of the Colonialism*, 15.
10. Akan speakers conceptualized asocial behavior as *bayi*, or "witchcraft," and participated in religious movements intended to identify and deal with offending parties. For a

historical analysis of one movement, see Jean Allman and John Parker, *Tongnaab: The History of an African God* (Bloomington: Indiana University Press, 2007).

11. Stephen F. Miescher, *Making Men in Ghana* (Bloomington: Indiana University Press, 2005); Birgit Meyer, *Translating the Devil: Religion and Modernity Among the Ewe in Ghana* (Edinburgh: Edinburgh University Press, 1999); Jon Miller, *Missionary Zeal and Institutional Control: Organizational Contradictions in the Basel Mission on the Gold Coast, 1828–1917* (Grand Rapids, MI: William B. Eerdmans Publishing, 2003); Mohr, *Enchanted Calvinism*.

12. C. G. Baeta, *Prophetism in Ghana: A Study of Some 'Spiritual' Churches* (London: Student Christian Movement, 1962); Hans W. Debrunner, *The Story of Sampson Oppong, the Prophet* (Accra: Waterville Publishing House, 1965); Robert W. Wyllie, "Pioneers of Ghanaian Pentecostalism: Peter Anim and James McKeown," *JRA* 6, no. 2 (1974), 109–122.

13. PRO CO 96/224: 28 April 1892, dispatch 144, enclosure from H. H. J. Bell, cited in Skinner, "Muslim Elites," 100, 106n52. For the description of Hausa immigration as "revolutionary," see Adamu, *Hausa Factor*, 166.

14. PRAAD, Cape Coast: ADM 1/23/353, no date, "Ahmadia Movement in the Gold Coast."

15. Debrunner, Fisher, and Fisher, "Early Fante Islam," *GBT* 1, no. 7 (1959), 29.

16. Jeffrey K. Taubenberger and David M. Morens, "1918 Influenza: The Mother of All Pandemics," *Review of Biomedicine* 17, no. 1 (2006), 69–79.

17. Patterson, "Influenza Epidemic," 502.

18. N. Smith, *The Presbyterian Church of Ghana: 1835–1960* (Accra: Ghana Universities Press, 1966), 159; Patterson, "Influenza Epidemic," 492.

19. Mohr, *Enchanted Calvinism*, 61.

20. For the classic example from southern Nigeria, see J. D. Y. Peel, *Aladura: A Religious Movement among the Yoruba* (London: Oxford University Press, 1968).

21. Mohr, "Capitalism, Chaos, and Christian Healing," 70–71.

22. Fafunwa, *Jama-at-ul Islamiyya of Nigeria at 60*, 4.

23. Members of the Pedro family still reside at Saltpond, but most of the family has moved to other coastal towns. My interviews produced only vague memories of Amadu Ramanu Pedro and his early years in the Gold Coast. Contemporaneous written materials and Fante memories are the basis for my argument about Pedro's role in the arrival of the Ahmadiyya.

24. "Ahmadiyya Mission News: Nigeria," *RR* 16, no. 1 (1917), 41.

25. Pedro added the initials "D.S.M." after his signature on a document, hinting at receipt of a medal in the British military. PRAAD, Cape Coast: ADM 1/23/353, 22 August 1921, Maulvi A. R. Nayyar to DC, attachment.

26. Fisher heard the memory about Pedro's involvement in the kola nut trade in the late 1950s. Debrunner, Fisher, and Fisher, "Early Fante Islam [continued]," *GBT* 1, no. 8 (1960) 28.

27. "Ahmadiyya Mission News: Nigeria," *RR* 16, nos. 10–11 (1917), 396.

28. *Aburofoo kokoo* was the term used in interviews conducted in 2005. I discussed usage with informants, such as Hakeem Kofi Yamoah at Ekrawfo, who confirmed that *kokoo* was the adjective. I also discussed the term with Maulvi Abdul Wahab Adam.

29. Fisher, *Ahmadiyyah*, 118.

30. Debrunner, Fisher, and Fisher, "Early Fante Islam," *GBT* 1, no. 7 (1959), 26, 31. Ahmadi Muslims in the late 1950s insisted to Fisher that Mahdi Appah had been at Ekrawfo when Lochmann visited. See Debrunner, Fisher, and Fisher, "Early Fante Islam [continued]," *GBT* 1, no. 8 (1960), 27–28. I conclude, as did Fisher on the basis of Lochmann's report, that Appah was not present when he visited. Note that my contention that Appah was an absent leader needing to reassert his authority in the late 1910s runs counter to current memories that emphasize that he was leader from the time of Sam's death to the arrival of the Ahmadiyya.

31. "Ahmadiyya Mission News: Nigeria," *RR* 16, nos. 10–11 (1917), 396.

32. Pedro's letter and provision of funds is noted but incorrectly connected to the Ahmadiyya community in Lagos. "Ahmadiyya Mission News: Nigeria," *RR* 16, nos. 10–11 (1917), 396.

33. "Ahmadiyya Mission for America," *RR* 18, no. 12 (1919), 405–406; and "News and Notes: Our London Mission," *RR* 20, no. 1 (1921), 39–40. See chapter 4 for the various plans to send an Ahmadi missionary to West Africa.

34. PRAAD, Cape Coast: ADM 1/23/353, 22 August 1921, Maulvi A. R. Nayyar to DC.

35. PRAAD, Cape Coast: ADM 1/23/353, 3 March 1921, Saltpond DC to CCCP.

36. "News and Notes: West Africa," *RR* 20, no. 4 (April 1921), 158–159.

37. PRAAD, Cape Coast: ADM 1/23/353, 3 March 1921, Saltpond DC to CCCP.

38. PRAAD, Cape Coast: ADM 1/23/353, 12 April 1921, Saltpond DC to CCCP.

39. Hanson interview at Ekrawfo: Hakeem Kofi Yamoah, 1 June 2005; Effah, "Ahmadiyya Movement in Ghana," 30.

40. "News and Notes: West Africa," *RR* 20, no. 4 (1921), 158.

41. PRAAD, Cape Coast: ADM 1/23/353, 12 June 1922, Acting Saltpond DC to CCCP.

42. PRAAD, Cape Coast: ADM 1/23/353, 12 April 1921, Saltpond DC to CCCP.

43. PRAAD, Cape Coast: ADM 1/23/353, no date, "Ahmadia Movement in Islam."

44. News and Notes: Our West African Mission," *RR* 20, no. 8 (1921), 332–335.

45. PRAAD, Cape Coast: ADM 1/23/353, attachment to 22 August 1921, Maulvi A. R. Nayyar to DC.

46. PRAAD, Cape Coast: ADM 1/23/353, attachment to 3 December 1921, Maulvi A. R. Nayyar to DC.

47. Hanson interview at Ekotsi: Usman Kojo Otoo and Kwesi Abdullah Saeed, 2 June 2005; "How Islam Ahmadiyyat was Introduced to the Citizens of Ekumfi Ekotsi in the Central Region of Ghana, Compiled by Bro. Usman Koko Otoo and Bro. Kwesi Abdullah Saeed" (manuscript given to the author by the compilers on 2 June 2005).

48. PRAAD, Cape Coast: ADM 1/23/353, 3 December 1921, Maulvi A. R. Nayyar to DC.

49. Acquah, "Impact of African Traditional Religious Beliefs," 157–160. Hamidu's son, Al-Hajj Hamied, is the current leader of Fante Muslim community at Obonster.

50. PRAAD, Cape Coast: ADM 1/23/353: no date, "Ahmadia Movement in Islam."

51. Guar-Gorman discussed other Fante Muslim communities in "Islam in Fantiland," 87–95.

6 Ahmadiyya Consolidation in the Gold Coast

MAULVI FAZLUL RAHMAN HAKEEM, recently arrived as the first residential Ahmadi missionary in the Gold Coast, stepped off the bus at Swedru, where it made a scheduled rest stop on its route. There Maulvi Hakeem met Steven J. Johnston, the thirty-year-old African manager of a British provisions store. Maulvi Hakeem discussed the Ahmadiyya with Johnston, a former Cape Coast resident whose parents hoped would become an Anglican priest but who instead pursued a business career. Maulvi Hakeem left an Ahmadi pamphlet with Johnston, and they corresponded as he read it and posed questions. Johnston eventually decided to join, took Jamal as his Muslim first name, and left his manager's position to work with the Ahmadiyya.[1] Not all new members uprooted themselves to work for the movement, but Johnston's experience in accepting the Ahmadiyya through personal contact and comparison occurred frequently. Ahmadi missionaries and lay members proselytized as they went about their daily activities, convincing family members, neighbors, coworkers, and strangers to embrace the Ahmadiyya. This effort increased membership from several hundred in 1921 to more than twenty thousand by the mid-1940s.

The Ahmadiyya in the Gold Coast had continuities with the early Fante Muslim community. One shared feature was Muslim proselytism through comparisons between the Christian Bible and Islamic beliefs and practices, a strategy adopted by Binyameen Sam and evident in Jamal Johnston's conversion by Maulvi Hakeem. Another was the establishment of English-language Muslim schools. The Ahmadiyya nevertheless introduced new practices, such as the use of pamphlets in evangelism and the teaching of Arabic. Ahmadi missionaries also stressed community discipline and fidelity to distinctive Ahmadi ideas and practices. Maulvi Hakeem and Maulvi Nazir Ahmad Ali, each serving two tours as the lone missionary-in-charge in the Gold Coast from 1922 to 1937, were younger than Maulvi Nayyar and on their first assignments as members of an initial cohort trained at the Ahmadiyya seminary at Qadian. They brought energy and enthusiasm to their proselytism, but they also were bound by the "Rules and Regulations" negotiated between Nayyar and Mahdi Appah in 1921. Assisting the residential Ahmadi missionaries was Binyameen Esau Keelson, the first general secretary of the Gold Coast branch, who staffed the headquarters at Saltpond until his retirement in 1937. Keelson illustrates the patterns of continuity and change: he was Mahdi Appah's cousin but also a Christian who accepted the Ahmadiyya during Maulvi Hakeem's first year in the Gold Coast.

This chapter analyzes the consolidation of the Ahmadiyya in the southern regions of the Gold Coast based on Ahmadi mission reports, British colonial documents, and memories.[2] The first section discusses Ahmadiyya organizational and educational institutions, including an Arabic school, a missionary-training center, and English-language schools. The next explores Ahmadiyya proselytism along the coast as residents in both Gold Coast towns and rural areas joined the movement. The final section concerns the changes that accepting the Ahmadiyya brought to its African members. It also discusses transitions as Maulvi Ali arrived in 1929 to serve two terms, broken by Maulvi Hakeem's return. The Ahmadiyya expansion to Asante and Wa is treated separately in chapters 7 and 8.

Building a Mission

Maulvi Fazlul Rahman Hakeem arrived at Saltpond in May 1922 and took up residence in a small mission house that Maulvi Abdul Rahman Nayyar and Amadu Ramanu Pedro had acquired. Hakeem's father, a member of a Punjabi family of Pashtun heritage, was a pioneering Ahmadi Muslim who sent Hakeem for religious education at the movement's headquarters at Qadian. Hakeem was unmarried and in his twenties when he accepted his first missionary posting abroad at Saltpond. Fante Ahmadi Muslims reportedly grasped his drive and energy from the outset: the *Review of Religions* noted, "Everyone is saying that 'Ahmadiyya movement means business.'"[3] Hakeem was both an organizer and proselytizer, whose strong leadership led Hausa-speaking Muslims to refer to the Ahmadiyya community as *hakeemawa* or "Hakeem's people" in Hausa. Hakeem served two lengthy tours in the Gold Coast, initially from 1922 to 1929, and again in the mid-1930s. Succeeding Maulvi Hakeem as missionary-in-charge was Maulvi Nazir Ahmad Ali, serving from 1929 to 1931 and again in the mid-1930s (he also had a third tour in the mid-1940s). These two missionaries were formative in putting the movement on firm foundations in their service as head of the mission at Saltpond during the early years.

Binyameen Esau Keelson was essential to the success of the initial Ahmadi missionaries (see figure 11, where he is wearing a fez and seated next to Maulvi Hakeem). Keelson, Mahdi Appah's cousin, was a Christian who had worked as a clerk at a British firm in the Gold Coast until Mahdi Appah convinced him to become an Ahmadi Muslim and manage the Ahmadiyya office in Saltpond. Keelson succeeded Amadu Ramanu Pedro as the general secretary in 1922 and became the confidant of both Maulvi Hakeem and Maulvi Ali, assuming the role of interpreter, providing local knowledge, managing the affairs of the office, and articulating the concerns of local Ahmadi Muslims to the missionary-in-charge.

When Maulvi Hakeem returned to Saltpond to begin his second tour of duty in 1931, he expressed joy at seeing Keelson, whom he described at the time as "my very old and intimate friend."[4] Keelson also developed excellent working relations with British colonial officials and managed affairs when Hakeem and Ali were away from Saltpond.

Memories focus on Binyameen Keelson's devotion to the Ahmadiyya. He reportedly embraced the End Times message and spoke frequently about Ghulam Ahmad's role as the Messiah. Proofs or signs of the End Times, according to those remembering Keelson, were the massive ocean steamers that frequented the Saltpond harbor. Others relate his emphasis on prophesies from the Bible, especially the passage in Revelations about the horsemen of the Apocalypse: in Keelson's preaching these biblical figures were not cavaliers but colonial-era railroad engines, ironclad and billowing fire and steam as they transported timber and cocoa through the rainforest. Keelson's exegesis of the Bible, an outgrowth of his Christian heritage, helped him connect with elderly Fante Muslims, as his practice echoed Binyameen Sam's preaching from the Bible. Keelson's family connection with Mahdi Appah also helped forge strong relations with Fante Muslims, the core of the Ahmadiyya in the early years. It was Keelson's organizational acumen, however, that is most remembered as he ran the office while serving as the cultural broker between Fante Muslims and the residential missionaries. Haleesah Esi Esuan, his wife, also is remembered as a pious Ahmadi Muslim who assisted Binyameen Keelson in hosting guests and proselytizing the Ahmadiyya among women in the early years.[5]

Residential Ahmadi missionaries quickly came to a cross-cultural understanding of Fante Ahmadi Muslims. This sympathetic perspective is reflected in a 1928 *Review of Religions* article. It discusses the efforts of Christian missionaries in Nigeria to end colonial restrictions on their proselytism in the north, where Muslims resided in large numbers and had autonomy through the "indirect rule" policies formulated by Frederick Lugard at the outset of British rule. Comparing northern Nigeria and the British Gold Coast, the Ahmadi commentary noted:

> The natives of northern areas of Nigeria are about the only race in Western Africa who still lead their lives in their own way, undisturbed by the onrush of Western Civilization. On the Gold Coast, on the other hand, where the people were led by the early Christian missionaries to commit the serious mistake of abandoning their religious system, wholly regardless of its healthy ethics, Western civilization has supplanted indigenous culture to such an extent that the people are feeling its weight almost as sorely as the people of Europe.[6]

The passage's reference to the "healthy ethics" of the "indigenous culture" in the Gold Coast is a remarkable concession for a proselytizing religious community. It also is notable for running counter to the ethnic and racial prejudices that divided Africans, Asians, and Europeans in the colonial era. The commentary's spirit no doubt expressed the emerging views of the movement as communicated by Maulvi Hakeem, who through his interactions with Binyameen Keelson and others, came to appreciate Fante culture.

Gold Coast officials remained suspicious of the Ahmadiyya mission throughout the early 1920s. Maulvi Hakeem professed loyalty to the British in an interview with the Saltpond district commissioner,[7] but official scrutiny of the Ahmadiyya continued as it had during Maulvi Nayyar's 1921 visits. British officers asked Hausa headmen about Hakeem's activities, and they reported what turned out to be false rumors of financial impropriety.[8] Back in London in 1923, Maulvi Nayyar wrote to the undersecretary of state for the colonies to request official recognition of the Ahmadiyya in West Africa, adding his concern about the negative attitudes toward the movement in the Gold Coast.[9] The request needed approval of the Saltpond district commissioner, who summoned Maulvi Hakeem for an interview: Hakeem reportedly told him that the Ahmadiyya sought only "to strengthen the faith of members and not get new converts," a deferential response reflecting tense relations more than an exchange of opinions. The district commissioner judged the Ahmadiyya to be "antagonistic to Protestantism," but he admitted that there was no basis in colonial policies to deny its request for recognition.[10] Over the following few years Maulvi Hakeem established good rapport with subsequent British officials at Saltpond and ultimately convinced the colonial government to fund Ahmadiyya schools in the district, as will be discussed later in this chapter.

The Ahmadiyya developed constructive relations with several African political leaders. While Hausa leaders in *zongos* remained critical of the movement, Fante *ahene* offered no objections and a few warmed to the Ahmadiyya presence.[11] Mahdi Appah's status as both an *odehyee* and Ahmadi Muslim no doubt was critical to this acceptance, and Binyameen Keelson's role in the office underscored this local connection. By the 1930s, Maulvi Hakeem, on his second tour, established personal connections to several Fante political leaders. He had particularly close relations with the *tufuhene* at Saltpond. Maulvi Hakeem first established a bond with Tufuhene Korsah, whom Provincial Commissioner A. C. Duncan-Johnstone described as "a modern chief, wealthy, educated and progressive."[12] These values coincided with the Ahmadiyya, and while Tufuhene Korsah did not become an Ahmadi Muslim, he supported it. His successor also had close ties with Maulvi Hakeem and even sought Hakeem's blessings at the Ahmadi mosque before his installation as *tufuhene*.[13] The support of Fante political leaders in towns and villages was critical to Ahmadiyya efforts to consolidate its position in the region.

Maulvi Hakeem and Binyameen Keelson established a hierarchical organization that wove dispersed Fante Ahmadi Muslim communities into a cohesive movement. They traveled footpaths to visit small villages and towns where most Fante Ahmadi Muslims resided, selecting local heads in rural contexts. These community leaders worked with Ahmadi councils in the villages and reported regularly to Keelson at Saltpond. They were responsible for religious and financial affairs, ensuring the regular performance of *salat* and securing financial contributions to support the Ahmadiyya mission. Muslim holidays were occasions when the Ahmadiyya community met together at Saltpond, but mothers with young children, elderly members, and others often remained in their rural communities. The *jalsa salana*, the annual meeting that was a central feature of the Ahmadiyya by the 1920s in India, was not practiced with the same high levels of participation in the Gold Coast during the early years, but eventually it became an important annual activity.[14]

The emphasis on regular financial contributions met with resistance from some members in the early years. Maulvi Hakeem noted the commitment of Fante Ahmadi Muslims in his early correspondence, but the British received reports of disgruntlement and opposition. Brahima, identified as a Fante Ahmadi Muslim from the commercial center of Sraha, reportedly made a donation to the Ahmadiyya when Maulvi Nayyar visited in 1921, but he refused to make additional contributions to Maulvi Hakeem. Another Fante Ahmadi Muslim, Issa from a fishing community near Saltpond, refused to give a second donation and reportedly told Maulvi Hakeem to return to India, drawing Hakeem's retort that Issa would have to pay his passage back.[15] These stories suggest resistance to regular contributions among some Ahmadi Muslims. The monthly contributions and a registry with names and contributed amounts rankled those who remembered Binyameen Sam's criticism of Methodist "ticket money." The early years probably saw a decline in membership as Maulvi Hakeem and Binyameen Keelson, in tandem with the local leaders, put pressure on members to contribute funds.

Fante Muslims remaining in the Ahmadiyya practiced Islam in ways that distinguished themselves from other Muslims in the Gold Coast. Residential Ahmadi missionaries stressed exclusivity in the performance of *salat* and encouraged the building of Ahmadi mosques as a means to do so, especially for Friday communal prayers. Building mosques also allowed Fante Ahmadi Muslims to honor the Ahmadiyya emphasis on cleanliness in the ritual space: instead of the sheep- and goatskin prayer mats widely used throughout West Africa, Fante Ahmadi Muslims performed *salat* on imported prayer rugs or mats made of local cloth.[16] The most prominent distinction was that Ahmadi Muslims crossed their arms during *salat*, whereas other Muslims followed Maliki practice and left their arms at their sides. Ahmadi funerals also broke from West African Muslim practices: instead of the elaborate rituals held over several weeks with a significant expenditure of funds, Ahmadi funerals were simple burials of the deceased in white cloth within hours of death. Ahmadi bylaws explicitly tied simple funerals with keeping expenses reasonable so that members could donate to Ahmadiyya missionary and educational activities.[17] Some Fante Muslims even adopted new clothing styles, dropping the *riga*-style robes of Hausa Muslims for the South Asian style of short gowns with collars.[18] With these external markers Fante Ahmadi Muslims distinguished themselves from other West African Muslims.[19]

Maulvi Hakeem devoted himself to providing education and opening schools. Within weeks of his arrival Maulvi Hakeem taught twenty students Arabic at Saltpond.[20] He later delegated responsibility for Arabic instruction to M. A. Ishaque, a young Fante Muslim who had become proficient in Arabic by studying with savanna Muslim scholars after Binyameen Sam's death. Maulvi Hakeem also founded a missionary training center at Saltpond. Ishaque, one of the initial seminary students, devoted himself to proselytization in a long career with the Ahmadiyya mission, including service as a missionary in the Northern Territories, as discussed in chapter 8. Memories of Ishaque's missionary career stress his effective responses to criticisms from other Muslims based on his ability to draw on specific verses in the Quran in support of Ghulam Ahmad's teachings. Ishaque, who went on hajj later in his life, is remembered as a model of erudition and moral standing by those who learned Arabic or accepted the Ahmadiyya under his guidance.[21]

The Talim-ul-Islam Ahmadiyya School, opened in 1924, had a standard British curriculum and also offered Arabic instruction as an elective. It met in an upstairs room of the mission house and had an initial enrollment of forty-seven boys and girls in the first to sixth levels taught by five teachers; the head instructor was a former teacher at the Wesleyan Methodist primary school at Cape Coast (see figure 1). Teacher salaries and other operations were funded completely by local contributions from Ahmadi Muslims, and students paid no fees in its first year. The interim British inspector of schools visited in September 1924: he was sufficiently impressed with the school's pedagogy to agree to its inclusion on the government-assisted list, and the school began to receive colonial subsidies in 1925. The inspector's report, however, recommended that the school expand from its cramped single-room and add desks, maps, and other educational aids.[22]

Maulvi Hakeem received £500 from the Ahmadiyya headquarters at Qadian to address the inspector's recommendations by building a new schoolhouse with improved instructional features.[23] The school's foundation stone was laid in February 1926 at a ceremony attended by the manager of the Saltpond branch of the British Bank of West Africa, who told the assembled group that the building under construction was testament to Maulvi Hakeem's "energy and enthusiasm, and to the able assistance of his Committee and all who are interested in the Ahmadiyya Movement."[24] The new building was completed in only a few months, and teachers and students shifted their classes there from the mission house in June 1926. The British inspector of schools visited in November 1926 and remarked that it was "a model for other schools in the district to copy" given its high level of instruction and excellent student performances in arithmetic, composition, and reading. The building also drew favorable commentary as the "best equipped in the Central Province."[25]

Others visited the Talim-ul-Islam Ahmadiyya School in its first years of operation. In June 1927, Maulvi Hakeem organized an opening in the presence of J. H. West, the Saltpond district commissioner. West had been a lower-ranked official when Maulvi Hakeem received critical British scrutiny in 1922. West addressed that past by noting that Maulvi Hakeem "came as a stranger to a strange land without a following, without a school, without pupils. During these five years he has built this school and has carried out his educational work. The school building is a testimony in itself to his labours."[26] This visit was followed by one from the governor of the Gold Coast in 1928. Maulvi Hakeem spared no detail in welcoming the governor: students were outfitted in uniforms, a banner welcomed the governor, and class sessions and other events occurred for him to observe (see figure 12). The establishment of the Talim-ul-Islam Ahmadiyya School was a crowning achievement for a movement that had been on the coast for less than a decade: it added an English-language Muslim school to a Gold Coast context that had been dominated by Christian missionary institutions.

The Ahmadiyya established other schools in the years ahead. Maulvi Hakeem and his successor, Maulvi Ali, founded primary schools in several rural villages. Ekrawfo was the first, established in the late 1920s, and three others were added in the early 1930s. These schools launched the Ahmadiyya into an educational mission for underserved areas and taught both Ahmadi Muslims and Christian students. The organizational capacity and financial resources of the Ahmadiyya in the Gold Coast sustained this effort, in contrast to the closings of the English-language Muslims schools founded by the Fante Muslim community in the late nineteenth century. By the early twentieth century the attitudes of Fante Ahmadi Muslims were closely aligned with the educational reformism of the Ahmadiyya in ways that differed from Binyameen Sam's era. This commitment to the movement also found expression in an active effort to recruit new members to the Ahmadiyya.

Ahmadiyya Proselytism

Maulvi Hakeem and Maulvi Ali were tireless in proselytizing the Ahmadiyya in the Gold Coast. They gave lectures, distributed pamphlets, and maintained a correspondence with interested persons. Residential missionaries also engaged strangers, as Maulvi Hakeem did when he met Jamal Johnston during a bus trip, as discussed in the introduction. Informal proselytism from lay Ahmadi members also was effective, as family members and in-laws often were persuaded by their relatives. Jamal Johnston, for example, convinced several family members to accept the Ahmadiyya shortly after he joined. Preaching and pamphlets helped the Ahmadiyya extend its reach to Christians and those educated in Christian missionary schools. Local missionaries and lay members also proselytized the Ahmadiyya message. Insight into the effort is offered in written materials from the early years. Maulvi Hakeem published two sermons given in the late 1920s for readers of the *Review of Religions*. These sermons reveal Hakeem's two-step approach to converting Christians: he first acknowledged shared values and other similarities between Islam and Christianity, and then he articulated the Ahmadiyya message in universal terms. An Ahmadi pamphlet from Maulvi Ali's era indicates that he adopted a similar approach to Ahmadi evangelism. These efforts resonated with the practice of West African cosmopolitans along the coast.

Maulvi Hakeem's essay "Islam and Christianity" illustrates the first step in this process. It begins by commenting on his Gold Coast experiences in which Christians mocked Muslims and stated that they were "doomed to perdition forever" as "the fuel of hell-fire." Professing love for Christians, it turns the biblical message toward Christians and insists that God's grace alone provided access to heaven. The essay then outlines shared areas of theological agreement before making the Ahmadiyya argument that Jesus survived the cross and died in India. After discussing several biblical passages in support of his view, the essay articulates the Muslim view that Jesus was a prophet and not the son of God, again citing biblical passages in support of its claims; it adds that the concept of the Trinity has no basis in the Bible. The essay ends by appealing to Christians and Muslims to accept one another: "we should be allowed to live in peace, with love and goodwill, so that we can become united and thus make progress and receive the blessings of God . . . whether one is doomed to hell or not is no business of anyone else." It follows with an appeal that Christians accept Muhammad as Muslims accepted Jesus.[27] Maulvi Hakeem's approach was to acknowledge the shared religious heritage of Christians and Muslims, to ask that Christians join Ahmadi Muslims in refusing to accuse others of being fated to death by hell's fire, and to nudge Christians into an engagement with Ahmadiyya ideas based on reading the Bible. Maulvi Hakeem's Biblicism harkened back to Binyameen Sam's preaching, but it added references to the Quran and to Ghulam Ahmad's teachings.

Maulvi Hakeem's essay "Islam" reveals the second aspect of his proselytism: the proclamation of Islam's outstanding aspects. The essay focuses on Islam's core beliefs and ends with its "ten beauties." These beauties included the purity of the Quran, the reasonableness of its theology, the simplicity of its rituals, the thoroughness and broad-mindedness of its scholars who drew on all prophets and made Islam the oldest religion, and its status as "an up-to-date religion."[28] In addition to the standard Muslim views of Islam's virtues, the essay adds an

Ahmadiyya dimension by insisting that Ghulam Ahmad's receipt of divine revelations allowed Islam to guide its followers in its engagements with the modern world. The Ahmadiyya took "the oldest religion" and made it "new." Maulvi Hakeem's preaching adopted an evangelical approach similar to the preaching of Samuel Crowther in the nineteenth century, as discussed in the book's introduction. While acrimonious encounters between Muslims and Christians defined the context in which Ghulam Ahmad founded the Ahmadiyya, Maulvi Hakeem did not bring that perspective to West Africa. He instead pursed the approach of cosmopolitans such as Crowther and Binyameen Sam in which universal human values and shared religious perspectives figured prominently in a conversation about religious beliefs and practices.

The Ahmadiyya produced pamphlets that the missionaries distributed in the Gold Coast during the 1920s and 1930s. One of these pamphlets survives in the Tamale archives in Ghana.[29] Maulvi Ali, Hakeem's successor, gave it to a British official in 1931, and it provides a glimpse into the message in these pamphlets. The four-page document proclaims in large font at the top: "BEHOLD! A LIGHT!" Above it is a statement in smaller font, extending in a semicircle: "A warner came upon the world and the world accepted him not, but God will accept him and establish his truth by mighty signs." The main text takes the form of an open letter from Maulvi Ali, who offers salutations to God and the reader before stating its intention to quote extensively from "the Holy Bible without which it would be impossible for you to understand me." Two paragraphs follow with citations from Old and New Testaments passages to claim that Christ was "a great Prophet and essentially a man" who survived the crucifixion and completed his mission to minister to the Israelites, even the "lost tribes" in India. The following two paragraphs introduce the Prophet Muhammad as one sent by God to fulfill biblical prophesies, which were referenced and interpreted. The next paragraph then discusses Ghulam Ahmad's role as a prophet and how biblical references to "the second advent of Jesus Christ" point to his role as the Messiah. The last paragraph starts with the appeal, "Lovers of Christ, I bring glad tidings to you that the beloved Christ has truly appeared in the person of Ahmad in Northern India," and concludes with the plea to "pray to God Who alone is the Helper that He Himself may guide you to the right path, before it is too late; because those who seek light from Him cannot remain in darkness. May Allah bless those who accept the truth."

The pamphlet made the case for the Ahmadiyya in English as the fulfillment of biblical prophesies and the enduring guidance God provided through the Messiah, Ghulam Ahmad. Pamphlets were common in Punjab, where exchanges in print media began in the late nineteenth century as Muslims, Hindus, and Sikhs responded to Christian missionary materials, but in the British Gold Coast the Ahmadiyya pamphlets introduced Muslim interpretations of

Christian teachings in printed English. While informed by Punjabi exchanges of the nineteenth century, the English-language pamphlets adopted a softer tone, one that did not assail Christian teachings pejoratively but used biblical quotations to argue for Ahmadiyya claims about the arrival of the Messiah. It appealed to a shared concern for Jesus and noted at one point in its argument for Jesus' survival of the crucifixion that "no lover of Christ can image that God paid no heed his heartrending prayers to be saved from an accursed death." Ahmadiyya proselytism, while similar to Binyameen Sam's use of the Bible to preach Islam, differed substantially: Sam pointed to Old Testament dietary and other laws shared by Islam and Judaism whereas the Ahmadiyya message focused on its claims that Ghulam Ahmad was the Messiah and stressed the fulfillment of biblical prophesies as well as continued access to divine guidance. The two-dozen references to biblical passages invited readers to read scripture and interpret the passages for themselves. This rhetorical move encouraged further exchanges through correspondence (with the Ahmadiyya mission headquarters address in the Gold Coast noted at the bottom).

The Ahmadiyya paid for advertisements in Gold Coast newspapers to draw attention to their message and provide an address to request their pamphlets. Those interested would receive the pamphlet in an envelope with a poster stamp affixed (see figure 13). The intended audience for the pamphlets were Christians who were open to questions about faith, and the goal was to engage them in written exchanges, ideally leading to acceptance, as illustrated by Jamal Johnston's experience with Maulvi Hakeem in 1922. Johnston and others then helped distribute Ahmadi pamphlets to other Christians whom they felt would be open to the invitation to read their Bible and reflect on the Ahmadiyya message. Through Johnston's efforts, other members of the coastal Christian elite became Ahmadi Muslims, including two brothers of the Arthur family of Anomabu, Noor Ahmad and Al-Hajj Mumtaz B. Arthur, and through them a member of the Arthur family of Cape Coast, Al-Hajj Muhammad W. E. Arthur.[30] Others converting through an engagement with Ahmadi materials were Muslim members of the colonial civil service, often serving at posts away from their homes when they saw an Ahmadi newspaper advertisement. The most effective means of proselytism was personal contact, but Hakeem and Ali worked to bring their message to others through the new print media, and these efforts proved successful in several instances.

Proselytism among Rural Fante Muslims

Rural Fante Muslims joined the Ahmadiyya in the years after pioneering Fante Muslims accepted during Maulvi Nayyar's visit in 1921. Several patterns emerge from memories of this expansion. News of the arrival of Maulvi Nayyar and the establishment of a mission at Saltpond created interest or perhaps curiosity in the movement. Communities sent small delegations of those deemed to have the best knowledge of Islam to discuss religious matters with Maulvi Hakeem at Saltpond. Those convinced returned to persuade heads of households. Once elders accepted the Ahmadiyya, then other family members and neighbors joined. This cascading expansion, with local actors playing pivotal roles, underscores the significance of laypersons in the expansion of the Ahmadiyya in rural areas. There sermons and pamphlets were not as relevant as word-of-mouth news about Ahmadi Muslims at Saltpond.

One direction of expansion was Gomoa, a region just east of the heartland of Binyameen Sam's Muslim community. Gomoa's small states did not have status as having been founded by Borbor Fante migrants, but its elite claimed Fante identity, and Akan culture was widely practiced by the nineteenth century. Binyameen Sam converted numerous traders in Gomoa, and more converted in the early twentieth century through the efforts of Hausa Muslims. Some were traders who came into contact with Hausa Muslims in Gomoa's commercial centers after the 1890s; many more were cocoa farmers who encountered Hausa Muslims in their travels outside Gomoa to acquire land for production. These Muslims did not join the meeting called at Mankessim by Mahdi Appah, and their awareness of the Ahmadiyya occurred only after the arrival of Maulvi Nayyar in 1921. Over the course of the 1920s, however, Gomoa became a major base of the Ahmadiyya.

This expansion is illustrated by events in Potsin. This small town was home to prosperous cocoa farmers who farmed outside the region but returned to Potsin after they accumulated wealth. One was Adam Kofi Quarm: his mother's brother was a subchief, and Quarm used his royal connections to gain land in Agona. His move outside Gomoa coincided with his conversion to Islam: he married a Muslim woman and sent his two eldest sons to an Arabic school run by Hausa Muslim scholars in Agona. Retired to Gomoa in the early 1920s, Quarm heard about the arrival of Maulvi Nayyar and sent his two eldest sons, Muhammad Kojo Inkoom and J. E. Adam, from their cocoa farms to learn about the Ahmadiyya at Saltpond. Persuaded by Maulvi Hakeem they in turn convinced their father to accept the Ahmadiyya. Eventually all of Adam Quarm's family became Ahmadi Muslims. Notably his youngest sons, U. B. Adam and Jibril Adam, trained at Saltpond to become Ahmadi missionaries.[31] Adam Quarm's oldest sons, Muhammad Kojo Inkoom and J. E. Adam, played roles as informal missionaries who convinced other cocoa farmers in Agona to join the Ahmadiyya.[32] Another Fante cocoa farmer in Potsin, Isa Quantson, became an Ahmadi Muslim, but his story differs from the previous example. He had studied Arabic with Hausa Muslim scholars and ran a small Quranic school in Potsin, where Quantson taught Adam Kofi Quarm's youngest sons. Quantson was not convinced to become an Ahmadi Muslim when Adam Quarm did, expressing concern about the practices advocated by the Ahmadiyya. Quantson finally joined after making the hajj; he reportedly arrived by steamer along the coast and went to meet Maulvi Hakeem at Saltpond before returning to Potsin to announce his decision.[33]

The Ahmadiyya spread into other regions. Large Ahmadi Muslim communities formed in Breman and Enyan, north of Ekumfi. Most were cocoa farmers who learned of the movement from Fante Ahmadi Muslim cocoa farmers and traders. The success of informal missionaries in this expanding frontier meant that religious discipline lagged behind Ahmadiyya expansion. Maulvi Hakeem admitted to difficulties in keeping contact with Ahmadi Muslims in distant rural areas, especially when they dispersed to their cocoa farms deep in the rainforest. Maulvi Hakeem occasionally sent Ahmadi youths who had memorized his sermons to distant villagers removed from regular religious guidance.[34] Maulvi Hakeem also trained several Africans to serve as missionaries to make frequent visits to these rural communities and ensure that Ahmadiyya discipline was practiced.

Ahmadi Muslims

The Ahmadiyya was a reformist movement that challenged West African Muslim norms in concrete, socially visible ways. Women were active in the Ahmadi community: the movement did not accept West African Muslim customs that discouraged girls from attending schools and prohibited menopausal women from praying at mosques. Gender inclusivity appealed to women who joined the movement in part because they could be active in religious activities in ways that women in other West African Muslim communities could not. Another Ahmadiyya practice that diverged from local norms was using African languages and English in delivering Friday sermons and in debating the merits of Islam with others. Ahmadi Muslims used Arabic in their conversations with West African Muslim scholars, but they were set apart by their willingness to use of African languages in contexts where other Muslims would not. This aspect of the Ahmadiyya gave the movement an advantage in proselytism, especially among Christians, and it also reinforced the reformism of the movement because members could read texts on their own and reflect on Ahmadi teachings.

Ahmadiyya distinctiveness also applied to Islamic ritual practices. As discussed earlier, the placement of arms during *salat* differed. Perhaps most significant to West African Muslim scholars was the Ahmadiyya rejection of "the practice of charms, magical writings, fortune telling, etc."[35] Many West African *mallams* sold amulets and herbal cures to Muslims and non-Muslims alike: this provision was not only a theological issue but also a practical one with financial implications.[36] Instead the Ahmadiyya asked members to provide funds for concrete activities organized by the movement, such as building new mosques and schools. These activities demonstrated differences more than minor variations in the performance of *salat*. The Ahmadiyya was in the forefront of Muslim condemnation of selling charms and providing esoteric cures, a feature of West African Muslim reformism in the decades that followed.

Other aspects of Ahmadiyya reformism were more challenging to new members. As discussed already, continued financial contributions met with resistance from some members. Hausa Muslims added their criticism and encouraged Fante Muslims not to pay by making false allegations of fraud by Ahmadi leaders. The opening of the Talim-ul-Islam Ahmadiyya School in 1924 helped dampen these rumors in British colonial circles and within the Ahmadiyya community itself. Funeral practices were another area of reluctant acceptance of the movement's expectations. Extensive rituals surround Akan remembrances of the deceased, and the requirement that Ahmadi Muslims mark such occasions with minimal ritual and not participate in non-Muslim funerals created tensions with non-Ahmadi relatives. Insistence on Islamic inheritance, too, went against the matrilineal principles associated with many Fante kin groups, and bilateral succession allowed Ahmadi Muslims to honor the Ahmadi insistence on providing for wives and direct descendants and to provide contributions to matrilineal relatives.[37] Cocoa entrepreneurs, among the initial group of Ahmadi Muslims, may well have welcomed the opportunity to pass more family wealth to direct descendants as opposed to more distant matrilineal kin.

The Ahmadiyya asked its members to join a movement that was gender and language inclusive but also exclusive with respect to other Muslims. Ahmadiyya exclusiveness reinforced their identity as a distinctive Muslim community and created internal social solidarity, but it also led to opposition from other Muslims, who often accused Ahmadi Muslims of not practicing Islam well. Criticism from other African Muslims was implicit in the reference to Ahmadi Muslims as *hakeemawa*, or "Hakeem's people." Other Muslim critics referred to Ahmadi Muslims as *tuuba*. This Hausa word, based on the Arabic term *tawba*, or "retreat," usually referred to someone who has returned to Islam, but in the Gold Coast it was an accusatory term that conveyed the sense that someone had left the correct path. The widespread invocation of *tuuba* in relation to Fante Ahmadi Muslims referenced the decision to accept the Ahmadiyya and not adopt savanna Muslim norms. Both *tuuba* and *hakeemawa* carried the meaning of inferior religious status.

Hewing to Ahmadiyya practices in the face of criticism from relatives and other Muslims was an aspect of Ahmadi discipline that came to define the community over time. Membership included engaging with an organizational structure of community leaders reporting to Saltpond. It also involved attending English-language schools and seeking employment on an equal footing with Christians educated in mission schools. Ahmadiyya discipline was most attractive to those who wished to gain the benefits that organizational rigor and educational institutions provided in the British colonial era. The movement remained small, but it was a community of aspirational Muslims who embraced their differences with other Muslims and pursued a new path.

Transitions

The late 1920s brought several transitions to the Ahmadiyya in the Gold Coast. One was that Mahdi Appah died in 1929. He was not the last of the first generation of Fante Muslims converted by Binyameen Sam, but Appah's death marked the end of an era. Another was that Maulvi Hakeem ended his first tour as missionary in 1929 and was replaced by Maulvi N. A. Ali. Binyameen Keelson continued as general secretary until 1937, performing the same intermediary tasks in the office and in relation to members visiting Saltpond, but with the added stature as having served in that capacity for seven years. Maulvi Ali's era is not fixed clearly in the memories of coastal Ahmadi Muslim families. Maulvi Ali resided for a much shorter period, literally half the number of years as Maulvi Hakeem. He also embarked on several initiatives in the Northern Territories, as is discussed in chapter 8. Maulvi Ali did not leave many records, but the available evidence suggests that he maintained an active presence and consolidated what Maulvi Hakeem had built in his first seven years in the Gold Coast.

One of the clearest signs of the consolidation of the Ahmadiyya on the coast occurred early in Maulvi Hakeem's second tour as missionary. Hakeem's attention shifted increasingly from the Gold Coast to Nigeria. Imam Arose had been in charge of the Ahmadiyya community in Lagos since the departures of the Alakurani, or "Quranic People," and of those leaving to join M. L. B. Agusto's rival Muslim movement during the 1920s. Maulvi Hakeem appreciated Arose's leadership, but he concluded after a visit that Ahmadi Muslims in Lagos were "in need of further training." Hakeem left Saltpond for an extended residence to instill greater Ahmadiyya discipline in Lagos and put the Gold Coast Ahmadiyya in the hands of its African leaders: Binyameen Keelson assumed Maulvi Hakeem's role as leader as well as continuing as general secretary, Jamal Johnston took over as manager of Ahmadiyya schools, and a committee of four members supervised financial affairs.[38] Maulvi Hakeem expressed extreme confidence in this group and affirmed African capacity and leadership in the Ahmadiyya.

The consolidation of the Ahmadiyya was evident in the building of new mosques and schools in the 1930s. For a religious movement that survived largely on the donations of its local members, the economic decline of the 1930s could have been devastating. Colonial reports suggest that some repairs on Ahmadiyya schools were delayed, but nonetheless the Ahmadiyya continued to construct new mosques and open additional primary schools. Perhaps the clearest evidence of continued vitality and financial support, and the highlight of Maulvi Ali's era on the coast, was the opening of a new mission headquarters at Saltpond in 1937. It had been started under Maulvi Hakeem in 1934 and took three years to accumulate sufficient funds to complete. Christian missions had impressive complexes at Cape Coast and Accra, supported with contributions from donors abroad, and the opening of a new Ahmadiyya mission at Saltpond signaled the movement's enduring presence. The new Ahmadiyya headquarters was all the more notable given its self-financing at a time of global economic downturn.

The opening of the new Saltpond headquarters in 1937 occurred at another moment of transition in the Ahmadiyya in the Gold Coast. Binyameen Keelson retired months earlier, and his replacement was Jamal Johnston, who had been manager and now assumed the larger role of general secretary. Johnston was not connected to pioneering Fante Muslim families, and his rise expressed a maturation of the movement with new members assuming prominent roles. Johnston worked with Maulvi Ali to organize a grand reception with close to three thousand Ahmadi Muslims in attendance.[39] This was the first major event since its founding, and it helped instill future participation in the annual *jalsa salana*. Maulvi Ali left shortly after the opening of the new headquarters, and he was replaced by Maulvi Nazir Ahmad Mubashir, who began what would be twenty-five years of service in the Gold Coast. Together Maulvi Mubashir and Jamal Johnston supervised the movement as the Great Depression gave way to the Second World War. Memories of this era are not as distinct at the early era. The postwar period, too, is remembered for the arrival of additional South Asian missionaries and the introduction of new approaches to proselytism. Maulvi Mubashir emphasized an organized approach to evangelism, in contrast to the previous reliance on lay missionaries, and he trained a new generation of African missionaries in new strategies, such as vigorous street preaching.

Maulvi Mubashir's leadership included memorable visionary experiences. One came early in his tenure in the Gold Coast and elevated his stature among Ahmadi Muslims. He reportedly responded to Muslim taunts that the End Times had not come by predicting the imminent occurrence of an earthquake as one of the Signs. Maulvi Mubashir made this claim in several public sermons at coastal towns in 1939, and shortly thereafter an earthquake shook the southern regions of the Gold Coast along an established fault-line. This event not only enhanced Maulvi Mubashir's stature within the Ahmadiyya but also led new members to join the movement as word of these events circulated.[40] Maulvi Mubashir's organizational changes in proselytism marked a transition in the movement, but he continued to emphasize Islam's shared heritage with Christianity as he insisted that the Ahmadiyya united believers in one religious movement.[41] Muslim engagement with Christians remained one of the enduring aspects of the Ahmadiyya as it thrived in the Gold Coast and expanded in the postcolonial era.

Conclusion

The Ahmadiyya competed with other religious movements in the Gold Coast religious marketplace. In southern Ghana, indigenous practices still held sway, Christian movements were gaining followers, and savanna Muslims had a presence. The Ahmadiyya stressed Muslim reformism and emphasized the End Times message of Ghulam Ahmad and his successors. Its missionaries and lay preachers engaged Christians by emphasizing the shared scriptural heritages of the two religions, and they succeeded in bringing many of them into the fold. The Ahmadiyya mosque at Ekrawfo (figure 8) reflects the historical sociology of the Ahmadiyya as a movement that integrated members of Binyameen Sam's Fante Muslim community. The Ekrawfo mosque is similar in style to local Christian churches with its tall steeple, but it is capped not with a Christian cross but an Islamic crescent moon.[42] Ahmadi Muslims, dismissed as *tuuba* by some Muslims, embraced their distinctiveness. The movement expressed a cosmopolitan perspective on religious matters, an ethos that had deep roots along the coast and came to be embraced by Ahmadi Muslims from the 1920s.

Notes

1. "Profile of Mr. Jamal Stephen Johnston, a Veteran in the Service of Islam-Ahmadiyyat in Ghana," *Khilafat Centenary Jubilee Souvenir* (Accra: Ahmadiyya Muslim Mission, 2008), 155–157; Hanson interview at Saltpond: Hadija Brown (née Johnston), 2 June 2005.
2. The early Ahmadiyya consolidation is not developed in Fisher's brief chapter in *Ahmadiyyah*, 117–120.
3. "Our Mission Abroad: West Africa," *RR* 21, no. 9 (1922), 303.
4. "Ahmadiyya Movement in Foreign Lands: West Africa," *RR* 32, no. 11 (1931), 588.
5. Hanson interviews at Accra, Saltpond, and Fomena: Maulvi A. Wahab Adam, Haroon Appiah, and Nazir A. Keelson, 28 May 2005, 2 June 2005, and 25 June 2005, respectively.
6. "Notes: Christian Missions and Northern Nigeria," *RR* 27, no. 2 (1928), 1–2.
7. PRAAD, Cape Coast, ADM 1/23/353: 12 June 1922, Saltpond DC to CCCP.
8. PRAAD, Cape Coast: ADM 1/23/353, undated, "Ahmadia Movement in Islam."
9. PRAAD, Cape Coast: ADM 1/23/353, 21 February 1923, Maulvi Nayyar to Under Secretary of State for the Colonies.
10. PRAAD, Cape Coast: ADM 1/23/353, 14 May 1923, "Ahmadia Movement . . . Application Requesting Government Recognition."
11. PRAAD, Cape Coast: ADM 23/1/353, 2 March 1925, Saltpond DC to CCCP.
12. PDJ: box 1, Monthly diaries, 11 September 1928.
13. Ahmadiyya Movement in Foreign Lands: West Africa," *RR* 33, no. 11 (1934), 442.
14. "Our Mission Abroad: West Africa," *RR* 21, nos. 10–11 (1922), 368–72; and "Ahmadiyya Movement in Foreign Lands: West Africa," *RR* 33, nos. 9–10 (1934), 399–402.
15. PRAAD, Cape Coast: ADM 23/1/353, undated, "Ahmadia Movement in Islam."
16. Point 24 of the 1921 bylaws reads: "Dirty sheep skins ought to be removed from mosques and to be replaced by good clean mats or carpets and houses of God must be kept clean."

17. Point 17 of the 1921 bylaws reads: "All unnecessary expenses on marriages and death are to be stopped, and money thus saved is to be devoted to mission work."
18. PRAAD, Cape Coast: ADM 21/1/353, undated, "Ahmadia Movement in Islam."
19. Information in this paragraph is drawn from several interviews: Hanson interview at Abura: Nana Abubakr Aidoo and others, 5 June 2005; Hanson interview at Breman Asikuma, Nuhu Bin Mahdi and others, 6 June 2005; Hanson interview at Immuna: Ahmad Saeed Anderson, with Abdullah Anderson and Al-Hajj Abubakr Anderson, 2 June 2005; Hanson interview at Mankessim: Maulvi Ahmad Jibraeel Saeed, 5 June 2005.
20. PRAAD, Cape Coast: ADM 1/23/353, 12 June 1922, Saltpond DC to CCCP.
21. Hanson interview at Ekotsi: Usman Kojo Otoo and Kwesi Abdullah Saeed, 2 June 2005; "How Islam Ahmadiyyat was introduced to the citizens of Ekumfi Ekotsi in the Central Region of Ghana" (manuscript given to the author by Usman Kojo Otoo and Kwesi Abdullah Saeed on 2 June 2005); Hanson interview at Mankessim: Maulvi Ahmad Jibraeel Saeed, 5 June 2005.
22. PRAAD, Cape Coast: ADM 23/1/353, 20 September 1924, "Report on Palim-ul-Islam Ahmadia school (Saltpond)."
23. PDJ: box 5, "The Ahmadiyya Movement in the Gold Coast, 1921–31."
24. "Mission News: Gold Coast," *RR* 25, no. 3 (1926), 22.
25. PRAAD, Cape Coast: ADM 23/1/353, 29 November 1926, "Report on the Ahmadiyya School."
26. "Educational Activities of the Ahmadiyya Community in Gold Coast," *RR* 26, no. 10 (1927), 16–17.
27. F. R. Hakeem, "Islam and Christianity," *RR* 25, no. 7 (1926), 20–29.
28. F. R. Hakeem, "Islam," *RR* 29, no. 3 (1930), 69–74.
29. PRAAD, Tamale: NRG 8/19/5, 25 June 1931, Maulvi Ali to CCNT, enclosure.
30. "The Two Brothers among the Veterans in the Service of Islam Ahmadiyyat," "Alhaj Mumtaz B. Arthur: Another Veteran in the Service of Islam-Ahmadiyyat," and "Profile of Alhaj Muhammad W. E. Arthur, Former National President of the Ahmadiyya Muslim Mission of Ghana," in *Khilafat Centenary Jubilee Souvenir* (Accra: Ahmadiyya Muslim Mission, 2008), 157, 164, 164–165.
31. Hanson interview at Gomoa Potsin: N. Inkoom (descendant of Adam Kofi Quarm), 31 May 2005; "History of Islam at Potsin" (manuscript given to author by N. Inkoom on 31 May 2005).
32. Hanson interviews at Gomoa Potsin: N. Inkoom and Sarah Anderson, 31 May 2005.
33. Hanson interview at Gomoa Potsin: Sarah Anderson (niece of Isa Quantson), 31 May 2005.
34. "Ahmadiyya Movement in Foreign Lands: West Africa," *RR* 33, nos. 9–10 (1934), 399–402.
35. Point 25 of the 1921 bylaws.
36. For the economic implications of Ahmadiyya preaching against amulets for other Muslims in the Gold Coast, see PDJ: box 5, "The Ahmadiyya Movement in the Gold Coast, 1921–31." Chapter 8 discusses the exchanges on this topic in Wa.
37. Hanson interview at Mankessim: Maulvi Ahmad Jibraeel Saeed, 5 June 2005; Christensen, *Double Descent*; George P. Hagan, "An Analytical Study of Fanti Kinship," *Research Review* 5 (1968), 50–90.
38. "Ahmadiyya Movement in Foreign Lands: West Africa," *RR* 33, no. 11 (1934), 443.
39. PRAAD, Cape Coast: ADM 23/1/353, (no day or month) 1937, Jamal Johnston, "Ahmadiyya Movement of the Gold Coast."

40. Hanson interviews with Jibreel Adam and Fatimah Yusuf: Mangoase, 2 June 2005 and Ebubonko, 5 June 2005, respectively.

41. Maulvi N. A. Mubashir, "The Debate: Which Is the Universal Religion, Islam or Christianity," *RR* 42, no. 11 (November 1943), 285–299 and "Did Jesus Die on the Cross to Bear the Sins of Mankind?" *RR* 44, no. 6 (June 1945), 96–101.

42. The mosque was renovated in 1952. Guar-Gorman, "Islam in Fantiland," 151n300. Informants assured me that the steeple and overall structure reflected the architectural style of the original mosque.

7 Ahmadiyya Expansion to Asante

Maulvi Fazlul Rahman Hakeem extolled the efforts of African lay preachers in the expansion of the Ahmadiyya in Asante. Maulvi Hakeem identified one by name, Nana Sadiq, whom he praised as the leader of the rapidly growing Ahmadi community in southern Asante during the 1920s.[1] Also acknowledging Nana Sadiq's leading role in Ahmadiyya proselytism was the British colonial officer A. C. Duncan-Johnstone.[2] Another was Ishmael Kwaku Addo of Asokwa, who was 101 years old when I interviewed in 2005. Ishmael Addo had been a Christian, as were many others in Adanse, where the Methodist mission had established a presence in the early twentieth century. Ishmael Addo remembered that he had just started farming cocoa when he met Nana Sadiq, an experienced cocoa farmer. They conversed about religious matters, and Nana Sadiq asserted that Christians and Muslims worshiped the same God and that the Ahmadiyya was a modern expression of Islam. Addo eventually revealed to Nana Sadiq his reoccurring dream about falling down a vast expanse, and Nana Sadiq interpreted it to mean that Addo was called by God to leave the Methodists and accept that the Messiah had come.[3] This conversation convinced Addo to become an Ahmadi Muslim.

Nana Sadiq, a goldsmith and cocoa farmer in Adanse, was married to Nana Salamat Akua Afiriyie. They were members of Asante royalty, and Nana Sadiq's older brother was the *ohene* of Baworo in the 1920s. Nana Sadiq and Nana Salamat lent their status as *adehyee* to the Ahmadiyya, and more important, they actively proselytized the movement, as did many other Ahmadi Muslims in Asante. In investigating this history, I uncovered another story: Nana Sadiq and other Ahmadi Muslims in Asante had accepted Islam in the early twentieth century, well before the Ahmadiyya arrived in the Gold Coast. Nana Sadiq reportedly converted to Islam after dreaming about robed figures emerging from the ocean.[4] Others also had visionary experiences that led them to accept Islam. These pioneering Asante Muslims formed the initial core of the Ahmadiyya as the movement spread north from the coast. The arrival of the movement in Asante, in these accounts, was not a rupture but a transition in their Muslim journey. Overlooked in the historical literature, this religious development is central to understanding the arrival of the Ahmadiyya in Asante.[5]

This chapter begins with an overview of the political, economic, and religious changes in Asante after 1874, including the adoption of Islam by small numbers of Asante cocoa farmers. It follows with discussion of informal proselytism by Nana Sadiq and other in rural areas of southern and eastern Asante. The chapter ends with the expansion of the Ahmadiyya to Kumasi. Here the Ahmadiyya took longer to become established, as a result of Muslim opposition to the movement in Kumasi's *zongo*, where savanna Muslim scholars expressed concern about its theology and practices. Asante Ahmadi Muslims persevered, however, and consolidated a vibrant movement in the Asante capital during the 1930s. I contend that Kumasi was a closed market for the Ahmadiyya until that point, prevented from open proselytism by the leader of the Kumasi *zongo* in the 1920s, Mallam Salaw. His departure, and other developments I discuss in this chapter, opened the religious marketplace in Kumasi and paved the way for a Muslim renaissance in the Asante capital starting in the middle decades of the twentieth century.

Asante in the Late Nineteenth and Early Twentieth Centuries

Asante was unsettled for decades after the British invasion in 1874. The Asante loss led to the secession of several provinces and to the installation of a new *asantehene*, Mensa Bonsu, but continued unrest culminated in the outbreak of a civil war and the installation of Asantehene Agyeman Prempe I. His reign was aborted, however, after the British invasion of Asante in 1896: the British annexed Asante as a protectorate and sent Prempe I into exile in the Seychelles. British rule led Yaa Asantewaa, the Queen Mother of Ejisu, to lead a revolt that the British suppressed militarily as they incorporated Asante formally into the Gold Coast in 1900. The British chief commissioner imposed direct rule in Kumasi and granted partial local autonomy to selected Asante provincial rulers to defuse the opposition. By 1924 the British felt sufficiently entrenched to allow Prempe I to return from exile, not as the *asantehene* but in the diminished role of *kumasehene* or ruler of Kumasi. Additional moves toward indirect rule occurred in the 1920s and especially in the early 1930s. Finally, too, the British administration recognized Prempe II, successor to Prempe I in 1931, in the restored role of *asantehene* in 1935. The British chief commissioner nonetheless still retained considerable influence for two more decades.[6]

Social and economic transformations accompanied these political changes. The heartland of Asante experienced a significant demographic decline during the last quarter of the nineteenth century, followed by a gradual recovery in the early twentieth century. The twentieth century also witnessed economic expansion, not only in established activities such as gold mining, now controlled by British firms, but also in new areas of African initiative such as cocoa farming. The rainforests in eastern and southern Asante were the first opened to cocoa, and later it spread to western Asante. Farmers relied on family labor and added wage laborers when cocoa plants matured and profits were assured.[7] Expanding cocoa production altered social relations in households by increasing reliance on women's labor, leading them to challenge matrilineal inheritance practices: wives of male cocoa farmers pushed for themselves and their children to receive the fruits of their labors rather than having it pass to matrilineal kin.[8]

Religious movements arose to express unease with these political, economic, and social transformations. Asocial behavior was understood to be witchcraft in the local imagination, and religious movement arose to identify asocial persons and provide ways to deal with the offending parties.[9] The first movement of the era, *domankama*, occurred in the wake of the British invasion of the 1870s and was directed against the *asantehene*, who used the army to crush the challenge. Other movements flourished after the cocoa boom and expressed concern over new forms of wealth accumulation and the challenges to matrilineal inheritance from women in cocoa households. These movements were diverse, and one appropriated deities from the savanna, reflecting Asante interest in the spiritual power of outsiders from the north at a time of social change. Between *domankama* and the movements of the 1920s was another witchcraft eradication movement, known as *aberewa*. Directed against the activities of Christian missions in 1907, *aberewa* was widespread but quickly dissipated. Not much is understood about this movement, but its decline seems to have opened the way to increased acceptance of Christianity in Asante in the years that followed.[10]

Christianity gradually gained influence. Christian missions had tried to establish a presence from the 1840s, but a succession of Asante rulers had resisted their efforts and kept Christian residents under tight control. The 1896 declaration of a British protectorate and deportation of Prempe I opened Asante to an evangelical wave. The Presbyterian Basel Mission and the Wesleyan Methodist Mission, both established along the coast, expanded to Asante. They were attacked during the Yaa Asantewaa revolt and again during the *aberewa* movement, but they gained converts during the 1910s and 1920s. Joining these two missions were the Catholic and Anglican missionary societies; the latter benefited from local interest after the baptism of Prempe I during his forced residence in the Seychelles. Independent Christian movements also emerged. One of the most influential was led by Sampson Oppong, who attracted as many as twenty thousand followers in the 1920s. Oppong preached in white robes, claimed to have renounced his status as an *okomfo*, and called on followers to follow the Christian God. Initially accepted by the Methodists, Oppong fell out of their ranks and led his own prophetic movement.[11]

The Muslim presence in Asante increased through immigration from the savanna after 1874 and especially during the early twentieth century.[12] Overt Muslim proselytism had been restricted for much of the nineteenth century, after Asantehene Osei Kwame was deposed for his alleged sympathies for Islam.[13] Most Muslim merchants remained at Asante's borders in savanna towns such as

Salaga; Kumasi only had a small residential community of Mande-speaking *mallams*, known as *asante nkramo*. After the British invasion of the 1870s Asante's main roads were opened to immigrant Muslim merchants, and over time Muslims began to settle in *zongos* throughout Asante.[14] The largest *zongo* was in Kumasi, where by the 1930s perhaps twelve thousand immigrants resided, working as traders and laborers in the expanding colonial town.[15] Residents of the Kumasi *zongo* constructed a common immigrant culture focused on the Hausa language as a lingua franca and the social customs they shared as former residents of the savanna. The practice of Islam also was an element of this immigrant culture in the Kumasi *zongo*, defined by the savanna Muslims norms articulated by Hausa Muslim scholars.[16]

British colonial officials devolved considerable power to *zongo* leaders in Kumasi. The chief commissioner developed an informal patronage system with several "headmen" in the *zongo*. After a devastating plague in 1924, British officials turned to Mallam Salaw, the Hausa headman, to assist in opening a new *zongo* to resettle recent arrivals and thereby relieve cramped living arrangements, which British officials believed contributed to the health crisis. Thereafter Mallam Salaw worked closely with British officials, who ultimately declared him *sarkin zongo* in 1927. The appointment gave Mallam Salaw greater authority and allowed him to intervene in the affairs of other *zongo* headmen. Riots against this change did not dissuade the British at first, but by 1932 resentment toward Mallam Salaw had increased, and a new outbreak of rioting forced Mallam Salaw's resignation and departure from Kumasi. British officials abolished the position of *sarkin zongo* and returned to the previous system of multiple headmen in the Kumasi *zongo*.[17]

Asante Acceptance of Islam in the Early Colonial Era

Asante conversions to Islam were rare in the early twentieth century and therefore are not a major theme in the historical literature. Many Ahmadi Muslims, however, claimed to have converted to Islam before the 1920s, and their acceptance is an element in family memories. These accounts emphasize the role of visionary experiences in the process of religious change. Although superficially similar to Binyameen Sam's account of his conversion to Islam decades earlier, Asante narratives pointedly do not refer to being converted by Hausa *mallams* attached to the colonial military. Asante Muslims were not open to contact with the Hausa Force and its local expression, the Gold Coast Constabulary; the latter's barracks in Kumasi was torched during the Yaa Asantewaa revolt, and for decades British efforts to recruit Asante into the military were fruitless, reportedly because of an unwillingness to join "an alien and hated body of men."[18] The Muslims in Asante accounts are Mande-speaking *mallams*, known as *karamokos*, many of whom were attached to the courts of *amanhene*. Many Asante Muslims were *adehyee*, and several used their royal contacts to acquire virgin forest lands to become pioneering cocoa farmers in southern and eastern Asante. Drawing on memories and colonial documents, this section presents the outlines of this religious transformation. It is a preliminary assessment, and future research hopefully can amplify this provisional account based on details from those who did not become Ahmadi Muslims.

Acceptance of Islam was facilitated by Asante openness to change during an unsettled period after several British invasions and the imposition of colonial rule. Already by the second half of the nineteenth century, Asante entered what Thomas McCaskie argued was "a period of derangement, of innovation, of compromises and confusion, of false starts and hopes, and, ultimately, of a decisive cognitive and material shift that was beyond the control of a much weakened state."[19] One innovation was related to the *nsumankwaahene*, the royal office that supervised both *akomfoo* and *asante nkramo*: Asantehene Prempe I reportedly allowed Muslims greater access to his children during the 1890s, according to informants interviewed by James Agyeman Duah in the early 1960s.[20] Ahmadi Muslim memories add that Tuudu, a leading *okomfo* under Prempe I, predicted that Islam would come to dominate Asante.[21] These memories combine to suggest that, in the wake of a contentious civil war, Asantehene Prempe I gave loyal Muslim scholars an expanded role in his court. To the degree that Kumasi court life set an example for royal households throughout Asante, this change liberalized interactions between Muslim scholars and younger members of royalty outside Kumasi in the first decades of the twentieth century.

Members of Asante royal families were in the vanguard of Asante subjects converting to Islam in the early twentieth century. One of those pioneering Muslims was Nana Sadiq, a member of the royal Bretuo clan associated with the Baworo *oman*. Then known as Kwame Boateng, Nana Sadiq had been a goldsmith serving Asantehene Prempe I in Kumasi and then was sent by the Asante ruler to Fomena, the capital of the southern Asante *oman* of Adanse, where he was as a goldsmith for Adansehene Kwabena Ofori (see map 6). Nana Sadiq's conversion did not occur at Fomena, according to family memories, but happened during one of his visits to the coast: "Nana saw in a dream men clad in long white robes emerging from the sea and walking towards him. They engaged him in discussion about Islam and taught him how to perform ablution and how to pray."[22] This memory is similar to the conversion narrative associated with Binyameen Sam, and one cannot discount the possible influence of Sam's story on accounts of the dream that led Nana Sadiq to convert to Islam.[23] What is important is what reportedly happened next: after the dream Nana Sadiq returned to Adanse and became close to Suleiman, a *karamoko* at the Adanse capital of Fomena, who gave him a Muslim name, Ahmad Abu Bakr Sadiq, and taught him Arabic and more details about Islam. Eventually Nana Sadiq received land to farm cocoa from

Adansehene Kwabena Ofori. At Tasliman in southern Adanse, Nana Sadiq was one of the pioneering cocoa farmers in Asante, and he reportedly proselytized Islam among fellow Asante cocoa farmers in the region during the early twentieth century.[24]

Another pioneering Asante Muslim was Kwabena Nti. His father was the *krontihene*, a political office in the Kokofu *oman*, an Asante state in which Asantehene Prempe I's clan played a role in court affairs. Kwabena Nti converted to Islam when he was in Asante Agona farming cocoa in the early twentieth century: he reportedly met a *karamoko* who provided esoteric services at the court at Asante Agona. Perhaps Kwabena Nti first developed an interest in Islam as a youth in Kokofu and then approached a *karamoko* in Asante Agona, where the distance from Kokofu afforded greater latitude for interactions. Kwabena Nti not only converted to Islam, taking Yusuf as his new first name, but also obtained knowledge of esoteric healing and soothsaying. Mallam Yusuf, as he was known locally, began a career providing esoteric services and, at midlife, settled at Peminanse, where he continued to offer Muslim healing to Akan speakers in southern Asante (see map 6).[25]

Mahama Kofi Dwumaah is another Asante cocoa farmer who adopted Islam during his time away from home. He had been baptized and given the Christian name Timothy at the Basel Mission church at Mampon in 1910 before leaving with his two brothers to farm cocoa in Asante Akyem. Dwumaah reportedly went missing one day, and for the following three days his brothers searched for him with a party of hunters from the nearby town of Domeabra. Unfound by this search, Dwumaah emerged from the rainforest and told his brothers that God had appeared and asked him to prostrate when he prayed. Kofi continued this practice, praying in Asante Twi and gaining the name *odomankoma nkramo* or "Muslim made by God." News of Dwumaah's conversion circulated in the region and led Dogo, a *karamoko* from a nearby town, to visit Kofi, give him Mahama as a Muslim name, and teach him how to perform *salat*. Mahama Dwumaah marked his new status as a Muslim by wearing a turban with a brass pin in the shape of a crescent moon. He continued to receive visions, not only about personal matters but also about public affairs, such as his prophesy that Prempe I would return from the Seychelles.[26]

This conversion story is corroborated by the British colonial officer A. C. Duncan-Johnstone, who encountered Mahama Dwumaah after his conversion to Islam. Based at Juaso in Asante Akyem, Duncan-Johnstone traveled to Domeabra and Kanongo in 1923. The *ahene* were providing forced labor to build colonial roads, but they faced opposition; at Kanongo, for example, several young men attacked the *ohene* during an evening funeral procession.[27] At Domeabra, close to Mahama Dwumaah's cocoa farm, Duncan-Johnstone met Dwumaah, whom he described as wearing "a brass crescent dangling over his turban" and claiming status as "the head of all the Ashanti Moslems." Dwumaah wanted Asante Muslims in Domeabra removed from the authority of the *ohene* and put under the jurisdiction of the *zongo*. Duncan-Johnstone refused, and the affair seems to have ended, as Dwumaah does not appear again in Duncan-Johnstone's diaries.[28] This encounter not only helps date Dwumaah's conversion to Islam and confirms memories of the brass crescent on his turban; it also suggests that converting to Islam meant joining a community of immigrant cocoa farmers who could band together in efforts to resist *ahene* demands on their labor.

These accounts of pioneering Asante Muslims share common features. Involvement in court life at several locales, including Kumasi and provincial capitals such as Baworo, Fomena, Kokofu, and elsewhere, gave Nana Sadiq and Mallam Yusuf opportunities to interact with the Muslim scholars associated with Asante rulers. In addition, their conversions, as well as the conversion of Mahama Dwumaah, occurred after travel from home in which distance from relatives allowed them to explore new ideas and convert to Islam. Royal connections also gave both Mallam Yusuf and Nana Sadiq grants of land to farm cocoa as members of the initial generation of cocoa farmers in Asante, but others were cocoa farmers, suggesting that this aspirational social group found something attractive in Islam. Perhaps it was the ritual practice of *salat*, which could be performed on cocoa farms. The appeal also may have included the ability to pass their cocoa wealth along the patrilineal line to direct offspring.

Notable in these stories is the prominent role of Mande-speaking *mallams* in the conversion of Asante Muslims. In some examples the names are forgotten, but not their status as *karamoko* who had esoteric knowledge and an ability to pass along information about *salat* and other aspects of Islam. These Muslim scholars were associated with local courts and would have been aware of the liberalization of Asantehene Prempe I's attitudes toward Muslim contact with royalty. All of them interacted with Asante cocoa farmers in contexts far from their homes, opening the possibility for interactions without social pressure from relatives. Whether Mande-speaking *mallams* engaged in an active effort to convert residents of Asante is an open question. Future research on this topic may provide a more comprehensive picture of Muslim religious change in Asante before the arrival of the Ahmadiyya.

Ahmadiyya Arrival in Asante

Fante Ahmadi Muslims brought news of the Ahmadiyya to Asante in the early 1920s during the course of their trading activities and cocoa farming. Memories assign a primary role to Kwabena Yusuf, an Ahmadi Muslim from Assin, north of Ekrawfo, who accepted the Ahmadiyya at Ekrawfo during Maulvi Nayyar's visit in 1921. Kwabena Yusuf reportedly informed Mallam Yusuf of Peminase, who then told Nana Sadiq of Adanse.[29] Mallam Yusuf and Nana Sadiq became Ahmadi leaders in southern Asante, so this account may truncate the process of transmission to emphasize their roles. What is clear is that the Ahmadiyya message of prophesy and reform appealed to Asante Muslim cocoa farmers who had come to Islam through visions and found appealing the movement's reformism and openness to English-language education. Nana Sadiq and Mallam Yusuf made Adanse and Kokofu, respectively, centers of the Ahmadiyya and bases from which the movement spread to neighboring Asante regions, such Mampon in eastern Asante (see map 6).

Nana Sadiq has the honorific designation as the first Ahmadi Muslim in Asante.[30] His decision to accept the Ahmadiyya occurred after learning of the Ahmadiyya and discussing the movement with his spiritual mentor, Suleiman, at the Adanse capital of Fomena. Suleiman reportedly confirmed that the Mahdi would return at the End Times and released his former student to become an Ahmadi Muslim, even though he did not join the Ahmadiyya himself.[31] Thereafter Nana Sadiq proselytized the Ahmadiyya in Adanse from his residence at Tasliman: it became an informal Ahmadi mission where those interested in the movement had meals and discussed religious matters. The constant arrival of visitors impressed Nana Sadiq's wives and children, who were instructed to be kind and generous to all strangers: this memory perhaps expresses how members of Nana Sadiq's household came to accept service to the Ahmadiyya. Several devoted themselves to the movement, most notably Nana Sadiq's third wife, Nana Salamat Akua Afiriyie. She is remembered as being engaged with women's groups, hosting meetings, organizing social welfare activities, and proselytizing the Ahmadiyya from her residences at Tasliman and Kumasi's Asante New Town neighborhood. Together Nana Sadiq and Nana Salamat Akua Afiriyie brought many Asante men and women into the movement.[32]

Women were pioneering Ahmadi Muslims in Asante. Nana Salamat Akua Afiriyie stands out in memories because of her royal status and active role, but memories in several families recount moving stories of pioneering women who accepted the Ahmadiyya. One reoccurring motif in memories is the destruction of religious objects associated with family shrines, usually in public acts such as lighting bonfires outside the family compound for neighbors to witness. These demonstrative acts, forceful expressions of a new religious identity, also had social implications in that they signaled a new spiritual relationship with ancestors in the matrilineal line.[33] As mentioned earlier, the expansion of cocoa production put women in new economic roles and led them to raise questions about matrilineal inheritance: women sought to secure a portion of cocoa wealth associated with their labor and prevent its seizure by matrilineal kin. The Ahmadiyya, with its acceptance of direct inheritance, from husbands to wives and from fathers to children, provided a religious basis for inheritance practices in which wealth was shared more equitably. Memories do not mention such pragmatic or mundane reasons for joining the movement, but stories of women destroying indigenous religious objects associated with matrilineal ancestors underscore the social transformations associated with accepting the Ahmadiyya during the cocoa boom of the early colonial era.

Adanse was a center for Ahmadiyya expansion to cocoa farms and commercial towns throughout southern Asante. Nana Sadiq regularly traveled to Brofoyedru, a market town on the main road from the coast to Kumasi, but he also visited smaller towns where cocoa farmers frequented (see map 6). Nana Sadiq became so involved in these activities that he entrusted his gold smithing to one of his apprentices, Papa Haroun, whom Nana Sadiq had convinced to become an Ahmadi Muslim. Nana Sadiq drew on his conversion story to urge others to accept the Ahmadiyya, adding details that helped press the points about prophesy and reformism associated with the Mahdi and Messiah.[34] His involvement with Ishmael Addo, discussed in the chapter's introduction, reveals that Nana Sadiq conversed with both Christian and Muslim cocoa farmers and was as effective with the former as the latter. Others were involved in Ahmadi proselytism in Adanse during the early years. Jamal S. Johnston regularly visited from the Ahmadiyya mission headquarters in Saltpond, bringing him into frequent contact with Nana Sadiq; Johnston eventually married one of Nana Sadiq's daughters. Another Ahmadi Muslim from the coast was Suleiman Kwame Adam of Anomabu, whose commercial activities took him to Brofoyedru. Suleiman Adam was not a trained Ahmadi missionary, but he nonetheless had learned Arabic and informally proselytized the movement. Through his contact with Nana Sadiq, Suleiman Adam later became a secretary for the *adansehene* at Fomena. Once settled permanently in Adanse, Suleiman Adam married Aisha Tiwaa, another of Nana Sadiq's daughters. Abdul Wahab Adam, one of their offspring, became an Ahmadi missionary and eventually rose through the ranks to become in 1974 the first Ghanaian to head the national branch.[35]

Kokofu was another center of Ahmadiyya proselytism in southern Asante during the early years. Mallam Yusuf was the initial agent as a pioneering Asante Muslim and the one who evangelized the Ahmadiyya from his residence in Peminase. Mallam Yusuf's decision to accept the Ahmadiyya reportedly was influenced by a dramatic recovery from an illness. He was ill and fell into a deep coma for so long that he was taken for burial, at which point Mallam Yusuf awoke from a dream: he was approaching a fork in a road where, on the left were Muslims dressed in distinctive clothing, and on the right were people clothed in rags. When Mallam Yusuf later heard about the Ahmadiyya, he reinterpreted the dream as pointing him to the left and a movement brought by Muslim strangers from afar. Mallam Yusuf abandoned the practice of esoteric Muslim healing and soothsaying and came to preach against those activities as superstitions.[36]

Mallam Yusuf actively proselytized the Ahmadiyya in Kokofu and neighboring regions. He traveled widely and convinced many cocoa farmers to become Ahmadi Muslims. Mallam Yusuf also played a role in convincing Nana Yaw Konkroma, the former *kofofuhene*, to accept the Ahmadiyya upon his return from exile with Prempe I in the Seychelles, where Nana Konkroma had converted to Christianity.[37] Nana Konkroma's acceptance of the Ahmadiyya, even though he never regained political office, added legitimacy to the movement in Kokofu and helped bring more residents to the movement.[38] Mallam Yusuf's proselytism extended beyond Kokofu to neighboring areas: he convinced Asante Muslims at Anwomaso to become Ahmadi Muslims, including the pioneering Ahmadi Muslims Papa Yakubu and Papa Malik Pepra.[39] Mallam Yusuf's primary focus was Kokofu, however, and one of his major accomplishments was securing contributions to have a large Ahmadi mosque built at Peminase, which was opened in 1928 at a ceremony attended by the residential missionary Maulvi Hakeem and Nana Kofi Aburi, the *ohene* at Peminase.

Eastern Asante was another region where the Ahmadiyya expanded among Asante cocoa farmers during the early years. Mahama Dwumaah was the leader of the Asante Muslims, and his acceptance of the Ahmadiyya helped expand the movement in the region. Dwumaah reinterpreted his earlier visionary experiences into a premonition of the arrival of the Ahmadiyya, and he reportedly had subsequent dreams about the appearance of the Mahdi. At the time of Dwumaah's acceptance of the Ahmadiyya, he had retired from cocoa farming in Asante Akyem and resided at Mampon, where he and other former cocoa farmers contributed funds to build a large Ahmadi mosque that impressed A. C. Duncan-Johnstone.[40] This British official, who had met Dwumaah earlier at Domeabra when Asante Muslims were seeking to be placed under the authority of the *zongo*, was concerned that Ahmadi Muslims might not accept subordination to Asante *amanhene*, but Duncan-Johnstone learned, after interviewing several Asante leaders in eastern Asante, that relations were quite positive.[41] After several encounters with Ahmadi Muslims, Duncan-Johnstone came to the conclusion that the Ahmadiyya was more attractive to the residents of Asante than the Islam practiced in *zongos* because it was a modern movement brought by strangers.[42]

The funeral of Nana Sadiq in 1935 was a major event for the Ahmadiyya movement in Asante. Many Ahmadi Muslims attended, including the residential Ahmadi missionary Maulvi Ali. It occurred at Tasliman, where Nana Sadiq asked to be buried instead of at his family home at Baworo; he reportedly worried that his extended family, most of whom were not Ahmadi Muslims, would not honor his request for the simple Ahmadi Muslim ceremony he preferred.[43] But Nana Sadiq's influence nonetheless extended to Baworo, where his older brother, the *ohene* of Baworo Ahmad Kwaku Dua, abdicated to accept the Ahmadiyya. This conversion spoke to Ahmad Kwaku Dua's religious commitment, but it equally signaled the growing strength of the movement. The Ahmadiyya was gaining momentum, and by the time of Nana Sadiq's death it started to make major inroads in Kumasi, the Asante capital, where it had been active since 1921, but without the same success as in rural areas.

Ahmadiyya Expansion to Kumasi

Maulvi Nayyar visited Kumasi in 1921, and Maulvi Hakeem made several visits in the 1920s, but opposition to the Ahmadiyya limited its expansion in Kumasi for more than a decade.[44] Mallam Salaw, the Hausa headman and then *sarkin zongo* in the Kumasi *zongo*, was a bulwark against the Ahmadiyya, and his resistance discouraged most from accepting the movement, including immigrants residing in the *zongo* and members of the *asante nkramo* at Suame. These Muslims rejected Ahmadiyya reformism, including its prohibition of Muslim esoteric healing and soothsaying, and they dismissed its claims that Ghulam Ahmad was the Mahdi and Messiah. Asante Ahmadi Muslims were not deterred, however, and they built a small following in two neighborhoods: Asafo and Asante New Town. Developments in the 1930s benefited Ahmadiyya efforts to proselytize and establish an institutional presence in Kumasi: their main opponent, Mallam Salaw, was deposed as *sarkin zongo* in 1932, and Asantehene Prempe II advocated for English-language education once back as supreme Asante leader beginning in 1935. The religious marketplace in Kumasi was opened to religious competition after the mid-1930s.

Initial Efforts

Maulvi Nayyar visited Kumasi in September 1921. He remarked that the Asante capital was "still under military administration," evident in his need to obtain British approval for his meetings and to rely on police as interpreters. Maulvi Nayyar met with several Asante *ahene*: he had a public meeting and visited several in private residences; one leader indicated interest in the Ahmadiyya but refused to make a public declaration "owing to political expediency."[45] Maulvi Nayyar also met a small delegation of visiting Muslim merchants from northern Africa and the Sudan, with whom he conversed in Arabic and cited references to the Quran and *ahadith* in support of Ahmadiyya teachings. Maulvi Nayyar also met with *zongo* "headmen" and *asante nkramo* in a private residence in the *zongo*. Maulvi Nayyar reported no conversions, but memories suggest that at least one *asante nkramo*, Mallam Qasim of Suame, accepted the Ahmadiyya. Others reportedly joined in the years that followed, but this group abandoned the movement when Maulvi Hakeem visited and explained the obligations of membership: *asante nkramo* were not ready to cease esoteric practices or to make regular financial contributions. Mallam Qasim remained an Ahmadi Muslim, however, and is remembered as one of ten pioneers of the movement in Asante.[46]

Mallam Salaw led opposition to the Ahmadiyya in Kumasi. This British-appointed Muslim leader in the *zongo* was born at Yeji, the capital of the Dagomba state in northern Ghana during the late nineteenth century: he was the son of a Hausa Muslim merchant from Katsina and a daughter of Dagomba royalty. Some Hausa opposed Mallam Salaw's appointment as headman in 1919 because his mother was not Hausa, but he had the support of the British.[47] Mallam Salaw also was the student of one of the most notable Hausa Muslim scholars of the era, Al-Hajj Umar ibn Abi Bakr of Kete-Krachi. Umar was a prolific writer who showered his former student with praise poetry throughout his political career.[48] Mallam Salaw used his position to thwart the efforts of the Ahmadiyya in Kumasi for a decade after Maulvi Nayyar's 1921 visit, often asking Al-Hajj Umar to lend his authority to local denunciations of the movement's claims.

When Maulvi Hakeem visited Kumasi in 1925, A. C. Duncan-Johnstone arranged a meeting between Maulvi Hakeem and Muslim leaders of the Kumasi *zongo*. Duncan-Johnstone was Mallam Salaw's patron and allowed him to bring a large delegation to his residence, including Al-Hajj Umar of Kete-Krachi. Maulvi Hakeem began his presentation with the Ahmadiyya perspective on the End Times and Ghulam Ahmad's role as the Mahdi and Messiah. This elicited no comment from the delegation, but when Maulvi Hakeem claimed that Jesus had survived the cross and died in India, Al-Hajj Umar abruptly stood up, spat on the floor, proclaimed that he would no longer listen to blasphemy, and departed. Mallam Salaw offered apologies to Duncan-Johnstone as he led the rest of the delegation out the door.[49] Given Al-Hajj Umar's scholarly stature and Mallam Salaw's rising position in the colonial administration, their opposition encouraged others Muslims in Kumasi to avoid Ahmadi Muslims and prevent them from proselytizing in the *zongo*.

Ahmadiyya evangelism nonetheless occurred in Kumasi outside the *zongo*. The effort focused on two Kumasi neighborhoods, Asante New Town and Asafo. Nana Salamat Akua Afiriyie's compound in Asante New Town was one place for Ahmadi Muslims to congregate, especially when she or Nana Sadiq visited Kumasi. Asafo was another meeting place, especially when Papa Yakubu and Papa Malik Pepra of Anwomaso visited relatives. This small but growing community of Ahmadi Muslims in Kumasi had no mosque, and Nana Sadiq headed a delegation of Asante Ahmadi Muslims who made their desire for an Ahmadi mosque in Kumasi known to Duncan-Johnstone in 1928. He advised Nana Sadiq to make a formal petition to the Kumasi Public Health Board and to accumulate funds for the project in a bank account. Maulvi Hakeem visited Kumasi for the second time shortly thereafter, and he repeated the Ahmadi request for a mosque at a private meeting with Duncan-Johnstone.[50]

Maulvi Hakeem's 1928 visit to Kumasi was memorable for the public debate on the merits of the Ahmadiyya. The event came as Mallam Salaw was at the height of his influence. Also present was a visiting Muslim scholar, Al-Hajj Duku, a Fulbe Muslim scholar who had studied for over a decade at the prestigious Al-Azhar university in Cairo and was on his way back to Senegal. Mallam Salaw convinced Al-Hajj Duku to challenge Maulvi Hakeem to defend Ahmadiyya doctrines publicly. Maulvi Hakeem accepted, and the event occurred in an open-air venue near the Kumasi *zongo*. It was attended not only by Muslims but also by Duncan-Johnstone, the British commissioner of police, the head of the Catholic mission in Kumasi, and several representatives of the *kumasehene*, including the head *okyeame*. Maulvi Hakeem and Al-Hajj Duku sat across from each other, behind small tables upon which copies of the Quran and other Arabic texts were stacked. Duncan-Johnstone described what occurred: "the Maulvi led off, and in a sonorous Arabic expounded his principles. Alhaj Duku, who was no match for him in theology, quickly abandoned the unequal context and contented himself with abuse." The event lasted two hours, until Maulvi Hakeem stated that Jesus was dead, whereupon Mallam Salaw "leapt to his feet and asked the European audience how they could sit calmly by and listen to such blasphemy against their own teachers." The audience then became "ugly," and the head *okyeame* finally stood, extolled the value of freedom of belief, and insisted that fighting was not allowed. His statement calmed the situation, and the event ended shortly thereafter.[51]

The public debate increased opposition to the Ahmadiyya in Kumasi. Mallam Salaw reportedly warned a British colonial official that he "could not be responsible for the peace" if the Ahmadiyya was not stopped from proselytizing. Duncan-Johnstone admitted surprise at the depth of Muslim opposition: he had never experienced "such feeling or rather religious fanaticism" and concluded that "the demonstrators must therefore have been extremely incensed."[52] Ahmadi Muslims remember being hooted at and stoned by other Muslims, aggressive actions that likely increased in the postdebate aftermath.[53] In this climate, the Ahmadi request to establish a mosque was denied, a decision influenced by Mallam Salaw, who sat on the Kumasi Public Health Board. Maulvi Hakeem wrote the administration to express his "great astonishment" at the outcome and asked, pointedly, whether a Christian request to build another church in Kumasi would have been refused.[54] Maulvi Hakeem's appeal was denied, and Mallam Salaw's continued membership on the board meant that the Ahmadi petition would not succeed until after 1932, when Mallam Salaw left Kumasi to resettle with his father's relatives at Katsina.[55] Al-Hajj Umar died in 1934, also removing his voice of opposition to the Ahmadiyya. In the absence of their primary opponents, the Ahmadiyya had an opportunity to push forward with greater hope for success in Kumasi.

Muslims in Kumasi during the 1930s

The public debate between Maulvi Hakeem and Al-Hajj Duku foreshadowed a new era of Muslim competition that opened in Kumasi during the mid-1930s. The short-term result, as argued already, did not produce an outpouring of local support for the Ahmadiyya, but Al-Hajj Duku's performance not only failed to win the neutral observers in the face of Maulvi Hakeem's debating skills; it underscored both the dynamism of the Ahmadiyya and the failure of the non-Ahmadi Muslim community in Kumasi to field an opponent of their own. In the years that followed, Kumasi became a center of activity for both the Ahmadiyya and other Muslim communities. A. C. Duncan-Johnstone observed that savanna Muslim scholars had been "shocked . . . out of their complacency" by the Ahmadiyya.[56] It would be facile to argue for a simple cause and effect of Ahmadi initiative and non-Ahmadi response, but clearly the persistent Ahmadiyya efforts to secure a presence in Kumasi was a factor encouraging change in the *zongo* and Suame, residence of the *asante nkramo*. The metaphor of the religious marketplace has utility in framing events in Kumasi after Mallam Salaw's departure, as the religious arena opened and competitors borrowed strategies from other groups.

The Ahmadiyya established an English-language school in Kumasi in the mid-1930s. Already in 1929 the movement had identified four acres of land for a school.[57] The proposed locale was Asafo, a Kumasi neighborhood some distance from the *zongo*, where a small Ahmadi community already had emerged. The initiative gained momentum after 1932. Not only was Mallam Salaw removed from the board but the British installation of Prempe II as *asantehene* in 1935 added a prominent advocate for educational initiatives; going forward Asantehene Prempe II supported Ahmadiyya efforts to build schools in Asante.[58] The Ahmadiyya also gained an effective advocate in Al-Hajj Joseph Cudjoe Hassan Atta, who worked as a project inspector in the engineering department of the Kumasi Town Council and became an Ahmadi Muslim in 1934. Hassan Atta's nickname, "Atta Commander," referenced his status as a decorated former soldier in the West African Frontier Force and someone with moral rectitude in approving building permits.[59] These developments led to the approval of the Ahmadiyya request to build an English-language primary school at Asafo in 1936.[60]

The Muslim community in the Kumasi *zongo* embarked on its own effort to improve Muslim education in Kumasi. Memories of this era credit the initiative to Mallam Usman, who reportedly recruited a prominent Muslim scholar to open an advanced Muslim school and train promising members of the younger generation. From this pedagogical effort emerged eleven Muslim scholars who later formed their own schools. Among the ranks of the "Big Eleven," as they came to be known, are Baba el-Wa'iz, Ahmed Nur Din, and Mallam Gilgali, founders of influential advanced Muslims schools, respectively the Wataniyya, al-Nuriyya al-Islamiyya, and Azariyya educational institutions. The emphasis in these schools was Arabic language instruction, and some of the institutions adopted new organizational forms, such as grouping students together by age and emphasizing language comprehension and not mere learning by rote.[61] These pedagogical developments mirrored Muslim reformist initiatives elsewhere in West Africa and were not a direct effort to adopt Ahmadi strategies, but nonetheless the Ahmadi school set an example that spurred a new generation of Kumasi Muslims to develop educational institutions based on long-standing Muslim norms in a newly competitive context.

Muslim competition extended to other realms. Ahmadiyya proselytism introduced preaching in local languages, whereas *mallams* in the savanna tradition used Arabic. More changes in the Ahmadiyya occurred under the leadership of Maulvi Mubashir and the cohort of South Asian Ahmadi Muslims who arrived in the late 1940s to expand the range and intensity of Ahmadi proselytism: they brought the preaching style of the religious marketplace in South Asia to the Gold Coast. One expression of the changes was the open-air preaching at Kejetia, a market in central Kumasi, under the direction of Maulvi Ihsanullah Malik, a Pakistani who headed the Kumasi mission beginning in the late 1940s.[62] On the other side, Big Eleven joined the Gold Coast Islamic Missionary Society, formed to enhance Muslim proselytism in the face of Christian and Ahmadiyya initiatives.[63] Religious competition extended to other areas, such as mosque building, with the construction of new Ahmadi and non-Ahmadi Muslim mosques in Kumasi during the 1940s, and schooling, with the Ahmadiyya opening a secondary school in 1950.[64] These examples are merely illustrative of changes in the postwar era, which opened a new chapter in the history of the Ahmadiyya, both in South Asia and in West Africa.

Conclusion

Several pioneering Asante Ahmadi Muslims told A. C. Duncan-Johnstone that they accepted the Ahmadiyya because Maulvi Hakeem was so convinced of the message that he left home to evangelize among strangers in West Africa.[65] Maulvi Hakeem no doubt played a role, but he credited the expansion of the movement to the proselytism of African lay preachers. Many of them were cocoa farmers who helped build a network of Ahmadi communities throughout southern and eastern Asante. Aspirational Asante cocoa farmers found the Ahmadiyya's inheritance practices well suited to the social and economic transformations in household labor associated with cocoa production. English-language education also was a draw. The Ahmadiyya eventually established a presence in Kumasi, but only after its main opponent, Mallam Salaw, had left his position of authority. Thereafter, the Ahmadiyya was free to take initiatives in the Asante capital, such as opening schools, building a mosque, and engaging in street preaching. But before these successes in Kumasi, Asante Muslims in rural areas had an even wider impact: Wala Muslims learned about the Ahmadiyya during travels to Asante cocoa farms and returned to proselytize the movement in Wa. Chapter 8 turns to that history.

Notes

1. "Ahmadiyya in West Africa," *RR* 25, no. 11 (1926), 4.
2. PDJ: box 2, diary entry for 16 February 1928.
3. Hanson interview at Asokwa: Ismael Kwaku Addo, 26 June 2005.
4. Sakeeka K. Bonsu and Abdul Noor Wahab, "In Search of the True Islam: the Story of Nana Sadick," *Khalifat Centenary Jubilee Souvenir* (Accra: Ahmadiyya Muslim Mission, 2008), 159.
5. Fisher's chapter on Ghana in *Ahmadiyyah* included no references to Nana Sadiq or to developments in Asante.
6. A. Adu Boahen, *Yaa Asantewaa and the Asante-British War of 1900-1*, ed. Emmanuel Akyeampong (Accra: Sub-Saharan Publishers, 2003); Thomas Lewin, *Asante before the British: The Prempean Years, 1875-1900* (Lawrence: Regents Press of Kansas, 1978); William Tordoff, *Asante under the Prempehs, 1888-1935* (London: Oxford University Press, 1965); Wilks, *Asante in the Nineteenth Century*.
7. Gareth Austin, *Labor, Land, and Capital in Ghana*.
8. Jean Allman, "Making Mothers: Missionaries, Medical Officers and Women's Work in Colonial Asante, 1924-45," *History Workshop*, no. 48 (1994), 23-47.
9. *Bayi* is the general Akan term for asocial behavior.
10. The history of these movements is discussed in Allman and Parker, *Tongnaab*.
11. Debrunner, *Christianity in Ghana*, 310-311; G. M. Haliburton, "The Calling of a Prophet: Sampson Oppong," *Bulletin of the Society for African Church History* 2, no. 1 (1965), 84-96.
12. For Muslims in colonial Asante, see Owusu-Ansah, Iddrisu, and Sey, *Islamic Learning*; Schildkroudt, *People of the Zongo*; Silverman and Owusu-Ansah, "Presence of Islam among the Akan"; Weiss, *Accommodation and Revivalism*.
13. Asantehene Osei Kwame's reign introduced public involvement for Muslims in Asante court life, but historians debate the degree to which he was inclined toward Islam. See Wilks, *Asante in the Nineteenth Century*, 253-254; and McCaskie, *State and Society*, 389n170.
14. Schildkroudt, *People of the Zongo*, 69.
15. PDJ: box 5, "The Ahmadiyya Movement in the Gold Coast, 1921-31."
16. Residents of the *zongo* engaged in diverse efforts to create a common immigrant culture over the decades. See Schildkroudt, *People of the Zongo*, 82-97.
17. PDJ: box 4, "Confidential Report to Chief Commissioner on the Status of Kumasi Chiefs." For the historical context, see Schildkroudt, *People of the Zongo*, 67-85.
18. Confidential diary of the chief commissioner, 29 January 1917, quoted in Schildkroudt, *People of the Zongo*, 71.
19. Thomas McCaskie, "Accumulation, Wealth, and Belief in Asante, I: To the Close of the Nineteenth Century," *Africa* 53, no. 1 (1983), 37.
20. James Agyeman Duah, *Nsumankwa Stool History* (Legon: Institute of African Studies, 1962), cited in Donna Maier, "Nineteenth Century Asante Medical Practices," *Comparative Studies in Society and History* 21 (1979), 74.

21. Hanson interview at Baworo: Nana Muhammad K. Duah, 24 June 2005; "How and Why the Tikrom-Baworo Jama'at of the Ahmadiyya Muslim Mission Was Established" (manuscript given to the author by Nana Muhammad K. Duah on 24 June 2005).
22. Bonsu and Wahab, "Nana Sadick," 159.
23. Evidence for the emergence of narratives about Nana Sadiq's conversion is not as extensive as evidence for the rise of Binyameen Sam's conversion narrative: one cannot know the longevity of stories about Nana Sadiq's visit to the coast nor the influence of Sam's stories, if any, on those of Nana Sadiq.
24. Bonsu and Wahab, "Nana Sadick," 158–163.
25. Hanson interview at Peminase: Dr. Mohammed bin Ibrahim, 23 June 2005.
26. Hanson interview at Mampon: Ibrahim Agyeman, Abdullah Nasir Boateng, and Al-Hajj Mahmud Bobrey, 25 June 2005; Abdullah Nasir Boateng, "A Brief History of the Establishment of the Ahmadiyya in Ghana," in *Khalifat Centenary Jubilee Souvenir* (Accra: Ahmadiyya Muslim Mission, 2008), 145–146.
27. PDJ: box 1, diary entry for 5 February 1923.
28. PDJ: box 1, diary entry for 26 September 1923.
29. Abudu, "Contribution of the Ahmadiyya Muslim Mission," 13; Effah, "Ahmadiyya Movement in Ghana," 33.
30. Bonsu and Wahab, "Nana Sadick," 160. Memories are not clear whether Nana Sadiq accepted the Ahmadiyya during Maulvi Nayyar's time, which Kumasi memories mention, or early in Maulvi Hakeem's first tour, which Nana Sadiq's family remembers. See note 45 for Kumasi memories.
31. Bonsu and Wahab, "Nana Sadick," 160.
32. Ibid., 162–163. Hanson interviews at Accra: Maulvi A. Wahab Adam, 24 July 2000 and 28 May 2005.
33. My interpretation of the local meaning of women's conversion stories benefited from my conversations with Maulvi A. Wahab Adam and Fatima Yusif. Hanson interview at Accra: Maulvi A. Wahab Adam, 28 May 2005; Hanson interview at Ebubonko: Fatima Yusif, 5 June 2005.
34. Bonsu and Wahab, "Nana Sadick," 161.
35. Maulvi A. Wahab Adam studied to become an Ahmadi missionary in Pakistan and then served in London and in various postings in Ghana before his appointment as Ameer and missionary-in-charge in Ghana.
36. Hanson interview at Kumasi: Abdullah Nasir Boateng, 25 June 2005.
37. Nana Yaw Konkroma, who took the royal name Asibe II, had the support of Prempe I to be reinstated as *ohene*, but the British continued to support Kofi Ado. See Lewin, *Asante before the British*, 207; Tordoff, *Asante under the Prempehs*, 80, 168, 388–389; McCaskie, *State and Society*, 412n108. Mallam Yusuf visited Nana Yaw Konkroma at Frobeye frequently because his brother, Daud Bafo, had married Nana Konkroma's daughter. Hanson interview at Peminase: Alhassan Atta, 23 June 2005.
38. Abudu, "The Contribution of the Ahmadiyya Muslim Mission," 15; Effah, "Ahmadiyya Movement in Ghana," 34.
39. Boateng, "The Establishment of the Ahmadiyya Muslim Mission at Asafo, Kumasi," 6, 14; Effah, "Ahmadiyya Movement in Ghana," 34.
40. PDJ: box 1, diary entry for 16 February 1928.
41. PDJ: box 1, diary entry for 9 March 1928.
42. PDJ: box 5, "The Ahmadiyya Movement in the Gold Coast, 1921–31."
43. Bonsu and Wahab, "Nana Sadick," 163.

44. Maulvi Nayyar provided a long description of his 1921 visit in *Review of Religions*, and Maulvi Hakeem's visits in 1925 and 1928 received considerable attention in the reports of the British officer A. C. Duncan-Johnstone. Maulvi Hakeem also may have visited Kumasi in 1922. See Abudu, "Contribution of the Ahmadiyya Muslim Mission," 14; Effah, "Ahmadiyya Movement in Ghana," 33.

45. "West Africa Mission," *RR*, 21, nos. 6–8 (1922), 206. According to Ahmadi memories in Kumasi, Nana Sadiq invited and hosted Maulvi Nayyar in 1921, and such a role would explain how Nayyar was able to meet with a delegation of *ahene*. Maulvi Nayyar reportedly designated Nana Sadiq as head of the Kumasi Ahmadi community. Maulvi Nayyar, however, does not mention these details in his report about his visit to Kumasi. Additionally, memories from Nana Sadiq's family do not include Maulvi Nayyar's Kumasi visit and instead family members mentioned that Nana Sadiq accepted the Ahmadiyya during Maulvi Hakeem's first tour. Maulvi Hakeem also referred to Nana Sadiq as head of the Adanse Ahmadi community and not head of the Kumasi Ahmadi community. For Kumasi memories, see Abudu, "Contribution of the Ahmadiyya Muslim Mission," 13–14; and Effah, "Ahmadiyya Movement in Ghana," 33–34; for memories from Nana Sadiq's family, see Bonsu and Wahab, "Nana Sadick," 160; for Maulvi Hakeem's representation of Nana Sadiq's role, see "Ahmadiyya in West Africa," *RR* 25, no. 11 (1926), 4.

46. Abudu, "Contribution of the Ahmadiyya Muslim Mission," 13; Morgan, "History of the Ahmadiyya Movement in Ashanti," 14; Effah, "Ahmadiyya Movement in Ghana," 33, 34.

47. Schildkrout, *People of the Zongo*, 198–205.

48. Al-Hajj Umar wrote numerous poems, and I refer to three here: Arabic Collection, Balme Library, University of Ghana at Legon, Ghana: mss. 239 (i), 239 (ii), 239 (iii). For Al-Hajj Umar, see the book's introduction, note 53.

49. PDJ: box 5, "The Ahmadiyya Movement in the Gold Coast, 1921–31."

50. The requests to build a mosque are in PDJ: box 1, diary entries for 14 and 28 April 1928, respectively.

51. PDJ: box 1, diary entry for 30 April 1928, and box 5, "The Ahmadiyya Movement in the Gold Coast, 1921–31."

52. Quotations from PDJ: box 5, "The Ahmadiyya Movement in the Gold Coast, 1921–31."

53. Effah, "Ahmadiyya Movement in Ghana," 34.

54. PRAAD, Kumasi: ARG 1/30/2/42, 2 July 1928, Maulvi Hakeem to Acting Chief Commissioner, Ashanti, quoted in Antoine, "Practice and Conversion," 86.

55. PDJ: box 2, diary entry for 26 September 1932.

56. PDJ: box 2, diary entry for 11 July 1932.

57. PRAAD, Kumasi: ARG 1/30/2/42, 5 September 1929, Maulvi Hakeem to Chief Commissioner, Ashanti, quoted in Antoine, "Practice and Conversion," 86.

58. Hanson interview at Accra: Maulvi A. Wahab Adam, 28 May 2005; Hanson interview at Kumasi: Ibrahim K. Gyasi, 22 June 2005.

59. Abudu, "Contribution of the Ahmadiyya Muslim Mission," 15; Ibrahim K. Gyasi, "The Mandela Icon and the Capitulation of the Ghanaian Intelligentsia," *Daily Guide*, 20 December 2013; Morgan, "History of the Ahmadiyya Movement in Ashanti," 18–19; Hanson interview at Kumasi: Ibrahim K. Gyasi, 22 June 2005.

60. Abudu, "Contribution of the Ahmadiyya Muslim Mission," 15, 26; Morgan, "History of the Ahmadiyya Movement in Ashanti," 19.

61. Owusu-Ansah, Iddrisu, and Sey, *Islamic Learning*, 80–81.

62. Abudu, "Contribution of the Ahmadiyya Muslim Mission," 16.

63. Owusu-Ansah, Iddrisu, and Sey, *Islamic Learning*, 80.

64. For the Ahmadiyya secondary school at Kumasi, see Abudu, "Contribution of the Ahmadiyya Muslim Mission," 26–27; Yusuf K. Agyare, "History of Talim-ul-Islam Ahmadiyya Senior High School, Kumasi, Ashanti Region, Ghana," in *Khalifat Centenary Jubilee Souvenir* (Accra: Ahmadiyya Muslim Mission, 2008), 116–120. For the Kumasi central mosque, see Ahmad Seidu, "Accountability in Religious Circles: Case Study of the Kumasi Central Mosque," MA thesis, Kwame Nkrumah University of Science and Technology, 2012.

65. PDJ: box 5, "The Ahmadiyya Movement in the Gold Coast, 1921–31."

8 Ahmadiyya Expansion to Wa

MALLAM YUSUF, a pioneering Asante Ahmadi Muslim from Peminase, crossed paths with Mallam Salih, an immigrant Muslim scholar from Wa. Salih, who ran an Arabic school for Wala migrants working on Asante cocoa farms, noticed that Yusuf performed *salat* differently from savanna Muslims. The two discussed religious issues, and Yusuf told Salih about the Ahmadiyya. Salih sought more information from Maulvi Ali, the Ahmadi missionary at Saltpond, who convinced Salih to accept the Ahmadiyya and become a missionary to establish the movement at Wa.[1] Salih and a small group of Wala Ahmadi Muslims faced stiff and sometimes violent opposition led by the Wala Muslim leadership. In 1934 a mob attacked Salih's residence, precipitating a riot and forcing him and others to leave Wa. British officials investigated the matter, and the chief commissioner of the Northern Territories allowed Salih and Wala Ahmadi Muslims to return because he would not allow "a few intolerant men" to alter British colonial policy regarding freedom of religious practice.[2]

Muslim disagreements at Wa concerned a range of Islamic ideas and practices. Savanna Muslim scholars adopted ritual recommendations in the Maliki tradition that Ahmadi Muslims did not follow: this difference was on display daily in the performance of *salat*, with differing placement of arms in the *rakat*. Ahmadi Muslims also prayed separately as a community on Fridays, failing to recognize the leadership of Wala Muslim elders in a public forum. Ahmadi Muslims condemned savanna Muslim norms, particularly the esoteric practices of *mallams* who offered predictions, protections, and cures. Attendance at English-language schools was not condoned by savanna Muslim scholars but was embraced by Ahmadi Muslims. Theological claims were another source of disagreement: savanna Muslims rejected Ahmadi assertions about Jesus' death and Ghulam Ahmad's status as the Mahdi and Messiah. Ahmadi Muslims faced opponents in Kumasi, but at Wa, where a much larger proportion of the population practiced Islam, Muslim scholars held much greater sway.

This chapter analyzes the Ahmadiyya arrival at Wa. It diverges from arguments in *Wa and the Wala* by Ivor Wilks on both chronological and interpretive matters.[3] Wilks conducted research when relations between Wala Muslim communities were tense, and he did not interview Ahmadi Muslims; I consulted a wide range of written and oral materials as well as key documents, unreferenced by Wilks, in the voluminous materials amassed during the British inquiry into the 1934 riot. These materials enable me to situate the Ahmadi initiative in Wa into broader Ahmadiyya efforts at proselytism in the Northern Territories.[4] The chapter begins with background on Wa. It follows with Maulvi Ali's activities in the Northern Territories and Mallam Salih's acceptance of the Ahmadiyya. The chapter then analyzes Salih's efforts to found an Ahmadiyya mission at Wa, illuminating the generational dimensions of the Ahmadi initiative, the reformist nature of the Ahmadi challenge, and the long struggle that concluded with an enduring Ahmadi presence at Wa through British intervention from the highest colonial circles.

Wa

Wa is a small town surrounded by farmlands in the savanna of today's northwestern Ghana (see map 1). Agriculture has been practiced in the region for more than three millennia, and working the land today are diverse farming communities speaking one of several West African languages, including Dagara, Sisala, and Walii. Beginning over three hundred years ago, groups of newcomers settled in and around Wa. Among these immigrants were farmers claiming origins in the Dagomba polity in today's central Ghana. Another group arrived from the Mamprusi polity in the northeast of today's Ghana (see map 2); this latter group formed the Nabihi, Wa's ruling elite. The ruler of Wa or "Wa Na" was a member of one of four Nabihi lineages and governed a small polity from a capital at Wa. Other newcomers to Wa were Mande-speaking Muslim migrants from the west. The first to arrive were Yerihi, organized in two descent groups with internal subdivisions. The second were Muslim scholars who formed the Limamyiri, a group divided into four scholarly lineages. Walii, the language spoken at Wa and surrounding villages, is related to Dagara, reflecting the region's history of absorbing newcomers through cultural exchanges and marriages.[5]

Walii speakers engaged in various productive and commercial activities. Lineages organized farming and craft production. Wa's market was served by local producers, regional traders bringing forest products, cattle herders from the savanna, and long-distance merchants interested in gold produced in the nearby Black Volta River basin. Local merchants served in brokerage roles for visiting merchants and trading on their own account. Various forms of dependency augmented lineages: captives from raids and wars were incorporated by Nahibi and Muslim families in subordinate positions within lineages. Occasionally Wala groups gave recent war captives as tribute to Asante agents, whenever they visited Wa. In the nineteenth century slavery and slave-trading increased, as did commercial traffic that brought Hausa-speaking merchants to Wa, where they settled in a *zongo*. These commercial links meant that Wa was a small but vibrant trading town in an agrarian order dominated by cavaliers.

Wa's residents recognized several spheres of spiritual authority. The initial immigrants from Dagomba believed that they had access to *tendalun*, spiritual powers associated with the earth. Dzandan, a small pond on the outskirts of Wa town, was a potent source, as were outcroppings of rocks and sacred groves in the countryside. Ritual experts known as *tendana* led activities to appease these spiritual forces and organized festivals to celebrate harvests. *Nalun* was a spiritual force introduced by the Nabihi, who asserted authority by defending Wa's residents from animal predators and human invaders through their cavalry power and access to *nalun*. Symbolic references to *nalun* were the animal skins upon which the ruler of Wa, or "Wa Na," sat when performing official duties; jumping over a cow at an annual harvest festival was a way for the ruler of Wa to demonstrate his power. Wala Muslims had access to another sphere of spiritual authority. *Salat* and other Muslim practices were exclusive to the Muslim community, but non-Muslims sought and received spiritual services from Muslims in the form of protective prayers and amulets. Wala Muslims also served the ruler of Wa in titled positions: the "Yeri Na," selected by the Yerihi, served on the ruler's advisory council and helped select a new ruler of Wa, and the imam of Wa, known as "Limam," offered Muslim prayers for the ruler of Wa and all Wa's residents.

Wa's Muslims largely tolerated these diverse spheres of spiritual authority. They limited their advocacy to peaceful means and directed most of their effort to internal reform of the Muslim community. In the mid-nineteenth century Muslim reformism led Limamyiri lineages to send promising sons for advanced study with prominent Mande Muslim scholars at Kong, a market town and Muslim center to the west. This initiative was followed by the opening of new Muslim schools and mosques at Wa. An affluent Wala Muslim financed the construction of a Friday mosque, built by a visiting Muslim architect from Kong. This Friday mosque marked a shift: previously Wala Muslims had prayed privately at residences or neighborhood mosques and thereafter Muslims performed *salat* as a community in a public affirmation on Fridays. This reformist initiative, directed at the Wala Muslim community but including a performance of Muslim piety for all to observe, was an example of gradualist approach to Muslim reformism.

Rivalry between Wala Muslim scholarly lineages increased during the nineteenth century. This rivalry was most intense between two Limamyiri branches, Dzedzedeyiri and Dondoli, known by the neighborhoods at Wa where they resided.[6] The Dzedzedeyiri branch provided the funding for the new Friday mosque, and its initial imams were members of this branch. The Dondoli branch established a new neighborhood outside of town, where they built a small mosque and founded a Muslim school to enhance their scholarly status. The arrival of militant Muslims from outside Wa exacerbated the Limamyiri rivalry. When Muslim reformers originally from Zerma in the Niger River bend started raiding non-Muslim populations north of Wa in the 1870s, some Dzedzedeyiri scholars supported them. When Samory Ture's armies made an eastward march in flight from French imperial armies, some Dondoli scholars supported them. The differing external alliances of the Limamyiri had implications in the era of European imperialism.

British Colonial Rule

The British imperial intervention led to Wa's incorporation into the Northern Territories of the British Gold Coast.[7] Britain, France, and Germany competed for control of the region during the late nineteenth century. The British initiative included diplomatic overtures, led by George Ekem Ferguson, a Fante civil servant who in the early 1890s used his cultural knowledge to negotiate treaties of friendship with several political elites, including the ruler of Wa. Samory Ture's advance from the west rendered this diplomatic initiative moot and brought French imperial forces into the region; German forces also were advancing into the savanna in the east. French, German, and British colonial forces separately defeated a series of African military threats in the savanna, leading to imperial negotiations over spheres of influence and ultimately Britain's formal declaration of protectorate status over the Gold Coast's Northern Territories in 1901.

The British colonial consolidation was supervised by the chief commissioner of the Northern Territories based at Gambaga and later at Tamale. Local British officials in district postings recruited African intermediaries to assist in the implementation of colonial edicts. At Wa the British relied on Mallam Ishaq, a Dzedzedeyiri Muslim scholar, who assisted in the collection of the caravan tax on goods circulating in the savanna. The tax was abolished shortly thereafter, but Mallam Ishaq continued in an intermediary role for two decades. But over time, colonial officials invested the ruler of Wa with enhanced authority, and by 1920 Wa Na Pelpuo III underscored the office's enhanced status by building a new palace in the center of Wa to mark his installation. Wa Na Pelpuo II commanded labor to build colonial roads and encouraged Wala men to migrate to British mines and other enterprises in the south, such as Asante cocoa farms. This labor migration was not accompanied by restrictive pass laws, and its voluntary nature gave considerable autonomy to migrants. Returning migrants made new assertions in their home communities in ways that challenged local elites and practices. Wala Muslim migrants, for example, made graphic demonstrations of their new identities in the 1920s, adopting the fez and wearing white robes of imported cloth to distinguish themselves from the clothing styles of Muslim elders.[8]

English-language educational initiatives in the Northern Territories lagged behind those efforts in the south. The colonial administration established only a few primary schools that were intended to educate sons of local political elites for service in the administration, although often leaders forced the sons of commoners to attend in the place of their sons.⁹ Wa had a small primary school, and students who wanted advanced education had to board at Tamale, which had the only English-language secondary school in the Northern Territories. Other options for English-language education were few in number, as Christian missions were restricted in their activities in the Northern Territories. At Wa, for example, British officials refused both Catholic and Wesleyan Methodist requests to establish missions in the early decades of the twentieth century.¹⁰ Muslim scholars continued to offer instruction in the Quran and tutorials for advanced students over the course of the colonial era.¹¹

British officials largely tolerated Muslims in the Northern Territories as long as they acknowledged that political and economic activities would be managed by African political intermediaries supervised by colonial officers. As Holger Weiss noted, British officials were disinterested in Muslim affairs and formulated "no guidelines to promote or restrict the religious and social life of the Muslims."¹² British officials occasionally rewarded Muslim intermediaries with authorizations to build new mosques and financial support to make the hajj. At Wa British officials still interacted with Mallam Ishaq but increasingly deferred to the superordinate position of imam of Wa, especially after Al-Hajj Muhammad bin Uthman Dun of the Dondoli branch was appointed in 1926. Wa Limam Muhammad Dun consolidated his influence when Ishaq died in 1931 by having a close companion, Al-Hajj Said Soribo, succeed Ishaq as imam of the Friday mosque.¹³ Muslims did not mount overt challenges to British colonialism. The lone instance was mounted by a Fulbe Muslim from Adamawa: Mallam Musa and his companions operated in the Northern Territories for a few years during the first decade of the twentieth century, preaching reformism and destroying indigenous religious sites associated with earth spirits. Eventually the British administration forced Musa and his lieutenants to leave, alleging that they preached about the Mahdi and were a disruptive force. Whether Musa actually invoked the Mahdi is unclear.¹⁴ Muslims at Wa and elsewhere nonetheless saw Musa's activities as preparing the way for the appearance of the Mahdi and looked for additional signs of the End Times.¹⁵

Initial Ahmadiyya Efforts in the Northern Territories

The Ahmadiyya launched its expansion to the Northern Territories during the 1930s. Informal proselytism had carried the message to Tamale by 1928, through the activities of D. A. Mahama, a teacher and Ahmadi Muslim at the Tamale secondary school.¹⁶ Maulvi Nazir Ahmad Ali, Maulvi Hakeem's replacement as missionary-in-charge in 1929, visited the Northern Territories in 1931 in an effort to receive British colonial approval to establish a mission in the region. Maulvi Ali visited Salaga, where his lectures were politely received, but its Muslim leaders did not attend in a public rebuke of the Ahmadiyya. Ali's tour continued with a stop at Tamale. The Muslims in the *zongo* were aloof, but the Dagomba political leadership, joined by the local Muslim scholar Al-Hajj Qudus and several hundred residents of Tamale, accepted the Ahmadiyya movement in a public ceremony led by Ali (see figure 14). British officials were informed of the development in a letter from Ali and did not oppose it, but they doubted the sincerity of the conversions.[17]

Maulvi Ali met the Northern Territories' superintendent of education, A. G. N. Thompson, at Tamale. His predecessor, A. H. Candler, was not receptive to the Ahmadiyya when made aware of Maulvi Hakeem's initiatives in Asante during the 1920s, but Thompson was open to the movement.[18] Maulvi Ali followed his meeting with Thompson by making a request to the chief commissioner of the Northern Territories, F. W. K. Jackson. Ali wrote Jackson that "Christian missionaries were allowed to work in the North in the service of humanity, according to their conviction, when there was not a single native Christian in the whole Protectorate . . . [and] I earnestly hope that Government will have no objection to our religious and educational work in the country."[19] Ali's request to proselytize and open a school received the approval of both the chief commissioner and the colonial secretary.[20]

Maulvi Ali sent the Fante Ahmadi Muslim M. A. Ishaque to establish a mission at Tamale in early 1932.[21] Ishaque was one of the first Africans to train to be an Ahmadi missionary at Saltpond, and his command of both English and Arabic was ideal for a posting where Muslim opponents articulated their criticisms in Arabic. But Ishaque's goal was to attract young men attending Tamale's secondary school with appeals in English. He probably worked with D. A. Mahama, the Ahmadi Muslim teaching in the secondary school.[22] They distributed English-language pamphlets that made comparisons between the Ahmadiyya and Christian teachings, but the effort did not meet with much success.[23] The mission closed within months of opening, and Ishaque politely wrote the chief commissioner a letter thanking him for the opportunity before he left Tamale.[24] The lesson from the effort to establish a Tamale mission was that successful Ahmadiyya proselytism in the Northern Territories required local support. Mallam Salih's acceptance of the Ahmadiyya in Asante created an opportunity for the movement to establish a mission at Wa.

Mallam Salih's Acceptance of the Ahmadiyya

Mallam Salih bin al-Hassan was a Wala Muslim scholar in the Dzedzedeyiri branch of the Limamyiri of Wa. His parents were Asani Kuri and Zeinab, the latter widowed from her marriage to the Dondoli scholar Mahama Taakula. Memories of Salih's youth speak to his intellectual abilities: Mallam Ishaq, the senior scholar in the Dzedzedeyiri branch in the early twentieth century, reportedly overheard Salih demonstrating his knowledge of an Arabic text and observed that he had the talent to become the next preeminent Limamyiri scholar, but that Salih needed to study outside Wa to prevent local scholars from obscuring his talents. Heeding this advice, Salih embarked on an itinerant career of studying with Muslim scholars outside Wa in the 1920s. By the early 1930s, he and his wife, Salmata Mwintuona, resided at Amumoso, a village in southern Asante, where Salih had his own school and lived among young migrants from Wa working on nearby cocoa farms.[25] Salih, in his midthirties at the time, met Mallam Yusuf of Peminase, one of the first Asante Ahmadi Muslims. Memories of Wala Ahmadi Muslims stress Salih's curiosity in the way Yusuf performed Muslim prayers with crossed arms.[26] Mallam Yusuf's descendants remember that Salih initially dismissed Yusuf's insistence that the Mahdi's missionaries were in the Gold Coast, but Salih became convinced when Mallam Yusuf retorted that Salih never expected to meet an Asante Muslim, but that Yusuf's conversion to Islam proved that it was the End Times.[27]

Maulvi Ali convinced Mallam Salih to join the Ahmadiyya. They first met during one of Maulvi Ali's tours of southern Asante. Salih remained unmoved after a brief encounter and visited Saltpond to have an extended discussion. For several days Salih engaged Maulvi Ali, who finally convinced him that the End Times had come, that Jesus had died, and that Ghulam Ahmad was the Mahdi and Messiah. Memories add that Salih's decision fulfilled local prophesies that a Dzedzedeyiri Muslim scholar would figure in the End Times.[28] Salih learned that he needed to abandon his provision of esoteric Muslim services, and thereafter he became a forceful proponent of Muslim reformism, preaching about the need to adopt the Ahmadiyya. As Salih prepared to become an Ahmadi missionary under Maulvi Ali's guidance, he returned periodically to Amumoso and converted other Wala Muslims to the Ahmadiyya, including his students and his wife, Salmata Mwintuona. He also convinced Wala Muslims visiting Amumoso, including Abd-al-Mumin, his brother, and Khalid, his cousin, both of whom would play important roles at Wa over the following decades.[29]

Ivor Wilks located Mallam Salih's decision to accept the Ahmadiyya into the context of Limamyiri rivalries and Salih's desire to elevate his religious stature in relation to the Dondoli branch.[30] Competition between Limamyiri branches influenced events: on the Dzedzedeyiri side, memories of Mallam Ishaq's statement about those trying to obscure Salih's talents probably shaped Salih's views, and on the Dondoli side, Wa Limam Al-Hajj Muhammad Dun appointed someone outside the Dzedzedeyiri branch as imam of the Friday mosque. But accepting the Ahmadiyya forced Salih to renounce much of his Muslim heritage, and the early years of his proselytism at Wa were difficult. Salih's thinking and motivations are not easily discerned from the available evidence, but his correspondence with Wa's Muslim leadership, discussed in the next section, suggests that he was moved deeply by Ahmadiyya reformism.

Maulvi Ali's encouragement certainly was a factor in Mallam Salih's decision to return to Wa. The Ahmadiyya agenda was to extend the movement into the Northern Territories, and the lesson from Tamale was that Ahmadiyya proselytism required someone from the local community to be effective. Salih's acceptance of the Ahmadiyya created an opening to found an Ahmadi mission at Wa just after the unsuccessful effort at Tamale. Ali wrote a letter of introduction for Salih in March 1933 to present to the British official at Wa. The main text of the letter included four points:

> 1) This is to state that the bearer, Mallam Salihu of Wa, is a preacher of the Ahmadiyya Movement. 2) He has been sufficiently instructed in the matter of loyalty to Native Chiefs as required by the British Government. This movement expects its preachers to be always on the side of law and order. 3) If as a result of religious differences the Movement forbids its adherents from saying their prayers in the leadership of other Muslims, it is requested that it may not be construed to mean disobedience on the part of Ahmadis to Chiefs and Imams. 4) Mallam Salifu will preach the Ahmadiyya doctrines to his fellow [residents of Wa].[31]

Maulvi Ali informed British officials that Salih was a preacher who would be obedient, but Ali anticipated potential opposition from Wala Muslim scholars over the issue of *salat*. The reaction that Salih received, however, transcended Maulvi Ali's concern about separate prayer and revealed the depth of hostility to the Ahmadiyya among Wa's Muslim elite.

Ahmadiyya Arrival

Mallam Salih returned to Wa in 1933. He was one of scores of young men leaving Asante for the Northern Territories at the time.[32] The economic depression of the early 1930s reduced hired labor on cocoa farms, and circular migration diminished as young men returned home to begin families with the wealth saved from their labors in Asante. Their experiences altered their views to titled Wala elites who demanded deference and made demands for labor. Nonetheless, the returning laborers still depended on family elders for many practical matters and were forced to accept less personal autonomy than they had in the south. The Ahmadiyya message articulated a religious challenge that combined with a broader generational desire for change.[33] The conflict that unfolded at Wa expressed not only religious issues but also the aspirations of youth and the efforts of Wa's elders to defend their status.

Wa's Muslim leadership acted quickly to subvert Mallam Salih's proselytism of the Ahmadiyya. Wa Limam Muhammad Dun was at the height of his influence in the mid-1930s, and he was aided by his close companion, Friday Limam Soribo, so entitled because he was the imam of the Friday mosque. They convinced parents of returning migrants to force their sons to renounce the Ahmadiyya. Most arriving before Salih agreed to renounce the Ahmadiyya, and those refusing to do so camped outside town. Salih traveled to Wa in late May 1933 with Mallam Yahya, related to Salih through marriage, and Khalid, his maternal cousin; the three were hosted by Karifa Salim, Khalid's brother.[34] Salih made a positive impression during his meeting with the district commissioner, H. Graham Ardron, on June 1, 1933, but his subsequent meetings with Wa Limam Muhammad Dun and Wa Na Pelpuo III went poorly, as did his visits to nearby villages.[35] Ahmadi Muslims allege that Wa's Muslim leadership organized plots against Salih's life that were thwarted by intrepid supporters.[36] These memories cannot be corroborated, but they allude to the intimidation that Salih and his followers faced.

British officials sided with the Muslim leadership at Wa. H. P. Dixon, the acting district commissioner serving during Ardron's leave, grew so alarmed that he sought the approval of his superiors to ask the Ahmadiyya to withdraw Salih from Wa.[37] Salih agreed, only leaving after Dixon gave him a letter acknowledging receipt of Maulvi Ali's introduction of Salih as an Ahmadi missionary.[38] Salih's departure did not reduce the pressure on other young Ahmadi Muslims, and they eventually left Wa and took refuge among Ahmadi Muslims in Asante.[39] Salih's return to Saltpond with Dixon's letter brought the matter before Maulvi Hakeem, who had replaced Maulvi Ali when Salih was at Wa. Maulvi Hakeem took a few months to assess the situation. Once convinced of Salih's character and integrity, Maulvi Hakeem vigorously defended Salih's rights in correspondence with Ardron, who had returned to duty as Wa's district commissioner.[40] Maulvi Hakeem also wrote the chief commissioner of the Northern Territories.[41] Through this correspondence Maulvi Hakeem cleared the way for Salih's return to Wa in mid-1934.

During Mallam Salih's year in exile from Wa, Friday Limam Soribo engaged in correspondence to reiterate the Muslim establishment's views. The Arabic correspondence no longer exists in original documents, but the chief commissioner of the Northern Territories received English translations made by Maulvi Hakeem in 1934.[42] These materials convey the gist of the debate between Wa's Muslim leadership and Salih. In late 1933 Soribo wrote to Ahmadi Muslims who had taken refuge in Asante. He argued that Salih had become a Christian and erroneously condemned legitimate Muslim practices such as making amulets, using the rosary to pray, giving *sadaqa* to Muslim leaders, and marrying multiple wives. Soribo ended his short epistle by reminding its readers that those who left Islam would not be rewarded on the Day of Judgment.[43] Soribo also wrote Salih in late 1933 and insisted that Wala Muslim leaders would reject any religion that was not identical to Islam.⁴⁴ These letters confirmed in writing what Salih and his supporters had heard before they were expelled from Wa.

Mallam Salih responded to Friday Limam Soribo in a lengthy letter revealing his grasp of Ahmadiyya teachings. Salih began by affirming his ties to Soribo as a fellow member of the Limamyiri. He then quoted from the Quran, including the verse that there is no compulsion in religion. Salih asserted that Ghulam Ahmad taught only what Muhammad revealed through the Quran, adding that the doors to revelation of previous prophets, including Noah, Abraham, Moses, and Jesus, were closed, but that Muhammad's door was forever open, an oblique reference to Ghulam Ahmad's claims to receive divine revelation. He closed this section of the letter with an assertion that Jesus had died and that Ghulam Ahmad's appearance as the Messiah was to verify Muhammad's revelation just as Jesus' appearance had affirmed Moses' revelation. Salih's response restated Ahmadi positions he had articulated earlier and expressed his continued fidelity to the movement.

Mallam Salih's letter also included a discussion about the need for Muslim reform. He asserted that God had sent Moses and Muhammad to the Jews and Arabs, respectively, to reform practices, and that Wa needed the same. Salih condemned local practices that he alleged were widely practiced by Wala *mallams*: adultery, foretelling the future, and making amulets. He argued that the manufacture of amulets at Wa used animal blood and was akin to the idolatry of animal sacrifice: this reference may be to mixing blood into the ink used for writing a verse from the Quran on the paper inserted inside the amulet. Salih added that accepting *sadaqa* or gifts to *mallams* at funerals was profiting from the dead and not Islamic. The letter ended with an assertion that the words of current Wala Muslim scholars were not the word of God and asked Muslims to accept that God sent the Mahdi to guide them.⁴⁵

Friday Limam Soribo wrote a lengthy response to Mallam Salih in early 1934. He insisted that Wala Muslim leaders followed the teachings of the Prophet Muhammad and enumerated their practice of the five basic requirements of Islam from *salat* through *zakat* to honoring the Ramadan fast. Soribo wondered why Salih was being stubborn and speaking ill of his former teachers and added that Soribo would keep his distance from a deceitful imposter who perhaps was working for the Anti-Christ. Soribo questioned how Salih could claim to follow the Mahdi if he also denied that Jesus was in heaven. Soribo raised the specter of a violent response to anyone speaking against Islam's prophets in a lengthy discussion that ended with the assertion that such acts were akin to war. He closed with a poem, written in a Sufi style, which reinforced his points about Salih's abandonment of Islam.⁴⁶

These exchanges reveal the substantive issues at stake in the conflict at Wa. Mallam Salih was a member of the Wala Muslim community who condemned local practices and pressed the eschatological claims of Ghulam Ahmad to be the Mahdi and Messiah. Friday Limam Soribo defended local Muslim practices and dismissed the Ahmadiyya by alleging that Ahmadi Muslims were Christians, or, worse, following the Anti-Christ. Soribo invoked the local Muslim establishment as his authority. Implicit in the exchanges was a generational cleavage between Soribo, Salih's former teacher, and Salih, a younger man who traveled and returned with news of the Mahdi.

Mallam Salih's Return and the 1934 Riot at Wa

Mallam Salih returned to Wa in August 1934.[47] Ahmadi memories stress that Wa Limam Muhammad bin Uthman Dun imposed draconian restrictions: Salih could not leave his residence, and members of his immediate family were prohibited from activities such as farming, shopping at the market, and collecting drinking water. When Karifa and Seidu, Salih's cousins and Ahmadi Muslims, disregarded these restrictions on August 14, they were attacked on the outskirts of town, bound, and taken to Wa Limam Muhammad, who lectured them before sending them to the ruler of Wa on the way to the district commissioner for arrest and imprisonment. Emboldened by this incarceration, a small group from Dondoli surrounded Salih's residence, climbed on its flat roof, and tried to strike him with a club when he stepped outside to investigate the noise. Two companions, Khalid and Yahya, came to Salih's defense and bloodied two of the attackers. Rumors circulated in Dondoli that the two had been killed: a large Dondoli group attacked residents and destroyed property throughout Dzedzedeyiri ward, which led its residents, Ahmadi and non-Ahmadi alike, to defend against the action.[48] District Commissioner Ardron and a police contingent arrived around two thirty in the afternoon, broke up the riot, and jailed several participants, including Salih, whom Ardron he later expelled from Wa.[49]

The riot was a pivotal event. It transformed a religious dispute into a broader social conflict and brought official attention to it. Mallam Salih's relatives had embraced kinship solidarity in his defense and, in the years that followed, they became Ahmadi Muslims and made Dzedzedeyiri ward a bastion of the Ahmadiyya at Wa. The riot also led to a British inquiry, the results of which were disseminated to senior officials. The report included numerous statements from the main protagonists. Friday Limam Soribo testified that "Mallam Salihu caused this fight by coming to Wa. His mouth is a knife, his wife's tongue is a knife."[50] Wa Limam Muhammad added:

> Mallam Salihu will not come [to Friday prayers] but stands on his housetop and makes his own call to prayer, and his wives go about abusing other people's wives. Mallam Salihu does not close his mouth abusing us. When one of our people dies we kill a cow and make sacrifice, as is our custom, and

Mallam Salihu goes about and says it is a fetish and pagan custom. Also our amulets which we wear around our necks, he derides them and says they are false.⁵¹

Salih insisted that he was nonviolent and held fast to his Quran without striking back during the riot. When asked about his dismissive statements to Wa's Muslim leadership, Salih responded that: "My teaching is the same, based on the Koran, but mine refers to the Prophet Muhammad, and what they like is only what they hear from their fathers." The testimony of these three figures reiterates the main points of the religious exchanges that Soribo and Salih had in their correspondence in the months preceding the riot and reveals the depth of feeling on both sides.⁵²

Wa Limam Muhammad underscored his testimony at the inquiry by sending a letter directly to the chief commissioner of the Northern Territories on behalf of Wa Na Pelpuo and himself.⁵³ Wa Limam Muhammad began by noting that he had been Mallam Salih's teacher, but his former student had not greeted him promptly upon arrival at Wa and then, when he did, Salih revealed himself to having renounced Islam. Wa Limam Muhammad reminded the chief commissioner that he had made the hajj and knew Islam well. He also tried to place blame for the violence on Salih: Wa's district commissioner had sent him away but he insisted on returning to Wa, only to precipitate the riot that Muslim elders had anticipated. Wa Limam Muhammad ended by asserting that "we are very old and do not want disturbances and riots among our children."⁵⁴ The letter implied that conflict would continue in the event of Salih's return, echoing Friday Liman Soribo's testimony that Salih's mouth was a "knife."

W. J. A. Jones, chief commissioner of the Northern Territories, had been troubled by what he learned about the 1934 riot at Wa, and Wa Limam Muhammad's letter only confirmed his impressions of the Muslim establishment's intransigence. Jones already had told the colonial secretary that the inquiry's report had disturbed him: "This is the first occasion on which to my knowledge religious differences have been the direct cause of a riot in the Gold Coast."⁵⁵ Jones was so concerned that he toured Wa in December 1934; Wa Limam Muhammad wrote to Jones after that visit, perhaps because he sensed that the chief commissioner was not supportive of the Muslim establishment's views. Wa Limam Muhammad's letter did little to change his opinion, and Jones recommended to the colonial secretary that Salih be allowed to return because "it would be a complete negation of government to permit ourselves to be dictated to by a few intolerant men."⁵⁶ The colonial secretary agreed.⁵⁷ District Commissioner Ardron, however, remained sympathetic to the ruler and the imam of Wa, and he communicated their opposition to the chief commissioner. Jones was unmoved and sharply upbraided Ardron.⁵⁸ The colonial administration was not an advocate for the

Ahmadiyya, but Jones and the colonial secretary adopted a neutral posture and demanded that the Wa district commissioner assume it as well.

Maulvi Hakeem welcomed the reopening of Wa to Ahmadiyya proselytism.[59] He did not send Salih back to Wa immediately and let tensions diminish as the two strategized about the next steps.[60] The delay had an unintended result: prominent Wala opponents of the Ahmadiyya died, Wa Na Pelpuo III in September 1935 and Wa Limam Muhammad in September 1936.[61] Their successors did not have the same stature or support: Wa Limam Muhammad's successor, Al-Hajj Malik ibn Uthman, was a notable scholar but not from the illustrious Dondoli branch of the Limamyiri, and Wa Na Pelpuo II's successor, Hamidu Bomi, carried the burden of having been imposed as the first ruler of Wa selected under the new, British-written constitution mandating a rotation between the Nabihi lineages. Hamidu Bomi's selection by rotation upset long-standing processes giving constituencies a voice in naming the new ruler of Wa, and he governed under a cloud of opposition from other Nabihi and was removed from office less than a decade later due to lack of popular support.[62] These two leaders opposed the Ahmadiyya, but without the same effectiveness of their predecessors. Salih's 1936 return occurred under propitious circumstances for the long-term success of the Ahmadiyya at Wa.

Consolidation of the Ahmadiyya at Wa

Mallam Salih informed the Northern Territories' chief commissioner of his intention to return to Wa in May 1936, and British officials made preparations to receive him in June.[63] Dressed in his military uniform and accompanied by an extra patrol of armed police, District Commissioner Ardron met Salih on the outskirts of town, escorted him to his headquarters, and accepted the February 1935 letter from the chief commissioner authorizing Salih's return.[64] It was a triumphant moment, as Ardron was the district commissioner who had arrested, jailed, and sent Salih from Wa in 1934. Wa Limam Muhammad was in the last months of his life, and no organized disruptions occurred that day or in the weeks that followed. The following few years, nonetheless, presented challenges to the Ahmadiyya community at Wa. While Salih never was expelled again, he and his followers endured harassment and occasional threats. Salih's freedom of movement in town also was limited at the outset, and Ahmadi Muslims could not preach in Dondoli and several other wards. The Ahmadiyya nevertheless grew, with membership rising to perhaps a hundred by 1939.[65] Most Ahmadi Muslims were from Dzedzedeyiri or those with family ties to Salih, such as Mallam Yahya and Khalid.[66]

Mallam Salih's residence in Dzedzedeyiri served as the Ahmadiyya mission at Wa. His compound had several large rooms surrounding a courtyard. Salih and his small group of Ahmadi Muslims prayed in one of the rooms, but they wanted to mark their return to Wa by building an Ahmadi mosque. The problem was that the Ahmadiyya community did not have permission to build such a structure. Ahmadi Muslims instead enlarged a room at Salih's compound and added a new door on the outer wall to provide a direct entrance for those coming from town. Wa Limam Al-Hajj Malik ibn Uthman objected to this development, arguing that it disturbed those passing by, and he asked the district commissioner to block the outer door and windows with wood planks. Ardron did not agree because the obstructions posed a safety hazard. Sensing the rising tensions at Wa, the district commissioner ordered a patrol to guard the Ahmadi mosque and asked for instructions from the chief commissioner. The latter agreed to allow the new structure to serve as a mosque, and the Wala Ahmadi community won a major concession.[67]

Other challenges arose. Ahmadi Muslims performed *salat* with crossed arms, and non-Ahmadi Muslims reportedly restrained their arms at their sides in the Maliki style when they prayed at the market or their farms. Implicit in the different performance styles was the Ahmadi insistence that members pray behind an Ahmadi *imam*, a challenge to the Muslim leadership at Wa made public every Friday when most Muslims headed to the central mosque and Ahmadi Muslims went in the opposite direction to Salih's residence. Ahmadi condemnation of the fabrication and use of amulets reportedly drew even more forceful responses from non-Ahmadi Muslims. Mallam Salih's preaching was relentless, accusing Wala *mallams* of profiting at the expense of a fraudulent practice.[68] Ahmadi memories reference several attempts to detonate a large amulet with explosives near the Ahmadi mosque: gunpowder was inserted inside an animal's head, but these incendiary devices reportedly never exploded.[69] At least once an amulet detonated successfully, reportedly as a protest against the ruler of Wa at the refuse incinerator, so Wala Muslims used these devices and may have tried them against Ahmadi Muslims to demonstrate forcefully against reformist arguments censuring esoteric practices.[70]

The most pressing challenge was the refusal of non-Ahmadi Muslims to marry Ahmadi Muslims. The issue was so serious that Mallam Salih included it as a complaint to the chief commissioner in 1943.[71] Most marriages at Wa at the time were arranged, and non-Ahmadi lineage elders prevented their children from making unions with Ahmadi Muslims. One reason for the prohibition was to keep those marrying into the Ahmadiyya from converting, and another, perhaps, was to reduce the births in the Wala Ahmadiyya community. Ahmadi Muslims in the Dzedzedeyiri branch no longer found partners in the other three Limamyiri branches.[72] Ahmadi Muslim memories nonetheless praise Salih's ability to address the problem: young Ahmadi couples began to practice patrilineal cross-cousin marriage, which was permissible but rarely occurred.[73]

Over time the increasing number of Ahmadi Muslims at Wa produced greater social diversity so that cross-cousin marriages did not endure.[74]

The Wala Ahmadi community formed a disciplined community that followed Ahmadiyya guidelines regarding financial support, education, and proselytism. Mallam Salih collected payments from members to support Ahmadi activities. The ruler of Wa attempted to prevent this collection by insisting that only the ruler of Wa could receive taxes, but the British sided with the Ahmadiyya and allowed the payments to continue. One of the new initiatives of the Wala Ahmadiyya was the opening of an Arabic school at Wa. Mallam Yahya, one of his first Wala Ahmadi Muslims and a learned scholar, taught Arabic to students beginning in the late 1930s and gained a large student following over the years.[75] The opening of an Ahmadiyya English-language school was delayed for decades, however, as it would have provoked opposition. Salih was aware of local sentiments: he sent one of his sons to the British school attended by Nabihi children being groomed for service in the colonial administration, but Salih had to withdraw him, because of the abuse his son received for attending a non-Muslim school.[76] Salih and other Wala Ahmadi Muslims sent their children to study in English-language schools in Asante, creating a new pattern of migration for educational purposes and not employment.

The Ahmadiyya provided Wala Muslim with new opportunities. Wala Muslim leaders prohibited women from performing *salat* at the mosque until they reached menopause, but Ahmadi young women prayed regularly with the men. Mallam Salih's wives, especially Salmata Mwintuona, taught the women the basic positions of the *rakat*, including standing, bowing, and prostration, as well as rudimentary Arabic so that they knew the verses of the Quran needed for *salat*. Salmata Mwintuona, remembered as the second Wala Muslim convert after Salih, assumed a leading role in advancing the movement. The Wa Muslim leadership was especially incensed that a young woman would be involved in a Muslim movement, and Friday Limam Soribo had testified before the British inquiry that Salmata Mwintuona's "tongue is a knife." In the years that followed, Wala Ahmadi Muslim women organized themselves to perform daily tasks such as cooking and caring for the young as a small cohort.[77]

The Ahmadiyya expanded from Wa to other communities in the Northern Territories beginning in the late 1930s. Mallam Salih drew on Dzedzedeyiri connections to make contact with families in villages outside Wa, such as Goripisi, and at towns farther afield, such as Tumu and Navrongo. Salih also forged strong links to the Ahmadi community at Tamale, where an Ahmadi mission was relaunched by Ahmad Samba Barwey Wemah, a teacher in the government secondary school.[78] Wemah had grown up in Tamale, the son of a West African Frontier Force soldier, and as a youth he joined the "Boys Brigade," a group that combined morning military drilling in emulation of their fathers with studies under the local Muslim imam. Wemah became an Ahmadi Muslim after a motor accident: he received medical treatment outside Tamale and met Al-Hajj Al-Hassan Atta, a former solider, who convinced him to accept the Ahmadiyya during Wemah's convalescence in Kumasi.[79] Once back in Tamale in 1937, Wemah built the Ahmadi mission successfully through his organizational skills and ability to connect with residents as someone with deep roots in Tamale. Salih regularly visited Wemah during frequent trips to petition the chief commissioner for support against Ahmadi opponents at Wa.

Mallam Salih faced a new proposal to move the Ahmadiyya from Wa in the early 1940s. When Salih returned from his first tour of the Northern Territories, opponents complained that Salih referred to non-Ahmadi Muslims as "infidels" and visited the Yeri Na to gloat after his son had become an Ahmadi Muslim.[80] Tensions increased over the next few weeks, as Muslims hurled epitaphs and threats back and forth near the Ahmadi mosque, leading the new chief commissioner to believe that lasting peace would be achieved only if Ahmadi Muslims moved their mission outside of town.[81] The chief commissioner's proposal was conveyed by the Saltpond district commissioner to Maulvi Nazir Ahmad Mubashir, who expressed interest.[82] Salih immediately travelled to Saltpond and met Maulvi Mubashir, who only recently had arrived as missionary-in-charge and did not know Salih nor the circumstances in Wa.[83] Convinced by Salih, Maulvi Mubashir and General Secretary Jamal Johnston engaged a local lawyer, who helped them write a petition in favor of the Ahmadiyya's right to proselytize at Wa in June 1941.[84] Salih also wrote to British officials in July 1941 insisting that he had the right to remain at Wa.[85] This coordinated effort dissuaded the chief commissioner from enacting his plan. Rioting followed at the end of Ramadan in October 1941, but again the violence dissipated, and the Wala Ahmadi Muslim community survived another challenge.[86]

The threat of expulsion led Mallam Salih and his followers to build a new mosque to anchor the movement in town. It still was in Salih's compound, but its walls were extended to accommodate a large, purpose-built structure. Construction began in mid-1941, and almost immediately new tensions arose.[87] Wa Na Hamidu Bomi had his men confiscate the wood, obtained locally, needed to support the mosque's earthen walls.[88] Salih imported beams from Asante, but they also were seized and given to the ruler of Wa's supporters; memories attest that these logs caught fire and became infested with insects, which Wala Ahmadi take as a sign of God's vengeance.[89] The Ahmadi mosque went up without any wooden support beams and somehow withstood the rainy season downpours.[90] With the mosque in place, Wa Na Sumaila, installed in November 1943, made one of his first acts a petition to remove the Ahmadiyya, arguing that "in a small town like Wa there cannot be two mosques or two sections of people serving God in different ways.... They are our sons but we want peace in the town and they should remove their mosque . . . outside of Wa."[91] Wa's district commissioner agreed, as did the chief commissioner, who wrote Salih directly with the suggestion.[92]

The Ahmadiyya headquarters in Saltpond acted to defend the Ahmadiyya presence at Wa. Maulvi Mubashir, General Secretary Jamal Johnston, and President M. A. Ishaque sent a formal petition in defense of the Ahmadiyya at Wa to the Gold Coast governor, Alan Cuthbert Maxwell Burns, in March 1944. The document asked the governor "to redress the wrongs done to the Wa Ahmadis from time to time and to allow them to practice and preach freely their religion to others." It reviewed the history of the Ahmadiyya in the Gold Coast, detailed the decade of problems at Wa, and referenced correspondence with British colonial officials that contravened the right to freedom of religion.[93] Governor Burns responded in late May 1944, defending British actions but also conceding the right of the Ahmadiyya to practice freely at Wa. Burns pointedly added that Ahmadiyya actions, such as building a new mosque, contributed to the problems, but affirmed that the Ahmadiyya "need have no fear that its freedom 'to make its own way' will be interfered with either by Government or the Native Administration."[94] Burns's letter concluded, importantly, with a promise to investigate the recent claims of the disturbance of peace by members of "any religious sect in Wa" and prosecute offenders in the courts.

This intervention into Wa affairs returned the British colonial administration to the neutral position of arbiter that it had taken immediately after the 1934 riots. This shift encouraged Wa Na Sumaila to be more accommodating to the Ahmadiyya thereafter: when the Dondoli scholar Muhammad Saghir, successor to Wa Limam Al-Hajj Malik ibn Uthman in 1943, launched a new campaign of harassment of Ahmadi Muslims, Wa Na Sumaila did not condone these actions.[95] Wa Na Sumaila's support gave Mallam Salih the confidence to make the hajj in late 1944. Salih pointedly made a modern pilgrimage, not following the precedence of the Dondoli scholars who traveled by foot across the Sahara: he traveled by ocean steamer and made the hajj in less than a year.[96] Salih left a Wala Ahmadi community that was more than six hundred strong in the mid-1940s, less than a tenth of Wa's overall population but a committed presence that would grow in the decades that followed.[97]

The postwar era ushered in new developments at Wa. In the late 1940s the Ahmadi Muslim Mumin Koray became the ruler of Wa, and his short time as leader revealed the tenuous hold that Ahmadi Muslims had at Wa. Mumin Koray was a member of a Nabihi lineage who gained an English-language education and independently joined the Ahmadiyya through correspondence with Maulvi Hakeem in 1929. He returned to become the ruler of Wa in 1949 after Wa Na Sumaila died.[98] When the Limam position opened, Wa Na Mumin Koray maneuvered to have Mallam Salih appointed, placing Ahmadi Muslims in the two most prominent roles of Wa's leadership. The appointment of Mallam Salih roiled the

Wala Muslim establishment, and he eventually decided to resign. These developments take the story into the era into the era of nationalist politics, beyond the purview of this book. Ahmadi Muslims in Wa still would experience intimidation and violence from other Muslims, but the Ahmadiyya presence no longer was in question at Wa.

Conclusion

Mallam Salih testified in 1934 that he held fast to his Quran as a riot unfolded around him, an event precipitated by the Muslim reformism he advocated and the violent reaction it produced. Salih was an insider challenging the savanna Muslim tradition with ideas from the Ahmadiyya; he also was a young man articulating a generational challenge to Wala elders. Wa Limam Al-Hajj Muhammad Dun and other Muslim leaders tried to subvert Ahmadiyya proselytism, and they received support in that effort from local British officials. The success of the initiative hinged on support from the Ahmadiyya mission at Saltpond: residential Ahmadi missionaries intervened at crucial moments and won official recognition of the Ahmadi mission at Wa from the chief commissioner of the Northern Territories and then from the Gold Coast governor. But on several occasions residential Ahmadi missionaries contemplated British proposals to remove the Ahmadiyya from Wa, and only the resolution and advocacy of Mallam Salih convinced the Ahmadi leadership to remain committed to a presence at Wa. This mission, as with Ahmadiyya expansion elsewhere in the Gold Coast, was the expression of African initiative: Wala Ahmadi Muslims faced their opponents with courage and conviction as they successfully consolidated the movement at Wa.

Notes

1. Salih, *Ahmadiyya Factor*, 123; Hanson interview at Peminase: Dr. Mohammed bin Ibrahim, 23 June 2005.
2. PRAAD, Tamale: NRG 8/19/6, 25 January 1935, CCNT to Colonial Secretary.
3. Ivor Wilks, *Wa and the Wala: Islam and Polity in Northwestern Ghana* (Cambridge: Cambridge University Press, 1989).
4. Weiss, *Accommodation and Revivalism*, locates Ahmadiyya expansion to Wa into the larger context of the Northern Territories, but he follows Wilks's chronology and does not draw on interviews with Ahmadi Muslims.
5. For a discussion of the complexities of ethnicity in northwestern Ghana, see Carola Lentz, *Ethnicity and the Making of History in Northern Ghana* (Edinburgh: Edinburgh University Press, 2006).
6. The Dzedzedeyiri branch descended from Limam Yakubu and the Dondoli branch descended from Limam Muhammad.
7. This section draws on Jeff D. Grischow, *Shaping Tradition: Civil Society, Community and Development in Colonial Northern Ghana, 1899–1957* (Leiden: Brill, 2006); Lentz, *Ethnicity*

and the Making of History in Northern Ghana; Weiss, *Accommodation and Revivalism;* and Wilks, *Wa and the Wala*.

8. Wa District annual report, 1923-24 (PRAAD, Accra: NRG 56/1/493), cited in Weiss, *Accommodation and Revivalism*, 223.

9. Roger G. Thomas, "Education in Northern Ghana, 1906-40: A Study in Colonial Paradox," *International Journal of African Historical Studies* 7, no. 3 (1974), 427-467.

10. Wilks, *Wa and the Wala*, 179.

11. Owusu-Ansah, Iddrisu, and Sey, *Islamic Learning*.

12. Weiss, *Accommodation and Revivialism*, 258.

13. Wilks, *Wa and the Wala*, 181.

14. Al-Hajj Umar of Kete Krachi stated that Musa claimed to be the Mahdi in an Arabic poem critical of the movement. Wilks found no evidence that Musa ever claimed to be the Mahdi. See Arabic Collection, Balme Library, University of Ghana at Legon, Ghana, ms. 109 (ii); Wilks, *Wa and the Wala*, 154-155. Also see Jack Goody, "Reform, Renewal and Resistance: A Mahdi in Northern Ghana," in *African Perspectives*, ed. Allen Christopher and R. W. Johnson (Cambridge: Cambridge University Press, 1970), 143-156; Weiss, *Accommodation and Revivalism*, 171-174.

15. Salih, *Ahmadiyya Factor*, 124-125.

16. PRAAD, Tamale: NRG 8/19/5, 9 January 1928, Superintendent of Education to Director of Education. The teacher is identified as D. A. Mahama in PRAAD, Tamale: NRG 8/19/5, 15 June 1931, Superintendent of Education to Director of Education.

17. PRAAD, Tamale: NRG 8/19/5, 25 June 1931, Maulvi Ali to CCNT (photograph enclosed); PDJ: box 5, "The Ahmadiyya Movement in the Gold Coast, 1921-31."

18. PRAAD, Tamale: NRG 8/19/5, 9 and 14 January 1928, Superintendent of Education Candler to Director of Education.

19. PRAAD, Tamale: NRG 8/19/5, 25 June 1931, Maulvi Ali to CCNT.

20. PRAAD, Tamale: NRG 8/19/5, 11 August 1931, CCNT to Colonial Secretary; 15 January 1932, Colonial Secretary to CCNT.

21. PRAAD, Tamale: NRG 8/19/5, 24 January 1932, CCNT to local head of the Ahmadiyya.

22. Two Ahmadi missionaries are mentioned in Weiss, *Accommodation and Revivalism*, 286. D. A. Mahama, the secondary school teacher, likely is the second missionary, serving in an informal role.

23. PDJ: box 2, diary entries for 5 June and 11 July 1932.

24. PRAAD, Tamale: NRG 8/19/5, 29 November 1932, M. A. Ishaque to CCNT.

25. Oral testimony on Mallam Salih's life is summarized in Salih, *Ahmadiyya Factor*, 89-98, 115-117, 123-126.

26. Interview with Khalid, Salih's maternal cousin and one of the early converts to the Ahmadiyya, recorded by his son, Mahmud, at Wa on 16 September 1993 (Mahmud Khalid provided me with an English translation from the testimony in Walii). Mona Fikry also interviewed Khalid in 1967 and translated the interview in Fikry, "Wa: A Case Study of Social Values and Social Tensions as Reflected in the Oral Traditions of the Walas of Northern Ghana," PhD diss., Indiana University, 1969, vol. 1, 207-214. Also see Salih, *Ahmadiyya Factor*, 123.

27. Hanson interview at Peminase: Dr. Mohammed bin Ibrahim, 23 June 2005.

28. Salih, *Ahmadiyya Factor*, 124-125.

29. Salih, *Ahmadiyya Factor*, 125-126; Khalid's 1967 interview in Fikry, "Wa," 209.

30. Wilks, *Wa and the Wala*, 181-182.

31. PRAAD, Tamale: NRG 8/19/5, 26 March 1933, Maulvi Ali to Wa DC.

32. Wilks put Salih's return in 1934, but colonial documents refer to his return in 1933. See PRAAD, Tamale: NRG 8/4/71, Informal Diary, Wa, 1, 9, 14 and 16 June 1933; and *Wa and the Wala*, 180. Wilks cited *Ahmadiyya Movement in Ghana* as his source, but it actually refers to 1933. Wilks might have been adopting the (inaccurate) chronology in J. C. Dough, "Wa and Its People," Institute of African Studies, University of Ghana at Legon, 1966, 51.

33. Wilks, *Wa and the Wala*, 182.

34. Khalid's 1967 interview in Fikry, "Wa," 211–212.

35. PRAAD, Tamale: NRG 8/4/71, Informal Diary, Wa, 1, 9, 14 and 16 June 1933.

36. Salih, *Ahmadiyya Factor*, 135–138.

37. PRAAD, Tamale: NRG 8/19/5, 16 June 1933, Wa DC to CCNT.

38. PRAAD, Tamale: NRG 8/19/5, 5 July 1933, Wa DC to CCNT.

39. Khalid's 1967 interview in Fikry, "Wa," 211–212.

40. Copies of the correspondence (31 December 1933, Maulvi Hakeem to Wa DC; 13 February 1934, Wa DC to Maulvi Hakeem; 7 June 1934, Maulvi Hakeem to Wa DC) are in PRAAD, Tamale: NRG 8/19/6, 27 August 1934, Ardron report, appendix A.

41. *Ahmadiyya Movement in Ghana*, 14.

42. The translations are in: PRAAD, Tamale: NRG 8/19/6, 30 August 1934, Maulvi Hakeem to CCNT, attachments.

43. PRAAD, Tamale: NRG 8/19/6, 30 August 1934, Maulvi Hakeem to CCNT, English translation of Soribo's first letter.

44. PRAAD, Tamale: NRG 8/19/6, 30 August 1934, Maulvi Hakeem to CCNT, English translation of Soribo's second letter.

45. PRAAD, Tamale: NRG 8/19/6, 30 August 1934, Maulvi Hakeem to CCNT, English translation of Salih's letter.

46. PRAAD, Tamale: NRG 8/19/6, 30 August 1934, Maulvi Hakeem to CCNT, English translation of Soribo's third letter.

47. PRAAD, Tamale: NRG 8/4/71, Informal Diary, Wa, 8 August 1934.

48. Salih, *Ahmadiyya Factor*, 179–181; Khalid's 1967 interview in Fikry, "Wa," 211–212.

49. PRAAD, Tamale: NRG 8/4/71, Informal Diary, Wa, 15 August 1934.

50. Soribo's testimony in PRAAD, Tamale: NRG 8/19/6, 27 August 1934, Ardron report.

51. Limam Muhammad's testimony in PRAAD, Tamale: NRG 8/19/6, 27 August 1934, Ardron report.

52. Salih's testimony in PRAAD, Tamale: NRG 8/19/6, 27 August 1934, Ardron report.

53. Wa Limam Muhammad wrote the letter in Hausa document in Arabic script; it no longer exists, but an English translation was made in the office of the Secretary of Native Affairs. See translation in PRAAD, Tamale: NRG 8/19/6, 15 January 1935, Secretary of Native Affairs to CCNT.

54. Translation in PRAAD, Tamale: NRG 8/19/6, 15 January 1935, Secretary of Native Affairs to CCNT.

55. PRAAD, Tamale: NRG 8/19/6, 10 September 1934, CCNT to Colonial Secretary.

56. PRAAD, Tamale: NRG 8/19/6, 25 January 1935, CCNT to Colonial Secretary.

57. PRAAD, Tamale: NRG 8/19/6, 8 February 1935, Colonial Secretary to CCNT.

58. PRAAD, Tamale: NRG 8/19/6, 25 March 1935, CCNT to DC Wa.

59. PRAAD, Tamale: NRG 8/19/6, 18 February 1935, CCNT to Head of the Ahmadiyya Mission; 31 March 1935, Maulvi Hakeem to CCNT.

60. Several scholars refer to Salih's return to Wa in 1935, but no contemporaneous documents refer to this arrival. Salih also does not mention a 1935 return in his 1936 petition to return to Wa. See PRAAD, Tamale: NRG 8/19/6, 9 May 1936, Mallam Salih to CCNT.

61. Wilks, *Wa and the Wala*, 174, 183.
62. Wilks, *Wa and the Wala*, 175–176.
63. PRAAD, Tamale: NRG 8/19/6, 9 May 1936, Mallam Salih to CCNT, and 29 June 1936, Wa DC to CCNT.
64. Dougah, "Wa and Its People," 53; Fikry, "Wa," 213–214. Also see Wilks, *Wa and the Wala*, 181.
65. *Ahmadiyya Movement in Ghana*, 15.
66. Salih, *Ahmadiyya Factor*, 225.
67. Salih, *Ahmadiyya Factor*, 223–224; PRAAD, Tamale: NRG 8/4/74, Informal Diary, Wa, 27 October 1937.
68. Transcript of Mahmud's 1993 interview with Khalid; Hanson interviews at Wa: Mahmud Khalid, 26 June 1997, Latif Khalid, 28 June 1997, and Zakaria Malik, 25 June and 17 August 1997.
69. Hanson interview at Wa: Zakaria Malik, 25 June 1997.
70. PRAAD, Tamale: NRG 8/4/96, Informal Diary, Wa, 2 April 1945.
71. PRAAD, Tamale: NRG 8/19/6, 23 November 1943, Mallam Salih to CCNT.
72. A few Limamyiri families still married into the Dzedzedeyiri branch, including the Limampalayiri and Vuori.
73. Wilks, *Wa and the Wala*, 94.
74. Yahya's 1967 interview in Fikry, "Wa," 215; transcript of Mahmud's 1993 interview with Khalid; Hanson interviews at Wa: Mahmud Khalid, 26 June 1997 and Latif Khalid, 28 June 1997.
75. Hanson interview at Wa: Farida Yahya and Ibrahim Yahya, 30 June 1997.
76. PRAAD, Tamale: NRG 8/4/74, Informal Diary, Wa, 29 June 1936; Salih, *Ahmadiyya Factor*, 104–105.
77. Hanson interview at Accra: Mohammed bin Salih, 25 May 1997.
78. PRAAD, Tamale: NRG 8/4/96, 25 June 1941, Mallam Salihu's tour; Salih, *Ahmadiyya Factor*, 223–34; Karim Wemah, "Mr. Ahmad Samba Barwey Wemah, 1894–1950: A Pioneer Ahmadi Muslim in Northern Ghana," in *Khilafat Centenary Jubilee Souvenir* (Accra: Ahmadiyya Muslim Mission, 2008), 151.
79. Wemah, "Wemah," 152. For the larger context, see Abdulai Iddrisu, "British Colonial Attitudes towards Islamic Education: A Case Study of the Northern Territories of the Gold Coast, 1890–1940," *Journal of the Institute of Education* 4, no. 2 (1998), 60–75.
80. PRAAD, Tamale: NRG 8/19/6, 30 November 1940, Wa DC to CCNT.
81. PRAAD, Tamale: NRG 8/19/6, 31 December 1940, CCNT to the Colonial Secretary.
82. PRAAD, Tamale: NRG 8/19/6, 4 February 1941, Maulvi Mubashir to Saltpond DC.
83. Mallam Yahya's 1967 interview in Fikry, "Wa," 214–215.
84. PRAAD, Tamale: NRG 8/19/6, 16 June 1941, Maulvi Mubashir to Saltpond DC; the barrister Mr. de Graft Johnson is mentioned in 14 June 1941, Saltpond DC to CCCP.
85. PRAAD, Tamale: NRG 8/19/6, 20 June 1941, Mallam Salih to Wa DC.
86. PRAAD, Tamale: NRG 8/4/96, Informal Diary, Wa, 25 October 1941.
87. PRAAD, Tamale: NRG 9/19/6, 7 June and 6 November 1941, Wa DC to CCNT.
88. PRAAD, Tamale: NRG 8/19/6, 20 November 1943, Mallam Salih to CCNT.
89. Salih, *Ahmadiyya Factor*, 233–234.
90. The earthen mosque was replaced by a cinder-block structure on land acquired in Dzedzedeyiri. Salih faced opposition from some who had grown attached to the earthen mosque: he reportedly ordered confidants to weaken the structure in secret so it would fall during the rainy season. Salih, *Ahmadiyya Factor*, 236–237.
91. PRAAD, Tamale: NRG 8/19/6, 2 December 1943, Wa Na et al to CCNT.

92. PRAAD, Tamale: NRG 8/19/6, 28 January 1944, CCNT to Mallam Salih.
93. PRAAD, Tamale: NRG 8/19/6, 23 March 1944, Ahmadiyya petition to the Governor, British Gold Coast.
94. PRAAD, Tamale: NRG 8/19/6, 30 May 1944, British Gold Coast Governor, to the Ahmadiyya Mission.
95. Mallam Yahya's 1967 interview in Fikry, "Wa," 215–216, 217; Wilks, *Wa and the Wala*, 184.
96. Wilks, *Wa and the Wala*, 156, 184.
97. PRAAD, Tamale: NRG 8/19/6, 22 May 1944, Wa DC to CCNT; *Ahmadiyya Movement in Ghana*, 17.
98. Hanson interview at Wa: Seydu Mumin, 30 June 1997; Wilks, *Wa and the Wala*, 185–190.

Conclusion

Several young men fled Ebubonko, a village in the Gold Coast, to avoid conscription into British military service abroad during the Second World War. Their hideout was in virgin rainforest, close to where they previously had farmed cocoa. One of the young men, Kobina Tawiah, left the hideout one day to purchase supplies at a nearby village and met an Ahmadi missionary popularly known as "Teacher Bain." Bashir ud-Din Bain was a former African Christian who had accepted the Ahmadiyya and trained to become a missionary.[1] Bain persuaded Kobina Tawiah to take him to meet the others, and during repeated visits to the hideout, Bain convinced the young men, all of whom were Methodists, to become Ahmadi Muslims by comparing passages in the Bible to teachings in the Quran. Teacher Bain also pointed to the Second World War as one of the signs of the End Times and reassured the men of the arrival of the Mahdi and Messiah. After the war the young men returned to Ebubonko and encouraged others to join the Ahmadiyya, including the women who eventually became their wives.[2] This development expressed the continued efficacy of Muslim preaching from the Bible, a religious practice started by Binyameen Sam and continued by Ahmadi missionaries in the twentieth century.

Independence came to several British colonies after the Second World War. British India split into Pakistan and India in 1947, and the Gold Coast gave way to the new nation of Ghana in 1957. The Partition, as the former event is known, was a wrenching experience, especially in Punjab, which was split between the two new nations: at least three hundred thousand Punjabi residents died in communal violence, and hundreds of thousands more crossed the India-Pakistan border to make new lives for themselves in Pakistan or India. Qadian was on the India side of the new boundary, and Khalifatul Masih Bashir ud-Din Mahmud Ahmad led most of the community to Rabwah in Pakistan, asking a few hundred Ahmadi Muslims to remain and guard Ghulam Ahmad's grave. In the decades ahead, however, it was Pakistan that presented the greatest challenge: the government instituted constitutional changes, first in 1974 that declared Ahmadi Muslims not to be Muslim and then in 1984 that added punitive measures if Ahmadi Muslims engaged in proselytism or represented themselves as Muslims by performing *salat* at Ahmadi mosques.[3] These actions, a culmination of growing opposition to the movement in Pakistan, led the Ahmadiyya Muslim Community to move its headquarters to London in 1984.[4]

Threats to the Ahmadiyya in South Asia led to increased proselytism elsewhere. The succession crisis of the 1910s was one example, the post-Partition era was another, and the current repression was a third. The first period brought the initial residential missionaries to the Gold Coast, the second led to an increased South Asian missionary presence during the middle decades of the twentieth century, and the third further expanded the South Asian presence, not only as missionaries and teachers but also as medical missionaries staffing new Ahmadi medical clinics and hospitals in Ghana. The postwar expansion of Ahmadi missionaries from South Asia led Humphrey Fisher to stress external control of the movement in West Africa and J. Spencer Trimingham to argue that the Ahmadiyya was a "maritime implantation" in West Africa. Both Trimingham and Fisher allowed the changes of the mid-twentieth century to obscure their view of African initiative in the movement's genesis in the West Africa.

This book contends that the arrival and consolidation of the Ahmadiyya in the Gold Coast was a culmination of African efforts to establish a Muslim community. Fante Muslims engaged in conversations across religious boundaries, first in becoming Muslims and then in accepting the Ahmadiyya. Joining the movement as equals, Fante Muslims negotiated the terms of their acceptance in the 1921 "Rules and Regulations" of the Gold Coast branch, which allowed for all financial contributions to be used for local purposes and led to the expansion of English-language schools and mosques, first along the coast and then in Asante and Wa, as the movement gained followers. The arrival of the Ahmadiyya in the Gold Coast was not the first chapter in the story of a "maritime importation" but the middle chapter of a longer one involving West African cosmopolitans who conversed with strangers about universal religious values. This conclusion looks backward, to summarize the book's conclusions, and then casts an eye forward to the postcolonial world appearing on the horizon as the young men from Ebubonko became Ahmadi Muslims.

Religious Change in the British Empire

Britain transformed a small imperial presence into sizable colonial realms in Africa and Asia during the eighteenth through twentieth centuries. The political and economic aspects of British rule were predominant, but the evangelism of Christian missionary societies contributed to the rise of religious marketplaces in which new understandings of personal choice won over converts and, in response, inspired local reformist movements. In Punjab, Christian proselytism was met first by Hindu and Sikh reform movements and then by the Ahmadiyya. It offered a path into the colonial social order for Muslims by establishing English-language schools and encouraging them to engage with others. Ghulam Ahmad asserted that he received revelation as the Mahdi and the Messiah, and his successors made claims to receive divine guidance. In British Punjab's competitive marketplace, the Ahmadiyya was a reformed Muslim movement led by charismatic leaders who attracted members from rural and urban contexts and established an enduring organization catering to the needs of aspirational Muslims.

In West Africa, British imperialism coincided with the abolition of the external slave trade and the expansion of cash cropping in the nineteenth century. British colonies, founded at Freetown in 1808 and Lagos in 1861, were associated with these developments. The Gold Coast experienced both abolitionism and cash cropping from the early nineteenth century, but it only became a formal colony in 1874 after the British invasion of the Asante Empire. Christian missionary evangelism created religious marketplaces in all three British colonies, resulting in the establishment of a small but significant Christian presence. Muslims operated in the marketplaces of Freetown and Lagos, but in the Fante states of the Gold Coast, they became influential only in the early 1870s when the Hausa Force and its *mallams* arrived from Lagos. The British victory over Asante encouraged coastal residents to explore the God of the victors, and while Christianity received most of the attention, Islam intrigued a few Fante Methodists. One of the latter was Binyameen Sam, a Biblicist who grasped that aspects of Islam were rooted in the Old Testament. Sam also was attracted by Muslim esoteric healing and was critical of certain Methodist doctrines and practices. He broke from Christianity to form a new religious community of Fante Muslims.

Changes in the Gold Coast religious marketplace in the early twentieth century shaped the arrival of the Ahmadiyya and its acceptance by Fante Muslims. The number of Christian movements increased, including several new African independent churches that broke from mission churches over issues of control, cultural expression, and prophesy. Muslims arrived from the savanna in increasing numbers, settling in *zongos* in the south. Muslim scholars criticized the beliefs and practices of the Fante Muslim community, and they began to win over young Fante Muslims after Binyameen Sam's death around 1909. The Ahmadiyya entered this marketplace in 1917, just before the 1918 influenza epidemic. The Ahmadiyya's End Times message resonated in the postinfluenza context, and the movement's promotion of English-language education appealed to Fante Muslims whose efforts had failed a decade earlier. Most Fante Muslims accepted the Ahmadiyya's reformism and End Times preaching. Once rooted in the Gold Coast, Fante Muslims spread news of the movement in urban-rural networks extending into the rainforest of Asante, and from there the Ahmadiyya expanded to Wa, where Wala Muslims evangelized the movement.

This analysis reveals patterns of religious change in the British Empire involving Muslim engagement with Christian missionaries. The Fante Muslim community in the Gold Coast and the Ahmadiyya in British India developed distinctive biblical interpretations in their interactions with Christians. This Muslim exegesis of the Bible, though having different expressions, was an element of their cosmopolitan engagement with Christian missionaries in the British Empire. These two religious movements converged to become one, a branch of the Ahmadiyya Muslim Community in the Gold Coast: this development combined the initial Ahmadiyya forays in global proselytism with the initiatives of West African Muslim cosmopolitans. Changes in practices and theology occurred in the Gold Coast, but it was not a rupture: the continuities help explain the embrace and enthusiastic proselytism of the Ahmadiyya by African converts. This case may be unique, but it suggests that religious change occurred through an affirmation of shared principles between Muslim missionaries and converts in the competitive religious marketplaces of the British colonial era. Scholarship on Christian missions in Africa has been at the forefront of acknowledging these complex religious interactions, and these lines of inquiry may yield similar insights on Muslim movements.

West African Muslim Cosmopolitans

Most expatriate Christian missionaries in the British imperial era were absolutists, convinced of the inferiority of other religious expressions, but their efforts opened the possibility for local cosmopolitans to transcend religious boundaries. One was Samuel Crowther, the first African bishop of the Anglican Church, who turned Biblicism into efforts to engage Muslims with shared stories in the Bible and Quran as a step toward possible conversion. Muslims were cosmopolitans, too, and historians are beginning to appreciate their activities. In West African coastal regions during the nineteenth century, Atlantic Muslims were shaped by the crucible of the transatlantic slave trade and conversed with Christians about universal human values. Two of these communities, both from Lagos, played instrumental roles in this history: the Hausa Force and its *mallams*, and Afro-Brazilian Muslims who were members of the first Ahmadiyya community in West Africa.

The Hausa Force was a Muslim community, even though most historians treat its Muslim identity as an illusory representation associated with British "martial races" thinking. Hausa Force members included Muslim immigrants from Freetown and savanna Muslims who had been enslaved, worked along the coast, and fled African masters to join the force in Lagos. Founded in the early 1860s, this colonial militia played a significant role in the British colony of Lagos and became the target of growing resentment of former masters who eventually convinced British officials to reorganize it after John Glover departed Lagos in the early 1870s. But before the force disbanded, some members served a tour of duty in the Gold Coast during the British invasion of Asante. The Muslim expressions of the Hausa Force, not well documented in Lagos, were evident during their Gold Coast deployment. Their *mallams*, too, provided esoteric services to others and in the process engaged with Christians, such as Binyameen Sam, about shared religious values.

Afro-Brazilian Muslims were members of an extensive West African coastal diaspora. The current literature acknowledges their ecumenical religious attitudes, but few have appreciated their wider role in religious change. Samuel Crowther's missionary journals point to a formative early encounter with an Afro-Brazilian Muslim, for whom we only have a first name, Mahamma: he approached Crowther as a fellow cosmopolitan and launched Crowther on his distinctive approach to evangelizing African Muslims. Another Afro-Brazilian Muslim was Amadu Rahman Pedro, who left Lagos for Saltpond and brought Fante Muslims into conversation with Maulvi Nayyar. In the crucial months before the first residential missionary arrived, Pedro managed the Ahmadiyya bank account and then helped connect Maulvi Hakeem with African Ahmadi Muslims. Pedro and other Afro-Brazilians broke from the Ahmadiyya in the years that followed, but they played a central role in the early history of the Ahmadiyya in West Africa.

Fante Muslims were cosmopolitans. They were not former slaves, such as Atlantic Muslims discussed already. Fante Methodists broke from Christianity in response to the preaching of Binyameen Sam, a Biblicist who found scriptural bases for Islam in Christian scripture. He convinced them that they could worship "the same God as the Wesleyans" but with "purer" devotional practices. They would have access to Muslim healing unavailable in the Christian tradition, avoid paying Methodist "ticket money," and maintain Fante practices such as polygyny. Sam's preaching occurred during a period of religious change after the British victory over Asante: some Fante Methodists were moved by this appeal to integrate aspects of their Christian heritage into their Fante Muslim expressions. This synthesis included an enduring Biblicism and a distinctive Fante Muslim visual culture that attached meaning to religious pictures of Old Testament prophets. These Muslim cosmopolitans joined the Ahmadiyya in 1921 as they continued to engage strangers about universal religious values.

Ahmadiyya Proselytism in the Gold Coast

The first Ahmadi residential missionaries in the Gold Coast relied on Africans to spread the message. Mahdi Appah negotiated the terms of the arrival and made sure that his cousin, Binyameen Essau Keelson, served as the first general secretary of the Ahmadiyya in the Gold Coast, placing a Fante Muslim in the mission headquarters from the outset. Other Fante Muslims served as informal missionaries and spread news of the Ahmadiyya along trade routes heading into the interior. Some of their first converts were Asante cocoa farmers, such as Nana Sadiq and Mallam Yusuf, who had become Muslims in the early twentieth century and then accepted the Ahmadiyya. Nana Sadiq was a tireless advocate of the Ahmadiyya, an informal missionary who convinced hundreds to become Ahmadi Muslims. Mallam Yusuf abetted the movement's expansion through his contact with Mallam Salih, who joined the Ahmadiyya, became an Ahmadi missionary, and endured strong opposition as he and his companions established a presence in Wa.

The Ahmadiyya established discipline over its members. Maulvi Hakeem identified leaders in each Ahmadi community with the assistance of Binyameen Essau Keelson; these leaders worked with local councils to ensure that Ahmadi Muslims observed prayer, followed Ahmadi rules, and made regular financial contributions. The effort proved successful, with only a few losses in the early years. Maulvi Hakeem sought to bring Ahmadi Muslims together to celebrate Muslim holidays in Saltpond, but he found it difficult to get all members to attend, especially as more Asante cocoa farmers joined: he sent young Ahmadi Muslim school children, who had memorized his sermons, to distant Ahmadi communities and forged ties that bound them as one movement. The Ahmadiyya requirement to make financial donations was in contrast with Binyameen Sam's preaching against Methodist ticket money and points to significant religious transformations associated with the Ahmadiyya.

The Ahmadiyya arrival introduced sectarian divisions in West Africa. Under Khalifatul Masih Bashir ud-Din Mahmud Ahmad, the Ahmadiyya Muslim Community insisted that its members pray only behind Ahmadi Muslims or, if traveling where none resided, perform *salat* separately from other Muslims. Underscoring the distinctiveness of Ahmadi Muslim identity in West Africa was the style of prayer: arms were folded instead of being extended in the Maliki tradition practiced in West Africa. Ahmadi Muslims differed in other ways. The 1921 "Rules and Regulations" cited practices to avoid, such as esoteric healing and protective amulets, and Ahmadi missionaries pressed this issue. Another distinction was the running of English-language schools. Theological issues, such as the death of Jesus, figured as well, but were less prominent than differences over Muslim practice and schooling.

Muslim opposition increased as the Ahmadiyya moved from the rainforest to the savanna, a development that encouraged Ahmadi missionaries to cultivate relations with British officials to ensure religious liberty. The initial British views of the Ahmadiyya were negative, but Maulvi Hakeem pushed forward and opened an Ahmadi English-language school at Saltpond that became a focus of admiring British administrators. Ahmadi missionaries were not alone in cultivating British officials: Mallam Salaw in Kumasi and Limam Muhammad in Wa also counted on local administrators who supported their opposition to

Ahmadiyya proselytism. In Kumasi, the removal of Mallam Salaw opened the way for Ahmadiyya expansion. In Wa, the effort was more difficult, but Mallam Salih convinced residential Ahmadi missionaries to support Wala Ahmadi Muslims and lobby senior administrators to overrule local officers. The Ahmadiyya astutely secured government assistance for their primary schools and demanded the protections afforded by religious freedom in the face of opposition to the movement among Muslim scholars in the savanna.

The Ahmadiyya in Ghana

The Ahmadiyya in contemporary Ghana retains a focus on local concerns while building stronger connections with the global Ahmadiyya community.[5] Supervising the branch from the 1970s have been Ghanaian Ahmadi Muslims. Shortly after Maulvi Mubashir's era ended a new period began with Ghanaian Ahmadi Muslims, descendants of pioneering Ahmadi Muslims in the Gold Coast, in top leadership roles. Maulvi Abdul Wahab Adam, one of the first Ghanaians to study at the Ahmadiyya seminary in Rabwah, was appointed in 1974 as the first local resident serving as missionary-in-charge in Ghana. Maulvi Wahab brought Ghanaian sensibilities to his leadership, such as mirroring the efforts of the early era and relying on lay missionaries: he sent them into regions of Ghana where no Ahmadiyya presence had been established, and they successfully increased membership significantly.[6] Maulvi Wahab also grasped the possibilities of new media and made inroads with broadcasts on Ghanaian public television. Maulvi Wahab's recent passing led to the appointment of another Ghanaian, Maulvi Mohammed bin Salih, as missionary-in-charge. Maulvi bin Salih, as regional missionary in the 1980s, spearheaded efforts to expand the movement into Burkina Faso, paralleling the efforts of his father, Mallam Salih, who founded the Ahmadi mission at Wa.[7] Maulvi bin Salih's leadership of the Ghanaian Ahmadiyya organization continues the recent pattern of Ghanaian leadership. It is rooted, as all Ahmadi missionary efforts have been from the start, on the active support and assistance of lay Ghanaian Ahmadi Muslims who volunteer time and make regular financial contributions to the Ahmadiyya.

The provision of education remains a primary Ahmadiyya activity. The increasing number of residential Pakistani missionaries after the Second World War supported this effort, but over time Ghanaian Ahmadi Muslims have assumed positions at these schools as teachers and headmasters. Currently the Ahmadiyya runs 85 preschools, 124 primary schools, and 51 junior secondary schools in Ghana.[8] These schools are open to students of all religious backgrounds. Operated in partnership with the Ghanaian government, many schools are in underserved rural areas. Some Ghanaian Ahmadi youths also studied at the Ahmadiyya seminary at Rabwah in exchanges that began in the late 1950s and produced a cohort of Ghanaian Ahmadi religious leaders. As Muslim opposition to the Ahmadiyya grew in Pakistan in the 1980s, the Ghanaian branch assumed an increasingly prominent role in the global movement. Ekrawfo, the former base of the Fante Muslim community, for example, became an Ahmadiyya seminary for students from West Africa and farther afield. Enhancing the Ghanaian branch's stature are the ties Khalifatul Masih Masroor Ahmad, the current successor, forged when he was a missionary in Ghana.

The Ahmadiyya added the provision of health care into its local operations. With funds from the global community, the Ahmadiyya in Ghana has established seven hospitals, all accredited by the Ghanaian government. Most are staffed by Ahmadi medical missionaries from South Asia, but a few Ghanaian Ahmadi Muslim physicians have served, and scores more worked as other medical staff. Other initiatives of Ahmadiyya include homeopathic medicine; the movement opened a clinic in Kumasi, the first homeopathic clinic run by the Ahmadiyya anywhere in the world, to produce medicines and to train homeopathic doctors.[9] Herbal medicine also is promoted by Ghanaian Ahmadi Muslims who produce and sell herbal compounds to address a range of illnesses. The combination of biomedical, homeopathic, and herbal approaches to healing is a distinctive medical presence and widens access to a broad range of users, both Ahmadi Muslims and others.

The Ahmadiyya message remains focused on Ghulam Ahmad's roles as the Mahdi and Messiah and on the divinely inspired leadership of his successors. Visionary experiences remain important to Ghanaian Ahmadi Muslims as well as to the South Asian Ahmadi missionaries who serve in Ghana. It is an element of their religious faith, and the successors to Ghulam Ahmad lead the community in part through the spiritual inspiration they receive in visions and dreams. Africans also had visionary experiences. Accounts of Binyameen Sam's visions, remembered today as the reason for his acceptance of Islam at the hands of a *mallam*, may not have occurred exactly as narrated, but these stories express the local view that a religious quest began in that era: visionary experiences and conversations across cultural frontiers brought two religious movements into one during the British colonial era.

Notes

1. Bashir ud-Din Bain's career as an Ahmadi missionary is discussed in Effah, "Ahmadiyya Movement in Ghana," 34, and Morgan, "History of the Ahmadiyya Movement in Ashanti," 15.

2. Hanson interview at Ebubonko: Fatima Yusif, 5 June 2005; "History of Ahmadiyya Muslims at Ebubonko, Compiled from Information from Fatima Yusif, Wife of (Late) Op. Yusif Kobina Tawiah."

3. Khan, *From Sufism to Ahmadiyya*, 160–165.

4. Religious and political persecution of Ahmadi Muslims in Pakistan is discussed in Antonio Gualtieri, *Conscience and Coercion: Ahmadi Muslims and Orthodoxy in Pakistan* (Montreal: Guernica Editions, 1989); and Khan, *From Sufism to Ahmadiyya*. Also see Simon Ross Valentine, *Islam and the Ahmadiyya Jama'at: History, Belief, Practice* (New York: Columbia University Press, 2008). Anti-Ahmadi sentiments also were expressed in Ghana. See, for example, S. P. Tayo, *Emergence of the Ahmadiyya Movement in West Africa (as a Truth-Seeker Sees It)* (Kumasi: n.p., 1974).

5. John H. Hanson, "Modernity, Religion, and Development in Ghana: The Example of the Ahmadiyya Muslim Community, *Ghana Studies* 12–13 (2009–2010), 55–75; Samwini, *Muslim Resurgence in Ghana since 1950*, 86–96, 147–172, 191–211; Skinner, "Conversion to Islam and the Promotion of 'Modern' Islamic Schools in Ghana."

6. Maulvi A. Wahab Adam, "New Openings of Preaching in Ghana," *RR* 81, no. 8 (August 1986), 5–18.

7. Maulvi Omar Farooq Yahya Sahib, "Establishment of Ahmadiyyat in Neighboring Countries through the Ghana Mission," in *Khalifat Centenary Jubilee Souvenir* (Accra: Ahmadiyya Muslim Mission, 2008), 194. Also see Fabienne Samson, "La guerre des ondes comme mode to proséltisme: La Ahmadiyya et les medias au Burkina Faso," *Ethnographiques* 22 (2011), http://www.ethnographiques.org/2011/Samson.

8. Ibrahim K. Gyasi, "The Contribution of the Ahmadiyya Muslim Mission to the Development of Education in Ghana," in *Khalifat Centenary Jubilee Souvenir* (Accra: Ahmadiyya Muslim Mission, 2008), 180–181.

9. Dr. Mohammed bin Ibrahim, "The Contribution of Ahmadiyya to Health Care Delivery in Ghana," in *Khalifat Centenary Jubilee Souvenir* (Accra: Ahmadiyya Muslim Mission, 2008), 183–187.

Glossary

aberewa. *Bayi*-eradication movement in early twentieth-century Asante; derived from *mberewa* or "old woman" in Akan languages

aburofoo kokoo. Foreigner with light skin pigmentation; from *aburofoɔ kɔkɔɔ* or "red foreigner" in Akan languages

abusua (pl. *mmusua*). Matrilineage or matrilineal clan; from Akan languages

alim (pl. *ulama*). Muslim scholar; from *'ālim/'ulamā'* for "learned one/s" in Arabic

ameer. Leader in the Ahmadiyya Muslim Community; from *amīr* or "commander" in Arabic

anjuman. Administrative body, such as an assembly or organization; from *anjuman* in Urdu

asantehene. Paramount ruler of the Asante Empire; from "ruler of Asante" in Akan languages

asante nkramo. Community of Mande-speaking Muslim scholars integrated into the Asante state as scribes, advisers, and physicians to the *asantehene*; corporate origins from the 1840s, and over time descendants have come to speak Asante Twi but still trace descent from the original Mande settlers; see *karamoko* and *nkramo*

bayat. Oath of allegiance; from *bay'at* in Arabic

bayi. Asocial behavior conceptualized as "witchcraft"; from "take away a child" in Akan languages; see *obayifo*

bida. Innovation, especially in religious beliefs and practices; implies "heresy" to some Muslim scholars; from *bid'ah* in Arabic

Brahman. Member of the Hindu priestly class; from *brāhmaṇa* in Sanskrit

dar al-ulum. Advanced school in the Deoband Muslim reformist network; from *dār al-'ulūm* or "house of knowledge" in Arabic

doab. Region in Punjab lying between two converging rivers; from *dōāb* in Urdu, derived from Persian

Eid al-Adha. Muslim holiday, second of two major holy days; celebrates submission to God's will as expressed through Abraham's willingness to sacrifice his son before God intervened though the Angel Gabriel; from *'īd al-aḍḥā* in Arabic

Eid al-Fitr. Muslim holiday, first of two major holy days; marks the end of fasting in the Muslim month of Ramadan; from *'īd al-fiṭr* in Arabic

End Times. Era before the Final Judgment in eschatological religions such as Christianity and Islam

Gabriel. One of several angels involved in communicating divine revelations to prophets in the Jewish, Christian, and Muslim traditions

gurdwara. Sikh temple or place of worship; from *gurduārā* in Punjabi

guru. Religious teacher, associated with the Hindu and Sikh traditions; from *gurū* in several South Asian languages, derived from Sanskrit

hadith (pl. *ahadith*). Report of the words or actions of the Prophet Muhammad transmitted orally from his companions; Muslim scholars produced collections of these reports, evaluating them for accuracy, and using them as a secondary source to the Quran; from *ḥadīth/aḥadith* in Arabic

hajj. Pilgrimage to the Holy Lands of Mecca and Medina, fulfillment of which is considered one of the five major obligations of Muslim piety; Al-Hajj is the honorific title given to one who has made the hajj; from *ḥajj* in Arabic

hakeemawa. Ahmadi Muslims, literally "Hakeem's people" in Hausa

imam. Leader of *salat*; from *imām* in Arabic

ishtihar. Public notice; from *ishtihār* in Urdu

jalsa salana. Annual convention of the Ahmadiyya Muslim Community; from *jalsa sālāna* in Urdu

jihad. Religious effort or struggle, ranging from inner spiritual development and moral advocacy to defensive military action against nonbelievers; from *jihād* in Arabic

karamoko. Muslim scholar; equivalent to *alim* and *mallam*; from *karamògò* in Mande languages

khalifatul masih. Title of Ghulam Ahmad's successors as head of the Ahmadiyya Muslim Community; from *khalīfat al-masīḥ* or "Successor of the Messiah" in Arabic

khalsa. Sikh order; from *khālsā* in Punjabi

khatam al-nabiyyin. "Seal of the prophets," a phrase in the Quran; many Muslim scholars interpret it to mean that the Prophet Muhammad is the last prophet, whereas Ghulam Ahmad (and others) argue that it makes reference to the Quran received by Muhammad as the last scripture; from *khātam an-nabiyyīn* in Arabic

madrasa. School; usually associated with religious education; from *madrasah* in Arabic

Mahdi. "Guided One" of the Muslim End Times; from *maḥdī* in Arabic

Maliki. Legal interpretive tradition ascribed to Malik ibn Anas (715–795); from *mālikī* in Arabic

mallam. Muslim scholar; used in various West African languages; from *muʿallim* in Arabic; see *alim*

maulvi. Muslim scholar; used in various South Asian languages; from *mawlawi* in Arabic

Messiah. "Deliverer"; from *masīḥ* in Arabic

mfantsefoo. Fante people; from *mfantsefoɔ* in Fante Twi

mirza. Title of a noble; from *mīrzā* in Urdu, derived from Persian

mobahala. Public debate in which God is invoked as the judge; from *mobahala* in Urdu, derived from *mubāhilah* in Arabic

mosque. Place where *salat* is performed; often a physical structure but can be any clean place where *salat* occurs; from *masjid* in Arabic

muezzin. Person calling Muslims to *salat*; from *muʾaḏḏin* in Arabic

mujaddid. Title of a Muslim reformer expected by Muslims to appear every century; from *mujaddid* or "renewer" in Arabic

mullah. Muslim scholar; used in various South Asian languages; from *muʿallim* in Arabic; see *alim*

nalun. Authority of rulers; associated with the rights to "eating the *nam*" or appropriating wealth and protecting the Wala people; from *nalun* in Walii

Nananom Mpow. "Grove of the ancestors"; from *nananom mpow* in Fante Twi

naskh. Abrogation; a classical Muslim scholarly concept employed in resolving contradictory statements in Islamic sources such as the Quran and *ahadith*; from *naskh* in Arabic

nkramo. Muslim; from *nkramo* in Akan languages, derived from *karamògò* in Mande languages

obayifo (**pl. abayifoo**). Asocial person, "witch or wizard"; from *ɔbayifo/abayifoɔ* in Akan languages

obirempon (**pl. abirempon**). Important person, "big man"; from *ɔbirɛmpɔn/abirɛmpɔn* in Akan languages

obosom (**pl. abosom**). Spiritual force or accessible god; from *ɔbosom/abosom* in Akan languages

odehyee (**pl. adehyee**). Royal; from *ɔdehyeɛ/adehyeɛ* in Akan languages

odonko (**pl. nnonkofoo**). Slave acquired from the savanna; from *ɔdɔnkɔ/nnɔnkɔfoɔ* in Akan languages

ohene (**pl. ahene**). Ruler; from *ɔhene/ahene* in Akan languages

okomfo (**pl. akomfoo**). Religious specialist; from *ɔkɔmfo/akɔmfoɔ* in Akan languages

okyeame (**pl. akyeame**). Spokesperson or linguist, from *ɔkyeame/akyeame* in Akan languages

oman (**pl. aman**). Settlement or town, and the political unit associated with it; from *ɔman/aman* in Akan languages

omanhene. Paramount ruler; from *ɔmanhene* in Akan languages

onyame. Creator; from *ɔnyame* in Akan languages

opanyin (**pl. mmpanyinfoo**). Elder; from *ɔpanyin/mmpanyifoɔ* in Akan languages

pir. Title for a Sufi leader; used in South Asia; from *pīr* in Urdu, derived from Persian

Quran. Islam's scripture; believed by Muslims to have been revealed orally to Muhammad and subsequently committed to writing; from *al-qur'ān* ("the recitation") in Arabic

Ramadan. Ninth month in the Islamic calendar; observed by Muslims as a month of fasting to commemorate the Prophet Muhammad's initial receipt of divine revelation; fasting during Ramadan is one of the five major obligations of Muslim piety; from *ramaḍān* in Arabic

rakat. One set of prescribed movements (standing, bowing, and prostration) in *salat*; from *rak'ah* in Arabic

riga. Robe or tunic; from *riga* in Hausa

sajjada nishin. Descendants of notable *pirs*; from *sajjāda nishīn* in Urdu, derived from Persian

salat. Muslim ritual prayer; affirmation of submission to God through the repetition of specific Quranic verses during a series of movements (each unit is known as a *rakat*); performed five times daily as one of the five major obligations of Muslim piety; from *ṣalāt* in Arabic

sarkin zongo. Title for the British-appointed leader of the Kumasi zongo in the early twentieth century; from "ruler of the *zongo*" in Hausa; see *zongo*

sati. The practice of self-immolation of widows on the funeral pyre of deceased husbands; from *sātī* in Hindi

shahada. Muslim profession of faith, stating publicly that there is only one God and Muhammad is a prophet; one of the five major obligations of Muslim piety; from *shahādah* in Arabic

shaykh. Title of a leader in a Sufi order; from *shaykh* in Arabic

shirk. Polytheism or associating others with God; from *shirk* in Arabic

shuddhi. Ritual purification; specifically a mass conversion ritual of the Sikh reformist movement, Arya Samaj; from *shuddhi* in Punjabi, derived from Sanskrit

Sufi. Muslim mystic following the spiritual path of Sufism; from *ṣūfī* in Arabic

***suman* (pl. *asuman*)**. Power object, such as an amulet, charm, talisman; from *sumaŋ/asumaŋ* in Akan languages

sura al-fatiha. First chapter of the Quran; its verses are repeated by Muslims during *salat*; from *sūrat al-fātiḥah* in Arabic

tendalun. Authority associated with *tendana*; from *tèŋgálun* in Walii

tendana. Religious specialist; associated with earth shrines; from *tèŋgána* in Walii

tibb. Classical Muslim medicine; believed to be based on the practice of the Prophet Muhammad; from *ṭibb* in Arabic

ticket money. Subscription to attend Methodist Sunday services, a practice during the nineteenth and early twentieth centuries

tufuhene. Subordinate *ohene*; from *tufuhene* in Akan languages

tuuba. Someone who needs to repent and return to what God commanded; from *tuuba* in Hausa, derived from *tawbah* in Arabic

Wa Limam. Leader of the Limamyiri of Wa; derived from imam

Wa Na. Ruler of Wa; see *nalun*

zakat. Religious alms or tithe for the poor; one of the five major obligations of Muslim piety; from *zakāt* in Arabic

zongo. Muslim neighborhood or ward; from *zongo* or "caravansary" in Hausa

Bibliography

Archives and Special Library Collections

Arabic Collection, Balme Library, University of Ghana at Legon, Ghana (materials formerly housed in the Institute of African Studies Library, University of Ghana at Legon, Ghana)
    Full references to materials cited are given in the notes. I worked from copies in Ghana as well as duplicate copies from the collection at the Melville J. Herskovits Library, Northwestern University, United States.
BM: Basel Mission Archive; Basel, Switzerland
    Full references to items cited are given in the notes. I consulted the English guides to the materials in the nineteenth century, including the valuable translations in "Abstracts from Correspondence in the Basel Mission Archive, 1852–1898, made by P. Jenkins." I then worked with microfilm copies of the original. I also drew on maps in the collection, which I received as PDF files from Basel.
CMS: Church Missionary Society Archive; Birmingham University Library, United Kingdom
    Full references to materials cited are given in the notes. I worked with microfilm copies of the original documents, focusing primarily on materials written by Samuel Crowther.
Humphrey J. Fisher materials; School of Oriental and African Studies Library, University of London, United Kingdom
    The files did not contain materials from Fisher's initial research in the 1950s but rather information from the 1970s when Fisher spent a year in West Africa. The information is invaluable for a history of the Ahmadiyya after independence in West Africa, but no materials are cited in this work.
PDJ: Papers of Lieutenant-Colonel A. C. Duncan-Johnstone; Bodleian Library of Commonwealth and African Studies, the University of Oxford, United Kingdom (materials formerly housed in the Rhodes House)
    Full references to materials cited are given in the notes. The papers are MSS Afr.s.593 in the Colonial Records Project.
PG: Papers of John Hawley Glover, 1861–1875; Cambridge University Library, United Kingdom (materials formerly housed in the Royal Commonwealth Society Library, London)
    Full references to materials cited are given in the notes. I consulted microfilm copies of the originals.
PRAAD: Public Records and Archives Administration Department; Accra, Cape Coast, and Tamale Depositories, Ghana (formerly National Archives of Ghana)
    Full references to materials cited are given in the notes. I consulted files specifically referencing the Ahmadiyya as well as general correspondence related to politics and educational policies.

PRO: Public Records Office; British National Archives, Kew, United Kingdom
   Full references to materials cited are given in the notes. I worked with Colonial Office files: for the Gold Coast from the 1870s to the 1940s and for Lagos from the 1860s to the 1870s. I also worked with War Office files for British invasion of the Gold Coast in the 1870s.
WMMS: Wesleyan Methodist Missionary Society Archive; School of Oriental and African Studies Library, University of London, United Kingdom
   Full references to materials cited are given in the notes. I consulted correspondence and reports pertaining to the Gold Coast from the 1930s to the 1920s, including materials associated with Thomas Birch Freeman.

Newspapers and Other Serials

African Times and Orient Review, 1912–1918, 1920
Islamic Review, 1913–1924
Review of Religions, 1902–1940

I also selectively reviewed: *Gold Coast Independent*; *Gold Coast Times*; *The Times* (London); and *West Africa* (London).

Unpublished Theses, Dissertations, Essays, and Conference Papers

Abdalla, Ismail Hussein. "Islamic Medicine and Its Influence on Traditional Hausa Practitioners in Northern Nigeria." PhD diss., University of Wisconsin, 1981.
Abudu, Richard Abu. "The Contribution of the Ahmadiyya Muslim Mission to the Development of Western Education in Ghana: A Case Study of the Asante Region." MA thesis, University of Cape Coast, 1998.
Acquah, Francis. "The Impact of Traditional Religious Beliefs and Cultural Values on Christian-Muslim Relations in Ghana from the 1920s through the Present: A Case Study of Nkusukum-Ekumfi-Enyan Areas of the Central Region." PhD diss., University of Exeter, 2011.
Adam, Imoru. "The Conflict of the Mosque in Tamale." BA honors essay, University of Ghana at Legon, 1978.
Antoine, Mikelle. "Practice and Conversion of Asante Market Women to the Ahmadiyya Muslim Mission in the Late Twentieth Century." PhD diss., Michigan State University, 2010.
Anvuur, Jonas. "The Evolution of Chieftaincy and the Problems of Skin Disputes in the Upper West Region." BA honors essay, University of Ghana at Legon, 1988.
Ayarna, Bashir Bahila James. "A Survey of the History and Impact of the Ahmadiyya Muslim Mission in Wa." MPhil thesis, University of Ghana at Legon, 1988.
Boateng, Francis. "Islam in the Adansi West District." BA honors essay, University of Ghana at Legon, 1993.
Boateng, Khadijah. "The Establishment of the Ahmadiyya Muslim Mission at Asafo, Kumasi, and Its Influence on the People." Long essay, postsecondary certificate, Kwame Nkrumah University of Science and Technology, 1990.

Brush, Stanley E. "Protestants in the Punjab: Religion and Social Change in an Indian Province in the Nineteenth Century." PhD diss., Stanford University, 1971.
Der, Benedict. "Missionary Enterprise in Northern Ghana, 1906–1975: A Study in Impact." PhD diss., University of Ghana at Legon, 1983.
Dretke, James P. "The Muslim Community in Accra (An Historical Survey)." MA thesis, University of Ghana at Legon, 1968.
Duffield, Ian G. "Dusé Mohamed Ali and the Development of Pan-Africanism, 1866–1945." PhD diss., Edinburgh University, 1971.
Essien, Kwame. "African Diaspora in Reverse: The *Tabom* People in Ghana, 1820s–2009." PhD diss., University of Texas at Austin, 2010.
Ferguson, Douglas E. "Nineteenth-Century Hausaland: Being a Description by Imam Imoru of the Land, Economy, and Society of His People." PhD diss., University of California at Los Angeles, 1973.
Fikry, Mona. "Wa: A Case Study of Social Values and Social Tensions as Reflected in the Oral Traditions of the Walas of Northern Ghana." PhD diss., Indiana University, 1969.
Guar-Gorman, Rasheed A. K. "Islam in Fantiland." MA thesis, University of Ghana at Legon, 1971.
Jenkins, Ray. "Gold Coast Historians and Their Pursuit of the Gold Coast Pasts, 1882–1917." PhD diss., University of Birmingham, 1985.
———. "West Indian and Brazilian Influences in the Gold Coast-Ghana, c. 1807–1914: Review and Reappraisal of Continuities in the Post-Abolitionist Links between West Africa and the Caribbean and Brazil." Paper, Society for Caribbean Studies conference, 1988.
Kasim, Waseem-Ahmed bin. "Identity and Islam as Reflected in Waala Relations with Their Dagaaba Neighbors from 1897 to 1966 in the Wa District of the Gold Coast." MA thesis, University of Ghana at Legon, 2010.
Mbillah, Johnson Apenad. "The Causes of Present Day Muslim Unrest in Ghana." PhD diss., University of Birmingham, 1999.
Mohadeen, Osuman. "The Influence of the Ahmadiyya in Wa." BA honors essay, University of Ghana at Legon, 1994.
Moles, Tarja. "The Evolution of the Ahmadiyya Community in the UK." PhD diss., Royal Holloway, University of London, 2009.
Morgan, M. A. "The History of the Ahmadiyya Movement in Ashanti." BA thesis, Kwame Nkrumah University of Science and Technology, 1990.
Quarcoopome, Samuel. "The Brazilian Community in Accra." BA honors essay, University of Ghana at Legon, 1970.
Rabiatu, Ammah. "The Position of Women in Islam: A Case Study of the Position of Muslim Women in Accra." BA honors essay, University of Ghana at Legon, 1981.
Sawada, Nozomi. "The Educated Elite and Associational Life in Early Lagos Newspapers: In Search of Unity for the Progress of Society." PhD diss., University of Birmingham, 2013.
Seidu, Ahmad. "Accountability in Religious Circles: A Case Study of the Kumasi Central Mosque." MA thesis, Kwame Nkrumah University of Science and Technology, 2012.
Silverman, Raymond. "History, Art, and Assimilation: The Impact of Islam on Akan Material Culture." PhD diss., University of Washington, 1983.

Songsore, Jacob. "Wa Town as a Growth Center, 1897–1973." PhD diss., University of Ghana at Legon, 1975.
Stewart, Charles C. "The Tijaniyya in Ghana." MA thesis, University of Ghana at Legon, 1965.

Published Books, Articles, and Essays in Edited Volumes

Abaka, Edmund. *Kola Is God's Gift: Agricultural Production, Export Initiatives, and the Kola Industry in Asante and the Gold Coast, c. 1820–1950*. Oxford, UK: James Currey, 2005.
Abler, Thomas S. *Hinterland Warriors and Military Dress: European Empires and Exotic Uniforms*. London: Bloomsbury Academic, 1999.
Abubakre, Razaq D., and Stefan Reichmuth. "Arabic Writing between Global and Local Culture: Scholars and Poets in Yorubaland (Southwestern Nigeria)." *Research in African Literatures* 28, no. 3 (1997): 183–209.
Adam, A. Wahab. "New Openings of Preaching in Ghana." *Review of Religions* 81, no. 8 (August 1986): 5–18.
Adamu, Mahdi. *The Hausa Factor in West African History*. Ibadan: Ibadan University Press and Oxford University Press Nigeria, 1978.
Addo-Aryee Brown, A. "Historical Account of Mohammedanism in the Gold Coast." *Gold Coast Review* 3, no. 2 (1927): 196–197.
Agyare, Yusuf K. "History of Talim-ul-Islam Ahmadiyya Senior High School, Kumasi, Ashanti Region, Ghana." In *Khalifat Centenary Jubilee Souvenir*, 116–120. Accra: Ahmadiyya Muslim Mission, 2008.
Ahmad, Chanfi. "The Wahubiri wa Kislamu (Preachers of Islam) in East Africa." *Africa Today* 54, no. 4 (2008): 3–18.
Ahmad, Ghulam. *The Will*. Tilford, UK: Islam International Publications, 2005.
Ahmad, Mubarak. *Our Foreign Missions*. Rabwah: Ahmadiyya Foreign Muslim Missions, 1965.
Ahmad, Tayyba Seema. *Ghulam Ahmad's Exposition of Jihad*. Tilford, UK: Islam International Publications, 1993.
Ahmadiyya Movement in Ghana. Saltpond: Ahmadiyya Movement, Ghana, 1961.
Ahmed-Rufai, Misbahudeen. "The Muslim Association Party: A Test of Religious Politics in Ghana." *Transactions of the Historical Society of Ghana*, n.s., no. 6 (2002): 99–114.
Ajayi, J. F. A. *Christian Missions in Nigeria, 1841–1891: The Making of a New Elite*. London: Longman, 1965.
———. "Nineteenth-Century Origins of Nigerian Nationalism." *Journal of the Historical Society of Nigeria* 2, no. 2 (1961): 196–210.
Akyeampong, Emmanuel Kwaku. *Drink, Power, and Cultural Change: A Social History of Alcohol in Ghana, c. 1800 to Recent Times*. Portsmouth, NH: Heinemann, 1996.
Allman, Jean. "Making Mothers: Missionaries, Medical Officers and Women's Work in Colonial Asante, 1924–45." *History Workshop*, no. 48 (1994): 23–47.
Allman, Jean, and John Parker. *Tongnaab: The History of an African God*. Bloomington: Indiana University Press, 2007.

Allman, Jean, and Victoria Tashjian. *"I Will Not Eat Stone": A Women's History of Colonial Asante*. Portsmouth, NH: Heinemann, 2000.
Amos, Alcione, and Ebenezer Ayesu. "'I am Brazilian': A History of the Tabom, Afro-Brazilians in Accra, Ghana." *Transactions of the Historical Society of Ghana*, n.s., no. 6 (2002): 35–58.
Anaman, Jacob B. *The Gold Coast Guide*. London: Christian Herald, 1902.
Anquandah, James. "Urbanization and State Formation in Ghana during the Iron Age." In *Archaeology of Africa: Foods, Metals and Towns*, ed. Thurston Shaw, 642–651. New York: Routledge, 1993.
Ansari, K. Humayun. *The Infidel Within: Muslims in Britain since 1800*. London: Hurst & Company, 2004.
———. "Making Transnational Connections: Muslim Networks in Early Twentieth-Century Britain." In *Islam in Inter-war Europe*, ed. Nathalie Clayer and Eric Germain, 31–63. London: Hurst and Company, 2008.
———. "The Woking Mosque: A Case Study of Muslim Engagement with British Society since 1889." *Immigrants and Minorities* 21, no. 3 (2002): 1–24.
Appiah, Kwame Anthony. *Cosmopolitanism: Ethics in a World of Strangers*. New York: Norton, 2007.
Arhin, Kwame. *West African Traders in Ghana in the Nineteenth and Twentieth Centuries*. London: Longman, 1979.
Atiemo, Abamfo. "'Singing with Understanding': The Story of Gospel Music in Ghana." *Studies in World Christianity* 12, no. 2 (2006): 142–163.
Austin, Gareth. *Labor, Land, and Capital in Ghana: From Slavery to Free Labor in Asante, 1807–1956*. Rochester, NY: University of Rochester Press, 2005.
Baer, Marc David. "History and Religious Conversion." In *The Oxford Handbook of Religious Conversion*, ed. Lewis R. Rambo and Charles E. Farhadian, 25–47. New York: Oxford University Press, 2014.
Baeta, C. G. *Prophetism in Ghana: A Study of Some "Spiritual" Churches*. London: SCM Press, 1962.
Ballantine, Tony. "Looking Back, Looking Forward: The Historiography of Sikhism." *New Zealand Journal of Asian Studies* 4, no.1 (2002): 5–29.
Balzani, Marzia. "Dreaming, Islam, and the Ahmadiyya Muslims in the UK." *History and Anthropology* 21, no. 3 (2010): 293–305.
———. "A Tale of Two Ahmadiyya Mosques: Religion, Ethnic Politics, and Urban Planning in London." *Laboratorium* 7, no. 3 (2015): 49–71.
Barry, Boubacar. *Senegambia and the Atlantic Slave Trade*. Translated by Ayi Kwei Armah. New York: Cambridge University Press, 1998.
Bartels, F. L. *The Roots of Ghana Methodism*. Cambridge: Cambridge University Press; Accra: Methodist Book Depot, 1965.
Basit, Asif M. "London's First Mosque: A Study in History and Mystery: Part 1." *Review of Religions* 107, no. 6 (2012): 30–46.
———. "London's First Mosque: A Study in History and Mystery: Part 2." *Review of Religions* 107, no. 7 (2012): 44–57.
Bayoumi, Moustafa. "East of the Sun (West of the Moon): Islam, the Ahmadis, and African America." In *Black Routes to Islam*, ed. Manning Marable and Hishaam D. Aidi, 69–78. London: Palgrave Macmillan, 2009.

Beard, Frederica. *Pictures in Religious Education*. New York: George H. Doran, 1920.
Beecham, John. *Ashantee and the Gold Coast, Being a Sketch of the History, Social State and Supersitions of the Inhabitants of those Countries with a Notice of the State and Prospect of Christianity Among Them*. Reprint, London: Dawsons of Pall Mall, 1968.
Bekye, Paul. K. *Dagaaba Christian Communities*. Wa: Wa Catholic Press, 1983.
Birtwhistle, Allen. *Thomas Birch Freeman: West African Pioneer*. London: Cargate Press, 1950.
Blyden, Edward W. *West Africa before Europe, and Other Addresses Delivered in England in 1901 and 1903*. London: C. M. Phillips, 1905.
Boahen, A. Adu. *Yaa Asantewaa and the Asante-British War of 1900–1*, ed. Emmanuel Akyeampong. Accra: Sub-Saharan Publishers, 2003.
Boateng, Abdullah Nasir. "A Brief History of the Establishment of the Ahmadiyya in Ghana." In *Khilifat Centenary Jubilee Souvenir*, 144–147. Accra: Ahmadiyya Muslim Mission, 2008.
Bonsu, Sakeeka K., and Abdul Noor Wahab. "In Search of the True Islam: The Story of Nana Sadick." In *Khilifat Centenary Jubilee Souvenir*, 158–163. Accra: Ahmadiyya Muslim Mission, 2008.
Brackenbury, Henry. *The Ashantee War: A Narrative Prepared from the Official Documents*, Vol. 1. London: W. Blackwood and Sons, 1874.
Braimah, B. A. R. "Islamic Education in Ghana." *Ghana Bulletin of Theology* 4, no. 5 (1973): 1–16.
Braimah, J. A., and Jack Goody. *Salaga: The Struggle for Power*. London: Longmans, 1967.
Breckenridge, C. A., S. Pollock, H. K. Bhabha, and D. Chakrabarty, eds. *Cosmopolitanism*. Duke University Press, 2002.
Brenner, Louis. *Controlling Knowledge: Religion, Power, and Schooling in a West African Muslim Society*. Bloomington: Indiana University Press, 2001.
———. "Histories of Religion in Africa." *Journal of Religion in Africa* 30, no. 2 (2000): 143–167.
———. "The Jihad Debate between Sokoto and Borno: An Historical Analysis of Islamic Political Discourse in Nigeria." In *People and Empires in African History: Essays in Memory of Michael Crowder*, ed. J. F. A. Ajayi and J. D. Y. Peel, 21–43. London: Longman, 1992.
Brunner, Daniel L. *Halle Pietists in England: Anthony William Boehm and the Society for Promoting Christian Knowledge*. Gottingen: Vandenhoeck & Ruprecht, 1993.
Burns, Alan. *History of Nigeria*, 7th ed. London: George Allen and Unwin, 1969.
Burton, John. *The Sources of Islamic Law: Islamic Theories of Abrogation*. Edinburgh: Edinburgh University Press, 1990.
Cardinal, A. W. *The Gold Coast, 1931: A Review of Conditions in the Gold Coast in 1931 as Compared to Those of 1921, Based on Figures and Facts Collected*. Accra: Government Printer, 1932.
———. *The Natives of the Northern Territories of the Gold Coast: Their Customs, Religion, and Folklore*. London: George Routledge and Sons, 1920.
Carneiro de Cunha, Marianno. *Da Senzala ao Sobrado: Arquitectura Brasileira na Nigéria e na Republica Popular do Benim*. São Paulo: Nobel Edusp, 1985.
Casely Hayford, J. E. *Gold Coast Native Institutions, with Thoughts upon a Healthy Imperial Policy for the Gold Coast and Ashanti*. London: Sweet and Maxwell, 1903.

Chestnut, R. Andrew. *Competitive Spirits: Latin America's New Religious Economy.* Oxford: Oxford University Press, 2003.
Chesworth, John A. "Fundamentalism and Outreach Strategies in East Africa: Christian Evangelism and Muslim *Da'wa.*" In *Muslim-Christian Encounters in Africa*, ed. Benjamin Soares, 159–186. Leiden: Brill, 2006.
Chidester, David. "Dreaming in the Contact Zone: Zulu Dreams, Visions, and Religion in Nineteenth-Century South Africa." *Journal of the American Academy of Religion* 76, no. 1 (2008): 27–53.
Chouin, Gérard L., and Christopher R. Decorse, "Prelude to the Atlantic Trade: New Perspectives on Southern Ghana's Pre-Atlantic History, 800–1500." *Journal of African History* 51, no. 2 (2012): 123–145.
Christensen, James Boyd. *Double Descent among the Fanti.* New Haven, CT: Human Relations Area File, 1954.
Claridge, W. Walter. *A History of the Gold Coast and Ashanti.* Vol. 2. 1915. Reprint, London: Frank Cass, 1964.
Clarke, Peter B. "Islamic Millenarianism in West Africa: A 'Revolutionary' Ideology?" *Religious Studies* 16, no. 3 (1980): 317–339.
———. *Mahdism in West Africa: The Ijebu Mahdiyya Movement.* London: Luzac Oriental, 1995.
Cohen, David William, Stephan Miescher, and Luise White. "Introduction: Voices, Words, and African History." In *African Words, African Voices*, ed. Luise White, Stephan Miescher, and David William Cohen, 1–27. Bloomington: Indiana University Press, 2001.
Cole, Gibril R. *The Krio of West Africa: Islam, Culture, Creolization and Colonialism in the Nineteenth Century.* Athens: Ohio University Press, 2013.
Comaroff, Jean, and John Comaroff. *Of Revelation and Revolution: Christianity, Colonialism, and Consciousness in South Africa.* Vol. 1. Chicago: University of Chicago Press, 1991.
———. *Of Revelation and Revolution: The Dialectics of Modernity on a South African Frontier.* Vol. 2. Chicago: University of Chicago Press, 1997.
Cooper, Barbara M. *Evangelical Christians in the Muslim Sahel.* Bloomington: Indiana University Press, 2006.
Crowther, Samuel Adjai. *Experiences with Heathens and Mohammedans in West Africa.* London: Society for Promoting Christian Gospel, 1892.
Crowther, Samuel A., and J. C. Taylor, eds. *The Gospel on the Banks of the Niger: Journals and Notices of the Native Missionaries Accompanying the Niger Expedition, 1857–1859.* London: Church Missionary Society, 1859.
Cruickshank, Brodie. *Eighteen Years on the Gold Coast, Including an Account of the Native Tribes, and Their Intercourses with Europeans.* Vol. 2. 2nd ed. New York: Barnes and Noble, 1966.
Daaku, Kwame Y. *Trade and Politics on the Gold Coast, 1600–1720.* London: Oxford University Press, 1970.
Danmole, H. O. "The Crisis of the Lagos Muslim Community, 1915–1947." In *History of the Peoples of Lagos State*, ed. Ade Adefuye, Babatunde Agiri, and Jide Osuntokun, 290–305. Lagos: Lantern Books, 1987.
———. "A Visionary of the Lagos Muslim Community: Mustapha Adamu Animashaun, 1885–1968." *Lagos Historical Review* 5 (2005): 22–48.

Danquah, J. B. *The Akan Concept of God: A Fragment of Gold Coast Ethics and Religion*. London: Lutterworth, 1944.
———. "The Historical Significance of the Bond of 1844." *Transactions of the Historical Society of Ghana* 3, no. 1 (1957): 3–29.
Dard, Abdur Raheem. *The Life of Ahmad, Founder of the Ahmadiyya Movement*. Tilford, UK: Islam International Publications, 2008.
Debrunner, Hans. *A History of Christianity in Ghana*. Accra: Waterville Publishing House, 1967.
Debrunner, Hans, H. H. A. Fisher, and Humphrey J. Fisher. "Early Fante Islam." *Ghana Bulletin of Theology* 1, no. 7 (1959): 23–35.
———. "Early Fante Islam [continued]." *Ghana Bulletin of Theology* 1, no. 8 (1960): 13–29.
Der, Benedict. "Church-State Relations in Northern Ghana, 1906–1940." *Transactions of the Historical Society of Ghana* 15 (1974): 41–61.
Dickson, K. A. "The 'Methodist Society': A Sect." *Ghana Bulletin of Theology* 2, no. 6 (1964): 1–7.
Dickson, Kwamina B. "Evolution of Seaports in Ghana: 1800–1928." *Annals of the Association of American Geographers* 55, no. 1 (1965): 98–111.
———. *A Historical Geography of Ghana*. Cambridge: Cambridge University Press, 1969.
Dolphyne, Florence. "Akan Language Patterns and Development." *Tarikh* 7, no. 2 (1982): 35–45.
Dougah, J. C. *Wa and Its People*. Legon: Institute of African Studies, University of Ghana, 1966.
Duffield, Ian. "Dusé Mohamed Ali, Afro-Asian Solidarity and Pan-Africanism in Early Twentieth Century London." In *Essays on the History of Blacks in Britain*, ed. J. S. Gundara and Ian Duffield, 124–149. Aldershot, UK: Avebury, 1992.
Dumett, Raymond. "African Merchants of the Gold Coast, 1800–1905: Dynamics of Indigenous Entrepreneurship." *Comparative Studies in Society and History* 25, no. 4 (1983): 261–264.
Effah, Yusuf K. "History of Ahmadiyya Movement in Ghana." *Review of Religions* 84, no. 10 (1989): 28–38.
Ephirim-Donkor, Anthony. *African Spirituality: On Becoming Ancestors*. Trenton, NJ: Africa World Press, 1997.
Elbourne, Elizabeth. "Word Made Flesh: Christianity, Modernity, and Cultural Colonialism in the Work of Jean and John Comaroff." *American Historical Review* 108, no. 2 (2003): 435–459.
Ellis, Alfred Burdon. *Land of the Fetish*. London: Chapman & Hall, 1883.
———. *West African Sketches*. London: Samuel Tinsley and Co., 1881.
Essien, Kwame. "*A abertura da casa Brasil*: A History of the *Tabom* People, Part 1." In *Back to Africa I: Afro-Returnees and Their Communities*, ed. Kwesi Prah, 179–186. Cape Town: Center for Advanced Studies of African Society, 2009.
Euba, Titilóla. "Muhammad Shitta Bey and the Lagos Muslim Community, 1850–1895, Part 1." *Nigerian Journal of Islam* 2, no. 1 (1971–1972): 21–30.
———. "Muhammad Shitta Bey and the Lagos Muslim Community, 1850–1895, Part 2." *Nigerian Journal of Islam* 2, no. 2 (1971–1972): 7–18.
Fafunwa, Aliu Babs. *Jama-at-ul Islamiyya of Nigeria at 60*. Lagos: n.p., 1984.
Falola, Toyin, and Kevin D. Roberts, eds. *The Atlantic World, 1450–2000*. Bloomington: Indiana University Press, 2008.

Fashinro, H. A. B. *Ahmadiyya as I See It*. Lagos: Irede Printers, 1995.
Feld, Steven. *Jazz Cosmopolitanism in Accra: Five Musical Years in Ghana*. Durham, NC: Duke University Press, 2012.
Findlay, G. G., and W. W. Holdworth. *The History of the Wesleyan Methodist Missionary Society*. Vol. 4. London: Epworth Press, 1921.
Finke, Roger, and Laurence R. Iannaccome. "Supply-Side Explanations for Religious Change." *Annals of the American Academy of Political and Social Science*, no. 527 (1993): 27–39.
First Report of the Anomaboe Temperance Society Total Abstainers. Birmingham, UK: Hudson and Son, 1864.
Fisher, Humphrey J. "The Ahmadiyya Movement in Nigeria." In *African Affairs*, ed. Kenneth Kirkwood, 60–88. Carbondale: Southern Illinois University Press, 1961.
———. *Ahmadiyyah: A Study in Contemporary Islam on the West African Coast*. London: Oxford University Press, 1963.
———. "Conversion Reconsidered: Some Historical Aspects of Religious Conversion in Black Africa." *Africa* 43, no. 1 (1973): 27–40.
———. "Dreams and Conversion in Black Africa." In *Conversion to Islam*, ed. Nehemia Levtzion, 217–235. New York: Holmes and Meier, 1979.
———. "Early Muslim-Western Education in West Africa." *Muslim World* 51, no. 4 (1961): 288–298.
———. "The Juggernaut's Apologia: Conversion to Islam in Black Africa." *Africa* 55, no. 2 (1985): 153–173.
———. "Planting Ahmadiyya in Ghana." *West Africa*, 30 January 1960, 121.
Freeman, Thomas Birch. *Journal of Various Visits to the Kingdoms of Ashanti, Aku, Dahomi, in Western Africa*. 2nd ed. London: J. Mason, 1844.
Friedmann, Yohanan. *Prophesy Continuous: Aspects of Ahmadi Religious Thought and Its Medieval Background*. Berkeley: University of California Press, 1989.
Furnish, Timothy. *Holiest Wars: Islamic Mahdis, Their Jihads, and Osama bin Laden*. Westport, CT: Praeger Publishers, 2005.
Fynn, John K. *Asante and Its Neighbors*. Evanston, IL: Northwestern University Press, 1971.
———. *Oral Traditions of Fante States*. 7 vols. Legon: Institute of African Studies, University of Ghana, 1974–1976.
Gbadamosi, T. G. O. *The Growth of Islam among the Yoruba, 1841–1908*. London: Longman, 1978.
Geaves, Ron. *Islam in Victorian Britain: The Life and Times of Abdullah Quilliam*. London: Kube Publishing, 2010.
George, Abosede A. *Making Modern Girls: A History of Girlhood, Labor, and Social Development in Colonial Lagos*. Athens: Ohio University Press, 2014.
Germain, Eric. "The First Muslim Missions on a European Scale: Ahmadi-Lahore Networks in the Inter-War Period." In *Islam in Interwar Europe*, ed. Natalie Clayer et al., 89–128. New York: Columbia University Press, 2008.
Gilbert, Michelle. "Names, Cloth and Identity: A Case from West Africa." In *Media and Identity in Africa*, ed. Kimani Njogu and John Middleton, 226–244. Bloomington: Indiana University Press, 2009.
Gillespie, W. H. *The Gold Coast Police*. Accra: Government Printer, 1955.
Gilmartin, David. *Empire and Islam: Punjab and the Making of Pakistan*. Oxford: Oxford University Press, 1989.

Gilmartin, David, and Bruce B. Lawrence, eds. *Beyond Turk and Hindu: Rethinking Religious Identities in Islamicate South Asia*. Gainesville: University Press of Florida, 2000.
Gilroy, Paul. *The Black Atlantic: Modernity and Double Consciousness*. Cambridge, MA: Harvard University Press, 1993.
Glover, Elizabeth R. S. "Early Days in Nigeria, I: The Niger Expedition of Half-a-Century Ago." *West Africa*, 12 May 1917, 256.
———. "Early Days in Nigeria, II: When Lagos was a Slave Market." *West Africa*, 19 May 1917, 266.
———. "Early Days in Nigeria, III: First Governor of Lagos." *West Africa*, 26 May 1917, 292.
———. "Early Days in Nigeria, IV: Opening Up the Road into the Interior." *West Africa*, 2 June 1917, 308.
———. "An Imperial Pioneer, V: A Campaign against the Ashantis." *West Africa*, 9 June 1917, 324.
———. "An Imperial Pioneer, VI: Close of the Ashanti Campaign and a Touching Farewell." *West Africa*, 16 June 1917, 339.
———. "An Imperial Pioneer, VII: A Sword of Honour and the Spirit of Africa." *West Africa*, 23 June 1917, 356.
———. *Life of Sir John Hawley Glover, R.N., G.C.M.G*, ed. Richard Temple. London: Smith, Elder & Co., 1897.
Glover, John H. "The Volta Expedition during the Late Ashantee Campaign." *Journal of the Royal United Service Institution* 18 (1875): 317–330.
Gocking, Roger S. *Facing Two Ways: Ghana's Coastal Communities under Colonial Rule*. Lanham, MD: University Press of America, 1999.
Gold Coast. *Census of the Population, 1911*. Accra: Government Printer, n.d.
———. *Census of the Population, 1948*. London: Crown Agents, 1950.
———. *Census Report 1921 for the Gold Coast Colony, Ashanti, and Northern Territories and the Mandated Territory of Togoland*. Accra: Government Printer, 1923.
———. *The Gold Coast Census, 1931, Appendices, Containing Comparative Returns and General Statistics of the 1931 Census*. Accra: Government Printer, 1932.
———. *Report on the Census of the Gold Coast Colony for the Year 1891*. London: Waterlow, 1891.
———. *Report on the Census for the Year 1901*. London: Waterlow, 1902.
Gomez, Michael A. *Black Crescent: The Experience and Legacy of African Muslims in the Americas*. Cambridge: Cambridge University Press, 2005.
———. *Exchanging Our Country Marks: The Transformation of African Identities in the Colonial and Antebellum South*. Chapel Hill: University of North Carolina Press, 1999.
Goody, Jack. *The Ethnography of the Northern Territories of the Gold Coast, West of the White Volta*. London: Colonial Office, 1954.
———. *The Interface between the Written and the Oral*. Cambridge: Cambridge University Press, 1987.
———. *The Logic of Writing and the Organization of Society*. Cambridge: Cambridge University Press, 1986.
———. "Reform, Renewal and Resistance: A Mahdi in Northern Ghana." In *African Perspectives*, ed. Allen Christopher and R. W. Johnson, 143–156. Cambridge: Cambridge University Press, 1970.

Green, Nile. *Bombay Islam: The Religious Economy of the West Indian Ocean, 1840–1915.* Cambridge: Cambridge University Press, 2011.
———. *Islam and the Colonial Army in India: Sepoy Religion in the Service of Empire.* Cambridge: Cambridge University Press, 2009.
Griffith, W. B. *The Far Horizon: Portrait of a Colonial Judge.* London: Stockwell, 1951.
Grischow, Jeff D. *Shaping Tradition: Civil Society, Community and Development in Colonial Northern Ghana, 1899–1957.* Leiden: Brill, 2006.
Gualtieri, Antonio. *Conscience and Coercion: Ahmadi Muslims and Orthodoxy in Pakistan.* Montreal: Guernica Editions, 1989.
Guha, Ranajit. *Dominance without Hegemony: History and Power in Colonial India.* Cambridge, MA: Harvard University Press, 1997.
Gyasi, Ibrahim K. "The Contribution of the Ahmadiyya Muslim Mission to the Development of Education in Ghana." In *Khilifat Centenary Jubilee Souvenir*, 180–181. Accra: Ahmadiyya Muslim Mission, 2008.
Hagan, George P. "An Analytical Study of Fanti Kinship." *Research Review* 5 (1968): 50–90.
Hanretta, Sean. *Islam and Social Change in French West Africa: History of an Emancipatory Community.* New York: Cambridge University Press, 2009.
Hanson, John H. "Ahmadiyya in West Africa." In *Oxford Islamic Studies Online*, ed. John Esposito. New York: Oxford University Press, 2012.
———. "Jihad and the Ahmadiyya Muslim Community: Non-violent Efforts to Promote Islam in the Contemporary World." *Nova Religio* 14, no. 1 (2007): 77–93.
———. "Modernity, Religion, and Development in Ghana: The Example of the Ahmadiyya Muslim Community." *Ghana Studies* 12–13 (2009–2010): 55–75.
Harding, Christopher. *Religious Transformation in South Asia: The Meanings of Conversion in Colonial Punjab.* Oxford: Oxford University Press, 2008.
Hastings, A. C. G., ed. *The Voyage of the Dayspring: Being the Journal of the Late Sir John Hawley Glover, R.N., G.C.M.G., Together with Some Account of the Expedition up the Niger River in 1857.* London: John Lane, 1926.
Hawkins, Sean. *Writing and Colonialism in Northern Ghana: The Encounter between the LoDagaa and "the World on Paper."* Toronto: University of Toronto Press, 2002.
Hempton, David. *Methodism: Empire of the Spirit.* New Haven, CT: Yale University Press, 2005.
Hill, Polly. "The History of the Migration of Ghana Cocoa Farmers." *Transactions of the Historical Society of Ghana* 4, no. 1 (1959): 14–28.
———. *The Migrant Cocoa Farmers of Southern Ghana: A Study in Rural Capitalism.* Cambridge: Cambridge University Press, 1963.
Hiskett, Mervyn. "Commissioner of Police v. Musa Kommenda and Aspects of the Working of the Gold Coast Marriage of Mohammedans Ordinance." *Journal of African Law* 20, no. 2 (1976): 127–146.
———. *The History of Islam in West Africa*, London: Longman, 1984.
———. *The Sword of Truth: The Life and Times of Shehu Usuman dan Fodio.* New ed. Evanston, IL: Northwestern University Press, 1994.
Hodgkin, Thomas. "Mahdism, Messianism, and Marxism in the African Setting." In *Sudan in Africa*, ed. Yusuf Fadl Hassan, 109–127. Khartoum: Khartoum University Press, 1971.

Hole, Charles. *The Early History of the Church Missionary Society for Africa and the East to the End of A.D. 1814*. London: Church Missionary Society, 1896.
Horton, Robin. "African Conversion." *Africa* 41, no. 2 (1971): 85–108.
———. "On the Rationality of Conversion: Part 1." *Africa* 45, no. 3 (1975): 219–235.
———. "On the Rationality of Conversion: Part 2." *Africa* 45, no. 4 (1975): 373–399.
Hugon, Anne. *Un protestantisme africain au XIXe siècle: L'implantation du méthodisme en Gold Coast (Ghana), 1835–1874*. Paris: Karthala, 2007.
Ibrahim, Mohammed bin. "The Contribution of Ahmadiyya to Health Care Delivery in Ghana." In *Khilifat Centenary Jubilee Souvenir*, 183–187. Accra: Ahmadiyya Muslim Mission, 2008.
Iddrisu, Abdulai. "British Colonial Attitudes towards Islamic Education: A Case Study of the Northern Territories of the Gold Coast, 1890–1940." *Journal of the Institute of Education* 4, no. 2 (1998): 60–75.
———. *Contesting Islam in Africa: Homegrown Wahhabism and Muslim Identity in Northern Ghana, 1920–2010*. Durham, NC: Carolina Academic Press, 2013.
Innes, C. L. *A History of Black and Asian Writing in Britain, 1700–2000*. Cambridge: Cambridge University Press, 2002.
Jalloh, Alusine, and David E. Skinner, eds. *Islam and Trade in Sierra Leone*. Trenton, NJ: Africa World Press, 1997.
Jegede, Ahmad Olayiwola. "History of the Ahmadiyyat in Nigeria." *Review of Religions* 88, no. 1 (1989): 19–26.
Johnson, Marion. "Pilgrim's Progress: Part 1." *Bulletin of the Ghana Geographical Association* 9, no. 2 (1964): 4–27.
———. "Pilgrim's Progress: Part 2." *Bulletin of the Ghana Geographical Association* 10, no. 1 (1965): 13–40.
Jones, Kenneth W. *Arya Dharma: Hindu Consciousness in Nineteenth-Century Punjab*. Berkeley: University of California Press, 1976.
Jonker, Gerdien. "A Laboratory of Modernity: The Ahmadiyya Mission in Inter-War Europe." *Journal of Muslims in Europe* 3 (2014): 1–25.
Kane, Ousmane. *Muslim Modernity in Postcolonial Nigeria: A Study of the Society for Removal of Innovation and Reinstatement of Tradition*. Leiden: Brill, 2003.
Kay, G. B. *The Political Economy of the Colonialism in Ghana*. Cambridge: Cambridge University Press, 1972.
Kea, Ray A. *A Cultural and Social History of Ghana From the Seventeenth to the Nineteenth Century: The Gold Coast in the Age of the Trans-Atlantic Slave Trade*. Lewiston, NY: Edwin Mellen Press, 2012.
———. "Modernity and Identity: William de Graft and John Halm and the Social Imaginary in Nineteenth Century Fanteland (the Gold Coast)." In *Mondes Akan/Akan Worlds*, ed. Pierluigi Valsecchi and Fabio Viti, 215–240. Paris: L'Harmattan, 1999.
———. "A Note on Muslim Visitors at Christiansborg (Gold Coast) in the Early Nineteenth Century." *Bulletin d'Information, Fontes Historiae Africanae*, 9–10 (1985–86): 77–79.
———. *Settlements, Trade and Polities in the Seventeenth-Century Gold Coast*. Baltimore: Johns Hopkins University Press, 1982.
Keay, John. *India: A History*. Rev. and expanded ed. New York: Grove Press, 2010.
Keelson, Haneef. *Early History of Ahmadiyyat in Ghana*. Accra: Ahmadiyya Muslim Mission, 2003.

Kemp, Dennis. *Nine Years on the Gold Coast*. London: Macmillan, 1898.
Khan, Adil Hussain. *From Sufism to Ahmadiyya: A Muslim Minority Movement in South Asia*. Bloomington: Indiana University Press, 2015.
Killingray, David. "Bald Biographies of the Barely Reclaimable: Native Officers of the Gold Coast Constabulary, 1874–1907." *Bulletin, Ghana Studies* 3 (1985): 9–16.
———. "Guarding the Extending Frontier: Policing the Gold Coast, 1865–1913." In *Policing the Empire: Government, Authority, and Control, 1830–1940*, ed. D. M. Anderson and David Killingray, 106–125. Manchester: Manchester University Press, 1991.
———. "Imagined Martial Communities: Recruiting for the Military and Police in Colonial Ghana, 1860–1960." In *Ethnicity in Ghana: The Limits of Invention*, ed. Carola Lentz and Paul Nugent, 119–136. London: Palgrave Macmillan, 2000.
———. "Repercussions of World War I in the Gold Coast." *Journal of African History* 19, no. 1 (1978): 39–59.
Kiong, Tong Chee. *Rationalizing Religion: Religious Conversion, Revivalism, and Competition in Singapore*. Leiden: Brill, 2007.
Kobo, Ousman Murzik. *Unveiling Modernity in Twentieth Century West African Reforms*. Leiden: Brill, 2012.
Kolapo, F. J. "'Making Favorable Impressions': Bishop Crowther's Niger Mission in Jihadist Nupe Emirate, 1859–1879." In *Religion, History, and Politics in Nigeria: Essays in Honor of Ogbu U. Kalu*, ed. Chima J. Koriah and G. Ugo Nwokeji, 29–51. Lanham, MD: University Press of America, 2005.
Kopytoff, Jean Herskovits. *A Preface to Modern Nigeria: The "Sierra Leoneans" in Yoruba, 1830–1890*. Madison: University of Wisconsin Press, 1965.
Landau, Paul. *The Realm of the Word: Language, Gender, and Christianity in Southern African Kingdom*. Portsmouth, NH: Heinemann, 1995.
Laotan, A. B. *The Torch Bearers, or Old Brazilian Colony in Lagos*. Lagos: Ile-Olu Printing Works, 1943.
Last, Murray. *The Sokoto Caliphate*. London: Longman, 1967.
Latham, Andrea. "The Relativity of Categorizing in the Context of the Ahmadiyya." *Die Welt des Islams* 48 (2008): 372–393.
Launay, Robert, and Benjamin Soares. "The Formation of an 'Islamic Sphere' in French Colonial West Africa." *Economy and Society* 28, no. 4 (1999): 497–519.
Lavan, Spencer. *The Ahmadiyyah Movement: A History and Perspective*. New Delhi: Manohar, 1974.
Law, Robin, ed. *From Slave Trade to "Legitimate" Commerce: The Commercial Transition in Nineteenth-Century West Africa*. Cambridge: Cambridge University Press, 1995.
Law, Robin, and Kristin Mann. "West Africa in the Atlantic Community: The Case of the Slave Coast." *William and Mary Quarterly*, 3rd ser., 56, no. 2 (1999): 307–334.
Lawal, Olakunde A. "Islam and Colonial Rule in Lagos." *American Journal of Islamic Social Sciences* 12, no. 1 (1995): 66–80.
Lawler, Nancy. *Soldiers, Airmen, Spies, and Whisperers: The Gold Coast in World War II*. Athens: Ohio University Press, 2002.
Lelyveld, David. *Aligarh's First Generation: Muslim Solidarity in British India*. Princeton, NJ: Princeton University Press, 1978.
Lentz, Carola. *Ethnicity and the Making of History in Northern Ghana*. Edinburgh: Edinburgh University Press, 2006.

Lentz, Carola, and Paul Nugent, eds. *Ethnicity in Ghana: The Limits of Invention*. London: Palgrave Macmillan, 2000.
Levztion, Nehemia. "Islam in the *bilad al-sudan* to 1800." In *History of Islam in Africa*, ed. Nehemia Levztion and Randall Pouwels, 63–92. Athens: Ohio University Press, 2000.
———. *Muslims and Chiefs in West Africa: A Study of Islam in the Middle Volta Basis in the Pre-colonial Period*. London: Oxford University Press, 1968.
Levztion, Nehemia, and Randall Pouwels, eds. *History of Islam in Africa*. Athens: Ohio University Press, 2000.
Lewin, Thomas. *Asante Before the British: The Prempean Years, 1875–1900*. Lawrence: Regents Press of Kansas, 1978.
Lindsay, Lisa. "'To Return to the Bosom of their Fatherland': Brazilian Immigrants to Lagos." *Slavery and Abolition* 15, no. 1 (1994): 22–50.
Lloyd, Allen. *The Drums of Kumasi: The Story of the Ashanti Wars*. London: Longman, 1964.
Loimeier, Roman. *Muslim Societies in Africa: A Historical Anthropology*. Bloomington: Indiana University Press, 2013.
———. "Patterns and Peculiarities of Islamic Reform in Africa." *Journal of Religion in Africa* 33, no. 3 (2003): 237–262.
Lovejoy, Paul. *Caravans of Kola: The Hausa Kola Trade, 1700–1900*. Zaria, Nigeria: Ahmadu Bello University Press, 1980.
Lynn, Martin. "Technology, Trade, and 'A Race of Native Capitalists': The Krio Diaspora of West Africa and the Steamships, 1852–95." *Journal of African History* 33, no. 3 (1992): 421–440.
Maier, Donna. "Nineteenth Century Asante Medical Practices." *Comparative Studies in Society and History* 21, no. 1 (1979): 63–81.
Mann, Kristin. *Slavery and the Birth of an African City: Lagos, 1760–1900*. Bloomington: Indiana University Press, 2007.
McCarthy, Mary. *Social Change and the Growth of British Power in the Gold Coast: The Fante States, 1807–1874*. New York: University Press of America, 1983.
McCaskie, T. C. "Accumulation, Wealth, and Belief in Asante, I: To the Close of the Nineteenth Century." *Africa* 53, no. 1 (1983): 23–43.
———. "Nananom Mpow of Mankessim: An Essay in Fante History." In *West African Economic and Social History: Studies in Memory of Marion Johnson*, ed. David Henige and T. C. McCaskie, 139–143. Madison, WI: African Studies Program, 1990.
———. *State and Society in Pre-Colonial Asante*. Cambridge: Cambridge University Press, 1995.
McIntyre, W. D. "British Policy in West Africa: The Ashanti Expedition of 1873–4." *Historical Journal* 5, no. 1 (1962): 19–46.
———. "Commander Glover and the Colony of Lagos, 1861–1873." *Journal of African History* 4, no. 1 (1963): 57–79.
McKenzie, P. R. *Inter-Religious Encounter in Nigeria: S. A. Crowther's Attitudes to African Traditional Religion and Islam*. Leicester, UK: Leicester University Press, 1976.
McKitterick, Meredith. *To Dwell Secure: Generation, Christianity, Colonialism in Ovamboland*. Portsmouth, NH: Heinemann, 2002.
Metcalf, Barbara Daly. *Islamic Revival in British India: Deoband, 1860–1900*. Princeton, NJ: Princeton University Press, 1982.

Meyer, Birgit. "Powerful Pictures: Popular Christian Aesthetics in Southern Ghana." *Journal of the American Academy of Religion* 76, no. 1 (2008): 82–110.

———. *Translating the Devil: Religion and Modernity Among the Ewe in Ghana*. Edinburgh: Edinburgh University Press, 1999.

Miescher, Stephen F. *Making Men in Ghana*. Bloomington: Indiana University Press, 2005.

Miller, Jon. *Missionary Zeal and Institutional Control: Organizational Contradictions in the Basel Mission on the Gold Coast, 1828–1917*. Grand Rapids, MI: William B. Eerdmans, 2003.

Mir, Farina. *The Social Space of Language: Vernacular Culture in British Colonial Punjab*. Berkeley: University of California Press, 2010.

Mohr, Adam. "Capitalism, Chaos, and Christian Healing: Faith Tabernacle Congregation in Southern Colonial Ghana, 1918–26." *Journal of African History* 51, no. 1 (2011): 63–83.

———. *Enchanted Calvinism: Labor Migration, Afflicted Spirits, and Christian Therapy in a Presbyterian Church*. Rochester, NY: University of Rochester Press, 2013.

Morgan, David. *Visual Piety: A History and Theory of Popular Religious Images*. Berkeley: University of California Press, 1998.

Motadel, David. "Introduction." In *Islam and the European Empires*, ed. David Motadel, 1–34. New York: Oxford University Press, 2014.

Mubashir, N. A. "The Debate: Which Is the Universal Religion, Islam or Christianity." *Review of Religion* 42, no. 11 (1943): 285–299.

———. "Did Jesus Die on the Cross to Bear the Sins of Mankind?" *Review of Religion* 44, no. 6 (1945): 96–101.

Naylor, Simon, and James Ryan. "The Mosque in the Suburbs: Negotiating Religion and Ethnicity in South London." *Social and Cultural Geography* 3, no. 1 (2002): 39–59.

Ntewusu, Samuel Aniegye. *Settling in and Holding On: A Socio-Economic History of Northern Traders and Transporters in Accra's Tudu, 1908–2008*. Leiden: African Studies Centre, 2012.

Obeng, Pashington. *Asante Catholicism*. Leiden: Brill 1996.

Oberoi, Harjot. *The Construction of Religious Boundaries: Culture, Identity, and Diversity in the Sikh Tradition*. Chicago: University of Chicago Press, 1994.

Oddie, Geoffrey A. *Imagined Hinduism: British Protestant Missionary Constructions of Hinduism*. New Delhi: Sage, 2006.

Odoom, K. O. "A Document on Pioneers in the Muslim Community of Accra." *Institute of African Studies Research Review* 7, no. 3 (1971): 1–31.

Olatunji, Ojo. "Afro-Brazilians in Lagos: Atlantic Commerce, Kinship and Trans-Nationalism." In *Back to Africa I: Afro-Returnees and Their Communities*, ed. Kwesi Prah, 232–260. Cape Town: Center for Advanced Studies of African Society, 2009.

———. "Islam, Ethnicity and Slave Resistance: Hausa 'Mamluks' in Nineteenth Century Yorubaland." In *Islam, Slavery and Diaspora*, ed. Behnaz A. Mirzai, Ismael Musah Montana and Paul E. Lovejoy, 103–124. Trenton, NJ: Africa World Press, 2009.

Oroge, E. Adeniyi. "The Fugitive Slave Question in Anglo-Egba Relations, 1861–1886." *Journal of the Historical Society of Nigeria* 8 (1975): 61–80.

O'Shaughnessy, Thomas. *Eschatological Themes in the Quran*. Manila: Ateneo de Manila University, 1986.

Oshineye, Brigitte Kowalski. "Migrations, Identities, and Transculturation in the Coastal Cities of Yorubaland in the Second Half of the Second Millennium: An Approach to African History through Architecture." In *Movements, Borders, and Identities in Africa*, ed. Toyin Falola and Aribidesi Usman, 126–149. Rochester: University of Rochester Press, 2009.

Owusu-Ansah, David. *Islamic Talismanic Tradition in Nineteenth-Century Asante*. Lewiston, NY: Edwin Mellen Press, 1991.

Owusu-Ansah, David, Mark Sey, and Abdulai Iddrisu. *Islamic Learning, the State and the Challenges of Education in Ghana*. Trenton, NJ: Africa World Press, 2012.

Page, Jesse. *Samuel Crowther: The Slave Boy Who Became Bishop of the Niger*. London: S. W. Partridge and Co., 1892.

Parker, John. *Making the Town: Ga State and Society in Early Colonial Accra*. Portsmouth, NH: Heinemann, 2000.

Patterson, K. David. "The Influenza Epidemic of 1918–19 in the Gold Coast." *Journal of African History* 24, no. 4 (1983): 485–502.

Peel, J. D. Y. *Aladura: A Religious Movement among the Yoruba*. London: Oxford University Press, 1968.

———. "For Who Hath Despised the Day of Small Things? Missionary Narratives and Historical Anthropology." *Comparative Studies in Society and History* 37, no. 4 (1995): 581–607.

———. *Religious Encounter and the Making of the Yoruba*. Bloomington: Indiana University Press, 2003.

Pellow, Deborah. *Landlords and Lodgers: Socio-Spatial Organization in an Accra Community*. Chicago: University of Chicago Press, 2008.

———. "The Power of Space in the Evolution of an Accra *Zongo*." *Ethnohistory* 38, no. 4 (1991): 414–450.

Pennington, Brian. *Was Hinduism Invented? Britons, Indians, and the Colonial Construction of Religion*. Oxford: Oxford University Press, 2005.

Perbi, Akosua A. *A History of Indigenous Slavery in Ghana: From the 15th to the 19th Centuries*. Accra: Sub-Saharan Publishers, 2004.

Person, Yves. "Guinea-Samori." In *West African Resistance: The Military Response to Colonial Rule*, ed., Michael Crowther, 111–143. New York: Africana Publishing, 1970.

Petersen, John. *Province of Freedom: A History of Sierra Leone, 1787–1870*. Evanston, IL: Northwestern University Press, 1969.

Peterson, Derek R., ed. *Abolitionism and Imperialism in Britain, Africa, and the Atlantic*. Athens: Ohio University Press, 2010.

Pietz, William. "The Problem of the Fetish, I." *Res*, no. 9 (1985): 5–17.

———. "The Problem of the Fetish, II: The Origin of the Fetish." *Res*, no. 13 (1987): 23–45.

———. "The Problem of the Fetish, III: Bosman's Guinea and the Enlightenment Theory of Fetishism." *Res*, no. 16 (1988): 105–123.

Pilaszewicz, Stanislaw. *Hausa Prose Writings in Ajami by Alhaj Umaru from A. Mischlich/H. Sölken's Collection*. Berlin: Dietrich Reimer, 2000.

Piot, Charles. "Atlantic Aporias: Africa and Gilroy's Black Atlantic." *South Atlantic Quarterly* 100, no. 1 (2001): 155–170.

Porter, Andrew. *Religion versus Empire? British Protestant Missionaries and Overseas Expansion, 1700–1914*. Manchester: Manchester University Press, 2004.

Powell, Avril Ann. "Duties of Ahmadi Women: Educative Process in the Early Stages of the Ahmadiyya Movement." In *Gurus and Their Followers: New Religious Reform Movements in Colonial India*, ed. Antony Copley, 128–156. New Delhi: Oxford University Press, 2000.
———. *Muslims and Missionaries in Pre-Mutiny India*. Surrey, UK: Curzon, 1993.
———. "Processes of Conversion to Christianity in 19th Century North Western India." In *Religious Conversion Movements in South Asia: Continuities and Change 1800–1900*, ed. Geoffrey A. Oddie, 15–55. London: Curzon Press, 1997.
Reade, William Winwood. "Extracts of Letters from W. Winwood Reade, Esq. to Andrew Swanzy, Esq., F. R. G. S., Relating to His Journeys in Western Africa." *Proceedings of the Royal Geographical Society of London* 13, no. 5 (1868–1869): 353–359.
———. *The Story of the Ashantee Campaign*. London: Smith, Elder & Co., 1874.
Reichmuth, Stefan. "Education and the Growth of Religious Associations Among Yoruba Muslims: The Ansar-Ud-Deen Society of Nigeria." *Journal of Religion in Africa* 26, no. 4 (1996): 365–405.
———. *Islamische bildung Und soziale Integration in Ilorin*. Münster: Lit Verlag, 1998.
Reynolds, Edward. *Trade and Economic Change on the Gold Coast, 1807–1874*. London: Longman, 1974.
Robert, Dana L., ed. *Converting Colonialism: Visions and Realities in Mission History, 1706–1914*. Grand Rapids, MI: William B. Eerdmans, 2008.
Robinson, David. *The Holy War of Umar Tal: The Western Sudan in the Mid-Nineteenth Century*. Oxford: Clarendon Press, 1985.
———. *Muslim Societies in African History*. Cambridge: Cambridge University Press, 2004.
———. *Paths of Accommodation: Muslim Societies and French Colonial Officials in Senegal and Mauritania, 1880–1920*. Athens: Ohio University Press, 2000.
Robinson, Francis. "Ahmad and the Ahmadiyya." *History Today* 40, no. 6 (1990): 42–47.
Rodney, Walter. "Gold and Slaves on the Gold Coast." *Transactions of the Historical Society of Ghana* 10 (1969): 13–28.
Roper, Geoffrey. "Arabic Printing and Publishing in England before 1820." *Bulletin (British Society for Middle Eastern Studies)* 12, no. 1 (1985): 12–32.
Ryan, Patrick J. *Imale: Yoruba Participation in the Muslim Tradition; A Study of Clerical Piety*. Missoula, MT: Scholars Press, 1978.
Salih, Mohammad bin. *A History of the Wala: The Ahmadiyya Factor*. Accra: Malam Salihsons, 2000.
Salmat, Purwez. *A Miracle at Woking: A History of the Shahjahan Mosque*. London: Phillimore, 2008.
Samwini, Nathan. *The Muslim Resurgence in Ghana Since 1950: Its Effects upon Muslims and Muslim-Christian Relations*. Berlin: Lit Verlag, 2006.
Sanneh, Lamin. "The Christian-Muslim Encounter in Africa." In *African Challenge*, ed. Kenneth Best, 101–110. Nairobi: Transafrica Publishers, 1975.
———. *Translating the Message: The Missionary Impact on Culture*. 2nd ed. Maryknoll, NY: Orbis, 2009.
Sarbah, John Mensah. *Fanti National Constitution: A Short Treatise on the Constitution and Government of the Fanti, Asanti, and Other Akan Tribes of West Africa*. 2nd ed. London: Frank Cass, 1968.

Schaumloeffel, Marco Aurelio. *Tabom: The Afro-Brazilian Community in Ghana*. Bridgetown, Barbados: Custom Books Publishing, 2009.
Schildkroudt, Enid. *People of the Zongo: The Transformation of Ethnic Identities in Ghana*. Cambridge: Cambridge University Press, 1978.
Schimmel, Annemarie. *Islam in the Indian Subcontinent*. Leiden: Brill, 1980.
Searing, James F. "The Time of Conversion: Christians and Muslims among the Sereer-Safèn of Senegal, 1914–1950s." In *Muslim-Christian Encounters in Africa*, ed. Benjamin Soares, 115–141. Leiden: Brill, 2006.
Seesemann, Rüdiger. and Benjamin Soares. "'Being as Good Muslims as Frenchmen': On Islam and Colonial Modernity in West Africa." *Journal of Religion in Africa* 39, no. 1 (2009): 91–120.
Shankar, Shobana. "A Fifty-Year Muslim Conversion to Christianity: Religious Ambiguities and Colonial Boundaries in Northern Nigeria, c. 1906–1963." In *Muslim-Christian Encounters in Africa*, ed. Benjamin Soares, 89–114. Leiden: Brill, 2006.
———. *Who Shall Enter Paradise? Christian Origins in Muslim Northern Nigeria, ca. 1890–1974*. Athens: Ohio University Press, 2014.
Sharkey, Heather J. "Empire and Muslim Conversion: Historical Reflections on Christian Missions in Egypt." *Islam and Christian-Muslim Relations*, 16, no. 1 (2005): 43–63.
———. "Missionary Legacies: Muslim-Christian Encounters in Egypt and Sudan during the Colonial and Post-Colonial Periods." In *Muslim-Christian Encounters in Africa*, ed. Benjamin Soares, 57–88. Leiden: Brill, 2006.
Shumway, Rebecca. *The Fante and the Transatlantic Slave Trade*. Rochester, NY: University of Rochester Press, 2011.
———. "The Fante Shrine of Nananom Mpow and the Atlantic Slave Trade in Southern Ghana." *International Journal of African Historical Studies* 44, no. 1 (2011): 27–44.
Silverman, Raymond, and David Owusu-Ansah. "The Presence of Islam among the Akan: A Bibliographic Essay." *History in Africa* 16 (1989): 325–339.
Simpson, Edward, and Kai Kress. "Cosmopolitanism Contested: Anthropology and History in the Western Indian Ocean." In *Struggling with History: Islam and Cosmopolitanism in the Western Indian Ocean*, ed. Edward Simpson and Kai Kresse, 1–41. London: Hurst, 2007.
Singleton, Brent D. "'That Ye May Know Each Other': Late Victorian Interactions between British and West African Muslims." *Journal of Muslim Minority Affairs* 29, no. 3 (2009): 369–385.
Skinner, David. "Conversion to Islam and the Promotion of 'Modern' Islamic Schools in Ghana." *Journal of Religion in Africa* 43, no. 4 (2013): 426–450.
———. "The Incorporation of Muslim Elites into the Colonial Administrative Systems of Sierra Leone, the Gambia and the Gold Coast." *Journal of Muslim Minority Affairs* 29, no. 1 (2009): 91–108.
Smith, N. *The Presbyterian Church of Ghana: 1835–1960*. Accra: Ghana Universities Press, 1966.
Smith, Robert S. *The Lagos Consulate, 1851–1861*. Berkeley: University of California Press, 1979.
Smith, William Cantwell. "Ahmadiyyah." *Encyclopaedia of Islam*. Second ed. Leiden: Brill, 1960.

Soares, Benjamin. "Muslim-Christian Encounters in Africa." In *Muslim-Christian Encounters in Africa*, ed. Benjamin Soares, 1–16. Leiden: Brill, 2006.
Soumounni, Elisée. "The Afro-Brazilian Communities of Ouidah and Lagos in the Nineteenth Century: A Comparative Analysis." In *Africa and the Americas: Interconnections During the Slave Trade*, ed. José Curto and Renée Soulodre-LaFrance, 231–242. New York: Africa World Press, 2005.
———. "Afro-Brazilian Communities of the Bight of Benin in the Nineteenth Century." In *Trans-Atlantic Dimensions of Ethnicity in the African Diaspora*, ed. Paul E. Lovejoy and David V. Trotman, 181–194. London: Continuum, 2003.
Southon, Arthur E. *Gold Coast Methodism*. London: Cargate Press, 1934.
Streets, Heather. *Martial Races: The Military, Race, and Masculinity in British Imperial Culture, 1857–1914*. Manchester: Manchester University Press, 2004.
Strickrodt, Silke. "The Brazilian Diaspora to West Africa in the Nineteenth Century." In *AfrikaAmerika: Atlantische Konstruktionen*, ed. Ineke Phaf-Reinberger and Tiago de Oliveira Pinto, 36–68. Frankfurt: Vervuert, 2008.
Sunaga, Emiko. "A Study of Urdu Print Culture of South Asia Since the Eighteenth Century." *Kyoto Bulletin of Islamic Area Studies* 6 (2013): 136–144.
Sundkler, Bengt, and Christopher Steed. *A History of the Church in Africa*. Cambridge: Cambridge University Press, 2000.
Tadhkirah: English Rendering of the Divine Revelation, Dreams, and Visions Vouchsafed to Hazrat Mirza Ghulam Ahmad of Qadian, The Promised Messiah and Mahdi, On Whom Be Peace. Translated by Muhammad Zafrullah Khan. Revised ed. Tilford, UK: Islam International Publications, 2009.
Talbot, Ian. *Punjab and the Raj, 1849–1947*. Riverdale, MD: Riverdale Company, 1988.
Tamuno, Tekena N. *The Police in Modern Nigeria, 1861–1965: Origins, Development and Role*. Ibadan: Ibadan University Press, 1970.
Taubenberger, Jeffrey K., and David M. Morens. "1918 Influenza: The Mother of All Pandemics." *Review of Biomedicine* 17, no. 1 (2006): 69–79.
Taves, Ann. *Fits, Trances, and Visions: Experiencing Religion from Wesley to James*. Princeton, NJ: Princeton University Press, 1999.
Tayo, S. P. *Emergence of the Ahmadiyya Movement in West Africa (As a Truth-Seeker Sees It)*. Kumasi: n.p., 1974.
Thapar, Romila. *Early India: From the Origins to AD 1300*. Berkeley: University of California Press, 2002.
Thomas, Lynn M. "Modernity's Failings, Political Claims, and Intermediate Concepts." *American Historical Review* 116, no. 3 (2011): 727–740.
Thomas, Roger G. "Education in Northern Ghana, 1906–40: A Study in Colonial Paradox." *International Journal of African Historical Studies* 7, no. 3 (1974): 427–467.
Tremearne, A. J. N. "Extracts from the Diary of the Late Rev. John Martin, Wesleyan Missionary in West Africa, 1843." *Man* 12 (1912): 138–143.
Trimingham, J. Spencer. *The Christian Church and Islam in West Africa*. London: SCM Press, 1955.
———. *A History of Islam in West Africa*. London: Oxford University Press, 1962.
Tordoff, William. *Asante under the Prempehs, 1888–1935*. London: Oxford University Press, 1965.

Turner, Richard B. "The Ahmadiyya Mission to Blacks in the United States in the 1920s." *Journal of Religious Thought* 44, no. 2 (2001): 50–66.

———. *Islam in the African-American Experience*. Bloomington: Indiana University Press, 1997.

Tuurey, G. *An Introduction to the Mole-Speaking Community*. Wa: Wa Catholic Press, 1982.

Umar, Muhammad Sani. "Muslims' Eschatological Discourses on Colonialism in Northern Nigeria." *Journal of the American Academy of Religion* 67, no. 1 (1999): 59–84.

Valentine, Simon Ross. *Islam and the Ahmadiyya Jama'at: History, Belief, Practice*. New York: Columbia University Press, 2008.

Vandeleur, Seymour. "Nupe and Ilorin." *Geographical Journal* 10, no. 4 (1897): 349–370.

van der Linden, Bob. *Moral Languages from Colonial Punjab*. Delhi: Manohar, 2008.

van der Veer, Peter, ed. *Conversion to Modernities: The Globalization of Christianity*. New York: Routledge, 1996.

———. *Gods on Earth: The Management of a Religious Experience and Identity in a North Indian Pilgrimage Centre*. London: Athlone Press, 1988.

Verger, Pierre. *Flux et reflux de la traite des nègres entre le Golfe de Bénin et Bahia de Todos os Santos: Du XVIIe au XIXe siècle*. Paris: Mouton, 1968.

Vertovec, Stephen, and Robin Cohen, eds. *Conceiving Cosmopolitanism: Theory, Content, and Practice*. Oxford: Oxford University Press, 2002.

Walker, F. Deaville. *Thomas Birch Freeman*. London: SCM Press, 1929.

Walls, Andrew F. "Africa as the Theatre of Christian Engagement with Islam in the Nineteenth Century." *Journal of Religion in Africa* 29, no. 2 (1999): 155–174.

———. "The Legacy of Samuel Ajayi Crowther." *International Bulletin of Missionary Research* 16, no. 1 (1992): 15–21.

Walter, Howard. A. *The Ahmadiya Movement*. London: Oxford University Press, 1918.

Ward, W. E. F. *A History of the Gold Coast*. London: George Allen & Unwin, 1946.

Ware, Rudolph T., III. *The Walking Qur'an: Islamic Education, Embodied Knowledge, and History in West Africa*. Chapel Hill: University of North Carolina Press, 2014.

Webster, John C. B. *The Christian Community and Change in Nineteenth Century North India*. New Delhi: Macmillan Company, 1976.

———. *A History of Dalit Christians in India*. San Francisco: Mellen Research University Press, 1992.

———. *The Nirankari Sikhs*. New Delhi: Macmillan, 1979.

———. *A Social History of Christianity: North-West India since 1800*. Oxford: Oxford University Press, 2007.

Webster, J. B. *The African Churches among the Yoruba*. Oxford: Clarendon Press, 1964.

Weiss, Holger. *Between Accommodation and Revivalism: Muslims, Society and the State in Ghana from the Colonial to the Postcolonial Era*. Helsinki: Finnish Oriental Society, 2008.

Wemah, Karim. "Mr. Ahmad Samba Barwey Wemah, 1894–1950: A Pioneer Ahmadi Muslim in Northern Ghana." In *Khilafat Centenary Jubilee Souvenir*, 152–155. Accra: Ahmadiyya Muslim Mission, 2008.

West, Gerald O. "Mapping African Biblical Interpretation: A Tentative Sketch." In *The Bible in Africa: Transactions, Trajectories, and Trends*, ed. Gerald O. West and Musa W. Dube, 29–53. Leiden: Brill, 2000.

West, Thomas. *The Life and Journals of the Rev. Daniel West, Wesleyan Minister and the Deputation to the Wesleyan Mission Stations on the Gold Coast, Western Africa.* London: Hamilton, Adams and Co., 1857.
Wherry, Elwood M. *Islam and Christianity in India and the Far East.* New York: Fleming H. Revell Co., 1907.
White, Luise, Stephan Miescher, and David William Cohen, eds. *African Words, African Voices.* Bloomington: Indiana University Press, 2001.
Wilks, Ivor. *Asante in the Nineteenth Century.* Cambridge: Cambridge University Press, 1975.
———. *The Northern Factor in Ashanti History.* Legon: Institute of African Studies, University of Ghana, 1961.
———. "The State of the Akan and Akan States." *Cahiers d'études africaines* 22, nos. 3–4 (1982): 231–249.
———. "The Transmission of Islamic Learning in the Western Sudan." In *Literacy in Traditional Societies,* ed. Jack Goody, 162–197. Cambridge: Cambridge University Press, 1968.
———. *Wa and the Wala: Islam and Polity in Northwestern Ghana.* Cambridge: Cambridge University Press, 1989.
Williamson, Thora, and Anthony Kirk-Greene, eds. *Gold Coast Diaries: Chronicles of Political Officers in West Africa, 1900–1919.* London: Radcliffe Press, 2000.
Wolseley, Garnet. *The Story of a Soldier's Life.* Vol. 2. London: Scribner's, 1904.
Wyllie, Robert W. "Pioneers of Ghanaian Pentecostalism: Peter Anim and James McKeown." *Journal of Religion in Africa* 6, no. 2 (1974): 109–122.
Yarak, Larry W. "New Sources for the Study of Akan Slavery and the Slave Trade: Dutch Military Recruitment in the Gold Coast and Asante, 1831–72." In *Source Materials for Studying the Slave Trade and the African Diaspora,* ed. Robin Law, 35–60. Stirling, UK: University of Stirling Press, 1997.
———. "A West African Middle-Ground: Elmina in the Nineteenth Century." In *Globalization and Urbanization,* ed. Toyin Falola and Steven J. Salm, 271–282. Trenton, NJ: Africa World Press, 2004.
Young, L. A., ed. *Rational Choice Theory and Religion: Summary and Assessment.* New York: Routledge, 1997.
Zachernuk, Philip S. *Colonial Subjects: An African Intelligentsia and Atlantic Ideas.* Charlottesville: University Press of Virginia, 2000.

Interviews

The author conducted the following interviews in Ghana:

Adam, Jibreel. Mangoase, 2 June 2005
Adam, Maulvi A. Wahab. Accra, 18 October 1996
———. Accra, 29 May 1997
———. Accra, 24 July 2000
———. Accra, 28 May 2005
Addo, Ismael Kwaku. Asokwa, 26 June 2005

Afful, Ahmad. Ekrawfo, 1 June 2005
———. Breman Askikuma, 6 June 2005
Agyare, Y. K. Kumasi, 13 July 2000
Agyeman, Ibrahim. Mampon, 25 June 2005
Aidoo, Nana Abubakr. Abura, 5 June 2005
Akyeampong, Abdul Malik Adu. Assin Asamankese, 3 June 2005
Ampong, Jibril. Breman Essiam, 2 June 2005
Anderson, Abdullah. Immuna, 2 June 2005
Anderson, Ahmad Saeed. Immuna, 2 June 2005
Anderson, Sarah. Gomoa Potsin, 31 May 2005
Appiah, Haroon. Saltpond, 2 June 2005
Atta, Abdul Hakeem, and Abdullah Apetse. Owuya, 2 June 2005
Atta, Alhassan. Peminase, 23 June 2005
Boateng, Abdullah Nasir. Kumasi, 14 July 2000
———. Kumasi, 22 June 2005
———. Mampon, 25 June 2005
Bobrey, al-haj Mahmud. Mampon, 25 June 2005
Boyela, Issa. Wa, 14 July 1997
Brown, Hadija (née Johnston). Saltpond, 2 June 2005
Dam, Kwesi Brahim, and Thaher Kwabina Andzie. Esebu-Ekrawfo, 4 June 2005
Duah, Nana Muhammad K. Duah. Baworo, 24 June 2005
Guar-Gorman, Rasheed A. K. Accra, 25 September 1996
Gyasi, Ibrahim K. Gyasi. Kumasi, 13 July 2000
———. Kumasi, 22 June 2005
Hassan, Sulieman bin. Mankessim, 2 June 2005
Ibrahim, Dr. Muhammad B. Peminase, 23 June 2005
Inkoom, Nuruddeen. Gomoa Potsin, 31 May 2005
Keelson, Nazir A. Fomena, 25 June 2005
Khalid, Latif. Wa, 30 June 1997
Khalid, Mahmud. Wa, 17 September 1996
———. Wa, 26 June 1997
Kuor, Yusuf Kweku Edu. Abura-Edukrom, 4 June 2005
Mahdi, Nuhu bin. Breman Asikuma, 6 June 2005
Malik, Zakaria. Wa, 25 June 1997
———. Wa, 8 July 1997
———. Wa, 17 August 1997
Mumin, Al-Hajj Alhassan. Wa, 11 September 1996
———. Wa, 26 June 1997
———. Wa, 2 July 1997
Mumin, Seydu. Wa, 30 June 1997
———. Wa, 7 July 1997
Otoo, Usman Kojo, and Kwesi Abdullah Saeed. Ekotsi, 2 June 2005
Quainon, Tahim. Wasabiampa, 6 June 2005
Saeed, Maulvi Ahmad Jibraeel. Mankessim, 5 June 2005
Salifu, Edwin Mumini. Wa, 15 September 1996
———. Wa, 25 June 1997

Salih, Maulvi Mohammed bin. Accra, 25 September 1996
———. Accra, 25 May 1997
———. Accra, 26 July 2000
Seinu, Ahmad. Wa, 12 September 1996
———. Wa, 26 June 1997
Yahaya, Farida, and Ibrahim Yahya. Wa, 30 June 1997
Yamoah, Hakeem Kofi. Ekrawfo, 1 June 2005
Yusif, Fatima. Ebubonko, 5 June 2005

Written Summaries of Memories

The author received the following texts, written summaries of memories, in the course of conducting interviews in the Central Region of Ghana in 2005. The author of the summary is provided when indicated in the text or from oral discussions when receiving the document.

Aidoo, Nana Abubakar. "History of Ahmadiyya in Abura-Edukrom."
Aidoo-Eduam, Abdul Latif, and Nurodeen Etuaful. "The History of Ahmadiyyat in Enyan Onyaadze."
Anderson, Ahmad Saeed. "Ahmadiyyat at Immuna."
Anderson, Ibrahim. "The History of Bronyibima Jamaat."
Anonymous. "Ahmadiyyat at Mando."
———. "Early History of Abura Ahmadiyyat Jamaat."
———. "Establishment of the Ahmadiyya Muslim Mission at Breman Bedum."
———. "History of Ahmadiyya Movement at Breman Essiam."
———. "A History of the Cape Coast Jamaat/Circuit."
———. "How the Ahmadiyyat in Islam Came to Otuam Town."
Appiah, Papa Harun. "Ahmadiyya in Saltpond."
Duah, Nana Muhammad K. "How and When Tikrom-Baworo Jama'at of the Ahmadiyya Muslim Mission Was Established."
Inkoom, N. "History of Islam at Potsin."
Keelson, Nazir A. "Brief History of the Ahmadiyya and the T. I. Ahmadiyya Secondary School in Fomena."
Mahdi, Nuhu Bin. "Advent of Chief Mahdi Appah, also Known as Kwadwo Aduagyir from Ekumfi Attakwaa, and Occupation of Breman Bedum Stool Land."
Ntsiako, Isa Kwesi. "A Short History of Islam Ahmadiyyat in Enyan Denkyira."
Oti, Sadique. "A Brief History of Ahmadiyya Muslim Jama'at in Pramso, Ashanti Region."
Otoo, Usman Koko and Kwesi Abdullah Saeed. "How Islam Ahmadiyyat was Introduced to the Citizens of Ekumfi Ekotsi in the Central Region of Ghana."
Yamoah, Hakeem Kofi. "The Advent of Ahmadiyyat in Ekumfi Ekrawfo."
[Yusif, Fatima.] "History of Ahmadiyya Muslims at Ebubonko, Compiled from Information from Fatima Yusif, Wife of (Late) Op. Yusif Kobina Tawiah."

Index

Page numbers in *italics* indicate maps and figures.

Abaasa, Methodist circuit of, 51
Abakrampa, 71
Abeka, Kwabena (Musa Kula Mulashi) (John Tobia), 60, 79, 87n1
aberewa, 201, 214n10
abirempon, 32
abolitionists, 38, 44; Hausa Force as, 47, 49–50
Abora, 35, 50
abosom, 31, 36–37, 38, 51–52, 53
Abu Bakr, Mallam, 60–61, 65, 68–71, 73, 75, 78, 89n34
Aburi, Nana Kofi, 208
Accra, 39, 42, *142*, *143*
Adam, Maulvi A. (Abdul) Wahab (Ameer), vii, viii, *150*, 207, 215n35, 246
Adam, J. E., 191
Adam, Jibril, 191
Adam, Suleiman Kwame, 207
Adam, U. B., 191
Adanse, 203–204, 206, 207
Addo, Ishmael Kwaku, 199, 207
adehyee, 33, 199, 202–203
Advisory Council (Ahmadiyya), 117
Afful, Ahmad, 66, 83–84
Afiriyie, Nana Salamat Akua, 199, 206, 210
African Times and Orient Review, 5, 123, 126–127, 131; "Colour Distinctions in Christian Churches," 127–128; letter to the editor from Lagos, 131
Afro-Brazilian Muslims, 1, 4, 7, 42, 77, 123, 244; in Lagos, 135–137. *See also* Agusto, M. L. B.; Mahamma; Martin, Jibril; Pedro, Amadu Ramanu
Agona, 78–79, *145*
Agusto, M. L. B. (Muhammad Lawal Basil), 19, 123, 128–129, 131–133, 140n45, 168, 194; and Jama'at-ul Islamiyya, 136, 137
ahadith/hadith, 98, 110–111, 112, 117, 135, 209
ahene, 32, 33, 34, 36. *See also* Ahmadiyya mission (Gold Coast): relations with *ahene*; *asantehene*
Ahl-i-Hadith movement, 107, 111

Ahmad, Bashir ud-Din Mahmud (Khalifatul Masih), 2, 95, 96, 114–116, 119, 240, 245; consolidation under, 116–118; London missionaries and, 125, 129
Ahmad, Ghulam, 2, 4, 14, 77, 95–96, 108–114, 240, 241; death and succession crisis, 95, 96, 115–118; divine revelations, 2, 20n7, 109–110; genesis of Ahmadiyya, 112–114; Lekh Ram and, 105, 108–109; London and, 119, 124; as Mahdi and Messiah, 95, 108–111, 113, 119, 169, 183, 189, 210, 247; as *mirza*, 108, 114; as *mujaddid*, 109–110; non-violence, 110–111; and *Proofs of the Ahmadiyya*, 108–109, 111; public debates, 102, 109, 111
Ahmad, Masroor (Khalifatul Masih), vii, 17, *150*, 247
Ahmad, Mubarak (Secretary, Ahmadiyya Foreign Mission Office), 128
Ahmad, Murtada (Ghulam Ahmad's father), 108
Ahmadiyya: *bayat*, 112–113, 115, 116; distinctiveness, 95–96; genesis, 95, 112–114; Ghulam Ahmad and, 108–112; *ishtihar*, 112, 117; *jalsa salana*, 113; as new sect in British India, 112, 117; nonviolence, adherence to, 111; proselytism, 119, 124; and Quran's reference to Ahmad, 95; schools, 95, 113; social diversity among initial followers, 114, 116; split after 1914 succession, 95, 96, 115–118. *See also* Ahmadiyya Anjuman Isha'at Islam; Ahmadiyya mission (Ghana); Ahmadiyya mission (Gold Coast); Ahmadiyya mission (Lagos); Ahmadiyya mission (London); Ahmadiyya Muslim Community
Ahmadiyya Anjuman Isha'at Islam, 115–116. *See also* Lahori Ahmadiyya movement
Ahmadiyya Foreign Missions Office, 128
Ahmadiyya mission (Ghana), 3; education, 246–247; healthcare, 247; leadership, 207, 215n35, 246
Ahmadiyya mission (Gold Coast): administrative structure, 173–175, 184–185; *bayat*, 172; distinctiveness, 175–176, 185–186, 192–193, 231,

277

Ahmadiyya mission (Gold Coast) (continued) 245; expansion to eastern Asante, 208–209; expansion to Kumasi, 209–213; expansion to southern Asante, 199, 205–208; expansion to Wa, 225–235; initial mission to Northern Territories, 222–223; invitation from Fante Muslims, 1, 17–18, 163–164, 168–171; missionary training and organization, 118, 174, 182, 186; Nayyar's visit, 1, 171–176, 209–210, 216n44; nonviolence, adherence to, 173–174, 229; opposition to, at Kumasi, 200, 209, 210, 211, 212; opposition to, at Wa, 218, 225–229, 230–232, 233–234, 235; Pedro's proselytism, 168–169; proselytism, 1, 183–184, 187–192, 200, 205–209, 210, 222–223, 225, 227, 230–231, 232–233, 240, 244–246; relations with *ahene*, 184, 208, 209, 212; Saltpond headquarters, 182, 194–195; schools, 1–2, 81, *149, 159,* 186–187, 192–195, 212, 217n64, 242. *See also* Ali, Maulvi Nazir Ahmad; Appah, Mahdi Adoagyir; Hakeem, Maulvi Fazlul Rahman; Johnston, Jamal (Steven J.); Keelson, Binyameen Esau; Nayyar, Maulvi Abdul Rahman; Pedro, Amadu Ramanu

Ahmadiyya mission (Lagos): administrative structure, 134–135, initial members, 131–133; opposition to, 135–136; schools, 134–135, splits, 135–137. *See also* Agusto, M. L. B.; Martin, Jibril; Pedro, Amadu Ramanu

Ahmadiyya mission (London), 2, 118, 119, 123, 124–126; influence of Dusé Mohamed Ali on Ahmadi missionaraies, 126–129. *See also* London

Ahmadiyya Movement in Nigeria, 136–137

Ahmadiyya Muslim Community, 2; administrative structure, 117; Anjuman-i-Taraqqi-Islam, 118, 122n89, 128; *bayat,* 117; consolidation under Bashir ud-Din Mahmud Ahmad, 116–118; headquarters, 19, 117, 240; missionaries, numbers abroad, 2–3, 19–20, 213, 241; missionary biographies, 139n31; Sadr Anjuman-i-Ahmadiyya, 116–117, 119. *See also* Ahmadiyya mission (Ghana); Ahmadiyya mission (Gold Coast); Ahmadiyya mission (Lagos); Ahmadiyya mission (London)

Akan state formation, 32

akomfoo/okomfo, 31, 36–38, 41, 52, 65, 74, 201, 203

Akonomnsu (Fante temperance movement), 64

akyeame, 35

Akyem Abuakwa, 42, 165

Alakurani ("Quranic People"), 134–135, 194

Ali, Maulvi Nazir Ahmad, *160,* 181, 182, 187, 188, 194, 208, 222–223, 225, 226

Ali, Muhammad, 114; and the 1914 split, 115–116

Aligargh movement, 106, 107, 131

Amini, Muhammad ("Kofi Maama"), 75

Amritsar, 105, 113; Great Temple at, 106

amulets, 9, 11, 31, 37, 133, 227, 231. *See also* esoteric practices

Anaman, Jacob B., 18, 28n110, 60–61, 64, 87n6, 89n34; Sam's interview with, 68–71

Anglo-Asante peace treaty of 1874, 46

Anglo-Vedic College, 104–105

Animashaun, Adamu, 135–136

Animashaun, Alfa Idris, 135

Anjuman-i-Punjab association, 101

Anjuman-i-Taraqqi-Islam, 118, 122n89

Ankorakwaa, 85

Anomabu (Anomabo, Anomaboe), 33, 60, 62, 70, 88n8, *145, 155*

Anomabu, Methodist circuit of, 50

Anwomaso, *147,* 208, 210

Appah, Mahdi Adoagyir: cocoa farming and, 84, 85, 169–170, 172; contributions to found Ahmadiyya mission and, 170–171, 172–173; conversion to Islam, 68–69, 74–75; death of, 194; grave at Ekrawfo, 17, *150;* Keelson and, 182; memories of, 17, 64–65, 67, 68; Muslim English-language schools and, 80, 81, 82–83; Lochmann's view of, 82–83; Mahdi as Muslim name, 75, 90n57; mosque at Wasabiampa, 84, 156; negotiations with Maulvi Nayyar, 19, 172, 173, 178, 244; reasserting authority over Fante Muslims, 163–164, 169–170, 178, 179n30; Sam, dispute with, 82–83, 84–85

Appiah, Joseph William Egyanka, 166, 168

Appiah, Kwame Anthony, 3, 5–6

Ardron, H. Graham, 226, 228, 229–230

"arena of belief," 35–36

Arose, Imam, 194

Arthur, Al-Hajj Muhammad W. E., 190

Arthur, Al-Hajj Mumtaz B., 190

Arya Samaj, 104–106, 108–109, 113, 118

Asafo (Kumasi neighborhood), 209, 210, 212

Asamang, Salomon, 71

Asante (Ashanti): acceptance of Islam, early colonial era, 202–205; Ahmadiyya arrival in, 205–207, 209–210, Ahmadiyya expansion in, 19, 199–200, 207–209, 210–213; British colonialism, *142,* 200–205; British invasion (1873–1874), 31, 45–46, *144,* 200, 242; cocoa production in, *147,* 200–201, 203–204, 205,

213; Muslim immigration to, after 1874, 201–202; restrictions on Muslims, 11–12, 31, 167; rise of, 11–12, 33, 143. See also *asante nkramo*; *asantehene*
Asante New Town (Kumasi neighborhood), 206, 209, 210
asante nkramo, 11–12, 202, 209–210, 214n12
asantehene, 11, 31, 36, 52, 200. See also Mensa Bonsu; Osei Kwame; Prempe I; Prempe II
Ashanti. See Asante
Asikuma, 84
aspirational Muslims, 4, 13, 118, 168–169, 193–194, 205
asuman, 37, 52, 75, 76
Athim, Abdullah, and debate with Ghulam Ahmad, 102
Atlantic Muslims, 8, 47, 244
Atta, Al-Hajj Joseph Cudjoe Hassan, 212, 233

al-Badr (Ahmadiyya publication), 113, 126
Baikie, W. B., 43
Bain, Bashir ud-Din, 240, 247n1
Bakr, Mallam Abu, 60–61, 65, 68–71, 73, 75, 78, 89n34
"barracks Islam," 8, 24n51, 32, 47, 54n7
Basel Mission, 18, 60, 78, 82, 201, 204; reports of Arabic Bible, 77–78; reports of Muslim visitors, 42, 59n115, 87n2
Bashir, Muhammad (of Bhopal), 111
Batala, 111, *148*
Baworo, *147*, 199, 203, 205, 208–209
bayat, 112–113, 115, 116, 117, 172
bayi (asocial behavior), 166, 178n10, 214n9. See also *aberewa*; *domankama*
Bedum, 80, 81
Beecham, John, 41, 63
Bible, 4, 6, 8, 13, 14, 39, 77, 78, 183. See also Bible, Arabic; Biblicists; Old Testament
Bible, Arabic, 6, 77–78, 91n70
Biblicists, 8, 13, 19, 53, 61, 62–64, 188, 244
"Big Eleven" Muslim scholars, 212–213
Black Atlantic, 4–5, 19. See also Atlantic Muslims
Blyden, Edward W., 81, 91n86, 130
Boateng, Kwame. See Sadiq, Nana
Bomi, Hamidu. See Hamidu Bomi
Borbor Fante, 32–33, 38, 74, 191
Boyle, Frederick, 48
Brahmans, 97–98, 104
Brahmo Samaj, 104
Brazil, 4, 7, 23n41, 130

Breman, 80, 83, *145*, 192
Breman Bedum, 80
Brenner, Louis, 24n56
British East India Company, 97, 100
British Gold Coast Colony. See Gold Coast colony
British India, 19, 99, 240; Hindu reform movements, 96, 97, 104–106, 241; Muslim reform movements, 95, 96, 106–107; Sikh reform movements, 96, 98–99, 104–106, 241. See also Punjab
Brofoyedru, *147*, 207
Burkina Faso, 246
Burns, Alan Cuthbert Maxwell (Governor), 234

"canal colonies," 100
Candler, A. H., 223
Cape Coast, 33, 45, *143*, *145*
Carey, William, 102
Casely Hayford, J. E., 40
cash cropping, 4, 35, 165–166, 201. See also cocoa production; palm oil production
cemetery: Ekrawfo, 17, 61; Qadian, 114, 117
Chishtiyya order, 98
Christianity: Asante and, 201; Gold Coast and, 38–41, 166; Punjab and, 99–100, 102–104; shared heritage with Islam, 6–7, 71–72, 79, 82, 86, 125, 128, 188, 190, 195–196, 242–243. See also marketplace, religious
Church Missionary Society, 6, 102
cocoa production, 84, 85, *147*, 165, 173, 192, 199–200, 200–201, 203–204, 205, 213; Hill on early Fante cocoa farmers, 92n94
Coke, Thomas, 38, 55n37
Comaroff, Jean, 13
Comaroff, John, 13
conversion, 14–15; and adhesion, 27n97; and baptism for Christians, 103; "deathbed conversion," 86; as matter of personal conscience, 99, 103, 176; and *shuddhi*, for Arya Samaj, 105; and "white birds" revelation, 124; and women's narratives, 75–76, 90n61
"conversion narratives," 65–68, 203
cosmopolitan, 3–5, 5–9, 21n17, 78, 82, 188, 189, 243–244. See also Bible; Christianity: shared heritage with Islam; Crowther, Samuel Ajayi; Islam: shared heritage with Christianity; Quran; Sam, Binyameen
cosmopolitanism, 5–6, 21n16; rival forms of, 95–96
Courier Journal (Louisville, Kentucky), 127

"criminal tribes," 118
Crowther, Samuel Ajayi, 6–7, 22n34, 22n35, 23nn36, 23n37, 77, 78, 189, 244
Cruickshank, Brodie, 39–40, 41

Dabiri (Alakurani leader), 134
Dagomba, 11, *143*, 210, 219, 223
Dard, Abdul Rahim, 125–126
Dayananda Anglo-Vedic Trust and Management Society, 104–105
De Graft, William, 39, 56n41, 63
debates, public, 102, 109, 111, 211
Deen, Ahmad, 131
Delhi, 97, 100, *148*
divine revelation, 2, 20n7, 109
Dixon, H. P., 226
doabs, 96, 98, 100
domankama, 201, 214n10
Domeabra, 204–205
Dondoli lineage, 220–221, 222, 224, 228, 235n6
Dowie, John, 109
Dua, Ahmad Kwaku, 208–209
Duah, James Agyeman, 203
Duff, Alexander, 102
Duku, Al-Hajj, 211, 212
Dun, Al-Hajj Muhammad. *See* Muhammad bin Uthman Dun, Al-Hajj
Duncan-Johnstone, A. C., 16, 27n101, 184, 199, 204–205, 208, 210–211, 212, 213, 216n44
Dusé Mohamed Ali, 5, 19, 123–124, 126–129, 131, 137, 139n19, *158*; as pan-Africanist, 126–129
Dwumaah, Mahama Kofi, 204–205, 208
Dzedzedeyiri lineage, 220–221, 223–224, 228, 230, 235n6

Early History of the Ahmadiyyat in Ghana (Haneef Keelson), 66, 67
Ebubonko, 240, 241
Egyaa, 61–62, 70, 88n8, *145*
Eid al-Adha, 48, 82, 83–84
Ekotsi, 76, 81, *146*
Ekrawfo, 50, 60, 74, 78–79, *145*, *146*, *156*, 163; English-language school, 80–82, 187; Nayyar's visit, 171–172
Ekrawfo cemetery, 17, 61
Ekrawfo narrative, 17, 28n107, 66–67, 87n5
Ekrofol, 58n105
Ekumfi, 62, 73–74, *145*, 192
elites: and African chiefs, 10–12; Fante, 33–36, 39, 41; Gold Coast, 164–165; "new elite," 101, 103–105, 113–114, 120n19; Punjab, 96, 98, 101, 103–105, 113–114

Ellis, A. E., 48
Elmina, 42, *142*, *154*
encounters, scholarly approach to Muslim-Christian, 12–13, 26n81
End Times, 3, 19, 103, 110–111, 195, 196, 242; influenza pandemic and, 167–168; Keelson and, 183; post-influenza epidemic, 163
Endow, Ekuwa, 67
English-language schools, 2, 8, 12, 35, 39, 80–83, 177, 186; Ahmadiyya, 1–2, 81, 84, 95, 113, *149*, *159*, 186–187, 192–195, 212, 217n64, 242; Anglo-Vedic College, 104–105; British assistance, 80–82, 134, 186, 245–246; Ekrawfo, 80–82, 187; Fante Muslim, 80–83, 187; Kumasi, 212, 213, 217n64; Lagos, 130–131; Nayyar and, 134–135, 174–175; Northern Territories, 221–222; Punjab, 101; Talim-ul-Islam School, *149*, *159*, 186–187, 193, 245. *See also* schools
Enyamen, 51
Enyan, 176–177, 192
esoteric practices, 9, 10–11, 15, 24n56, 31, 52, 53, 65, 67–68, 69, 70, 76, 80, 85, 98, 99, 116, 120n14, 167, 204, 209, 220, 231, 242, 244; Ahmadiyya preaching against, 2, 170, 175, 177, 192–193, 197n36, 207, 209–210, 218, 224, 227, 225; "barracks Islam" and, 8, 48. *See also* amulets; healing; *mallams*; Sufi expressions
Essikuma, 52
Esuan, Haleesah Esi, 183

Faith Tabernacle Congregation, 167–168
Fakhruddin, Shah, 98
Fante indigenous religious practices, 35–38; and "double rupture," 64; and Fante Muslims, 75, 76
Fante Muslims, 1, 3–4, 138, 163, 242, 244; as cosmopolitans, 8–9, 244; English-language schools, 80–83, 187; expansion, 78–83; formation, 3, 52, 73–78, 241, 244; generational divisions among, 83–86; indigenous religions practices and, 75, 76; Nayyar and, 171–173; social groups, 76, 84; split after acceptance of Ahmadiyya, 176–177. *See also* Appah, Mahdi Adoagyir; Sam, Binyameen
Fante people (*mfantsefoo*), 32; Borbor Fante, 32–33, 38, 74, 191; cocoa production, 84, 85, 92n94, 165, 173, 192; indigenous religious practices, 35–38. *See also* Fante Muslims; Fante states
Fante states, 5, 12, 32–34, *143*; founding and Nananom Mpow, 32–33, 36; Muslim residents in, 41–42; political order, 37–38; postwar religious change, 50–52; social rank, 33–34

See also Wesleyan Methodist mission (Gold Coast)
al-Fazl (Ahmadiyya publication), 117
Ferguson, George Ekem, 221
"fetish," 36, 39, 53n1, 55n23
Fisher, Humphrey J., vii, 75, 179n30, 214n5; Agusto, interview with, 136; on Ahmadiyya at Lagos, 123; on conversion, 14, 27n97; on dreams, 28n108; on Ekrawfo logbook, 81; emphasis on "overseas control and expatriate management," 2–3, 241; on Nayyar, 133; on Nyakro's dream, 164, 169, 178n1; oral interviews, 16, 66, 83, 84, 85, 87n5, 179n26; reliance on Lochmann, 18, 61, 87n6
Fomena, *147*, 203
forts, coastal, 33, 35, 45–46
Foster, G. F., 45, 49
Freeman, H. S., 42
Freeman, Thomas Birch, 38–40, 50–52, 56n57, 73; on Muslims at Gyinankoma, 60, 64–65; on Muslims from Lagos, 56n57, 87n3
Freetown, 4, 6–8, 22n35, 43, 91n70, *143*
Friday Limam, 222. *See also* Said Soribo, Al-Hajj
Friedmann, Yohanan, 115
Fulbe Muslims, 222
funerals, 175, 185–186, 193, 208, 227, 228–229

Garvey, Marcus, 126
Gerard, Ensign, 49
Ghana, xiii, 1, 3, 16, 19–20, 240, 246–247. *See also* Gold Coast colony
Ghartey, R. J., 64
Gilroy, Paul, 4–5
Glover, John H., 18, 42–44, 57n65, 57n69, 68, 70, *152*, 243; British invasion of Asante and, 46, 50; Gold Coast Constabulary and, 46–47
Gold Coast Armed Police Force, 46
Gold Coast colony, xiii, 1, 46, *142*, *147*; administrative structure, 164–165; declaration of, 31, 35, 46; Muslim migration to, 12, 25n71, 25n72, 25n75, 41–42, 69–70, 85–86, 166, 166–167. *See also* Asante: British invasion (1873–1874); Ghana; Northern Territories
Gold Coast Constabulary, 32, 45, 46–47, 48, *153*, 202. *See also* Hausa Force; West African Frontier Force
Gold Coast Guide, 1902, 18, 60–61
Gold Coast Islamic Missionary Society, 213
gold mining, 33
Gomoa, 78–79, *145*, 172, 191
Gonja, 11, *143*
Green, Nile, 15, 24n51, 54n7

Griswold, Hervey D., 112
Guar-Gorman, Rasheed A. K., 6, 16, 71, 81, 92n100, 178n1
Gurdaspur district, 108
gurus, 98
Gyan, Jibraeel, 83
Gyan, Kwesi (James Ainoo), 75
Gyinankoma, 60, 62, 73–74, 88n11, *146*

hadith. *See* ahadith/hadith
hajj, 222, 229, 234
al-Hakam (Ahmadiyya publication), 113
Hakeem, Maulvi Fazlul Rahman, 1, 9, 128, *149*, *158*, *159*, 245; Biblicism, 188; consolidation of Ahmadiyya and, 181–192; expansion to Asante and, 199, 209, 210–211, 216n44; and Lagos, 136–137; and Nana Sadiq, 199, 216n45; proselytism, 181, 187–190; public debate with Al-Hajj Duku, 211, 212; sermons in *Review of Religions*, 188–189; Wa and, 223, 226, 230, 234
hakeemawa, 182, 193
Hamidu (of Obonster), 68, 177
Hamidu Bomi (Wa Na), 230, 233
Hamied, Al-Hajj, 65, 68, 88n27, 89n33, 180n49
Hammond, John Oboboam, 86
Harage, 84
Haroun, Papa, 207
Harris, William Wadé, 166
Hausa Force, 3, 4, 8–9, 42–50, 68–69, 89n40, *152*, 243–244; as abolitionists, 47, 49–50; "barracks Islam," 8, 32, 47; buglers, 44–45, 47, 48; as cosmopolitans, 8, 243–244; daily routine, 47–48; genesis, 43–45; as "Glover's Hausa," 43, 57n61, 57n69; Gold Coast deployment, 45–47; Kanuri Muslims in, 69; Muslim expressions in Gold Coast, 47–50; Muslim identity, 44–45. *See also* Glover, John H.; Hausa Muslims
Hausa Muslims, 11, 78, 86, 167, 186, 191, 193, 202, 219; "headmen" and British colonial rule, 167, 202; "revolutionary era" of immigration to Gold Coast, 166–167. *See also* Hausa Force; zongo
Hayford, Isaac, 62, 63, 88n8
healing: Binyameen Sam and, 65, 67, 72–73; *mallams* as healers, 8, 31, 50, 52, 53, 61, 65, 68, 69–70, 167, 177, 218; new Christian movements and, 163, 166, 167–168; split among Fante Muslims and, 177. *See also* esoteric practices
Hennessy, Pope, 49
Henty, George Alfred, 48, 49
Hindu reform movements, 96, 97, 104–106, 241
Hinduism, 97–98

Horton, Robin, 14
Hugon, Anne, 40–41, 55n39, 56n47, 64
Husain, Muhammad (of Batala), 111
hymns: Methodist, 28n110, 39, 40; Fante Muslim, 76–77, 82

Ibn Arabi, 109
Ihsanullah Malik, Maulvi, 213
Ilorin, 23n37, 130
imperialism, British: Asante and, 200; Christian evangelism and, 13, 15, 35, 99, 166, 241; Gold Coast and, 35; Lagos and, 129–130; Muslims and, 5, 241–242; Punjab and, 97, 100–101; religious change and, 12–13, 35, 241–243. *See also* marketplace, religious
India, 19, 240. *See also* British India; Punjab
indirect rule, 183, 200, 202
infertility, healing for, 66, 67, 75, 80
influenza pandemic, 86, 163, 167–168, 169
inheritance, 32, 175, 193, 201, 205, 206–207
Inkoom, Muhammad Kojo, 191
Ishaq, Mallam, 221, 223–224
Ishaque, M. A., 83, 85, 176, 177, 186, 223, 234
ishtihar, 112, 117
Islam: Asante and, 201–205; British imperialism and, 5, 241–242; Gold Coast and, 41–42; lack of racial and social distinctions in, claims of, 127–128, 183–184; Punjab and, 98, 106–107; shared heritage with Christianity, 6–7, 71–72, 79, 82, 86, 125, 128, 188, 190, 195–196, 242–243; Wa and, 220–221. *See also* marketplace, religious
Islamic Review, 125, 127, 128

Jackson, F. W. K., 223
jalsa salana, 113, 185, 195
Jama'at-ul Islamiyya, 136, 137
"Java Hill" neighborhood, 42
Jesus: Ahmadiyya view of, 188, 189, 210, 211, 227; Ghulam Ahmad's teachings about, 109, 110, 126; Hindu views of, 104; "Tomb of Jesus Christ" at Srinagar, 110, 157
jihad, nonviolent concepts of, 111, 174
"jihad of the sword," 10, 11
Johnston, Jamal (Steven J.), 181, 187, 188, 195, 207, 234
Jones, Kenneth W., 114; definition of "acculturative movements," 99–100
Jones, W. J. A., 229–230

Kadama, 69
Kairanawi, Rahamatullah, 102

Kamal ud-Din, Khwaja, 5, 114, 115–116, 124–125, 127–129, 137, 139n28
Kanuri Muslims, 69
karamoko, 202–205
Karim, Abdul (Hausa Force officer), 43
Kea, Ray, 55n38, 63
Keelson, Binyameen Esau, *158,* 181–183, 184, 194, 244
Keelson, Haneef, 66, 67
Khalid (Salih's cousin), 224, 226, 228, 230, 236n26
khalifatul masih: as divinely inspired, 2, 115, 247; and consolidation of the Ahmadiyya Muslim Community, 116–118; Nur ud-Din as first, 115. *See also* Ahmad, Bashir ud-Din Mahmud; Ahmad, Masroor; Nur ud-Din
khalsa community, 98–99, 105
Khalsa Sikhs, 98–99, 108
Khan, Muhammad Zafarullah, 124
Khan, Sayyid Ahmad, 102
Killingray, David, 32
Kimberly, Lord, 46
Kintu, 64
Kokofu, *147,* 204, 205, 207–208
kola nut trade, 42, 56n58, 168, 179n26
Konkroma, Nana Yaw, 208, 215n37
Koray, Mumin. *See* Mumin Koray
Korsah, Tufuhene, 184
Kroboase, 81, 83
kumasehene, 200, 211
Kumasi (Kumase), 11, 12, 19, 31, 50, *142,* 200–202, 246; Ahmadi schools, 212, 217n64; Hakeem in, 209, 210–211, 212, 216n44; Muslims in during 1930s, 212–213; Nayyar's visit, 209, 215n30, 216n44, 216n45; opposition to Ahmadiyya, 200, 209, 210, 211, 212; rioting in *zongo,* late 1920s, 202
Kwamosa, Nana, 176–177

Lagos, Nigeria, 1, 4, 18, 119, *143,* 194; Abu Bakr and, 78; Alakurani people, 134–135; Elegbata neighborhood, 134–135; founding of Ahmadiyya branch, 131–133; Hausa Force in, 42–44; Muslims in colonial civil service, 190; Muslims in early twentieth century, 129–131; schools, 131–132, 134–135; split in Ahmadiyya community, 135–136
Lahore, 2, 96, 101, 102, 104, 106, 112, 113, 115–116, 125, 137, *148*
Lahori Ahmadiyya movement, 2, 5, 95, 115–116, 125, 137. *See also* Ahmadiyya Anjuman Isha'at Islam

Lala Munshi Ram, 105
languages: Akan, 32, 33; Arabic, 9, 186, 192, 213; Dagara, 219; Fulfulde, 9; Hausa, 9, 11; Mande, 11, 202, 205; Punjabi, 96; Sanskrit, 97; South Asian, 101; Urdu, 113; Walii, 219
Lavan, Spencer, 114, 115, 116
legal system, British, 34, 35
Leitner, William, 125
Lekh Ram, 105, 108–109
Leveson, Major, 43, 44, 57n71
Limamyiri lineage, 219, 220, 224
literary devices, 65, 71
lithographic press, 101, 104, 166
Lochmann, A. J., 18, 28n111, 61, 70, 71, 72, 78–79, 80, 87n5, 87n6, 87n7, 88n11, 92n97, 167; Appah, view of, 82–83
London: Ahmadiyya Muslim Community headquarters, 240; base for Ahmadiyya expansion in 1920s, 2, 126; Muslims in, 124–125. *See also* Ahmadiyya mission (London); Dusé Mohamed Ali; Sadiq, Mufti Muhammad; Sayal, Muhammad Fateh
Ludhiana, 102, *148*

Maclean, George, 63
Mahama, D. A., 222, 223, 236n22
Mahamma (Afro-Brazilian Muslim), 6–7, 77
Mahdi, 110; Ahmadiyya rejection of "warrior Mahdi," 173–174; Appah's Muslim name, 75, 90n57; Ghulam Ahmad's claims to be, 2, 110–111; Mallam Musa and, 222, 236n14; Nana Sadiq's proselytism and, 207; Salih's proselytism and, 227, 228; songs about arrival of, 172; Wala Muslim prophesies, 224
Majid, Abu, 127, 139n19
Malik ibn Uthman, Al-Hajj (Wa Limam), 230, 231, 234
Maliki tradition, 9, 185, 218, 231
mallams, 3–4, 8, 11, *151, 153*; challenges to, 175; Hausa Force and, 32, 48–49; on Hausa Force payroll, 44, 45, 47; as healers, 8, 31, 50, 52, 53, 61, 65, 68, 69–70, 167, 177, 218. *See also* esoteric practices
Mamprusi, 11, *143*, 219
Mande Muslims, 11–12, 202–205, 219
Mando, 51, 71, 75, 91n91, *146*
Mankessim, 32–33, 35, 36, 50–51, *145, 146*
Mann, Kristin, 42–43
Mansah, Rukiyya Akua, 75–76, 89n31
marketplace, religious: as approach, 15–16; in Fante states during the mid-nineteenth century, 35–42; in Gold Coast during the early twentieth century, 166–168; influenza pandemic and, 163, 167–168; in Kumasi during the mid-1930s, 212–213; in Punjab during the mid-nineteenth century, 99–107
"martial races," 8, 24n50, 32, 44
Martin, Jibril, 136–137
Martin, John, 36, 37
matrilineal inheritance, 32, 175, 193, 201, 205, 206–207
McCaskie, Thomas, 36, 41, 54n15, 55n22, 203
McKellar, Dr., 49
Meeting for Promoting Christian Knowledge, 38, 63
Mensa Bonsu (Asantehene), 31, 100
merchants: Muslims from savanna, 25n71, 166–167, 201–202; nineteenth-century Fante, 34, 165; Punjab, 97
Messiah, Ghulam Ahmad as, 95, 108–111, 113, 119, 169, 183, 189, 210, 247
messianic movements, 51, 75
Methodism, 38. *See also* Wesleyan Methodist mission (Gold Coast)
Methodist Book Depot, 82
Methodist Society, 63–64, 78, 88n23, 88n24; and "double rupture," 64
mobahala, 109
modernity, 13; Ahmadiyya as a "modern Muslim movement," 1–2
Mohammed Salihu, 131
Morgan, David, 72
Moses, 60, 109, 227
mosques, 17, 47, 74, 185, 194–195; Accra, 58n87; Ekrawfo, 87n5, *156*, 196, 198n42; Gold Coast Constabulary, 47, *154*; Harage, 84; Kumasi, 213; Lagos, 131; Mampon, 208; Okepopo, 135; Peminase, 208; Shitta Bey, 131; Wa, 220, 231, 233–234, 238n90; Wasabiampa, 80, 84, *156*; Woking, 5, 125, 137
Mubashir, Maulvi Nazir Ahmad, 195, 213, 234, 246
Mughal Empire, 13, 96–97, 98–99, 100
Muhammad (Prophet), 95, 98, 109, 110, 189
Muhammad bin Uthman Dun, Al-Hajj (Wa Limam), 222, 224, 225–226, 228–229, 230, 235, 237n53, 245
Muhammad Saghir (Wa Limam), 234
Mumin Koray (Wa Na), 234
Musa, Mallam (Ekrawfo), 69, 85
Musa, Mallam (middle Volta River region), 222, 236n14

Musama Disco Christo Church, 166
Muslim evangelism, 14, 26n93
Muslim Juvenile Society (Lagos), 132
Muslim Literary Society (Lagos), 132
Muslim migration: to Asante, 201–202; to Gold Coast, 12, 25n71, 25n72, 25n75, 41–42, 69–70, 85–86, 166, 166–167. See also *asante nkramo*; Naino, Mallam; Salaw, Mallam; Tibu, Mallam
Muslim militant movements, 10
Muslim reform movements, 5, 12, 106–107, 131, 136–137, 212–213; Ahmadiyya as, 95
Muslim savanna tradition, 9–11, 18, 24n52, 84–85, 86–87, 175, 196, 213, 218; at Ekrawfo, 164
Muslim social justice, 50
Muslim-Christian relations, approaches to, 12–13, 26n81. See also marketplace, religious
Mwintuona, Salmata, 224, 232

Nabihi lineages, 219, 220, 232, 234
Naino, Mallam, 42, 89n34
nalun, 220
Nanak, Guru, 98
Nananom Mpow, 33, 36, 38, 41, 51
naskh, 111
Native Jurisdiction Ordinance of 1878, 164
Nayyar, Maulvi Abdul Rahim, 1–2, 3, 5, 17, 18, 85, 125, 126, 244; as "Ahmadi Muslim Missioner, West Africa," 171; assertion of common bonds between Africans and Asians, 128, 139n24; Gold Coast visits, 163, 168, 169, 171–176, 178; Kumasi visit, 209, 215n30, 216n44, 216n45; in Lagos, 19, 133–137; preaching style, 133–134, 135; surveillance of, in the Gold Coast, 171, 172
"new elite," 101, 103–105, 113–114, 120n19
Nigeria, 4, 5, 10, 194. See also Lagos, Nigeria
nkramo, 53n1. See also *asante nkramo*
nnonkofoo, 34, 41–42, 49, 220
Northern Territories (Gold Coast), 1, 5, 12, 142, 165, 186, 194, 221; initial Ahmadiyya proselytism in, 222–225. See also Tamale; Wa
Notovich, Nicholas, 110
nsumankwaahene, 203
Nur ud-Din (Khalifatul Masih), 112, 115, 125
Nyarko, Yusuf, 86, 163–164, 168, 178n1

Obonster, 68, 81, 88n27, 146, 176–177
obosom. See *abosom*
Obowa, Ekua, 85
odehyee. See *adehyee*
odonko. See *nnonkofoo*

Ofori, Kwabena (Adansehene), 203–204
ohene. See *ahene*
Okepopo mosque, 135
okomfo. See *akomfoo/okomfo*
Old Testament, 60, 71–72, 77, 244. See also Bible; Quran: comparisons with Bible
onyame, 36, 37
onyankupon ("Great Friend"), 36
Oppong, Sampson, 201
Osei Kwame (Asantehene), 201, 214n13

Pakistan, 19, 215n35, 240, 246–247
palm oil production, 4, 34, 44, 88n9; Binyameen Sam and, 60, 61, 62, 76, 78, 79
pamphlets, Ahmadiyya, 189–190
pan-Africanism, 123, 126–129, 137
Partition, and the Ahmadiyya Muslim Community, 19, 240, 241
patrilineal cross-cousin marriage, 231–232
patron-client relationships, 42–44, 97, 202
Pedro, Amadu Ramanu, 1, 123, 132, 138, 163, 168–171, 179n23, 179n25, 179n26, 182, 244; Nayyar and, 171–172, 174, 176
Peel, John, 13, 23n38
Pellow, Deborah, 89n34
Pelpuo II (Wa Na), 221
Pelpuo III (Wa Na), 221, 229
Pepra, Papa Malik, 208, 210
Pfander, Karl Gottlieb, 102
Picot, T. B., 31
pigs, uncleanly for Muslims, 47
pirs, 98, 108, 109, 113. See also esoteric practices
polygyny, 60, 67
Potsin, *145*, 191–192
Powell, Avril Ann, 114, 116
Prempe I (Asantehene), 200, 201, 203
Prempe II (Asantehene), 200, 209, 212
Presbyterians, American, 102, 103, 112
proselytism: Ahmadiyya, 1, 8–9, 119, 124, 168–169, 171–172, 183–184, 187–192, 200, 205–209, 210, 222–223, 225, 227, 230–231, 232–233, 244–246; Ahmadiyya advertisements, 190; Ahmadiyya pamphlets, 189–190; Ahmadiyya targeting of English-speaking world for, 127; by Binyameen Sam, 74–75, 77–79; Christian, and British imperialism, 13, 15, 35, 99, 166, 241; Christian, in Punjab, 102–104; Crowther's approach, to Muslims, 6–7, 22n34, 22n35, 23n36, 23n37; Fante Muslim, as expression of cosmopolitan approach, 79–80; Methodist, 35, 38–41; Muslim efforts often neglected, 13–14; new

Ahmadiyya approaches in the 1940s, 195, 213; restrictions on Muslim, in Asante, 11–12, 31
Punjab, 19, 95–96, *148*; 1857 revolt, 100, 101, 102; British colonial rule, 100–101; Christian missionaries, 99, 102–104, 119; *doabs*, 96, 98, 100; esoteric practices, 99, 120n14; Hinduism, Islam, and Sikhism, 97–99; kin-based groups, 100; "new elite," 101; nineteenth century, 96–99; Partition, 240; religious marketplace, emergence of, 99–106; Sufi mystical experiences, 95

Qadian, 2, 108, *148*, 171, 240
Qadian cemetery, 114, 117
Qasim, Mallam, 209–210
Quansah, Ogyadziyi, 81
Quantson, Isa, 191–192
Quarm, Adam Kofi, 191–192
Quilliam, Abdullah, 124, 131
Quran: Alkaurani movement and, 134, 135; comparison with Bible, 4, 6–7, 77–78, 110, 181, 188, 189; esoteric practices and, 9, 24n56, 48, 67, 227; as "legislative" revelation, 109; Muslim education and, 9, 12; *naskh*, 111; reference to Ahmad as Muhammad's beautiful manifestation, 95; *sura al-fatiha*, 76; used by Salih to defend Ahmadiyya, 227, 229, 235

Rabwah, 240, 246–247
racial discrimination, 129–130, 166, 169, 183–184
rainforest, 11–12, 32, 33; and cocoa production, 84, 200; and palm oil production, 34
Ramadan, 82
Rashid ud-Din, 119
Reade, William Winwood, 48, 56n58, 58n89, 72
reform movements, as response to British imperialism and Christian proselytism, 15, 241. *See also* Ahmadiyya; Hindu reform movements; Muslim reform movements; Sikh reform movements
Reichmuth, Stephan, 123
religious marketplace. *See* marketplace, religious
religious pictures, 71, 72, 89n45
"Resolutions" of the Gold Coast Ahmadiyya, 173–174, 176
Review of Religions, 16, 113–114, 117, 136, 182; Agusto's writings, 132; on Fante Ahmadi Muslims, 183; Hakeem's sermons, 188; pan-Africanism in, 127–128; report of Pedro's activities, 168–169

Rossall, Richard, 74
Rowe, Samuel, 49, 50
Roy, Rammohun, 104
Royal Niger Company, 129
"Rules and Regulations" (1921 bylaws of the Gold Coast Ahmadiyya), 173, 174–176, 178, 181, 197n16, 197n17, 197n35, 241, 245

sacred groves, 36–37; Nananom Mpow, 33, 36, 38, 41, 51
Sadiq, Mufti Muhammad, 5, 22n27, 125, 126, 129, 133, 140n57, *157*
Sadiq, Nana (Kwame Boateng), 199, 203–204, 215n23, 215n30, 216n45, 245; death of, 208–209
Sadr Anjuman-i-Ahmadiyya (Supreme Council of the Ahmadiyya), 114, 115, 116–117, 119
Sahajdhari Sikhs, 99
Said Soribo, Al-Hajj (Friday Limam), 222, 226–228, 228, 229, 232
sajjada nishin, 98, 108, 116. *See also* esoteric practices
Salaga, 11, 12, *142*, 167, 222–223
salat, 73, 76, 112, 127, 205; placement of arms during, 175, 185, 192, 218, 224
Salaw, Mallam, 200, 202, 209–211, 245, 246
Salih, Mohammed bin, 16, 246
Salih bin al-Hassan, Mallam, 218, 245; acceptance of Ahmadiyya, 223–225; and consolidation of Ahmadiyya at Wa, 230–235, 237n60, 238n90; correspondence with Said Soribo, 226–228; return as Ahmadi missionary at Wa, 225–226, 237n32; riot at Wa, 1934, 228–230
Saltpond, 1, 52, 62, 86, *144*, *145*, *146*; Nayyar at, 171–172; Talim-ul-Islam School, *149*, *159*, 186–187, 193, 245
Sam, Binyameen, 3, 8, 12, 14, 16, 60, 176, 240, 242; Appah, dispute with, 82–85; before acceptance of Islam, 61–64, 67, 88n11; as Biblicist, 8, 19, 60, 61, 70, 188, 190, 244; birth, 61, 87n8; conversion to Islam, 3, 17, 20n15, 53, 60–61, 64–73, 87n6, 87n7, 89n40; conversion to Islam, narratives of, 17, 28n107, 66–67, 87n5; as cosmopolitan, 78, 82; death, 85, 92n97; English-language schools and, 80–83; gravestone, 17, 61, 87n8, 92n97; healing powers, 65, 67, 72–73; informal preaching, 75; interview with Anaman, 68–71; and Mallam Tibu, 69–70, 89n40; as palm oil broker, 60, 61, 62; proselytizing Christianity, 62, 74; proselytizing Islam, 60, 74–75, 77–78, 78–79; visionary experiences, 17, 61, 65–66, 67; "voice" and "words," 18

samanadze, 37
Sapara, Dr. Orisha, 128, 131–132, 139n28
Saraswati, Dayananda, 104–105
Sarbah, John Mensah, 36, 37
sarkin zongo, 202, 209. *See also* Sallaw, Mallam
Saro, 7–8, 130, 133, 134, 136
sartorial practices, 34, 37, 48, 71–27, 76–77, 186, 221
savanna tradition. *See* Muslim savanna tradition
Sayal, Muhammad Fateh, 125, 129, 138n12
schools: Ahmadi, 1–2, 81, *149*, *159*, 186–187, 192–195, 212, 217n64, 242; Arabic, 12, 130–131, 177; Christian, 81, 102–103; Lagos, 131–132, 134–135; logbooks, 81–83; Methodist commitment to, 39. *See also* English-language schools
Secretariat of Native Affairs, 164
self-presentation, and new forms of wealth, 34, 221
Sheibu (*mallam*), 68
Shitta, Muhammad, 7–8, 130–131, 134
Shitta Bey mosque, 131
Shumway, Rebecca, 38
Sierra Leone, 130. *See also* Freetown; Saro
Sikh reform movements, 96, 98–99, 104–106, 241
Sikhism, 97, 98–99
Singh, Gobind, 98
Singh, Ranjit, 97, 98–99, 100, 108
Singh Sabha reform movement, 105
Skinner, David, 28n111, 89n34 slaves: Akan, 33–34; British ideas about "Hausa," 8; as Methodist converts, 40–41; *nnonkofoo*, 34, 41–42, 220. *See also* Atlantic Muslims
Smith, Joseph, 63
social rank: Fante states, 33–34; Methodists, 40; Punjab, 97, 100–101
Sokoto Caliphate, 10, 11, *143*
Solomon, John, 71
Soribo, Al-Hajj Said. *See* Said Soribo, Al-Hajj
sources, vii–viii, 16–18, 19, 27n101, 28n107, 28n111, 28n112, 58n105, 61, 87n5, 88n27, 124, 138n13, 164, 179n23, 182, 199, 202–203, 205, 214n23, 216n44, 216n48, 218–219, 226–227, 236n25, 236n26, 237n53. *See also* Ekrawfo narrative
Sraha, 172
Srinagar, 110, *148*, *157*
stamp, Ahmadiyya, *159*, 190
Sufi expressions: Ahmadiyya as reforming, 2, 95, 108, 113; as dominant Muslim tradition in Punjab, 98, 107: influences on Ahmadiyya, 95,

108, 119n3. *See also* esoteric practices; *pirs*; *sajjada nishin*
Suleiman (*karamoko*), 203, 206
Sumaila (Wa Na), 233, 234
"sweepers," 114

Tagore, Debendranath, 104
Tagore, Hemendranath, 104
Talim-ul-Islam School, *149*, *159*, 186–187, 193, 245
Tamale, *142*, 221, 222–223
Tashhīdh al-adhlān (Ahmadiyya publication), 117
Tasliman, 204, 206, 208
Tat Khalsa Sikhs, 106, 118
Tawiah, Kobina, 240
Taylor, Alan, 64
Taylor, John Eldred, 126
Tekyiman, 32–33, 36, *142*
temperance movements, 64
tendalun, 220
Thompson, A. G. N., 223
Tibu, Mallam, 52, 59n115, 69–70, 89n40
"ticket money," Methodist, 40, 51, 60, 64, 177, 185
Tijani, Mallam, 83
Times of Nigeria, 135
The Times (London), 48, 127
Tiwaa, Aisha, 207
Townsend, Reverend, 6–7
trade networks, 11, 33–34, 96
transatlantic slave trade, 4, 6, 7, 8, 10, 33–34, 242; abolitionists, 38, 44, 47, 49–50; and Atlantic Muslims, 8, 47, 244; condemned in Ahmadiyya works, 128; Lagos, 42; *nnonkofoo*, 34, 41–42, 220
Trimingham, J. Spencer, 2, 5, 241
Truth Seeker, 127
Ture, Samory, 221
tuuba, as term of dismissal, 193, 196
Tuudu (*okomfo*), 203

Umar ibn Abi Bakr, Al-Hajj (of Kete-Krachi), 9, 24n53, 210, 211, 216n46, 236n14
United States: Ahmadi missionaries in, 5, 129; "colour prejudice," 128; Mufti Sadiq mission to, 125, 129, 133; Zion, John Dowie's utopian community, 109
The Unknown Life of Christ (Notovich), 110
Usman, Mallam, 212
Uthman dan Fodio, 10

Vedas, 97–98, 104
visionary experiences, vii, 17, 28n108, 247; acceptance of Ahmadiyya and, 199, 207; acceptance of Islam in early twentieth-century Asante and, 199, 203, 204; Ahmadiyya and, 17, 247; Ghulam Ahmad and, 95, 109–110; Methodists and, 71–72; Nyarko and, 163–164, 169–170; public memories of Sam's, 17, 61, 65–66, 67, 247
visual culture, 71–72, 244
Volta River region, middle, 11–12, 219
voluntary associations, 64, 101, 130

Wa, 1, 5, 19, 219–221, 242; Ahmadiyya arrival, 225–228; Ahmadiyya consolidation, 230–235; British colonial rule, 221–222; opposition to Ahmadiyya, 218, 225–229, 230–232, 233–234, 235; patrilineal cross-cousin marriage, 231–232, 238n72; riot of 1934, 218, 228–230, 235. See also Northern Territories (Gold Coast)
Wa Limam, 220. See also Malik ibn Uthman, Al-Hajj; Muhammad bin Uthman Dun, Al-Hajj; Muhammad Saghir
Waliullah, Shah, 98
Walls, Andrew, 6–7
Wa Na, 220. See also Hamidu Bomi; Mumin Koray; Pelpuo II; Pelpuo III; Sumaila
Wasabiampa, 80, 84, *145*, *147*, *156*
Wemah, Ahmad Samba Barwey, 232–233
Wesley, John, 38
Wesleyan Methodist mission (Gold Coast), 31, 35, 38–41, 50–52, 55n38, 55n40, 62–63, 70, 73–74, 86, *155*, 166, 167, 186, 201; African missionaries, 56n42; Biblicism, 62–64; dissident communities, 63–64; Nananom Mpow and, 41; "revival," 50–52, 53n3, 58n105, 70; social rank, 40; "ticket money," 40, 51, 60, 64, 177, 185
Wesleyan Methodist Missionary Society, 38, 39, 55n37, 63
West, Daniel, 71–72
West, J. H., 187

West, William, 40
West African Frontier Force, 46, 232–233
West Indian Regiment, 35
Wherry, Elwood M., 102
Wilks, Ivor, 218, 224, 235n4, 236n14, 237n32
The Will (al-wasiyah), 114
Winneba, 78, *142*, 177
Woking mosque, 5, 125, 137
Woking Muslim Trust, 125
Wolseley, Sir Garnet, 46, 50, 70
women: Ahmadiyya, 192, 206; Asante, 199; conversion to Islam, 75–76, 90n61, 183; destruction of indigenous religious objects, 76, 90n61, 206, 207; Wala, 232. *See also* Afiriyie, Nana Salamat Akua; Endow, Ekuwa; Esuan, Haleesah Esi; Mansah, Rukiyya Akua; Mwintuona, Salmata; Obowa, Ekua; Tiwaa, Aisha; Yansewa, Haleema Adjoa
World War I, 133, 167
World War II, 240

Yaa Asantewaa revolt, 200, 201
Yahya, Mallam, 226, 232
Yakubu (Hausa Force officer), 43
Yakubu, Mallam, 85–86, 92n100, 176–177
Yakubu, Papa, 208, 210
Yamoah, Hakeem Kofi, 66
Yansewa, Haleema Adjoa, 66–67, 68, 76, 89n31
Yaw, Akyeampon, 45
Yeboawa, Kwaabo, 80
Yusuf, Mallam (Kwabena Nti), 204–208, 218, 224, 245

Zenoah, Harri (Hausa Force officer), 43, 69, 89n37
Zion (John Dowie's utopian community, United States), 109
zongos, 12, 167, 202, 205, 208, 214n16
Zouave uniform, 44, 57n70

JOHN H. HANSON is Associate Professor of History at Indiana University, where he is also Director of the Africa Studies Program. He is the author of *Migration, Jihad, and Muslim Authority in West Africa: The Futanke Colonies in Karta* and co-editor (with Maria Grosz-Ngaté and Patrick O'Meara) of *Africa*, 4th edition. He is also an editor of *History in Africa: A Journal of Debates, Methods, and Source Analysis*.

www.ingramcontent.com/pod-product-compliance
Lightning Source LLC
Chambersburg PA
CBHW050432240426
43661CB00055B/2352